Prophets in Action

Itero

Reprints in the Service of the Scholarly Community
www.ehs.se/itero

Series Editor
Thomas Kazen

No. 3

Åke Viberg

Prophets in Action

An Analysis of Prophetic Symbolic Acts
in the Old Testament

Enskilda Högskolan Stockholm

Itero – Reprints in the Service of the Scholarly Community

Books still in demand should not get out of print, and with today's techniques there is no defence. With the reprint series *Itero*, the Biblical Studies department at Stockholm School of Theology would like to make books available for free online and at a very low cost in print. Part of the background is the fact that several faculty members have published their studies in series that were cancelled. With the publishing market in constant flux, series migrate, and volumes still in demand can suddenly become unavailable. This is unsatisfactory. In collaboration with the authors, we are now republishing a number of such volumes and we will consider publishing other out-of-print titles, for which authors hold the copyright. This is entirely a non-profit project. Files may be downloaded at www.ehs.se/itero and books can be bought through most major internet bookshops.

University College Stockholm – Stockholm School of Theology

University College Stockholm (Enskilda Högskolan Stockholm) is a major Swedish provider of education in Human Rights and Democracy, as well as in Theology/Religious Studies. EHS offers Bachelor's Master's and Doctoral programmes. The university college was founded in 1993 through a merger of educational institutions with roots dating back to 1866. Stockholm School of Theology is the common designation for the two theological departments: Religious Studies and Theology, and Eastern Christian Studies. Stockholm School of Human Rights and Democracy is the designation for the programmes in Human Rights and Democracy.

© 2007 Åke Viberg. © 2021 Åke Viberg & Enskilda Högskolan Stockholm.
Reprint edition. Previously published by Almqvist & Wiksell International.

ISBN: 978-91-8890-615-1

Cover design by Carl Johan Berglund. Typeset in EB Garamond.
Printed by BoD – Books on Demand, Norderstedt, Germany.

Stockholm School of Theology
University College Stockholm
Åkeshovsvägen 29, 168 39 Bromma, Sweden
www.ehs.se

Preface to the Itero Reprint Edition

I am grateful for the opportunity to make this book available in print yet again, especially since it has not been available for purchase for some time. Hopefully it can still serve its purpose to further our understanding of the prophetic literature of the Old Testament.

Stockholm 26 October 2021

Åke Viberg

Table of Contents

Abbreviations and Technical Remarks   **12**

A. Introduction   **13**

The Purpose, Problem and Hypothesis   13

Previous Studies of Prophetic Symbolic Acts   14

Linguistic Terminology   19

Metonymy   *19*

Metaphor   *19*

Idiom   *20*

Speech-act theory   *21*

Non-Linguistic Terminology   22

Convention/Conventional   *23*

Symbol, icon, index   *24*

Act   *26*

'Prophetic symbolic act'   *27*

A Wider Frame I: Nonverbal Communication   30

Introduction   *30*

Empirical study of nonverbal communication   *31*

Study of nonverbal communication in literature   *33*

A Wider Frame II: Symbolic Acts in the Ancient Near East   36

ARM 26.206: The Symbolic act of a muhhûm   *38*

Text, Nonverbal Communication and 'Textual World'   40

The Texts   43

Some Practical Issues Regarding the Analysis   54

B. Ahijah Tears the Mantle of Jeroboam (1 Kings 11:29-31)   **55**

Introduction   55

Analysis of 1 Samuel 15:27 and 24:5, 12   57

Introduction   *57*

Analysis of 1 Samuel 15:27   *61*

Analysis of 1 Samuel 24:5, 12   *65*

The Text   67

Earlier Studies   68

Performance   73

The Symbolism of the Act   74
Summary and Conclusions   82

C. Isaiah Goes Naked (Isaiah 20)   83

Introduction   83
The Text   83
Analysis   85
    Structure   *85*
    Historical background   *85*
    Literary coherence   *90*
    Symbolic meaning of the act   *96*
    The symbolic structure of the symbolic act *98*
Summary and Conclusions   101

D. Prophetic Symbolic Acts in the Book of Jeremiah   102

Introduction   102

1. The Hidden Girdle (Jeremiah 13:1-11)   105

The Text   105
Analysis   106
    Structure   *106*
    Literary coherence   *107*
    Performance of the act   *111*
    Symbolic meaning of the act   *113*
Summary and Conclusions   117

2. The Smashed Jar (Jeremiah 19:1-2, 10-11)   118

The Text   118
Analysis   119
    Literary coherence   *119*
    Performance of the act   *121*
    Symbolic meaning of the act   *124*
Summary and Conclusions   127

3. Wearing a 'Yoke-Collar' (Jeremiah 27:2-3; 28:10-11)   128

Introduction   128
The Text   130
Analysis   132

Literary coherence 132
Performance of the act 134
Symbolic meaning of the act 140
Summary and Conclusions 144

4. Buying a Piece of Land (Jeremiah 32:6-15) 145

The Text 145
Analysis 148
Introduction 148
Structure and literary coherence 149
Legal terminology 150
An application of speech-act analysis 153
Performance and symbolic meaning of the act 155
Summary and Conclusions 158

5. Putting Stones in the Clay (Jeremiah 43:8-10) 159

The Text 159
Analysis 160
Structure and literary coherence 160
Procedure of the act 161
Symbolic meaning of the act 161
Summary and Conclusions 168

6. Sinking the Scroll in the River (Jeremiah 51:59-64) 169

The Text 169
Analysis 171
Structure and literary coherence 171
Performance of the act 175
Symbolic meaning of the act 176
Summary and Conclusions 181

E. Prophetic Symbolic Acts in the Book of Ezekiel 182

1. Building a Siege (Ezekiel 4:1-3) 182

The Text 182
Analysis 183
Performance of the act 183
Symbolic meaning of the act 185
Summary and Conclusions 189

2. Laying on One Side (Ezekiel 4:4-8)   **190**

The Text   190
Analysis   191
Summary and Conclusions   195

3. Preparing a Meal (Ezekiel 4:9-12)   **196**

The Text   196
Analysis   196
Summary and Conclusions   199

4. Splitting Hairs (Ezekiel 5:1-4)   **200**

The Text   200
Analysis   201
Summary and Conclusions   207

5. Preparing to Leave (Ezekiel 12:3-7)   **208**

The Text   208
Analysis   209
Summary and Conclusions   213

6. Acts of Emotions (Ezekiel 12:17-20; 21:11-2, 17, 19)   **214**

The Text   214
Analysis   215
Summary and Conclusions   221

7. Not Mourning for a Wife (Ezekiel 24:15-24)   **222**

The Text   222
Analysis   224
Summary and Conclusions   228

8. Joining two Pieces of Wood (Ezekiel 37:15-22)   **229**

The Text   229
Analysis   230
Summary and Conclusions   236

F. The Marriage of Hosea (Hosea 1:2-3; 3:1-4)   **237**

Introduction   237
The Text   243

Analysis 244

Summary and Conclusions 249

G. Crowning a High Priest (Zechariah 6:9-15) 250

Introduction 250

The Text 251

Analysis 253

The structure of the text 253

The performance of the symbolic act 256

Why was a high-priest crowned? 261

How many temples are involved? 263

The symbolism of the prophetic act 265

Depositing the crown in the temple 268

Summary and Conclusions 270

H. General Conclusions 271

I. Bibliography 273

Abbreviations and Technical Remarks

Abbreviations and technical remarks have been used in accordance with the *SBL Handbook of Style* (1999).

Dates are B.C.E., unless otherwise stated.

A. Introduction

The Purpose, Problem and Hypothesis

The purpose of this study is to enhance our understanding of the particular group of symbolic acts that are performed by so-called prophets in the Old Testament. What did these characters intend with their various symbolic acts? I will attempt to show that these prophetic acts are part and parcel of their prophetic message, nonverbal communication that extends the rhetorical arsenal these prophets made use of in their struggles to persuade. Some scholars have described these acts as 'street theatre', and even though it is a poor comparison, there is definitely a clear analogy between these prophetic acts and what we would describe as 'street theatre', or even 'pantomime'. No doubt, we are seeing them in action.

The task of this study will be accomplished through an exhaustive exegetical analysis of the texts that describe these acts, with a particular focus on the symbolism involved. The goal will be to formulate the purpose and function of these acts, together with a description of the acts and how they have been construed by means of various forms of symbolism.

In order to reach this goal, we will prepare ourselves in this introduction by looking back at earlier studies of these symbolic acts. We will then start our journey towards a functional definition of 'prophetic symbolic act' as well as a relevant model for analysing something nonverbal in literary form. We will start by defining some important linguistic terminology that will be used in the analysis, since we are concerned with texts, and then turn to non-linguistic terminology used in the analysis, since we are concerned with understanding acts that are nonverbal. The goal will be to formulate a working definition of what is meant by a 'prophetic symbolic act'. The study of these acts also need to be set in the larger context of the study of nonverbal communication, both studied empirically as well as described in literature. Another larger context that needs to be understood is the study of nonverbal communication in texts from the ancient Near East. The only prophetic symbolic act available to us from the ancient Near East, namely from Mari, will be studied in order to shed some light on both the function of the prophetic symbolic acts from the OT, but also provide them with at least some form of comparative material. This will take us to a point where we are ready to formulate a model for how we should approach symbolic acts, on the one hand nonverbal, but on the other hand only available to us in literary form. This model will centre on the use of the concept of 'literary world'. Then follows the selection of the texts that will be included in the analysis. The selection of texts from the most recent studies on the subject of prophetic symbolic acts will be compared in order to show how differently scholars argue when they decide on the relevance of various texts, and to set the present analysis in relation to previous studies. Finally, some practical issues regarding the analysis will be dealt with.

Previous Studies of Prophetic Symbolic Acts

Earlier studies on these symbolic acts can easily be divided in three categories, due to the thorough study made by Fohrer in 1953, later published in a second, enlarged edition 1968[1], namely studies made before Fohrer, Fohrer's groundbreaking study, and studies made after Fohrer.

The earlier studies by Van den Born and Groenman were primarily occupied with the question whether these prophetic acts were actually performed or not.[2] This discussion has naturally remained in focus, but it should be decided less on the basis on particular preconceptions of ancient Israelite prophets and their activities, and more on the exegetical analysis of the texts that actually describe these acts. These acts were also largely considered to be equivalent to or closely related to magical acts, and the reasoning was heavily dependent on certain views of 'Hebrew mentality', anywhere the divine 'word' was supposed to have been almost a concrete entity which, once spoken through the prophet, would achieve its own fulfilment.[3] However, this view has later been heavily criticized for its undue emphasis on certain preconceived ideas of how ancient societies

---

[1] Fohrer (1968).

[2] Born (1935), Groenman (1942b), Groenman (1942a), Born (1946).

[3] E.g. Lods (1927), Robinson (1927). For further references see Friebel (1999: 41, n 80). This view persists among scholars, e.g. Carroll (1986: 295) and Stacey (1990: 267), 'words were not simply a code for communication, they were centres of power', and the otherwise well-informed study by Jeffers (1996: 91-2). Jeffers exemplifies with 1 Kgs 22:11, where Zedekiah makes horns of iron. But she fails to note that the act of fabricating the horns is in no way indicated to be understood in a symbolic way, nor is something said of wearing the horns. The horns themselves are symbolic, as the texts make perfectly clear, 'with these you shall gore the Syrians'. There is probably an element of magic involved in this act, but it is definitely not symbolic.

must have reasoned in a more 'concrete' and less 'abstract' sense than later cultures.[1]

Fohrer attempts to put an end to the earlier attempts to equate these acts with magical acts by postulating an evolutionary model. They are said to have been magical in their origin, but when used by Yahwistic prophets, the power is no longer believed to come from the prophets but solely from God. This makes the form similar to that of ancient Near Eastern acts of sympathetic magic, but the function unique to Yahwistic religion.[2] Fohrer's attempt to find a particular form in the descriptions of these acts have been largely successful and has been followed, mostly because it is so self evident;

1) God commands the prophet to perform a particular act,
2) the act is performed by the prophet, and
3) the act is explained by the prophet.[3]

However, as befits a trained form-critic, Fohrer tends to use this scheme in order to evaluate whether certain described acts are prophetic acts, and the scheme becomes a test as to whether an act is a proper prophetic symbolic act, which is going too far in the form-critical agenda.

After having gone from a close association if not identification between prophetic symbolic acts and magical acts, to a view where the two are more clearly contrasted as one developing from the other, the natural step would then be to consider the two categories to be wholly separate without any genetic connection. The first scholar to proposing this was Lang, when he identified these prophetic acts with 'street theatre'.[4] According to Lang, there was a group of prophetic acts that had nothing to do with magic whatsoever. Instead, these acts were meant to persuade through the use of nonverbal means, comparable to modern 'street theatre'. Amsler also follows Lang in seeing the 'actes prophétiques' as something distinctly different from magical acts.[5] Schökel even went

---

[1] See particularly the criticism from Barr (1961) and Thiselton (1974).

[2] Fohrer (1966b), Fohrer (1968). Lindblom (1962: 172) held to a similar view, even in the Swedish original, although with a lesser emphasis Lindblom (1934: 303).

[3] Fohrer (1968: 18-9).

[4] Lang (1978: 166-88), Lang (1981b), Lang (1981a: 88-9), Lang (1983b: 81-9), Lang (1985: 7-8), Lang (1986), Lang (1997). Of course there were others before Fohrer who held to this view, e.g. Gunkel (1917), but it was clearly the minority view in contrast to a clearly developing consensus view that was eventually formulated in a compromise by Fohrer.

[5] Amsler (1980), Amsler (1985).

so far as to describe these acts as 'pantomimes'.[1] Friebel has also followed this view, in his extensive study of the 'sign-acts' of Jeremiah and Ezekiel and their suasive-rhetorical capacity.[2] According to Friebel, there are no magical aspects involved in these acts. Instead they are means of persuasion, instrumental in the work of the prophets, 'but once the verbal words and nonverbal sign-acts are stripped of the nonexistent "inherently efficacious power", then they can truly be considered "rhetorical" communication devices.'[3] It is evident that this has rapidly become the new consensus.[4] The purpose of this study is therefore not to ask whether these acts are magical, but in what sense they can be said to be symbolic.

However, there are some variations on this new consensus, and Stacey's study is the most prominent.[5] He holds that these acts are not magical, but still they stand in a close relation to magical acts, similar to the view of Fohrer.[6] They are not communicative in the sense of Lang's 'street theatre', indeed they are not in any sense meant to convey a message, which is, according to Stacey, a very modern notion of what communication is all about.[7] Instead, these dramas stand over against reality in the sense of representing, interpreting and revealing its inner nature and manifesting its totality. The prophetic act and the reality it depicts stand beside each other as two aspects of one whole, originating in God's will. The acts do not cause any form of reality into being, but works with what already is at hand. This excludes any form of efficacious function of the prophetic act, as Fohrer argued.[8] However, it is very difficult to pinpoint what Stacey is actually arguing for, since his style is elusive and at times quite idiosyncratic. How can a drama be interpretative and yet not be communicative, and how can it do all this without apparently be in the need of an audience?[9] It wo-

---

[1] Schökel (1988: 113).

[2] Friebel (1999: esp. 11-61), see also further below, pp 28-30, for a criticism of Friebel's study.

[3] Friebel (1999: 47, also 41-51).

[4] See e.g. Uehlinger (1987: 135, 140), Clements (1988: 118), Greene (1989: 166), Thondiparambil (1989), Matthews, and Benjamin (1993: 215-6), Allen (1994: 65-6).

[5] Stacey (1990). For similar attempts to deal with acts of Jesus, see Bowker (1964), Hooker (1997).

[6] Stacey (1990: 257-8). It is strange that although Stacey spends much time arguing against the magical interpretation, he still ends up on the side of Fohrer.

[7] Stacey (1990: 265-6).

[8] Stacey (1990: 277-80).

[9] Hutton (1995: 255) similarly complains that Stacey's work is 'plagued by a number of problems.' Friebel (1999: 47, n 96) rightly criticizes Stacey for arguing from a metaphysical perspective, and for his failure to explain the function of the acts.

would seem that in Stacey's view these acts function similarly to visions, but even visions are put to use by the prophets in their rhetorical strategies to make their audiences react enough to change their ways of life. What is lacking in Stacey's study, beside a sufficient theoretical basis, is an explanation of the function of the prophetic act. It may mirror reality, but why did the prophets choose to perform them in those particular ways at particular moments?

Hutton attempts to go beyond what he sees as the two extremes of Fohrer on the one hand and Lang on the other. He understands prophetic action as consisting of both speech and symbolic act and to function as a form of curse.[1] As opposed to Stacey, he is occupied with the question of the function of the prophetic act. The words have power, according to Hutton, but not in the sense of being parts of magical acts in a new Yahwistic context, as Fohrer argued. Instead, he understands the words, and in extension also the prophetic acts, of the prophets in the sense that 'in the *conventional perception* that in certain socially recognized contexts and when performed by socially recognized persons, words have power.'[2] It would seem that Hutton's view is very close to that of Lang, if only with an acute awareness of the fact that the prophet played an important part in ancient Israelite society as an intermediate figure, who could speak curses because of his divine status and legitimation. However, Hutton's study is hampered by the fact that he mixes prophetic utterances and acts, which e.g. makes his use of illocutionary and perlocutionary functions[3] less useful categories for explaining the functions behind prophetic activity. It would seem that Hutton is doing two things in his study, on the one hand arguing that the force behind prophetic curses can be explained by means of speech act theory, and on the other hand trying to tie this in with the understanding of prophetic symbolic acts, which is less convincing and in need of further theoretical elaborations.[4]

Overholt takes quite a different approach to these texts, mainly because his aim is to understand those prophetic acts that are normally not included among

---

[1] Hutton (1995: 256-7).

[2] Hutton (1995: 254). Hutton (1995) relies on Thiselton (1974) and Mitchell (1987) for the use of illocutionary and perlocutionary aspects of language. See also Friebel (1999: 44-5, 47, n 95) and Houston (1993).

[3] Hutton's use of the concept 'perlocutionary' is insufficient, since it refers to all consequences pertaining to the person or persons acted upon, and not only emotions. The simplest perlocutionary act for an OT prophet would be that his people believed him and followed him. For a similar use of speech act theory in explaining prophetic curses in Jeremiah, see Anderson (1998a), and Anderson (1998b) for a broader view on the function of curse.

[4] Friebel (1999: 47, n 95) is correct in his criticism of Hutton that not all prophetic symbolic acts are future-oriented, nor are they all negative in their content.

symbolic acts of the prophets. Overholt begins by identifying the overall rubric of 'prophetic acts of power', as acts that 'refers to reported actions of prophetic figures that in their narrative context appear somehow unusual, extraordinary, or miraculous'.[1] Within this group, to which he counts over 60 instances in the OT, he further recognizes two subgroups; first, those acts that are within the capabilities of anyone to perform, and these are the acts that are usually regarded as 'prophetic symbolic acts', e.g. by Fohrer, Friebel, Stacy and in this study. These acts are called 'symbolic actions'. Second, Overholt collects those texts that describe actions by prophets that seem to go against the laws of nature, or what is normally expected of a person. These texts are mainly collected from the stories concerning Elijah and Elisha in 1 and 2 Kgs, and this is the category that Overholt is primarily interested in. The conclusion Overholt reaches is that these, apparently supernatural acts, had the social function of legitimating the prophets as intermediaries between the divine and the human in that particular society.[2]

It should be clear from this overview of previous studies that the magical aspect of these acts have come much into question, and is more or less regarded as a meaningless issue, since the difference between magic and religion is no longer meaningful enough to be upheld.[3] The question is, rather, whether these prophetic acts served any particular religious purpose or not, as a possible subsidiary aspect to the function of each particular act. I have earlier made the distinction between e.g. legal symbolic acts as conventional acts, and the prophetic symbolic acts as non-conventional, or innovative.[4] This categorisation has the advantage of focusing on the function of the acts and not on any preconceived notions of whether they were meant to function in a particular religious sense. In the analysis below it will be shown repeatedly that these acts, although very much innovative in their totality, are nevertheless constructed by the use of various items of conventional meaning. But the end product in the form of the prophetic symbolic act is something inherently different, as will become clear in the following analysis.

---

[1] Overholt (1989: 87).

[2] Overholt (1989: 96).

[3] See e.g. Stacey (1990: 234-59),

[4] Viberg (1992: 11-2). Friebel (1999: 57-61) now makes a similar distinction between conventional, or ritualistic acts and individualistic or idiosyncratic acts.

Linguistic Terminology

We will start defining our basic terminology with the linguistic one, which is necessary since the prophetic symbolic acts are only available to us in literary form. The terms that have been selected here are the ones that are most crucial to the analysis, and it is vital that they are used unambiguously. The terms that we will define here are metonymy, metaphor and idiom, and some terminology related to speech-act theory, such as performative, illocutionary and perlocutionary.

Metonymy

The basic characteristic of metonymy is the associative relation between the signifier and the signified.[1] A mantle may associate to the person that usually wears it, and the heavens may be a metonymy for God. The figure of metonymy is not restricted to the textual level, but can be found on higher levels of discourse, such as expressions, paragraphs or even whole texts, but then it is usually described semiotically as index, although Elam speaks of 'scenic metonymy' in the area of theatre and drama.[2]

Another characteristic of metonymy is that it functions within one semantic field and does not cross over or relate to different fields, which is the case with metaphors.[3]

Metaphor

The basic characteristic of metaphor is the analogical relation between the signifier, or the vehicle, and the signified, or the tenor.[4] A word or expression which in its literal use stands for one item, is applied to a different item, without mak-

---

[1] For definitions, see e.g. Kittay (1987: 295), Eco, and Sebeok (1983: 244-6) and Caird (1980: 136-7). Buzy (1923) is also largely occupied with this question. For the comparison with index, see Elam (1980: 28).

[2] Elam (1980: 28.)For this more overarching use of metonymy and also of metaphor, see e.g. Jakobson (1971: 254-9), Hedley (1988), Dévényi (1996), Panther, and Radden (1999), Spiegelman, and Teaching Company. (1999), Barcelona (2000).

[3] So Kittay (1987: 291). Cf. Culley (1981: 60), "A metaphorical world is separate but analogous, a member of a paradigm of conceivable worlds, while a metonymical world is contiguous with or part of our own, unexplored but governed by the same laws."

[4] For definitions, see e.g. Caird (1980: 66) and Soskice (1985: 15). For more elaborate discussions, see e.g. Eco, and Sebeok (1983: 254-6) and Kittay (1987: 24). Kittay's study will be regarded as the basis for metaphoric theory in this study. For studies of metaphor in relation to the Bible, see, e.g., Soskice (1985), Macky (1990), Perdue (1991).

ing the comparison explicit, in which case it would be called a 'simile'. The metaphor only functions when the signifier has or is given a certain symbolic meaning. The metaphorical expression 'God is king' is only understood if the symbolic meaning of the signifier, 'king', is understood as well. It is the analogical connection between this symbolic meaning, e.g., 'the one who rules', and the apprehension of that which is signified, here 'God', that creates the metaphorical meaning. The metaphor as a literary trope can therefore be described as a literary reuse or application of symbols in an analogical sense.[1] Since the symbol is also a process of signification, where 'king' signifies 'rule' in an analogical sense, the one who rules is associated with the rule itself, it can easily be seen that the process of signification, or semiosis is an endless process in principle.

The metaphor, as well as the metonymy, can be more or less conventional, even to the point of loosing the awareness of the discrepancy between the vehicle and the tenor, which is when an idiom is born, see below.[2] Between the extremes of newly created metaphors and idioms, we find metaphors of more or less conventional status.

Idiom

A synchronic as well as a diachronic explanation can be given to idioms.[3] The synchronic explanation states that an idiom is a standardized expression, which, although made up of several words, nevertheless functions semantically as one lexical item.[4] From a diachronic viewpoint, however, there is some uncertainty regarding the terminology. What might be called 'true' idioms would be expressions that can not be revitalized by substituting one of its parts with a synonym, in contrast to what is called frozen, or dead metaphors.[5] Saying "They tried to sugar the medicine" can revitalize the frozen metaphor "They tried to sweeten

---

[1] So e.g. Sigrist (1993: 384).

[2] The literature on 'metaphor' is so huge one hesitates even to start referring; Kittay (1987) will in the following be used as a basic and reliable study, together with Ricoeur (1978).

[3] For a technical definition, see Cruse (1986: 37-9). For further discussions, see Gläser (1988) and Sornig (1988). For a very narrow definition, see Ward (1986: 95-9).

[4] So e.g. Sornig (1988: 282). Contrast e.g. Barré (1990: 46-7), who seeks to interpret the idiom *nāṣā' nepeš* by focusing on its lexemic parts and not its linguistic use.

[5] So Cruse (1986: 41-4), who argues for this distinction. For a thorough discussion of dead metaphors, see Cooper (1986: 118-39) who prefers not to call them metaphors at all, but polysemes. This is a terminological problem, as in Nielsen (1989: 51), " in such an event a dead metaphor is concerned, i.e. a metaphor that does not at present function as a metaphor." However, how can a metaphor remain a metaphor when it does not function as such?

the pill". However, the idiom "John pulled his sister's leg" can not be revitalized by saying "John tugged at his sister's leg."[1] On the other hand, it would be natural to assume that most idioms originated as metaphors, but their metaphorical use has slipped out of the current language, or evolved beyond understanding. The difference between a frozen metaphor and an idiom is then a matter of semantic opacity.[2]

An idiom can also be the result of a metonymy, as well as metaphor.[3] This is another reason why the term 'idiom' should not be used synonymously with dead or frozen metaphor. Idiom is therefore used in this analysis as an overall concept, whereas dead or frozen metaphor is restricted to those idioms that have come into being through metaphorization, and this is often observable through the possibility of revitalizing them into live metaphors.[4] However, in dealing with an ancient language, the issue of revitalizing frozen metaphors becomes almost impossible in practise.

An idiom is thoroughly conventional, since there is no room for innovations as to its meaning or use. As soon as its status as fully conventional, i.e., only used in its primary meaning, is reduced by the intrusion of some form of secondary, or figurative meaning, the expression turns into a metaphor or metonymy. As will be shown below in the analysis, this has some very important implications for how the prophets used certain items of conventional meaning particular to their culture in the construction of their symbolic acts, which then by necessity had to be figurative and innovative. However, the mere use of items of conventional meaning brought with them certain associative meanings that were particularly useful in order to create a sense of recognition and understanding, even to the point of legitimation. These associative meanings were used in order to counter the often new and sometimes even shocking message that the prophet invested into his act.

Speech-act theory

Particular forms of conventional utterances are those that create a social fact, a change in social reality. By 'social reality' is meant a particular perception and construction of reality that is shared among a particular group or society.[5] This

---

[1] The examples are from Cruse (1986: 41-4).

[2] See de Ward (1977: 116), who notes that the borderline between metaphor and idiom is "fluid".

[3] So Kittay (1987: 297).

[4] So Kittay (1987: 297-9), Nielsen (1989: 52-3) and Eco (1984: 127). The term Catachresis is often used to refer to both frozen metaphors as well as metonymies.

[5] See e.g. Berger, and Luckmann (1966), Aijmer (1987), Searle (1995).

can only occur under particular circumstances that are strictly regulated by social conventions. Such an utterance is called 'performative', since it seems to perform something beyond being merely informative.[1] Among such performative utterances two categories are usually distinguished, namely illocutionary and perlocutionary. An illocutionary act is an utterance, which attempts to change how people think or act, but whether or not the illocutionary act succeeds, or not it has still been performed. A perlocutionary act, on the other hand, does change something by its very utterance, and therefore if it does not succeed, it has not been performed. A perlocutionary act can therefore also be termed a 'perlocutionary effect', since the effect may not have been intended. An illocutionary act can be more or less convincing, and its capacity to convince and make a change is termed 'illocutionary force'. This force is usually created by means of social conventions and expectations related to a particular social reality that is created by and relies on such conventions. An utterance can therefore have an illocutionary force with the intention of accomplishing a perlocutionary effect.

Normally, this terminology and speech-act theory in general is limited to verbal communication, but it has often been suggested, already by Austin himself, that it can also be used to describe nonverbal communication, or better, that performative acts can be accomplished by using nonverbal means.[2] Since it is a form of communication, albeit nonverbal, and since it is used with a clear intention of creating an effect on its audience, both emotive, cognitive as well as physical, and since the prophetic symbolic acts consistently operate by means of conventions which are used to build a specific social reality, these acts will be analysed by means of this terminology, when it is found relevant.

Non-Linguistic Terminology

Since prophetic symbolic acts are described as being nonverbal, there is also a need for a set of tools that enable us to analyse the acts as such. The terms that we will define here are 'convention/conventional', 'symbol', 'index', 'icon', and

---

[1] See Austin (1975), Lyons (1977: 7325-33) for this summary of terminology related to speech-act theory.

[2] So e.g. Lyons (1977: 726), 'it is arguable that there are certain non-linguistic communicative acts that would satisfy Austin's definition of speech-acts', Austin (1975: 119-22), Tambiah (1985: 78-80), Allwood (1987), Hillers (1990), Houston (1993), Downing (1995), Lang (1997).

finally the term 'act'. It should be noted that this terminology is strictly speaking inclusive of all discourse, which means that it could in principle be used to analyse text as well. This will then lead us to a workable definition of a prophetic symbolic act.

Convention/Conventional

Even though 'convention/conventional' is not restricted to the non-linguistic sphere but can also be used in relation to language, it will mostly be used in this study in relation to the area of the nonverbal. But the term does cross over this border, which only goes to show how useful it is to also be aware that both the verbal as well as the nonverbal make up human discourse.

A 'convention' is a social agreement and construction, made over time in a particular cultural context, and is presumed true and meaningful more or less unintentionally. The 'conventional' use of an act, or simply a 'conventional act' is therefore an act that by necessity has been performed before, and which has become, through a consensus agreement over a long period of time, a natural part of a particular society's construction of their social reality.[1] Berger describes this as the process of institutionalisation through reciprocal typification of habitualised behaviour.[2] Any such typification forms a social institution. This can be taken further into the area of speech act theory discussed above, which presumes that certain utterances are conventional, i.e., institutionalised. A convention, or institutionalised behaviour, is just as much experienced from within that particular society as an objective reality as the effect of a performative utterance. Searle speaks similarly of 'institutional facts', existing only within systems of 'constitutive rules', and forms a subclass of what he terms 'social facts' that must involve 'collective intentionality'.[3]

The terms *'legitimate'*/*'legitimation'* will sometimes be used in the analysis as they tie in closely with the concepts of 'convention' and 'social construction'. Once the conventions or institutionalised behaviours are transmitted to a new generation or a new group that has come into a social structure from without, they are experienced as traditions and parts of their memory. Therefore these conventions have to be legitimised sufficiently in order to integrate the new

---

[1] See e.g. Lewis (1969).

[2] Berger, and Luckmann (1966: 54-5).

[3] Searle (1995: 1-2, 24-9). It should be noted that Searle distinguishes between 'constitutive rules' and 'convention', since 'convention' implies arbitrariness. However, the distinction is not particularly useful, and it is not recognized in this study. Alternatively, it could be said that 'rules' form a subclass to 'conventions'. Cf. Saussure, et al. (1983: 100-1) for his use of 'convention' in the sense of 'collective habit'.

group into the social world wherein this convention is an objective reality, which only goes to show the limits of conventions.[1]

Symbol, icon, index

What is a symbolic act? This is a question that must be answered in a satisfying way before we can go on with the proper analysis of the relevant texts in the OT. The most acute problem with defining a symbolic act is not, however, related to the acts as such, but to the confusion that exists regarding the meaning and use of the elusive term 'symbol'. The term is used by scholars in various fields with quite different meanings.[2] So before we can ask what a symbolic act actually is, we must first decide what we mean by thee term 'symbol' and its derivatives 'symbolic' and 'symbolize'.

In a very basic sense a 'symbol', as well as well as 'sign', could be something, usually concrete and particular, that stands for something else, usually abstract and generalised.[3] However, it is when we try to understand this process of representing that various systems exist to charter the various possibilities for both 'sign' and 'symbol'. In the areas of linguistics and semiotics the two terms are not used interchangeably, however. Instead, either 'sign' is a subclass to 'symbol',[4] or vice versa.[5] Although the former has been held, it is the latter that is most often used, and Saussure and Peirce personify the two alternatives for this class.

Saussure's model for explaining the relationship between what is represented, or signified, and that which represents, or signifies, is that it forms, in its dyadic structure, the 'sign', and it is arbitrary. He uses 'symbol' in the sense of having some form of natural connection between the signifier and what is signified, and hence, it does not form part of what Saussure regarded as the basic task of 'semiology'.[6] Firth follows Saussure by attempting to differentiate between 'signal' and 'symbol', as 'to class as symbols those presentations where there is

---

[1] Berger, and Luckmann (1966: 61-2, 92-4). See also Austin (1975: 103-4) from the point of view of speech act theory, who notes that whereas the illocutionary act is conventional, the perlocutionary act can not be, since it depends on the reaction of the person acted upon. Instead, legitimation as a form of secondary socialisation has to be set in motion.

[2] For a convenient overview, see Heisig (1987), cf. also Firth (1973).

[3] Similarly, e.g. Gorman (1990: 22-3).

[4] So e.g. Geertz (1973: 208, n 19), Malmberg (1977: 21).

[5] See Eco (1986) for a useful overview of various alternatives.

[6] Saussure, et al. (1983: 67-8).

much greater lack of fit – even perhaps intentionally – in the attributions of fabricator and interpretator.'[1]

Peirce system, however, is a system that is much more complicated and different in principle, where the sign[2] does not consist of a dyadic relationship but of a triadic one. This system, often characterized by obscurity, has however certain advantages to this analysis, particularly since triadic structure of the sign facilitates the detailed analysis of the prophetic symbolic acts. It should also be noted that Peirce worked with a very broad semiotic approach, encompassing all forms of communications, whereas Saussure limited himself to the linguistic code. In order to correctly understand Peirce, I will quote him extensively;

> A sign, or *representamen*, is something which stands to somebody for something in some respect or capacity. It addresses somebody, that is, creates in the mind of that person an equivalent sign, or perhaps a more developed sign. That sign which it creates I call the *interpretant* of the first sign. The sign stands for something, its *object*. It stands for that object, not in all respects, but in reference to a sort of idea, which I have sometimes called the *ground* of the representamen.

A 'sign' is then to Peirce a triadic constellation, of which 'representamen' and 'object' would be the equivalents of Saussure's signifier and signified. What is not found in Saussure's model, and makes Peirce's system different in principle from Saussure's, are the two terms 'interpretant' and 'ground'. 'Interpretant' is to Peirce another sign in the mind of the person, an idea and perhaps we should say the meaning[3] of the sign, in a particular moment, referring to a particular object.[4] A flask of oil ('representamen') could evoke in our minds various things, such as cooking ('object') if one is hungry, squeaking doors ('object') if there is one at home, or water ('object') if one is thirsty. In ancient Israel, on the other hand, they might have thought of how they looked ('object') because of its cosmetic use, or even of anointing the king ('object'). The interpretant is then the idea in the mind that is evoked by the sign, and which points to a certain object.[5]

---

[1] Firth (1973: 60, 66-7), and also, 'in the interpretation of a symbol the conditions of its presentation are such that the interpreter ordinarily has much more scope for exercise of his own judgement -the alternatives in the situation may be much less circumscribed.'

[2] Peirce (1931: 2.303), a 'sign' is 'anything which determines something else (its *interpretant*) to refer to an object to which itself refers'. For studies on Peirce and his system, see e.g. Eco, and Sebeok (1983), Sheriff (1989), Hausman (1993), Ochs (1998).

[3] The term 'meaning' is here used similar to 'sense', which would make 'object' similar to 'reference', the terminology of Frege, see Lyons (1977: 177-86)

[4] See e.g. Aichele (1997: 63-7).

[5] See Aichele (1997: 65).

The concept of 'ground' is best taken in the sense of context, or communicative setting in which the interpretant occurs.[1]

There can be three kinds of signs; 'icon', 'index' and 'symbol'.[2] An icon is a sign, which is connected to its object by virtue of its own character, i.e., on the basis of analogy. An index works on the basis of association, which requires a direct relation between the representamen and its object, but no particular characteristics. The symbol works on the basis of convention, or general rule, i.e., the only reason why a red light (representamen) stands for 'halt' is because we have agreed to view it that way. It is particularly this triadic way of construing various forms of representations that is the value of Peirce's model to this analysis.

However, there is a problem of terminology, since Peirce's use of 'symbol' in the sense of the conventional is uncommon. We will therefore make two important distinctions as to the use of the term 'symbol'. First, we will use terms such as convention/conventional instead of symbol/symbolic in Peirce's sense, which also ties in to what has been said earlier regarding the linguistic terminology and also helps connect the symbolic analysis to the use of speech act analysis. We will ask if the prophetic symbolic act achieves its meaning by means of analogy, i.e., if its symbolism is iconic, or by means of association and have an indexical symbolism, or by conventional rules and institutions. Second, we will restrict the use of 'symbol' to secondary, or figurative meanings.[3] This is obvious in the case of the prophetic acts, since they are not simply meant to demonstrate what they actually perform physically, but are intended to convey something else, beyond their mere physical performance. That secondary, or figurative, use is termed here 'symbolic', in agreement with e.g. Saussure and as it is the more common use of the term.

Act

Mostly for the sake of completeness, we will define the term 'act', since there is no real need to delve into the technicalities of 'action theory' or 'social interactionism'. We will use the term 'act' in the very broad sense of when an individual, conscious of his/her doings, intentionally brings about a physical change of some kind, to some end, in a given context. One limitation that is strictly not necessary in this definition is the demand for a physical change. However, it is introduced in order to clarify that it is not a matter of verbal acts, but only non-

---

[1] So Sheriff (1989: 56).

[2] Peirce (1931: 2.247-9, 292-307).

[3] See e.g. Sigrist (1993: 384), who defines a 'geste symbolique' as a 'signe figuratif'.

verbal. This definition excludes various unconscious acts, although it does not exclude very basic acts, such as opening a door. But these very simple acts are eliminated when the accompanying terms 'symbol' and 'prophetic' are added, since they put their particular demands on the act in order for it to categorized as a prophetic symbolic act.

'Prophetic symbolic act'

Now that we have reached a workable definition of the terms involved, we can continue by asking what it means for an act to be symbolic. A simple answer to this question would be as follows:

> 'A symbolic act is an act that conveys a meaning that transcends the meaning related to its physical accomplishment.'

However, in order to avoid confusion, this definition should include references to the fact that it is the actual performance of the act that is relevant, and the fact that the act performs a particular *function*. This would lead to a more expanded definition:

> 'A symbolic act is an act whose performance has the function of conveying a secondary meaning that transcends the primary meaning related to its physical accomplishment.'

For an act to be prophetic we mean simply that it is used as a means by the prophet in his communication of the word he has received from his God to his people, as a recognized intermediate figure. It is used by the prophet together with his verbal communication. This means that not everything the prophet does can be a prophetic symbolic act, since there has to be an indication in the text that it is part of his task as God's messenger.

In order to limit our definition to prophetic symbolic acts, the following definition will be followed;

> 'A prophetic symbolic act is an act whose performance by a prophet has the function of conveying a secondary meaning that transcends the primary meaning related to its physical accomplishment. This meaning forms an inherent part of that prophet's message as a divine messenger, and functions in cooperation with and as an integrated part of his verbal teaching.'

In the light of this definition, we are able to select those texts that describe prophetic symbolic acts. Of course this definition is done in close contact with the analysis of the texts, and it is in and as a consequence of this analysis, that will follow below, that this definition has been worked out and the texts have been selected.

A Critical View of Friebel, 'Jeremiah's and Ezekiel's Sign-Acts'

The most comprehensive analysis of prophetic symbolic acts so far is the recent volume by Friebel, which deals only with the acts by Jeremiah and Ezekiel.[1] His view on the magical or non-magical character was mentioned above, but because of the scope and theoretical ambitions in his study, it deserves a particular analysis, and especially since there would appear to be some serious flaws in his theoretical approach.

Friebel makes use of research on nonverbal communication in order to sharpen his understanding of the 'sign-acts' of Jeremiah and Ezekiel, and he also notes that there are two levels of interpretation, the literary and the nonverbal.[2] He then states that he chooses to understand the persuasive aspect of the acts on the nonverbal level, without describing how it can be that we can understand a nonverbal act through the means of text. The consequence is for Friebel's study, that every text is simply presumed to describe the act precisely as it took place, and it is understandable therefore that Friebel chooses to simply assume the reliability of the literary renderings of these acts. He then uses the quite technical terminology of 'coding' in order to understand the symbolic acts, as if they were indeed available. This also has consequences for his use of semiotics.

In his section on terminology, Friebel follows basically the same semiotic terminology as is followed here, except that he does not acknowledge that it is a semiotic model, and also that it originates from Peirce, instead he follows a variant formulated by Hawkes.[3] Unfortunately, Hawkes uses Peirce's terms differently from Peirce himself, which creates confusion. For example, the 'interpretant' is for Peirce a second sign that is created in the mind of the person experiencing the first sign, whereas Hawkes identifies the two, a confusion that also involves the term 'ground', which to Hawkes seems to play the role of Peirce's 'interpretant'.[4] Admittedly, there are different schools of semiotics that have evolved from the way Peirce presented his system, and it does create a terminological confusion. A related problem is the fact that Friebel does not seem to make a difference between 'arbitrary' and 'conventional', since a sign that is 'arbitrarily coded' is at the same time conventional. Since arbitrary in this context comes from Saussure's semiotic model, where it denotes the choice of a word when it is used for the first time, it should have been distinctly separated from the more Peircian term conventional, which denotes the present status be-

---

[1] Friebel (1999).
[2] Friebel (1999: 12-3).
[3] Friebel (1999: 37-8).
[4] Friebel (1999: 38, n72).

tween the sign and its interpretant. Here Friebel unfortunately makes another mistake, as fatal as it is strange, namely of equating 'figurative' with 'arbitrary' and 'conventional'.[1] Although there is a large amount of variations in linguistic terminology, there is no discussion as to how to use the term 'figurative'. It always denotes that which is not conventional, but where the relationship is apparent in either an iconic or an indexical way. A word is used figuratively, i.e. in its secondary sense, when it is used metaphorically or metonymically, but when it is not, it is used in its primary sense.[2] It is strange to see such a misunderstanding in a work otherwise so impressive as Friebel's. The problem occurs when he uses a linguistic term, 'figurative', and uses it to classify what is not linguistic but nonverbal. 'Figurative' then refers according to Friebel to what is 'symbolically', i.e., arbitrarily, reused. In Jer 13, Jeremiah purchases a girdle, and to Friebel the girdle has only figurative meaning, in the sense of arbitrary,[3] but the emphasis on the clinging of the girdle to the body indicates an iconic relationship to the intimate relationship between the people and its God. All in all, it would have been better if the two sets of terminology had been kept apart. Another example where this creates confusion is when he refers to Polk's expression 'the metaphor/parable's world'.[4] The point, which Polk is trying to make, is similar to that of Paul Ricoeur, namely that by means of imagination a metaphor may enable the reader to understand one 'world' by the use of another. But to Friebel, this means that his category 'figurative acts' are related to this category because they demanded more from the audiences. But the fact is that the acts based on 'arbitrary' or conventional means are always the simplest to understand, simply because they are based on agreement. When no such agreement exists, the meaning must be based on either iconic or indexical meaning. To Friebel, there seems, strangely enough, to be a third possibility, where the prophet challenges his audience without conventional means, but also without using icons or indexes, which is simply impossible if one hopes for any success in any form of communication. Had Friebel remained consistently with Peircian terminology, this confusion would not have occurred. This confusion also keeps Friebel from understanding the prophet's subtle use of items of conventional meaning in the construal of the symbolic acts, since according to Friebel the acts are 'representational' or 'figurative'. This categorisation, which is simply not meaningful, since these acts are made up of various forms of symbolism and can therefore not be so easily labelled.

Friebel also seems to misunderstand the terminology of speech-act theory, as it can relate to nonverbal communication.[5] When the potter makes his pottery, it

---

[1] Friebel (1999: 38).

[2] See e.g. Waard, and Nida (1986: 152), Abrams (1993: 66-70).

[3] Waard, and Nida (1986: 103).

[4] Friebel (1999: 435), Polk (1983: 572-3).

[5] Friebel (1999: 378-80).

is to Friebel a performative act, in contrast to prophetic symbolic acts, which are communicative and therefore not performative. Again, Friebel misunderstands the basic terminology and turns it upside down. Performatives are always interpersonal, and not something that can describe what a potter does to his clay. On the other hand, it is precisely the prophetic symbolic act, which can function as an illocutionary act, since it has the intention, or force, to change the feelings and actions of the audience. That can hardly be the case with a piece of clay.

Friebel also seems to disregard the difficult issues of textual criticism and Dtr language in the book of Jeremiah, something one can hardly afford to do in such a technical study as Friebel's.

A Wider Frame I: Nonverbal Communication

Introduction

The purpose is here to broaden the scope of analysis of symbolic acts by understanding how nonverbal communication at large is analysed, and by that learn how to understand what is nonverbal. The value of this approach lies in understanding the place of the analysis of legal symbolic acts in the more general field of nonverbal communication.[1] It will aid the analysis not the least in avoiding mistakes easily made if research in neighbouring areas is not considered.[2] The empirical study of nonverbal communication will also be scrutinized in order to find some tools that will be valuable in the analysis. Then the focus narrows down to nonverbal communication as it is presented in literature, which is a step closer to what is being studied here. An even narrower view will then be taken, as studies of nonverbal communication in literature from the ancient Near East, including the OT, are brought to the forefront. Finally, the attention will turn to studies concerning prophetic symbolic acts in the literature from the ancient Near East, including the OT.

---

[1] For a definition, see Kendon (1981: 3), where it is said to consist of "all of the ways in which communication is effected between persons when in each other's presence, by means other than words." For works on the area of nonverbal communication in general, see e.g. Key (1980), Key (1982), Birdwhistell (1970), Morris (1979), Sebeok (1981), Efron, and Veen (1972) and Poyatos (1983: 69), who has a more technical definition.

[2] For a similar overview, see Friebel (1999: 34-40), although Friebel makes the mistake of not taking the survey into the study of nonverbal communication in literature, which is of obvious use to a study of prophetic symbolic acts described in texts.

Empirical study of nonverbal communication

In the literature regarding the empirical study of nonverbal communication there does not seem to be any consensus as to how to structure the different forms, although some basic distinctions can be found. There seems to be at least two ways of structuring nonverbal communication, a semiotic and a functional.[1] They are mostly combined in order to describe the different forms of nonverbal communication, but in order to suit this analysis they will be handled separately here.

The semiotic distinction distinguishes between how the acts achieve their meanings, i.e. their coding, for which there are three basic alternatives, and we recognize the Peircian triad.[2] First, an act can be iconic, whereby the performance of the act is in some way analogical to its meaning.[3] Second, an act can also be indexical whereby the act points to its meaning by way of some association that leads in that direction.[4] The third possibility is the conventional act.[5] In this third category, the relationship between the act and its meaning is not observable but agreed upon within the culture. The meaning is then often said to be conventional or arbitrary, although these two terms are not strictly synonymous in this context.[6] We recognize this use of the terms icon, index and conventional from the definitions given above, and which will be used in this study.

For example legal symbolic acts can be called conventional acts, since their legal meaning is not observable, but agreed upon within the cultural sphere.[7] However, it is not a matter of either or in deciding between the iconic/indexical on the one hand and the conventional on the other. It is more of a scale, from a

---

[1] The distinction is borrowed from Kendon (1983: 15).

[2] Kendon (1983: 15) describes these three categories as pointing, characterizing or depicting and conventional or symbolic.

[3] See e.g. "Physiographic" used by Efron, and Veen (1972: 11) and "Iconic" by Bolinger (1975: 20), Ekman, and Friesen (1969) and Poyatos (1983: 98, 116, 126-7).

[4] See e.g. "Deictic" used by Efron, and Veen (1972: 11) and Poyatos (1983: 114-6).

[5] This is called "Semiotic gestures" by Barakat (1969: 110-1), "Lexical gestures" by Bolinger (1975: 19), "Emblematic/Symbolic" by Efron, and Veen (1972: 11), "Symbolic gestures" by Morris (1979: xvi-xvii) and Kendon (1983: 15), and "Emblems" as coded arbitrarily by Ekman, and Friesen (1969) and Poyatos (1983: 98).

[6] It depends upon whether the act from an etic or emic perspective. From an etic perspective, conventional can be used synonymously with arbitrary. From an emic perspective, the conventional is often given an explanation that is more iconic/indexical than arbitrary. For a similar view, see Lyons (1977: 104-5). Lewis (1969: 70), in a basic study of the concept of 'Convention', holds that it is redundant to speak of an arbitrary convention, since a convention is by necessity always arbitrary.

[7] See my earlier study, Viberg (1992).

low form of coding of the indexical/iconic, since it is based on observable similarities and associations, to a higher form of coding, where there is nothing but the cultural code to rely on in order to discover the meaning of the act. A result of higher coding is that the performance is no longer needed to recognize the meaning. Instead, it is needed to mark boundaries to other similar acts. The performance of these acts then become harder to understand indexically/iconically, since legal symbolic acts are highly coded acts and it is the particular cultural code of law that is relevant in order to understand their function. However, this does not mean that these legal symbolic acts can not under particular circumstances still contain some indexical/iconic meaning, although it will always be subsidiary to the legal function.

Since legal symbolic acts are culturally conventional, they are not apt to be transposed across cultural boundaries, but instead they are culture specific. It is important to note that this applies to the meaning of the acts and not their procedure. Similar acts are given different meanings in different cultures, and the same would apply to legal symbolic acts.[1] It must therefore be the cultural context in which the acts occur that has the prime authority in providing them with meaning, and naturally this applies to prophetic symbolic acts as well.

Prophetic symbolic acts, in contrast, are not and can not be conventional, since they form part of one individual's message and are not to be repeated. The prophetic acts are often construed by means of various items that are taken from contexts that are highly conventional, but as a prophetic act, it can not be conventional but must be described as either iconic or indexical. This does not mean that a prophetic symbolic act can not be both a symbolic act and at the same time a conventional act. We find an example of this in Jer 32, where Jeremiah's act is both a conventional legal act of land-purchase, and a prophetic symbolic act with a highly innovative and also controversial meaning.

Another way of structuring nonverbal communication is to use a functional distinction. Some acts are used together with speech and others are not.[2] When an act is used with speech this relation, which can vary in kind, is then of relevance for the meaning of the act. The act can merely duplicate the verbal part, thus complementing the verbal part in some way, without being redundant.[3] The act can also illustrate what is being said, which ties it in much closer with the

---

[1] See e.g. Barakat (1969: 111), "Once removed from the original cultural context the semiotic gestures require different meanings."

[2] See e.g. Ekman, and Friesen (1969: 53), Efron, and Veen (1972: 10-1), Bolinger (1975: 19), Morris (1979: xvi) and Poyatos (1983: 99).

[3] So Poyatos (1983: 99).

verbal part.[1] On the other hand, an act, which functions without any speech, is itself communicative.[2] It is particularly the conventional acts which functions in this way, i.e. as substitutes for speech. This becomes easier to understand when the conventional character of words in their primary senses is taken into consideration.[3]

To sum up, the following points are relevant from the area of nonverbal communication for the study of prophetic symbolic acts;

1. A distinction should be made between iconic, indexical and conventional acts. The prophetic symbolic act can not be conventional, and must be described by means of index and icon.
2. The proper way to understand a prophetic symbolic act is through observing its procedure and how the act is construed by using various conventional means, in contrast to conventional acts.
3. All symbolic acts are culturally specific, which is why the comparative use of similar acts from other cultures is to be used with caution.
4. The relation between an act and speech that is used in relation to the performance of the act is important, since the act is then not functioning communicatively of itself but in relation to this speech.

Study of nonverbal communication in literature
So far nonverbal communication has been dealt with as it is available for empirical study. However, this study is concerned with nonverbal communication as it is presented in literary form. It is therefore the textual world, presented through the use of written language, that constitutes the situation of the nonverbal communication and not the real world analysed by means of empirical study.[4]

---

[1] For the term 'Illustrator', see e.g. Poyatos (1983: 103-4).

[2] The term most commonly used is "Emblem", so e.g. Ekman, and Friesen (1969) and Poyatos (1983: 98). Kendon (1983: 16), however, labels this category "Autonomous gestures".

[3] So e.g. Barakat (1969: 110).

[4] For the concept of 'textual world', see e.g. Vorster (1985: 60-1), who uses the term 'Narrative world' and Ricoeur, and Thompson (1981: 112), "Hermeneutics can be defined no longer as an inquiry into the psychological intentions which are hidden beneath the text, but rather as the explication of the being-in-the-world displayed by the text. What is to be interpreted in the text is a proposed world which I could inhabit and in which I could project my ownmost possibilities." A similar case can be made for a "ritual world", so Gorman (1990: 15).

The study of nonverbal communication within literature is a rather well trodden subject,[1] as well as that of nonverbal communication within other art forms such as painting and sculpture.[2] However, when different scholars try to categorize nonverbal communication in literature, they arrive at much the same categories as was found above regarding the empirical study of nonverbal communication. Smith, e.g., distinguishes between gestures that function together with speech and those that function independently.[3] The latter category is further separated into conscious and unconscious gestures. Barasch, on the other hand, distinguishes between natural, i.e. spontaneous gestures over against conventional, which are said to be cultural products as well as culture specific.[4] Although the term natural is unfortunate, it could well be compared to Ekman's distinction between acts that are common human experiences and those that vary with different cultures.[5] Poyatos has given a valuable survey of the different ways nonverbal communication can be used in literature, and what follows is a summary of his survey.[6]

1. An act is described together with an explanation of its meaning, which is the most usual method and therefore what we should expect to find in literature. This is also the case with prophetic symbolic acts. Since they are innovative and not conventional, they have to be supplied with an explanation that is given to the prophet to declare as openly as he performed the act. When the understanding of the act can not rely on conventions and institutional facts, the prophet must resort to verbally explaining his act.

2. An act is described without an explanation of its meaning, thus leaving the reader to understand it by means of contextual signals. This is the usual way legal symbolic acts are given in the OT, due to their conventional status. The reason is that the legal function of these acts was considered by the author to be very much a part of the cultural context, i.e. culturally conventional, and since this context was thought to be shared by the readers, no further verbal explanation was thought to be required. However, because of the cultural as well as the chronological distance, the modern interpreter is in the difficult position of hav-

---

[1] See e.g. Wespi (1949), Smith (1976), Benson (1980) and Poyatos (1983: 277-314), the most thorough and theoretically satisfying work. The study of nonverbal communication in the OT and other ancient Near Eastern literature will be taken up below.

[2] See e.g. Barasch (1987) and Sittl (1890).

[3] Smith (1976: 21-7).

[4] Poyatos (1983: 98: 113-5).

[5] Ekman, and Friesen (1969).

[6] Poyatos (1983: 308-10).

ing to transform his own interpretive cultural context into the author's context in order to understand these acts properly.

3. An explanation of the meaning of the act can be included without mentioning the nonverbal part. This is a use, which is almost impossible to detect when studying ancient texts as the OT. One possible example would be the oath. Since the act of raising the hand is sometimes used with the legal function of enacting an oath, the mere mentioning of the fact that an oath has been taken could be taken to infer that the act was performed. This would, however, demand that the act was mandatory in oath taking and not optional. Such a conclusion can not be drawn because of the limited amount of occurrences available of the act and the limited insight available into the oath taking at large within the culture mirrored in the OT. Such an insight would, in practise, demand the use of informants, or at least a vaster material than the one we have from the OT.

4. An expression that usually comes together with the nonverbal part is mentioned, although the nonverbal is not. This is also a use, which is practically impossible to detect in the study of ancient texts. The problem is simply how to know that an expression is always used with a nonverbal part. This would again demand the use of an informant.

The major difference between studying nonverbal communication empirically and in literary form is the importance of the literary context in understanding the meaning. The act should be seen as part of the literary whole to be understood by the interpreter.[1] It is as if the information concerning the acts comes not from eye-witnesses but second-handedly, through a description of the acts in literary form.[2] Of course this does not exclude the importance of studying the cultural, social and historical contexts of the text in question and how knowledge of these are expected to be found with the reader. This can be said to be included in understanding the meaning of literature in a wider and more profound sense.[3]

The nonverbal communication can be analyzed similarly to the way the empirical study was performed only if the barrier of the linguistic code is neglected.

---

[1] Cf. Bal (1988: 154). This is a fundamenal idea that is returned to several times in this introduction.

[2] For a technical description of the process whereby the author decodes his signs, reduces them to the verbal code and the following decoding act by the reader, see Poyatos (1983: 290-3).

[3] Cf. Prince (1982: 105-9), who speaks of a code of written narrative with different subcodes, e.g. cultural, symbolic and hermeneutic, using Barthe's terminology. As far as the author and the reader use similar sets of codes the text can, with its descriptions of acts, be understood similarly.

All information concerning the act is by definition achieved through analyzing the text, which describes the act. This is why the semiotic terminology given above, icon, index and conventional is supplanted in this study by a terminology which is similar but more limited to the linguistic code, namely metaphor, metonymy, idiom and conventional meaning.[1]

A Wider Frame II: Symbolic Acts in the Ancient Near East

So far the empirical analysis of nonverbal communication as well as its occurrence in literature have been surveyed. The next step is the analysis of nonverbal communication in literature from the ancient Near East and in particular, the OT. The tendency is here that the theoretical base of the analyses becomes poorer the further away from the empirical study of nonverbal communication this survey gets.

The major work on nonverbal communication in the ancient Near East is Gruber's two volume work from 1980.[2] It concerns gestures relating to supplication, prayer, obeisance, greeting, sadness, mourning,[3] anger and joy. The analysis is performed by analyzing texts from the three areas of Biblical Hebrew, Ugaritic and Akkadian. Gruber's study tends to emphasize emotive aspects[4] and is somewhat lacking in its theoretical base.[5] This is most evident in its failure to distinguish between idiomatic and non-idiomatic use, as well as the question whether an idiomatic expression originally described a gesture, which Gruber seems to take for granted. He has no discussion of concepts such as metaphor and metonymy, which should be included in such a study where the material is solely textual and mostly figurative. The fact that the analysis covers so much data as from three different cultural spheres raises the question whether the same act can be taken to mean the same thing across cultural boundaries. Furthermore, since the large amount of data does not permit a close contextual analysis, Gruber's work runs the risk of transferring a meaning across cultural boundaries and constructing meanings on the basis of, e.g., different body parts

---

[1] See Nida (1983: 87-9). For the iconic function of the metaphor, see e.g. Bolinger (1975: 218) and Ricoeur (1978: 199-200).

[2] Some further studies in this area by Gruber are Gruber (1978), Gruber (1980), Gruber (1983). A much older and briefer study is Vorwahl (1932).

[3] See the recent study of mourning in the ancient Near East and the OT, Pham (1999).

[4] So Kruger (1989: 55).

[5] So Carena (1981: 12), who complains about the lack of insight into semiotic theory and the use of comparative method.

that are involved in an act, an essentially etymological procedure that should be-long to a passed era of study. Otherwise, however, Gruber's work is a massive inventory of nonverbal communication in ancient Near Eastern literature.[1]

Another work, dealing with nonverbal communication within a limited text of the OT, is Carena's work from 1981. It is an investigation of the nonverbal communication within the prophetic stories of Elijah and Elisha in 1 Kgs 16:29 - 2 Kgs 13:25. Carena includes all forms of nonverbal communication. His approach is semiotic, in the sense that he regards all communication within the textual world, both the verbal and the nonverbal, as communicative and there-fore in need of de-codification by the interpreter.[2] The major strength of Carena's study is its thorough theoretical base, which results in an analysis through a grid of twelve categories. The use of semiotics and in particular the semiotic grand view which incorporates both verbal and nonverbal communica-tion is endorsed in this analysis. However, in contrast to Carena's study, this analysis is much more concerned with the contextual analysis. This is then, by contrast, the weakness of Carena's work, namely that he does not show how he has achieved his results.

Legal symbolic acts from the ancient Near East together with the OT have been studied by Viberg[3] and Malul.[4] These acts are, as have been mentioned above, thoroughly conventional and must be distinguished in principle from such innovative symbolic acts as those of the OT prophets. A third category also exists, namely cultic acts. They share with legal symbolic acts the conventional character.[5]

Even though prophecy is a well-known phenomenon from the ancient Near Eastern literature,[6] there is as yet no study of prophetic symbolic acts from the ancient Near East, no doubt because there appear to be only one example known, and that single text is quite recently published.[7] Nevertheless, this ex-ample may nevertheless bring some light to our study of the similar acts in the OT, so a closer study may be called for.

---

[1] A more promising approach is taken by Kruger (1989: 54-5).

[2] Carena (1981: 12).

[3] Viberg (1992).

[4] Malul (1988). See also Munn-Rankin (1956), Greengus (1969), Draffkorn Kilmer (1974)

[5] See e.g. Rowley (1956), Jacobsen (1975), Gorman (1990).

[6] See Huffmon (1992) for a survey with further literature.

[7] ARM 26.206, see Durand (1988).

ARM 26.206: The Symbolic act of a muhhûm

1 *a-na [be-lí-ia]* 2 *qí-[bí-ma]* 3 *um-ma [ia-qí-im-*^d*IM]* 4 *ìr-[ka-a-ma]* 5 1 ^lú*mu-uh-hu-u[m ša* ^d*da-gan]* 6 *il-li-kam-ma ki-[a-am iq-bi]* 7 *um-ma šu-ú-ma w[u-di mi-nam]* 8 *ša zi[im-ri-li-im]* 9 *a-ka-al* 1 *si[la i-di-in-m]a* 10 *lu-ku-ul* 1 *sila [ad-di-in]-šum-ma* 11 *ba-al-ṭú-us-sú-ma [i-n]a [p]a-an a-bu-lim* 12 *[i]-ku-ul- šu* 13 *ù lú-meš su-* gi 14 *i-na pa-an a-bu-ul-li-im* 15 *ša sa-ga-ra-tim*^ki 16 *ú-pa-hi-ir- ma* 17 *ki-a-am iq-bi um-ma šu-ú-ma* 18 *ú-ku-ul-tum iš-ša-ka-an* 19 *a-na a-la-né-e ru-gu-um-ma* 20 *a-sà-ak-ka-am li-te-er-ru* 21 *lú ša ri-i-sa-am i-pu-šu* 22 *i-na a-lim*^ki *li-šu-ṣú-ú* 23 *ù a-na ša-la-am be-lí-ka zi-i[m-ri-li-m]* 24 1 *túg tu-la-ab-ba-ša-an-ni* 25 *an-ni-tam iq-bé-e-em-m[a]* 26 *a-na ša-la-am be-lí-[ia]* 27 1 *túg ú-la-ab-b[i-is-sú]* 28 *a-nu-um-ma te-[er-tam ša]* 29 *id-bu-ba-a[m aš-ṭúr-ma]* 30 *a-na ṣe-er [be-lí-ia]* 31 *áš-tap-ra-[am]* 32 *ù te-er-ta-šu i-na sí-na sí-mì-iš-tim* 33 *ú-ul iq-bé-e-em i-na pu-hu-ur* lú šu-gi 34 *te-er-ta-šu id-di-in*[1]

Say to my Lord; This says Yaqqim-Addu, your servant. A *muhhûm* of Dagan came to me and said: 'What shall I eat that belongs to Zi'mri-Lim? Give me a lamb and I will eat it!' I gave him a lamb and he ate it alive[2] in front of the Gate. He gathered the elders in front of the Saggaratum Gate, and said: 'There will be a 'consumption'.[3] Call the cities, and let them return the sacred items. A man who makes an assault, let them expel him from the city. And, for the good of your Lord, Zimri-Lim, you should clothe me with a garment.' This is what he said to me, and for the good of my Lord, I clothed him with a garment.[4] The message which he spoke to me, I have written down and sent it to my Lord. He did not speak his message secretly but gave his message in the assembly of the elders.[5]

The text is a letter to Zimri-Lim, the king of Mari, from his governor in Sagga-ratum, Yaqqim-Addu. It describes how Yaqqim-Addu was approached by a cer-

---

[1] Durand (1988: 434-5).

[2] Both Huffmon (1997: 13), from whom the translation is taken, and Gordon (1995b: 77) translates *balṭussu* as 'raw', when it actually means 'alive', AHw 100b, so also the editor of the text Durand (1988: 388), 'tout vivant', and Sasson (1994: 311).

[3] The word *ukultum* means here 'plague', see AHw 1406b, known in the Mari texts through the expression *ukulti ilim*. Huffmon (1997: 13) translates 'plague', but we follow Sasson (1994: 311, n 43) in order to clearly bring out the wordplay.

[4] This should not be taken as a symbolic act, but as a request from the *muḫḫûm* for acceptance of his status, see Sasson (1994: 311), Huffmon (1997: 14). There is no need to follow Astour (1992) and deduce from the request for a garment that the *muḫḫûm* was naked while he performed the symbolic act.

[5] See also Durand (1988: 434-5), Huffmon (1997: 13).

tain *muḫḫûm*, an 'ecstatic', or simply 'prophet'.[1] The *muḫḫûm* asks for a lamb, and it is given him. He then starts to eat it, apparently while it was still alive, in front of the city gate for all to see. The elders of the city were then gathered at the gate, to hear the interpretation of this symbolic act. The *muḫḫûm* then declares that there will come a plague, lit. *ukultum*, 'consumption', which is a deliberate wordplay on his request to eat, *akālum*.[2] As the lamb was suddenly struck by disaster, so will it be for Mari and Zimri-Lim. The act is clearly a symbolic act, very much in line with what we know from Jeremiah and Ezekiel, although as far as we know, neither of them performed such a grotesque act. Sasson understands the act to be an act of sympathetic magic, without providing any for argument why it should be so.[3]

The iconic symbolism of the act works on the basis of analogy, emphasized through the wordplay. There does not seem to be anything in the text itself that would necessitate a magical interpretation of the act, however. Indeed, since this is the only symbolic act that we know of from a *muḫḫûm* or any other category of divinatory figures from the Mari texts, there is nothing to compare with and to be able to conclude that the act is 'sympathetic magic'. There is also the very unusual emphasis on the fact that the *muḫḫûm* delivered his message in public

---

[1] AHw 582b, *maḫḫûm/muḫḫûm*. The form *muḫḫû(tu)m* is peculiar to Mari, since in Babylonian and Assyrian texts and a few times in Neo-Assyrian texts the normal form is *maḫḫû(m)*, see Durand (1988: 386-8), Parpola (1997: 9-10), Nissinen (1998: 9). Cf. also Malamat (1987: 39). It is worthy of note how Nissinen (1998) and Parpola (1997) uses 'prophecy' and 'prophet' quite freely when they discuss Assyrian texts. Cf. also Nissinen (1993). However, Noort (1977: 9-34, 92) is hesitant to using 'prophetic' for the examples from Mari, and he is especially against any form of evolutionary model where the Mari-texts constitute the older form of what we find in the OT. A critical distance to using 'prophet' can also be found in deJong Ellis (1989: 129-33), but she is hesitant because the term has usually denoted a west-semitic phenomenon, and been loaded with hidden assumptions from the modern interpreter's background. Both of these have been shown to be unfounded by the volumes by Nissinen and Parpola.

The opposite mistake can also occur, if the OT is not to be compared with the same descriptions as other ancient Near Eastern phenomena, but must always have its own terminology. A relevant example is the recent debate as to whether or not the OT prophets were not actual prophets but poets. Nevertheless, why can they not have been both? See e.g. Auld (1983), Carroll (1983), Geller (1983), Williamson (1983), Auld (1993), Gordon (1995b), Gordon (1995a), Boadt (1997). The discussion has received new energy from the discovery of the Akkadian/Amorite isomorph to Hebrew *nābî'*, 'prophet', namely *nābû/munabbiātu*, see Fleming (1993a), Fleming (1993b).

[2] This must have meant that the *muḫḫûm* spoke in Akkadian and not in Amorite. Whether that means that he was not native Amorite is uncertain.

[3] Sasson (1994: 311).

and not only to Yaqqim-Addu. It would seem best, therefore, to categorize it as a dramatic symbolic act, used by the *muḫḫûm* in order to enhance his message, and without any apparent magical significance.

The similarities with the prophetic symbolic acts from the OT are obvious.[1] It is performed by an intermediate figure with an already recognized status of being able to reveal divine messages, particularly messages of threat as in this case. It is also symbolic in the sense that the mere performance is not relevant, and the intimate connection with the verbal message through a word-play emphasizes the symbolic interpretation. The emphasis on the public performance is also similar, since an audience is necessary to communicate both verbal as well as nonverbal messages.

Text, Nonverbal Communication and 'Textual World'

With the help of how nonverbal communication should be studied, both empirically as well as in literature, how should we then go about analysing nonverbal communication in the form of prophetic symbolic acts, available only as they are in the textual form of various parts of the OT? Should concepts and technical apparatus akin to the verbal or to the nonverbal level be used? The choice that we have to make is whether to analyse the acts themselves, in their setting or discourse context of nonverbal communication, or in their literary settings where they are described. If we decide to focus on the descriptions of the acts we immediately run into the problem of not being able to distinguish between fictional and non-fictional acts. Whether or not the acts were performed they still form parts of the text, and therefore the study remains a textual study. To be fair, one has to admit that no study of the OT can be anything other than a textual study, since there is nothing but text.[2] What varies is how we see and define the analogical relationship between what the text describes, and the physical world. Do we e.g. consider the prophet Jeremiah to be not only a character in the text of the book of Jeremiah, but also a historical figure in late pre-exilic Judah? If so, then an historical analogy exists between the literary character Jeremiah and a historical character Jeremiah. But how do we go about determining whether there is such an analogy?

---

[1] So e.g. Gordon (1995b: 77), even though Gordon speaks somewhat carelessly about 'prophetic symbolism' unfortunately relying on Stacey (1990).

[2] Not counting the very meagre archaeological and epigraphical material available.

The text has to be studied with all the means necessary in order to understand its verbal communication, and it is only in and through this close study of the text that the understanding of a possible historical character can be understood as well. However, when we attempt to understand the symbolic act as nonverbal communication, a second arsenal of analytical tools is brought in. To be more correct, the acts that then are analysed are seen in and through the '*textual world*'[1] of the text, the imaginary form of reality, which is mirrored to us in and through the text. When we recognize the importance of this textual world we also have to emphasize that all possible referential status of texts are indirect, i.e., from the textual world to the real world through the means of text.

All we can be sure of when it comes to the issue of historicity, is that the prophet performs his symbolic act in a particular textual world. Any possible relationship between the real world and the textual world, i.e., any possible historicity of the prophetic symbolic acts, must rely on how the textual world refers to the real world. Questions that can be asked at this point are e.g. whether the textual world seems to project its narrative into the real world, and whether there is an amount of overlap between the two worlds, i.e., if we can recognize the real world in the textual world and vice versa. However, from a textual point of view, we can only come as far as to say that the text describes a world that is possible to us. At this point it is valuable to see how Ricoeur distinguishes between on the one hand the text as a structured *work* or *event*, construed by the means of literary techniques, and on the other hand the *world*, or *meaning*, of the text, in the sense of what the text is about.[2] It is in order to keep these two aspects apart that we will use different sets of terminology, one literary and one semiotic.

It is interesting to note that in the area of theatre and drama, this question of various levels has been the object of intensive study. A particular semiotic approach, similar to the one used here, speaks of possible worlds, the world-creating operations of texts and the demands that texts make on their readers to make these worlds come into being.[3] Elam speaks e.g. of the 'dramatic world' and how it is construed in the dramaturgical process, as part of the 'possible

---

[1] E.g. Nel (1995). The expressions 'narrative world', e.g. Vorster (1985), and 'literary world', e.g. Stulman (1995), are sometimes used interchangeably with 'textual world'. Cf. also Polk (1983: 572-3), who speaks of the world of the metaphor or parable.

[2] See particularly Ricoeur (1976: 92-3), 'What has to be appropriated is the meaning of the text itself, conceived in a dynamic way as the direction of thought opened up by the text. In other words, what has to be appropriated is nothing other that the power of disclosing a world that constitutes the reference of the text.' and Ricoeur, and Thompson (1981: 137-8).

[3] Elam (1980: 98-101).

worlds'[1] of the drama.[2] The text equals the script, which presents the textual world, i.e. the dramatic world, to the reader. The dramatic world is therefore re-presented in the script as a possible world, whereas on the stage we can see the possible world itself. The same would have been the case for the people in Jerusalem in the 8th century, who saw the prophet Isaiah waking around naked. To us, this story is available in the form of a text, which represents the textual world in which Isaiah walks. This can also be described by using Plato's distinction between 'mimesis', the imitation of verbal communication in the textual world, and 'diegesis', the narrative descriptions of all forms of nonverbal communication, since they can not be imitated by means of text.[3] The prophetic symbolic acts must therefore be parts of the diegesis of the textual world. From this follows, that everything that is described and not merely imitated in the text is also subject to various literary conventions that come into play when the description of a symbolic act is created. This is the best explanation why we are told in some instances that a prophetic symbolic act has been performed but not in others. The particular literary style, intention and structure create certain strictures on how the description should be represented.[4] It need have nothing to do with whether the act was performed or not, whether in the textual world or in the real world. This means that in order to understand a possible world one has to understand the particular culture in which it is represented textually, which in this study would mean that these prophetic symbolic acts have to be understood more on the basis of the actual analysis of the texts in which they are described, rather than on any preconceived ideas as to their nature and function.[5]

Elam distinguishes between possible worlds as 'hypothetically actual constructs' and imaginary worlds, which remain explicitly remote.[6] The imaginary worlds are not meant to be realized in the mind of the reader/audience, whereas

---

[1] The concept of 'possible worlds' opens up yet further areas of interesting research that are valuable for the interpretation of both texts as well as symbolic acts within texts, see e.g. Ryan (1991), Ronen (1994).

[2] Elam (1980: 98-9).

[3] See Chatman (1978), Aichele (1997: 119-20), Plato, *Republic*, X.

[4] Aichele (1997: 121), 'Every story is also necessarily incomplete, for no story can describe every detail of the story-world from every possible point of view' and '... "the true story" - the fully and correctly referential story - can never be told.'

[5] Elam (1980: 98-101: 101), 'A *semiotic* ... theory of possible worlds is concerned with the "world-creating" operations of *texts* and the conceptual labours they call for from their decoders ... . The textual worlds of concern to the semiotician are determined by *cultural* rather than logical models, and must be investigated according to the interpretative process required for their constitution rather than according to formal calculi.'

[6] Elam (1980: 110-1).

the possible worlds are. When the prophets Elijah and Elisha perform various miracles in 1-2 Kgs, the one more strange than the other, it is tempting to understand these acts as imaginary worlds, not meant to be anything other than distant echoes of other worlds, and without both capacity and intention to be realized in the mind of the reader. Instead, they function as the divine legitimation for these prophets. These acts are therefore different in most respects from the prophetic symbolic acts studied here, since the latter are always within the boundaries of being realized.

The logical step beyond this is to look at the world offered in and through the symbolic act itself, a 'symbolic world' inside the textual world, although a suitable term would have been dramatic world. That symbolic world is the meaning of the symbolic act, what it signifies or represents. Our theoretical approach therefore works on the basis of three layers; first, the text that describes the symbolic act; second, the performance of the act within the textual world; and third, the symbolic reference or representation of the act within the symbolic world of the act.

The Texts

Earlier studies have largely agreed on what the relevant texts are, but some differences remain, and therefore there is need for clarifying the criteria and applying them to all the texts that have been suggested. I have included the major modern studies on these acts, and marked those texts that each study regards as a relevant text.

It should be noted that Overholt does not set out to study the prophetic symbolic acts as the rest of these scholars do, but with the intention to study the acts performed by intermediaries in order to legitimate their social position. However, it is interesting to see how his selection compares with the rest nevertheless, not the least because it will contribute to the question why these prophets performed these acts in the first place. This also ties in with the current discussion concerning what a prophet in ancient Israel actually was, and if there is any meaningful way of distinguishing between a prophet and various other intermediators, such as diviners.[1]

---

[1] See Overholt (1989), Petersen (1991), Barstad (1993), Grabbe (1993), Gordon (1995a), Gordon (1995b), Grabbe (1995), Wood (1995), Gitay (1997), Petersen (1997).

Text	Viberg	Friebel	Amsler	Fohrer[1]	Stacey	Overholt[2]
1 Sam 15:27				x?[3]	x	
1 Kgs 11:30	x	x	x	x	x	x
1 Kgs 17:13-6						x[4]
1 Kgs 17:21						x
1 Kgs 18:31					x	
1 Kgs 18:34-5				x	x	
1 Kgs 18:36-8						x
1 Kgs 18:42					x	
1 Kgs 18:46					x	
1 Kgs 19:19				x	x	x
1 Kgs 19:21			x	x	x	
1 Kgs 20:37						x
1 Kgs 22:11			x	x	x	x
2 Kgs 1:9-16						x
2 Kgs 2:8,14,24						x
2 Kgs 2:12					x	
2 Kgs 2:21						x
2 Kgs 2:23-5						x
2 Kgs 4:1-7						x
2 Kgs 4:33-5						x
2 Kgs 4:41						x
2 Kgs 5:26-7						x
2 Kgs 6:1-7						x
2 Kgs 6:15-20						x
2 Kgs 13:15-7		x	x	x	x	x
2 Kgs 20:7						
2 Kgs 20:11/Is 38:8						x
Is 7:3			x	x	x	x
Is 7:10-17				x	x	x
Is 8:3,18			x	x	x	x
Is 20:2	x	x	x			x
Jer 13:1-11	x	x	x	x	x	
Jer 16:1-4		x	x	x	x	x
Jer 16:5		x		x	x	x

[1] Fohrer (1968)

[2] Overholt (1989).

[3] Fohrer (1968: 20, n 1) has some doubts since Samuel is not clearly depicted as a prophet.

[4] This text belongs to Overholt's category of prophetic acts that goes beyond the laws of nature and serves the purpose of legitimating the prophet in his role.

Jer 16:8		x		x	x	x
Jer 18:1-4					x	
Jer 19	x	x	x	x	x	x
Jer 25:15-29				x	x	
Jer 27	x	x	x	x	x	x
Jer 28:1-17	x	x	x			
Jer 32:1-15	x	x	x	x	x	x
Jer 35		x	x		x	x
Jer 36					x	
Jer 43:8-13	x	x	x	x	x	x
Jer 51:59-64	x	x	x	x	x	x
Ez 2:8-3:3				x	x	x
Ez3:22, 24:25, 33:21		x	x	x	x	x
Ez 4:1-3	x	x	x	x	x	x
Ez 4:4-8	x	x	x	x	x	x
Ez 4:9-13	x	x	x	x	x	x
Ez 5:1-4	x	x	x	x	x	x
Ez 6:11		x			x	x
Ez 12:1-16	x	x	x	x	x	x
Ez 12:17		x	x	x	x	x
Ez 21:6,12		x	x	x	x	x
Ez 21:8-17,28-32		x	x	x	x	x
Ez 21:18-22	x	x	x		x	x
Ez 24:1			x	x	x	x
Ez 24:3-14			x	x	x	
Ez 24:15-24	x	x	x	x	x	x
Ez 37:15-28	x	x	x	x	x	x
Hos 1:1-3,3;1-2	x	x	x	x	x	x
Hos 1:3-9			x		x	x
Mic 1:8				x?[1]	x	x
Hab 2:2						x
Zech 6:9-15	x	x	x	x	x	x
Zech 11:4-17				x?[2]	x	x

What stands out from this survey is the rather large agreement on the selection of texts from the prophetic books, as well as the more or less total exclusion of

---

[1] Fohrer (1968: 71-2) is uncertain.

[2] Fohrer (1968: 73) is uncertain.

the miracle-stories from 1-2 Kgs. Fohrer's argument, that most of these acts were magical acts, and as such remnants from that form of prophetic acts that had otherwise managed to overcome the magical character and become true symbolic acts as they were performed by Yahwistic prophets in later time, is reasonable.[1] However, it should be complemented with Overholt's more functional approach,[2] namely that these apparently magical acts were of a somewhat different genre, i.e., they had a different purpose than the more traditional acts found in the prophetical books. As a way of distinguishing these two groups, aside from the obvious form-critical differences, the magical character should be replaced with the more functional sociological characterization, not because it is wrong but because it a criteria that is built not on function but on the worldview of the performers and the audiences.

Fohrer does include some of the texts from 1-2 Kgs, and these are examples that Fohrer regards as something like borderline cases, prophetic acts that have just about managed to climb out of the magical context in which they have belonged. The fact that Stacey includes many of these texts, even though he is opposed to Fohrer's interpretation of these acts as originally magical, should be contributed to his very inclusive definition of 'prophetic drama' as it borders on any form of nonverbal activity by the prophets. However, his somewhat idiosyncratic methodology makes it difficult to find a rational reason for his selection of texts, e.g. his inclusion of 1 Sam 15:27, an act which he admits was performed by accident![3]

It is also clear from this survey that our present analysis is quite strict in its definition, since there are several texts that are included by all or most all others but are excluded here. Friebel, who has a rather similar restrictive definition, almost always shares this strict selection.[4] The one, basic principle behind this more restrictive approach is the quite rigorous requirement to find a clear description of an act what was in all probability performed, or more correctly, is intended to be performed in the textual world. Some acts simply can not be held to perform an act that symbolically denotes something beyond its own performance, e.g. 1 Kgs 19:21, and others are not symbolical but divinatory, i.e., they are efficacious and not symbolic, e.g. 2 Kgs 13:15-7. In fact, the only prophetic

---

[1] Fohrer (1968).

[2] Overholt (1982), Overholt (1989), Overholt (1990).

[3] Stacey (1990: 78-9). For an interpretation of this text in connection with the prophetic symbolic act by tearing Ahijah's robe in 1 Kgs 11:30, see Viberg (1998).

[4] Friebel (1999).

symbolic act from 1-2 Kgs that is recognized in this analysis is found in 1 Kgs 11:30.

When it comes to the prophetic books there is a larger agreement among scholars, but still it is clear that this study is more restrictive and demands more from texts as far as indications of performance, prophetic relevance and symbolic value are concerned. Name giving is, e.g., not regarded here as a symbolic act (Is 7:3, 8:3, 18, Hos 1:3-9), since no performance of an act is described, as is the case in e.g. Ruth 4:16-7.[1] Strictly speaking, the name giving in these texts is not symbolic but only the names are, which also excludes any act of shouting out the names as prophetic symbolic acts.[2] The act of name giving is minutely described in relation to Isaiah's writing the child's name on a board, but there is nothing in the text that would indicate that anything other than the name is being used in a symbolic sense. It may be that the writing on the board is meant to be taken in a symbolic sense, but I can not find any clues that would point in such a direction.

The description of the act is introduced with the familiar phrase קַח־לְךָ, "take …", which is often used to introduce descriptions of prophetic symbolic acts, e.g. 1 Kgs 11:31, Ez 4:1, 3, 9, 5:1, etc. However, that does not mean that we can use that as an indication itself that the act that follows is symbolic, since the phrase often introduces ordinary acts with no intention of being used in a symbolic sense, e.g. Jer 36:2. Isaiah writes the name of the future child on the board and makes it public, and that act may very well be described as a prophetic act, in the sense that he does it on God's command and as part of his prophetic activity. However, there is nothing in the text that would indicate that the writing on the board, the public display in front of witnesses are meant to be taken in a secondary, symbolic sense, beside the public display of the name. The name itself, on the other hand, is clearly meant to be taken in a secondary sense as a description of the future fate of the people, but that does not apply to the act whereby the name is displayed. If we compare with Ez 37:16, קַח־לְךָ עֵץ אֶחָד וּכְתֹב עָלָיו, "Take a stick and write on it", we find a similar introduction. But although the phrase here introduces a prophetic symbolic act, that does not follow necessarily from the introductory phrase, but from the fact that the sticks are later being used in an act that is clearly meant to be understood as a symbolic act by means of various textual indications. In Is 8:1f, however, no such indications can be found,

---

[1] So Viberg (1992: 166-75).

[2] An Assyrian prophet from Arbela was called *la dāgil-ili*, 'One who does not see God', probably a name taken or given to the prophet in order to refer to the Assyrian nation as a whole, see Parpola (1997: l-li).

and therefore the act must be understood as an act of public display commanded by God, but not meant to be taken in any symbolic sense.

Mic 1:8 describes common, conventional acts of mourning, not in any way particular to the prophet or his message. They convey nothing else but their conventional meaning. For this to have been a prophetic symbolic act, it would have had to mean something more than the conventional meaning. There are also no indications as to whether these mourning were ever performed. This view is also shared with Friebel, Amsler, and to a certain extent, Fohrer. Hab 2:2 is not recognized by anyone else but Overholt, who does not provide any explanation for the inclusion of this text, which simply describes an act of writing. This act is not in any way indicated to be symbolic, as is also recognized in all other studies. Zech 11:4-17 presents a vision, describing some form of act with two sticks. But the visionary context clearly excludes any possibility for this text to describe a symbolic act, as is recognized by Friebel, Amsler and to a certain extent also Fohrer.

What is left, then, are the texts from Jeremiah and Ezekiel, and here we are dealing with prophets that were clearly accustomed to performing symbolic acts as part of their prophetic activity, and that in itself requires more when it comes to put any such text into question. However, it is only in and through a detailed analysis of all the relevant texts that a reliable selection can be made of 'prophetic symbolic acts', along the principles laid down in the definition above. Therefore, all the possible texts from Jeremiah and Ezekiel will be argued for or against in the light of what we define as a 'prophetic symbolic act'.

The Book of Jeremiah

Jer 13:1-11:[1] The story of Jeremiah and the linen girdle bears several marks of having been performed as a prophetic symbolic act; the command to perform a visible act, the detailed description of the act, and the following interpretation in the form of an oracle. However, it does have certain problems, such as the lack of an audience and the understanding of 'Euphrates'. But on the whole, the act should be understood as a prophetic symbolic act.

Jer 16: 1-9: The absence of action is not itself an action, a principle that we will have to come back to on several occasions in this study. There is a clear connection between Jer 16:1-9 and Ezek 24, with the exception that Jer 16:1-9 does not refer to any actions on Jeremiah's part, only his abstaining from action.

---

[1] Those texts presented in bold characters are the instances that are considered prophetic symbolic acts, and they are therefore included in the analysis below.

What we have in Jer 16 could be called 'Symbolic behaviour', which would include even the refusal to perform certain expected, conventional acts, but is does not constitute a symbolic act. We find somewhat of a confirmation of this conclusion from v. 10, where God is saying that Jeremiah 'will have preached all these words', i.e., no nonverbal behaviour is referred to, but verbal. Furthermore, when the people ask their question, they ask why God has pronounced such a great misfortune over them, i.e., another clear indication that what has preceded has been a verbal activity on Jeremiah's behalf, and not a nonverbal. Jeremiah's message that the people should abstain from performing the conventional rituals of mourning is itself a symbol of how they should regard the fall of Jerusalem as just, and therefore in no need to be mourned for.

Jer 18:1-4: Jeremiah's visits to the potter's house are regarded by Stacey as a prophetic symbolic act. However, there are several reasons for not regarding it as such. First and foremost, it is not Jeremiah himself that is performing the act, but the potter; to be a case of prophetic symbolic act, it has to be performed with intention of being a prophetic symbolic act, and although we can not excavate ourselves down through time to the mind of Jeremiah, we can in this instance know for sure that there was no such intention. Jeremiah only interprets the potter's ordinary work in a symbolic manner. It is therefore a case of prophetic symbolism, but not a prophetic symbolic act.

Jer 19: Here we find a proper case of prophetic symbolic act, where Jeremiah again goes to the potter. However, this time with the intention of not only interpreting symbolically what he sees, but of actually performing an act himself with will afterwards be understood in a symbolic way.

Jer 25:15-29: The story of the cup of wrath, being handed out by Jeremiah to various nations could not be taken as a symbolic act. The cup is said to be taken from the hand of God and given to surrounding nations to drink. It could be argued that this is all to be taken symbolically, and that Jeremiah could very well have performed some acts where he handed out a cup of wine. However, such an understanding would have to require certain indications from the text in that direction, indications that in this case are missing. Furthermore, there is no mentioning of an audience, and no following interpretation. When it is said in v. 15 that Jeremiah is to take אֶת־כּוֹס הַיַּיִן הַחֵמָה הַזֹּאת, 'this cup of the wine of wrath', it would appear to indicate a reference to what precedes in the oracle of Jer 25. Indeed, 25:9-10 speaks about punishing the people surrounding Israel, which then was taken up in the following vision, almost in the form of a parable. The conclusion must be that as far the text tells us, the handing out of the cup of wrath was not performed symbolically by Jeremiah, but was used as a parable in his preaching.

Jer 27:1-3; 28:10-11: This is a clear example of a prophetic symbolic act, and it is also provided with a clear, historical setting as well. What is particularly interesting is that we are provided with the act of the prophet Hananiah, who breaks the joke of Jeremiah as a prophetic symbolic act, but with the opposite message from Jeremiah's.

Jer 32:6-15: This is another clear and unambiguous example of a prophetic symbolic act. The only problem is that no audience is mentioned, although that may be presumed to be present. The very concrete description of the conventional act of buying a piece of land is an important indication that this act was performed. Furthermore, that the purchase was ordered by God and received a following interpretation (v. 15) are indications that help to classify this as a prophetic symbolic act.

Jer 35: This chapter does not describe a prophetic symbolic act, contrary to the views of Friebel, Amsler and Stacey. As we saw in regard to Jer 18, the act of someone else can not be taken as a symbolic act by the prophet who is standing by. He may be using the act symbolically, but not even that appears to be the case here. The behaviour of the Rechabites is taken up by Jeremiah as a worthy example of obedience to God, to be followed by his own people. It is a case of an act that is understood symbolically by the prophet and put to use in his ministry, but that does not make it a prophetic symbolic act.

Jer 43:8-13: Although the interpretation of this symbolic act is more difficult than most prophetic symbolic acts, there is nothing that would indicate that it was not performed as such. The description is concrete and receives an interpretation in a following oracle.

Jer 51:59-64: This is a highly unusual form of symbolic act. It is not the prophet himself that is to perform the act, since he is instructing a man called Seraiah to perform the act. Furthermore, Seraiah is to accompany the king as he goes to Babylon, and there Seraiah is to perform the act of sinking the scroll in Euphrates. Is this then a symbolic act, and if so, is it prophetic? It must be emphasized that there is no indication as to whether the act was ever performed or not. What the text provides us with is a description of the act, given by Jeremiah to Seraiah. Whether Seraiah ever got to Babylon and performed the act is unknown. On the other hand, the intention of the act was clearly to perform a prophetic symbolic act, although the prophet had to use a Seraiah as an extension of his hand, as it were. The case is therefore not the same as in Jer 18, where Jeremiah used the act of the potter in a sense in which it had never been intended. However, had the act been performed by Jeremiah it would clearly have been a prophetic symbolic act, and it is with these reservations that we will include this text.

The Book of Ezekiel

Ezekiel is the OT prophet that is described as performing the most prophetic symbolic acts. However, it is not the amount of acts performed by Ezekiel that has bewildered scholars as much as the nature of the acts. They are more elaborate in their performance, and in a number of instances there is a genuine difficulty in trying to determine whether what is described is in fact a prophetic symbolic act, meant to be understood as having been performed, or a vision. In order to distinguish an act from a mere form of symbolism, it has to be born out of the literary context certain significant indications that clearly show that it is a description of an act that is referred to. It is these indications that sometimes appear to be missing in Ezekiel, or appear difficult to distinguish from indications of visions.[1]

2,8-3,3: This is a description of a vision and not a prophetic symbolic act. In 2:8 Ezekiel is told to open his mouth and receive what God is giving him, and in 2:9 Ezekiel says, 'I saw a hand reaching out towards me'. These initial indications show that it is a matter of vision and not an act. When Ezekiel says in 3:3 that what he ate was sweet as honey, it is still a reference to the visionary context, and an indication in this direction is the fact that the taste of the scroll is used symbolically for the quality of the message which God has given to Ezekiel.

3:22-25: No prophetic symbolic act is involved in this text, even though it is believed to do so by Friebel, Amsler, Fohrer, Stacey and Overholt. God explains to Ezekiel how he is to be stricken by dumbness (see also 24:25-7; 33:21f), and forced to reside in his home, until he is to begin preaching again.[2] The basic indication that no symbolic act is involved is that no performance is given any

---

[1] There is also the view, shared by only a few scholars today, that the prophetic symbolic acts of Ezekiel were in effect only literary creations, described *as if* they had been performed. The most recent exponent of this view is Davis (1989b: 71), who ends up by saying that 'It is best to remain agnostic about whether any of the sign-actions was actually performed. One can only say that, while a number of them present great difficulties for a literal interpretation, they are all comprehensible and effective as literary devices.' For a critical evaluation of Davis position, see Darr (1994: 15-7), cf. also Davis (1989a) and the critical response by Darr (1989).

[2] I follow Zimmerli (1976: 158-9) et al. in considering the use of 'binding with chains' and 'strike with dumbness' as metaphorical utterances.

form of secondary meaning, either explicit or implicit. We have no way of knowing whether this dumbness was a physical impairment that struck Ezekiel, or whether he deliberately imposed it on himself. There may very well be symbolic value to the dumbness itself, but that does not involve a performance. Again, the lack of action does not constitute a symbolic act. What is symbolic in that case is instead a situation, a constellation of certain factors, but no performance, and therefore it can not be a symbolic act.

4:1-17: This text clearly describes a whole set of prophetic symbolic acts, that together form a cluster with one and the same basic message.

5:1-4: This is a clear example of a prophetic symbolic act, and it works in close conjunction with the prophetic symbolic acts in 4:1-17.

6:11-14: These acts are surely meant to be performed, but they are not prophetic symbolic acts. They are mere gestures, examples of that form of nonverbal communication that works in conjunction with verbal communication in order to enhance the value of the spoken message. As conventional gestures, these acts can be said to be symbolic since they do signify something beyond their mere performance. However, there are two things that distinguish these conventional gestures from prophetic symbolic acts. First, their complete conventional status distinguishes them from prophetic symbolic acts, since the latter category is always innovative, however dependent they may be on older conventional procedures. Second, there has to be some relevance to the prophetic context for an act to be considered as a prophetic symbolic act. A gesture of lamentation on the other hand, brings nothing that is relevant to the specific context of a prophetic ministry, but could be performed by any member of society.

12:1-16: This is a clear example of prophetic symbolic act. The prophet goes off, symbolising exile. The secondary meaning is clearly brought out by the literary context. The act is also free of any risk of being a mere conventional gesture, and the act has a direct link to the prophetic ministry, since it is a symbolic act that presumably no one else would be likely to perform.

12:17-20; 21:6-7, 12, 14: These are probably prophetic symbolic acts but of a less dramatic form, for two reasons. First, they only emphasize what is brought out by the accompanying verbal communication, and second, they are everyday conventional acts invested with an unusually small amount of dramatic emphasis for prophetic symbolic acts. However, they do symbolize something else, as in 21:6-7, where Ezekiel is said to sigh. His sigh, however, is not his own natural sigh in that particular situation but symbolizes the sighing at the time of Jerusalem's fall.

21:18-20: This is no doubt a description that is meant to be taken as something that was performed, even though it is seen as such by other scholars. However, it is not a prophetic symbolic act since the act whereby the simple map is made is not in itself in any way given a symbolic value by any form of indicators. It is the finished product that symbolizes something else, namely the crossroad at which the foreign king is standing, deciding on which road to take.

21:8-17, 28-32: This is not a description of a prophetic symbolic act but a metaphorical description of the violence that is about to fall on Jerusalem. There are no indications in the text to the effect that Ezekiel is supposed to perform anything in relation to a sword. His reaction is that of the observer in Jerusalem, displaying grief and sorrow at the sight of the oncoming destruction. Again, we take a more restrictive view on the text than other scholars.

24:1-3: There is nothing that would indicate that this presents a prophetic symbolic act. The act of writing down the name of the day does not in itself signify something else, and it is doubtful if there even is something symbolic about the product of the act, the written memory of the day that the king of Babylon rushed forward towards Jerusalem.

24:3-14: Although this text has been seen by some to describe a prophetic symbolic act (Amsler, Fohrer, Stacey), it does not. Instead, it does precisely what it says, namely מְשֹׁל מָשָׁל, 'fabricates a parable' (v. 3), or perhaps it should be called an allegory. There are several indications that points to the conclusion that this is not meant to be taken as a description of a symbolic act. The cauldron is said to be made of copper, an unlikely item to be found in early sixth century Judah (v. 11). Furthermore, what would appear to be a description of a symbolic act in vv. 3b-5 is explicitly said in v. 3a to be spoken by Ezekiel to the people, i.e., nothing is said about performing what is described. What is said in vv. 3b-5 is an ironic description of the feeling of security that Ezekiel knew could be found in Jerusalem. Whether it was originally a work-song is impossible to know for sure.[1]

24:15-24: Although it is doubtful whether lack of conventional action can be seen to constitute prophetic symbolic act, this example does contain some activity on Ezekiel's behalf as well. Therefore it would be best to consider this as a prophetic symbolic act.

37:15-28: This is a clear example of a prophetic symbolic act. It could be argued that it is only the final product of the act which has any symbolic value,

---

[1] For the most satisfying solution to all the technical problems in Ez 24:3-14, see now Block (1991).

but the emphasis in the text on being 'in the hand' of the prophet precludes any doubt as to the symbolic character of the act of unifying the two sticks itself.

Some Practical Issues Regarding the Analysis

The analysis that follows will deal separately with each of the texts that describe a prophetic symbolic act. However, some texts contain more problems than others, e.g. in the areas of textual criticism (Jeremiah), historical analysis and redaction history (Isaiah, Kings, Ezekiel), and some symbolic acts are more complex in their symbolism than others, e.g. the complexities in Zechariah 6:9-15 against the simplicity of Ez 4:9-13. This means that the amount of space given to each text varies. This is so in order to come to terms with each and every one of the prophetic symbolic acts, without ever neglecting the fact that it is only in and through the texts that they can be understood.

B. Ahijah Tears the Mantle of Jeroboam (1 Kings 11:29-31)

Introduction

Hardly anyone would deny that DtrG as a whole has been construed with the use of at least some earlier traditions. With a greater or lesser degree of force, these earlier traditions have then been tuned in to conform to the overarching theme.

Only a part of these texts concern a prophetic symbolic act (1 Kgs 11:29-31). But I have chosen to deal with certain other texts as well, namely those which do not describe a prophetic symbolic act, but still a symbolic act, namely 1 Sam 15 and ch. 24. It is only by seeing all these acts together that we can properly understand the overall theme into which the story of Jeroboam and the prophet Ahijah was put, and only so can the how and why regarding the oracle related to that act be understood.

Needless to say, making use of individual narratives in the DtrG begs the question of how far the Dtr went in constructing the overall story, and to what extent individual narratives were created de novo or not. But although one could hold, as is the view taken here, that the Dtr made use of a variety of stories, one still has to ask the question whether the story goes back to an historical event or not. These two questions, the extent of Dtr literary creativity and possible historical substratum, will be tackled when relevant in the following analysis.[1]

The symbolic acts in 1 Sam 15 and 24 are not prophetic in the sense in which we use the term in this study. Nevertheless, they are symbolic acts used with an ideological intent in a literary work where prophets are held in the highest esteem, and also perform symbolic acts, as in 1 Kgs 11:29-31.

A particular category of prophetic symbolic acts found in DtrG is the form, which I have elsewhere termed 'divine anointing'.[2] Since I have analysed these acts before, I will not include them here, only to say that it is evident that symbolic acts were used to a significant degree in DtrG, and as far as possible they emphasize those performed by a prophet. Why, then, were the symbolic acts in 1 Sam 15 and 24 preserved? First of all, we must note again the part these traditions play in the overarching theme that has been worked out quite meticulously in DtrG, namely how a divided mantle can symbolize a divided kingdom. It is

---

[1] See Viberg (1998) for a discussion of the way Dtr has treated the theme.

[2] Viberg (1992: 89-119).

probable that the theme was sparked off by any one of the traditions involved, and the story in 1 Kgs 11:29-31 could have been that spark that set off the people behind DtrG in their creative literary writing.

Although the symbolic acts in 1 Sam 15 and 24 are not performed by prophets, they are nevertheless performed by kings, or at least king to be. The point of view of Dtr appears to have been that the primary issue was whether it served the purpose of the overall story or not. If they were not performed by prophets but still contributed in a significant degree to the overall point of view of the story, so be it. The symbolic act in 1 Sam 15:27 may not be performed by a prophet, but it is performed in front of a seer, Samuel! And the new and surprising message of the act, unintentional as it may have been, is provided by Samuel, who interprets the act in a clearly different way than does Saul. Needless to say, in his interpretation by Samuel we are actually hearing the Dtr, construing this act into an important part of the overall theme.

Any possible pre-Dtr form of these narratives is lost to us. What we have available are the symbolic acts as they have been put to use in the ideological construction of Dtr, but then that is the problem we constantly encounter in trying to understand prophetic symbolic acts. However, any understanding and use of such an act is better than none. The belief, still strong in some circles of biblical scholarship, that an earlier context for a particular text can be unearthed with exegetical skills and a vivid imagination, is largely fruitless. We are left with the text before us, and any indication of an earlier context must be rooted in that text. Otherwise we are left with the imaginative but very subjective judgements of scholars. In recent years, we have seen a healthy shift in focus regarding the attempt to venture beyond and below the available text. It is now more or less well recognized that the focus should be on the present text and the attempt to explain that text. Any attempt to focus on an earlier, non-existing text is bound to end up in subjective judgements that can not be substantiated with certainty. The burden of proof for the existence of a textual history lies on the one who argues that it is possible to reach beyond the present state of the text.

A more productive and verifiable way of understanding the text is to try to situate it ideologically and sociologically. These attempts have in recent times become the most fruitful ways to further our understanding of the biblical text, and then we come back to the texts in 1 Sam 15 and 24. The best we can do is not to try to extrapolate these texts from their present contexts, but rather to do the opposite, and analyse how they function in their respective contexts. Any conclusion as to whether these traditions regarding symbolic acts have existed in a literary form earlier than in the present contexts must be based on indications in these contexts.

Analysis of 1 Samuel 15:27 and 24:5, 12[1]

Introduction

The study of Jirku is an example of older exegetical research concerned with these symbolic acts.[2] He begins by noting that according to the belief in ancient Israel, and which is witnessed to in the Old Testament, there is an inherent magical power in clothing, and he particularly emphasizes the magical nature of the hem of the mantle together with the mantle itself.[3] He explains the act in 1 Sam 15:27 by noting the fact that the hem of Samuel's mantle stands for the destiny of Saul, which Saul himself violates.[4] Concerning 1 Sam 24:5, 12 Jirku holds that David, by cutting off the hem of Saul's mantle, wanted to gain power over him, and it was the hem of the mantle that was thought to provide David with that power.[5]

Jirku does not work with comparative material, but tries with certain theories concerning magic to explain why the mantle in particular is being used and why it is used in this particular way. It is here that later scholarship disagrees with Jirku. Even if many scholars today would agree that the origin of the use of the mantle in such an act as in 1 Sam 15:27, it is more the symbolic meanings of the mantle, the hem of the mantle, the whole act of grasping the hem of the mantle and the act of cutting the hem of the mantle, that are of interest.

Hylander understands 1 Sam 15:27 as a conscious act by Samuel by which he tears off the hem of Saul's mantle. This would then be Samuel's way of achiev-

---

[1] See also my earlier study Viberg (2005).

[2] Jirku (1917/18).

[3] Jirku (1917/18: 109), 'Es ist eine im Alten Testamente weitverbreitete Anschauung, daß in Kleidungsstücken geheimnisvolle Kräfte verborgen liegen könne."

[4] Jirku (1917/18: 117), ' ... der Zipfel eines Kleides für das Schicksal eines Menschen von entscheidender Bedeutung sein kam." Stephens (1931: 61) also prefers a magical interpretation, 'Apparently the act had some magical power by which the man could be the more certain of receiving the blessing which he sought."

[5] Jirku (1917/18: 118), 'Bevor David es wagen konnte, Saul zu töten, wollte er erst Macht über ihn gewinnen. Und dies erreichte er dadurch, daß er den Zipfel an Sauls Gewande in seinen Besitz brachte." This is also the view of Noth (1971: 241). For the opposite interpretation, see Hönig (1957: 153).

ing a concrete, nonverbal illustration of what he later explains verbally in v. 28.[1] This means that according to Hylander, there is no example in the text of the symbolic act of grasping the hem of the mantle, but more an example of a prophetic symbolic act.[2] Mettinger has followed Hylander in his interpretation of 1 Sam 15:27, and emphasizes the continuity between the mantle of Saul which is torn apart and the kingdom of Saul, which is also 'torn' away from him. Mettinger also puts the symbolism of the act in connection with the symbolism of Jonathan's act of transferring his mantle, among other things, to David in 1 Sam 18:3.[3]

Conrad compares with those Mari-texts that describe how certain prophets have their hair and the hem of their mantle cut off. This symbolic act would mean that the king of Mari, who decides that such a thing should be done, makes these prophets harmless to him as prophets, since it means that they will be under his authority. It was his way of gaining control over potentially dangerous critics. The hair and the hem of the mantle would then stand for the fact that the prophet is no longer capable of functioning properly in his role as prophet, until the king releases him.[4]

Conrad holds it unlikely that Saul the king would submit himself to Samuel the prophet, which leads him to this alternative interpretation. To Conrad, then, Saul is trying to make Samuel appear dubious, and perhaps as a false prophet, by exercising his royal authority and cutting off the hem of Samuel's mantle. According to Conrad, this might well be the cause of the hostility between the

---

[1] Hylander (1932: 200), 'Der machtbegnadete Seher nimmt dem Verworfenen das Zeichen seiner Würde, den Königsmantel, den er zerreisst, und gibt dazu die deutenden Worte, dass so Jahwe es seinem Königreiche ergehen lassen wird."

[2] Fohrer (1968: 20, n 1) hesitates to classify this act as a symbolic act of the prophets, mainly because Samuel is not unambigously described as a prophet. His doubts in that case, however, are unfounded.

[3] Mettinger (1976: 34), '... the tearing of the robe in 15,27 refers to Saul's robe whether it was Saul himself or (more probably) Samuel who tore it. The rending of (15,27) and handing over of (18,4) a piece of the royal apparel would symbolize the transference of kingship from Saul and his son to someone else, to David." For an interpretation of the act in 1 Sam 18:3 as reflecting a legal symbolic act, see Viberg (1992: 127-35).

[4] Conrad (1969: 278), '...das Abschneiden von Haar und Mantelsaum bei den unbekannten Propheten in Mari eine gewisse Schutzhandlung des Königs und des Staates darstellt, eine Schutzhandlung gegen solche, die aus falschen Beweggründen, mit behaupteten Träumen und falscher Botschaft zum König kommen, die also in betrügerischer Absicht ihre Träume vorbringen." So also Munn-Rankin (1956: 92).

two of them.[1]

It is important to note that Conrad does not view the act in 1 Sam 15:27 as an example of the symbolic act of grasping the hem of the mantle. Instead, he understands the act, in line with the Mari texts he uses, as an example of the symbolic act of cutting the hem of the mantle. However, he is then faced with the problem of explaining how a symbolic act which contains both the grasping of the hem as well as cutting it off, should be compared with a symbolic with act which only covers the latter part, the cutting of the hem.[2]

Yet another problem with Conrad's view is that the text of 1 Sam 15:27 actually says וַיַּחֲזֵק, 'and he grasped', which definitely does not point in the direction of the symbolic act of cutting the hem of the mantle. On the contrary, it may point towards the symbolic act of grasping the hem of the garment. Brauner has also criticized Conrad for his way of using the Mari texts.[3] Yet another difficulty with Conrad's view is that Saul's comment afterwards in v. 30 does not fit in with an attempt on his part to dishonour Samuel. All this makes Conrad's interpretation of 1 Sam 15:27 unlikely. However, his interpretation becomes much more interesting when we come to 1 Sam 24:5, 12, where it explicitly said that David cuts off the hem of Saul's mantle.[4]

Brauner's own interpretation of 1 Sam 15:27 is more traditional compared with Conrad's view.[5] Brauner holds that it is an example of the symbolic act of grasping the hem of the mantle. According to the parallels that Brauner makes use of, the act points to some form of treaty, where the lower part, the vassal,

---

[1] Conrad (1969: 280), 'Saul benutzt zu ihrer Abwehr die Mittel, die König und Staat - wie in Mari - seit eh und je gegenüber ihren Propheten gehabt haben. Er reißt dem Propheten den Mantelsaum ab, entehrt und entmachtet ihn auf diese Weise. Ja, vielleicht kann man sagen, daß er ihn seiner Amtswürde entkleidete."

[2] Conrad (1969: 278, n 24) is aware of this problem, but he does not provide an explanation. Noth (1971: 240) holds that it might very well have been enough with just one of the two, but he provides no examples to substantiate his view.

[3] Brauner (1974: 37, n 9).

[4] Noth (1971) treats the same Mari texts that Conrad uses, but Noth sensibly enough applies them to 1 Sam 24, and not 1 Sam 15. So also Gordon (1980). Klein (1983) leans towards the same direction, 'Hence the taking of the robe in the present context is a sign of restraint and innocence....". This leaves open the question whether the act was meant to have another meaning outside of its present literary context. For the use of the act of cutting the hem of the garment in the context of divorce, see Finkelstein (1975: 240), 'For the sequence of actions entailed by the divorce procedure, which include the cutting of the sissiktu by the man, ... there can be no doubt therefore that this symbolic act was required to validate a divorce", see also Munn-Rankin (1956: 92), Greengus (1969: 514).

[5] Brauner (1974). His view is taken up by e.g. McCarter (1980: 268), Greenstein (1982: 217-8), Klein (1983: 150).

submits himself to the other part and thereby asks for the treaty. This means for Brauner that Saul submits himself to Samuel in 1 Sam 15:27 and asks him to remain with him.[1] Brauner argues on the basis of both Akkadian texts and the one relevant Ugaritic text, *KTU* 1.6.II:9-11.[2]

Grønbæck summarizes the four possible ways of understanding 1 Sam 15:27; first, Saul tears off the hem of his own mantle, second, Saul tears off the hem of Samuel's mantle, third, Samuel tears off the hem of his own mantle, and fourth, Samuel tears off the hem of Saul's mantle.[3] Grønbæck dismisses the first alternative, and holds that the second alternative presupposes a change in subject, which would have been made explicit in MT. To Grønbæck it is therefore basically reasons based on syntax that speaks against the first two alternatives, leaving him with alternatives three and four. He shows that מְעִיל, 'mantle', could very well be a royal mantle, part of the royal apparel.[4] However, Grønbæck agrees with Conrad in that it would be unlikely for the king to submit to the prophet, which leaves him with only one alternative, namely that Samuel tears off the hem of his own mantle. This would then not be a case of any of the two symbolic acts of grasping the hem of the mantle and cutting it off the mantle. It would then be an otherwise unknown act, but presumably with a symbolic significance. It would then make it similar to the prophetic symbolic acts.[5]

McCarter follows the view of Brauner in regard to 1 Sam 15:27[6] and Met-

---

[1] Brauner (1974: 38), 'Clearly, Saul supplicates Samuel, importunes him not to abandon him and submits himself of Samuel's (and God's) authority - all, both in word and in the deed of taking hold of Samuel's cloak. ... it is Samuel then who grasps the tearing of the garment to pronounce the penitent Saul's fate." So also Finet (1969: 126), 'En revanche, lorsque Saül veut agripper le pan du manteau de Samuel, c'est un geste de supplication. Car sisir - et non couper - la frange du manteau de quelqu'un, c'est quete une protection, se soumettre, faire allégeance." See also Munn-Rankin (1956: 92) regarding this symbolic act, which in the wider ancient Near Eastern arena can be both a legal symbolic act, e.g. *KAI* 215:11, as well as a non-legal act, e.g. KTU² 1.6.II:9-11, see also Viberg (1992: 127).
[2] For this text, see e.g. Moor (1987, n 422), who calls the act of Anat an act of supplication, and compares it the with the act in 1 Sam 15:27, in line with Brauner's interpretation.
[3] Grønbaek (1971).
[4] However, in this supposed identification Grønbæck makes the simple mistake of confusing sense with reference. The sense of 'mantle" is its general meaning, applicable to all sorts of mantles, royal or not, whereas the reference of 'mantle" may very well be exclusively royal.
[5] Grønbaek (1971: 42).
[6] McCarter (1980: 384). He compares 1 Sam 15:27 with 24:5, 'The situation here is not, however, the same. The piece of Saul's robe that David cuts away is to serve as proof of David's refused opportunity to strike down his king and thus of his loyalty to him." So also Stoebe (1973: 440). According to Stoebe, it is not likely that a symbolic/magical significance of the act would have been forgotten, which is why he does not prefer that view.

tinger's view of a legal symbolism when it comes to 1 Sam 18:3-4, although with a certain hesitation.[1] McCarter understands David's act in 1 Sam 24:5 as an attempt to prove that although he could have killed Saul, he did not because of his loyalty to Saul. He therefore sees no relevant parallel between 1 Sam 24:5 and the well-known conventional symbolic act of cutting the hem of the garment.

Analysis of 1 Samuel 15:27

וַיִּסֹּב שְׁמוּאֵל לָלֶכֶת.   As Samuel turned to go away, he caught
וַיַּחֲזֵק בִּכְנַף־מְעִילוֹ וַיִּקָּרַע   hold of the hem of his robe, and it tore. [2]

There are basically four ways to interpret this verse, as was noted above. First, Saul tears off the hem of his own mantle, second, Saul tears off the hem of Samuel's mantle, third, Samuel tears off the hem of his own mantle, and fourth, Samuel tears off the hem of Saul's mantle. As far as I know, no one has argued for the first alternative. There is a linguistic problem in the text, since Hebrew syntax formally agrees with all four alternatives. One would have thought that if Saul was the subject of the verb וַיַּחֲזֵק, 'and he grasped', it would have been made explicit, but it is not required. However, there are certain clues in the text itself that points in a certain direction. First, it says that Samuel turns around to walk away, second that someone grasps the hem of someone's mantle, and third that the hem tore. It is certainly reasonable to argue that there is an intimate relationship between these three statements, i.e., that they are dependent upon each other.

If Samuel, according to alternative four above, is understood as grasping and tearing the hem of Saul's mantle, there are at least two objections to be made. First, if Samuel turns around to walk away, the natural understanding of that statement is that he is walking away from Saul. It then becomes hard to understand how he can grasp and tear the hem of Saul's mantle at the same time that he is walking away from him. Second, the text seems to give the impression that someone intended only to grasp the hem, and that it tore by accident.[3] If Samuel

---

[1] Mettinger (1976: 39).

[2] We have chosen a consecutive translation of ו, 'and", here, mostly because it would suit all possible interpretations. But it is quite possible, and even likely that it should be translated adversatively, 'but it tore", which is preferred by e.g. Stoebe (1973: 289).

[3] The verb used, קרע, 'tear", in niphal occurs 5 times, Ex 28:32; 39:23, 1 Sam 15:27; 1 Kgs 13:3, 5. In Exodus it concerns cloth that is accidentally torn apart, which is relevant to 1 Sam 15:27.

were supposed to be performing the act it would be hard to understand that the text would describe a failure on his part.[1] Instead, it would have to be something intentional on Samuel's part, but then it could have been formulated in a much easier way, and not as if it was an accidental occurrence. This way of arguing shows Conrad's view to be unacceptable.

The two arguments above also speak against the third alternative, that Samuel would be tearing the hem of his own mantle. Why would he leave while performing a symbolic act, and why would the text give the impression that the hem of Samuel's mantle was torn by accident?

That leaves us with the second alternative, that Saul tears the hem of Samuel's mantle. It does justice to all three statements that are made in v. 27; Saul grasps the hem of Samuel's mantle, and as Samuel begins to walk away, it is easy to understand how it tears by accident. Yet another argument in favour of the alternative is that vv. 27 and 28 both start with Samuel as the explicit subject. In v. 28 Saul is referred to by a pronoun, and it would be natural for him to be referred to in this same way in v. 27.

When we look at Samuel's statement afterwards in v. 28, he says that 'Yhwh has torn the kingdom of Israel from you this very day'. If Samuel sees the kingdom as being symbolized by the hem of the mantle, then the analogy on which the symbolism is based does not quite fit in, since the hem is torn from Samuel's mantle and not Saul's.[2] However, it is doubtful whether we should demand the analogy to be so strict. The central issue, which forms the basis for Samuel's statement in v. 28, is the fact that the hem of the mantle was torn, rather than whose mantle it was. It is then the very act itself that is used in an analogical way by Samuel.

Textual criticism also supports the first alternative. Both LXX, Syr and 4QSam all have Saul as explicit subject to וַיַּחֲזֵק, 'and he grasped'. It is hardly likely that the name Saul would have disappeared by some mechanical error. Instead, the easiest solution is to consider LXX, Syr and 4QSam as examples of how 1 Sam 15:27 was understood when those texts were written.[3]

There is one other instance in the OT which mentions the symbolic act of grasping the hem of the garment, namely Zech 8:23. Ten men from various na-

---

[1] McCarter (1980: 270) holds that 'The prophetic narrator is principally concerned in these stories with obedience to the (prophetically transmitted) word of Yahweh". Veijola (1975: 102, n 156) wonders if 1 Sam 15 does not stem from prophetic circles, so also Birch (1976: 107). For a different view, see e.g. Donner (1983: 25), who considers 1 Sam 15 to postexilic.

[2] This is argued by Hylander (1932: 200), Mettinger (1976: 37, n 7).

[3] So e.g. Klein (1983: 146).

tions will וְהֶחֱזִיקוּ בִּכְנַף אִישׁ יְהוּדִי, 'grasp the hem of a Jehudite', and beg for his company. From the context it is clear that their act is one of supplication and submission.[1]

If we turn to extra biblical material, there is a well-known symbolic act expressed in Akkadian as *qaran ṣubāt PN ṣabātu*, 'grasp the hem of the mantle of PN' or *sissikta/sikka ṣabātu*, 'grasp the hem'.[2] This symbolic act means, while performed by a vassal in the making of a treaty, that he submits to the suzerain and promises obedience.[3] The act also occurs in more private legal contexts, and then it has the meaning of someone trying to limit the freedom of, or even exercise power over, someone else.

In earlier research the *qaran/sissiktu(m)* has been considered as some special item on the mantle, as e.g. the 'hem'. However, Malul has shown that this is not the case.[4] The *sissiktu/sikku* was not a hem of a mantle, but a form of clothing. The corner of the mantle was referred to by *qannu/qaran subāti*. A conclusion that Malul draws is that it is not a matter of a separate 'hem, but simply the corner of the mantle. The piece of clothing was called *sissiktu*, but with time the name of the piece of clothing came to signify, by means of metonymy, that particular part that was used in legal symbolic acts.[5]

A particular text that mentions the act of grasping the hem of the garment comes from the Ugaritic Baal epic KTU 1.6.II:9-11, where Anat performs the following act:

tiḫd . mt b sin . lpš .	She grasped Mot by the hem of (his) mantle,
tšṣqn[h] b qṣ . all .	she constrained (him) by the end of (his) robe.

Anat is looking for her brother Baal, who has been killed by Mot. Finally, she

---

[1] So e.g. Meyers, and Meyers (1987: 441). See also Kalluveettil (1982: 26-7). For the resumption of the verb חזק in Zech 8:23, see Joüon, and Muraoka (1991: 647, n 2).

[2] See AHw 2, 1050-1, and 3, 1067.

[3] See Munn-Rankin (1956: 91), "'To hold or carry the sissiktum' suggests a menial action and was undoubtedly a symbolic gesture performed by a vassal in acknowledgment of the authority of his suzerain. ... To 'seize the qarnu or the garment' had the same significance.' In the case of a treaty on a parity level, the symbolic act that was used was *sissikta raqāsu*, 'bind the hem'. It probably meant that something, symbolizing the agreement, was tied to the hem. See e.g. Korosec (1967: 148), 'L'autre locution sissiktam rakasum provient sans doute d'un geste symbolique indiquant la formation du lien entre les parties contractantes."

[4] Malul (1986).

[5] Malul (1986: 34), 'Thus, the functioning of the lap-garment in certain very common legal symbolic acts may well have caused, by way of metonymy, its name to be restricted to only that part of it which was frequently involved in the various symbolic acts."

goes to Mot and uses this symbolic act in her plea for the release of her brother.[1] It is clear that Anat's purpose with her symbolic act was to amplify her prayer for Baal's release. The act therefore signifies the humble request from the lower to the higher.

Yet another interesting case of the act of grasping the hem of the mantle can be found in KAI 215:11:

bḥkmth wbṣdqh py ʾḥz	Because of his wisdom and loyalty, he grasped
bknp mrʾh mlk ʾšśwr	the hem of his lord, the king of Assur.

The inscription was made by Barrakib, son of Panammuwa II of Samʾal, an Aramean city-state between Charchemish and Karatepe. In line 11 is described how Panammuwa submits as a proper vassal to his lord, the Assyrian king. His submission is described in two ways; first by the use of the concept of *ṣdq*, and second by means of the symbolic act of grasping the hem of the king's mantle, *ʾḥz bknp mrʾh mlk ʾšśwr*.[2] What should be noted is the similarity in wording and expression between 1 Sam 15:27, KTU 1.6.II:9-11 and KAI 215:11.

The conclusion that can be drawn is that what is found described in 1 Sam 15:27 is a symbolic act, which is well known from the ancient Near Eastern context of ancient Israel. The act signified submission and could even function as a legal symbolic act in the making of a vassal-suzerain treaty. To 1 Sam 15:27 this means that Saul, in despair over the fact that Samuel is abandoning him, makes use of a symbolic act, which he hopes, will soften the anger of Samuel. Tragically, however, his submission is by accident turned into something completely different, something that Samuel is the first to make use of.

At this point there is another lesson to learn from the extra biblical material. 1 Sam 15:27 emphasizes, quite ironically, that the hem of the mantle is torn.[3] What lies behind this is the identification of yet another symbolic act, well-known from the ancient Near Eastern context, that of cutting the hem of the garment, *sissikta batāqu*.[4] This symbolic act had at least two functions, divorce and

---

[1] See Greenstein (1982), Gaster (1961: 220-1).

[2] See Haulotte (1966: 77), Brauner (1974: 38, n 11).

[3] The irony can also be found in KTU² 1.6.II:9-11. Anat is said to grasp the hem of Mot's mantle in order to request for her brother's freedom, in all humility. Later, however, it is said in ll. 30-31 that *tiḫd bn. ilm.mt*, 'She grasped Mot, the son of El", and slaughters him. The irony resides in the use of the verb *aḥd* in the form *tiḫd* in both cases. That the two acts are consciously made parallel is clear by the fact that they are both preceeded by three lines describing Anat's longing for her brother.

[4] AHw 1, 1145, esp. 114.1.b.

and controlling prophets. In the context of divorce, the man cut off the hem of the woman's mantle, thus in effect terminating the marriage.[1] A somewhat different use was made of this symbolic act in Mari, as was mentioned above.[2] The sudden shift from the symbolic act intended by Saul, expressing humility, to the symbolic act that is reflected in the accident of the torn mantle, constitutes the basis for Samuel's final comment in v. 28. It is likely that this accident provided Samuel with a good illustration of his evaluation of Saul, namely that he was questioning and maybe even opposing Samuel's prophetic authority. This sudden twist from an act of humble request to what seemed similar to an act of defiance is probably meant to be understood as ironic by the author.[3] Probably Samuel is meant to understand the accidentally created allusion, but it is from the author's point of view that we get the full picture of the seemingly humble king, who is no longer in a position to hide his true intentions.

Analysis of 1 Samuel 24:5, 12

The symbolic act of cutting the hem of the garment also becomes relevant in trying to understand what David does to Saul in 1 Sam 24:5, 12. Why does David cut off the hem of Saul's mantle? Is there perhaps an intentional link on the author's behalf between 24:5, 12 and 15:27?

The expressions that are used in 15:27 and 24:5 are quite similar; 15:27 has וַיַּחֲזֵק בִּכְנַף־מְעִילוֹ, 'and he grasped the hem of his garment', and 24:5 has וַיִּכְרֹת אֶת־כְּנַף־הַמְּעִיל, 'and he cut off the hem of the garment'. This similarity between the expressions, together with the fact that Saul figures so prominently in both instances, makes it likely that the similarity is intentional. In 1 Sam 15:28 Samuel gives his final verdict, inspired by the accidental tearing of the mantle, by saying that Saul's kingdom will be torn from him and given לְרֵעֶךָ, lit. 'to your neighbour', or better, 'to someone else'. It is clear to the reader, as well as to Samuel, that this 'someone' is none other than David.[4] Saul's ignorance of this fact provides the scene with an ironic twist. He who had the reputation that

---

[1] See e.g. Finkelstein (1975: 240), Petschow, RLA 3, 321, Munn-Rankin (1956: 92).

[2] For this phenomenon, see Ellermeier (1968), Heintz (1968), Huffmon (1968), Nötscher (1968), Moran (1969), Ross (1970), Koch (1972), Dietrich (1973), Craghan (1975), Noort (1977), Malamat (1980), Schmitt (1982), Lafont (1984), Malamat (1987), Durand (1988), Gordon (1993).

[3] 'Author' is here used in a somewhat heuristic sense. We might as well speak of the 'implied author', or the 'Deuteronomist'.

[4] This is also spelled out later in 1 Sam 28:17, when Samuel, back from the dead, quotes himself in a final reproach to Saul, וַיִּקְרַע יְהוָה אֶת־הַמַּמְלָכָה מִיָּדֶךָ וַיִּתְּנָהּ לְרֵעֲךָ לְדָוִד, 'Yhwh tore the kingdom from your hand and gave it to your neighbour David."

no man in Israel was טוֹב מִמֶּנּוּ, lit. 'better/more beautiful than he' (1 Sam 9:2), is now told that his kingdom will pass on to someone who is הַטּוֹב מִמֶּךְ, 'better/more beautiful than you', and he does not even know who it is. The use of 'better/more beautiful than' in both cases is a clear indication that the irony is intended.

In 15:28 Samuel saw the hem that was torn from his mantle, as a symbol of the kingdom, which, he declared, was about to pass from Saul. This prophetic utterance is fulfilled in a comic sense in 24:8, when David cuts off the hem of Saul's mantle. The actual event of 15:27 is here repeated, but with an intrusion of David, the רַע Saul was ignorant of. And the irony continues in 24:5, since Saul is still unaware of what is happening.

Scholars have had different opinions as to whether David's act in 24:5 displays loyalty to the king, 'Look! I could have done it, but I did not!', or whether it is an example of the symbolic act discussed above, *sissikta batāqu*, 'cut the hem of the mantle'. The first alternative may seem rather evident, but it runs into difficulties in explaining, first, the oracle in v. 5, which appears to be God's go ahead for David to kill Saul, and, second, David's display of bad conscience in vv. 6-7. In the light of these two obstacles, the first alternative becomes at least insufficient as an explanation. It is clear that what David does in 24:5, 12 must have meant something more than just showing his loyalty to Saul as the anointed one. David must have done something harmful to Saul, although not physical.[1] It is precisely here that the symbolic act of *sissikta batāqu*, 'cut the hem of the mantle' becomes relevant, since the act symbolized taking authority over someone else. Saul grasped the hem of Samuel's mantle *wayyiqqāraʿ*, 'and it tore' (1 Sam 15:27), God would קָרַע, 'tear', the kingdom from Saul (1 Sam 15:27), and David וַיִּכְרֹת, 'cut', the hem of Saul's mantle.

Afterwards David is struck by bad conscience, and regrets his action towards Saul (1 Sam 24:6-7). What he regrets is the intention inherent in the symbolic act, which was tantamount to rebellion against the anointed king. This means that the symbolic act was indeed part of the rebellious act of David towards Saul and not something done by David to prove his new, loyal intent towards the king.[2]

It seems as if the author wanted to show how David, the king to be, is put to the test by God himself and manages to uphold his integrity, although with a

---

[1] So e.g. Noth (1971: 241).

[2] McCarter (1980: 387, n 2) instead chooses to consider vv. 5b-6 as an addition. However, the text can be understood as it stands, if the symbolic act is interpreted as a conventional symbolic act, well known from the cultural context.

certain doubt since he does cut off the hem of Saul's mantle. David is encouraged by his men to finish Saul off, since he does cut off the hem (1 Sam 24:5, 8, 11). However, in chapter 25 David learns from a woman how to hand over revenge and judgement to God. This is then implemented in David's own life i 26:9, when he is put to the same test as in chapter 24. 1 Sam 25 would then serve a proleptic purpose to chapter 26.[1] These three chapters would then make sense in the order in which they stand, and chapters 24 and 26 do not have to present the same occurrence.[2]

The Text

29 וַיְהִי בָּעֵת הַהִיא
וְיָרָבְעָם יָצָא מִירוּשָׁלַ͏ִם וַיִּמְצָא
אֹתוֹ אֲחִיָּה הַשִּׁילֹנִי הַנָּבִיא[a]
בַּדֶּרֶךְ[d] וְהוּא[b] מִתְכַּסֶּה בְּשַׂלְמָה
חֲדָשָׁה וּשְׁנֵיהֶם לְבַדָּם[c] בַּשָּׂדֶה
30 וַיִּתְפֹּשׂ אֲחִיָּה בַּשַּׂלְמָה הַחֲדָשָׁה
אֲשֶׁר עָלָיו וַיִּקְרָעֶהָ. שְׁנֵים עָשָׂר
קְרָעִים 31 וַיֹּאמֶר לְיָרָבְעָם
קַח־לְךָ עֲשָׂרָה קְרָעִים כִּי כֹה
אָמַר יְהוָה אֱלֹהֵי יִשְׂרָאֵל הִנְנִי
קֹרֵעַ אֶת־הַמַּמְלָכָה מִיַּד. שְׁלֹמֹה
וְנָתַתִּי לְךָ אֵת עֲשָׂרָה הַשְּׁבָטִים[d]

29 About that time, when Jeroboam was leaving Jerusalem, the prophet Ahijah the Shilonite found him on the road. Ahijah had clothed himself with a new garment. The two of them were alone in the open country 30 when Ahijah laid hold of the new garment he was wearing and tore it into twelve pieces. 31 He then said to Jeroboam: Take for yourself ten pieces; for thus says Yhwh, the God of Israel, 'See, I am about to tear the kingdom from the hand of Solomon, and will give you ten tribes.

Textual notes

[a] LXX prefers to read the more clarifying ὁ Αχιας.

[b] LXX emphasizes the seriousness on behalf of the prophet by adding καὶ ἀπέστησεν αὐτὸν ἐκ τῆς ὁδοῦ, 'and he removed him from the road' after ἐν τῇ ὁδῷ, 'on the road". Some scholars hold the opposite to be the case, namely that the phrase was lost in the transmission of the Hebrew text due to haplography by homoeoteleuthon, (בדרך ... הדרך), so e.g. Noth (1968: 242-3), Gray (1970: 290), Knoppers (1993: 183, n. 29). However, Wevers (1950: 303) has supplied a convincing explanation for the phrase as an addition, according to which LXX is rationalising when it concludes that if the two

---

[1] So e.g. Gordon (1980). Mettinger (1976: 37) talks about the skopos of the text, before a Dtr redaction, as being 'David's future kingship and his freedom from blood-guilt."

[2] Against e.g. Klein (1983: 236). Koch (1969: 132-48) considers chapter 24 to be original and chapter 26 as a later development from chapter 24. For the opposite view, see e.g. McCarter (1980: 386). Grønbaek (1971: 168f) holds it to be a matter of two independent traditions.

are first on the road and then in the field, they must have left the road. Wevers simply notes that being on a country road in that time was practically the same as being in the fields.

c This is missing in LXX^B,L, but added by LXX^O. MT is preferable for two reasons. First, the text does not seem to make sense without it, stating only the obvious that they were in the open, whereas the statement that they were alone has a specific purpose. Second, the Greek μόνοι, 'alone" could have been lost in the transmission due to haplography by homoeoteleuthon (ἀμφότεροι - μόνοι). DeVries (1985: 147), however, regards LXX^B,L as the original.

d It could be that the article is secondary since it does not occur in LXX. However, the opposite explanation is preferable, namely that the article has been left out, the reason for which is not clear. The article makes sense, since the ten pieces have been mentioned earlier in v. 31.

Earlier Studies

In trying to understand the symbolic act by the prophet Ahijah in 1Kgs 11:29-31, we must first note the rather chaotic state of the text in 1Kgs 11:26-40, something that has long been noted.[1] This is not the place to deal with the intricate issue of the redaction history of the deuteronomistic history, but only to note how various solutions have implications for the understanding of the symbolic act in vv. 29-31.

Scholars have mainly followed one of two alternative paths in trying to smoothen out the rugged texture of 1 Kgs 11:29-40. Either the text is on the whole considered to be a creation by Dtr, except for the odd few glosses that have caused the obvious inconsistencies, or it is thought to be based on some older, often prophetic, source that has been exposed to various forms of redaction, mostly by Dtr.[2]

The most well-known proponent of the first view is Noth in his commentary on 1 Kgs 1-16 in 1968, who considered 11:29-39 to be the work of Dtr, except

---

[1] See in particular Noth (1943: 114), Seebass (1963), Plein (1966), Noth (1968: 245-6), Dietrich (1972: 15-20, 54-5, 62, 137), Seebass (1976), Trebolle Barrera (1980: 143-8), Weippert (1983), Vanoni (1984), DeVries (1985: 148-9), Campbell (1986: 25-32), Provan (1988: 100-5), Trebolle Barrera (1989: 129-35), McKenzie (1991: 41-7). For an attempt to more fully appreciate the literary artistry of the text in its extant form, see Cohn (1985).

[2] For some general overviews of the various alternatives when it comes to the redaction history of the DtrG, see e.g. O'Brien (1989: 3-15), Knoppers (1993: 17-54), McConville (1993: 78-90).

for some minor glosses.[1] This approach has been further refined in various ways by Dietrich and Cross.[2] According to Dietrich, a story in 'dtrG' which concerned the rebellion that Jeroboam mounted against Solomon according to 1 Kgs 11:26, originally in 11:29-39, has been replaced with a prophetic story belonging to 'dtrP', consisting of vv. 29-31, 33a, 34a, 35aba, 37abgb.[3] The frame of the original 'dtrG' story in vv. 26-8, 40 would have been retained, however.[4] This story has then been added to with various explanations and corrections in vv. 32, 33b, 34b, 35bb, 36, 37aα, 38abα. This second layer is according to Dietrich no story of its own, but it does come from one single author and has a distinctly nomistic tendency. Dietrich identifies this second layer with his nomistically orientated deuteronomistic redaction, 'dtrN'.[5] To say, therefore, that Dietrich views 1 Kgs 11:29-39 as deuteronomistic needs some further qualifications in order for it not to be misleading, since he breaks down the deuteronomistic language into various redactional layers. A similar solution has been suggested by Provan. An original Dtr passage in vv. 29-31, 33, 34a, 36-38 has been reworked by a Dtr editor in two basic ways. First, v. 32 has been added in order to shift the emphasis from the active prophet to the Davidic covenant, together with vv. 34bα, 35 a-bα, 39. Second, the verb forms in v. 33 have been altered from the singular, referring to Solomon, to the plural, which now refer to the people of Jerusalem. This is evident from the end of v. 33, כְּדָוִד אָבִיו, 'as his father David', where the pronoun refers to what was originally a singular object earlier in the verse, namely Solomon. In recent times the pendulum has begun to swing away from a multitude of deuteronomistic redactions towards Noth's view that there was only one author behind the deuteronomistic history, and perhaps the best example of this recent trend is a work from 1991 by McKenzie. His book is an attempt to move away from various earlier intricate and sometimes very confus-

---

[1] Noth (1968). However, in Noth (1943), he held to the alternative view, namely that Dtr had taken over an earlier story about Ahijah and Jeroboam.

[2] Dietrich (1972: 15-20, 28-9, 54-5, 62, 137), Cross (1973: 287-9). A good critique of the analysis of Dietrich can be found in Mayes (1983). Cross does not deal particularly with 1 Kgs 11:29-31 in his short study, but the main points are that he sees a basic work by a deuteronomistic author, Dtr[1], mostly the same as Noth's author of DtrG. The difference lies in Cross's recognition of a later, exilic deuteronomistic editor, 'dtr[2]', to account for what Cross believed was a theme that could not be reconciled with a pre-exilic date. The recent work of Knoppers (1993: 51-2) proposes a similar view.

[3] Cf. McKenzie (1991: 91).

[4] So e.g. Veijola (1975: 43).

[5] Dietrich (1972: 28-9).

ing redaction-historical solutions.[1] McKenzie's conclusion is the same as that of Noth, namely that vv. 29-39 is the work of Dtr. The inconsistencies in the text are attributed to glosses and mistakes in the transmission of the text, and he sees no clear tendency among the glosses to suggest one or two writers behind them.

It is clear that on the basis of this view, a greater degree of variation and creativity is attributed to Dtr than is the case with the second alternative.[2] Usually this creativity extends to creating the narrative in 11:29-39, as is the view of McKenzie.[3] His line of argument, that when the style is smoothly deuteronomistic it is less likely to rely on an earlier tradition, is open to some rather serious criticism, however. What if Dtr chose to reformulate, or even to take over something that already was formulated in a way similar to the style of Dtr? Surely Dtr did not create his style completely himself, but relied on a way of writing and evaluating history already known to him.

The second alternative centres on the existence of a narrative concerning the encounter between the prophet Ahijah and Jeroboam.[4] This basic narrative is considered by some to form part of a larger 'prophetic' source.[5] This alternative grows out of a genuine problem, namely why prophetic stories situated in the north are found in a work from the south. The answer given is that Dtr would have made use of this source by incorporating various parts of it into his own narrative frame at strategic places, often altering the original tendency and emphasis of the added text. In contrast to the view of Dietrich, then, the prophetic strand can be found behind the deuteronomistic history, and not as a layer imposed upon it. Adherents of this view have usually worked out very elaborate solutions to how the text of 1 Kgs 11:29-39 has been conflated into its poor present status, sometimes with more than one redaction present in the text. One example is Weippert, who sees a basic, pre-Dtr kern in vv. 29-31, 37, 38bαβ, 40a.bα. She has made a rather strong case for seeing this basic kern in the form of a royal oracle with the purpose of providing a divine legitimation of a throne pretender who otherwise lacks access to the throne by means of proper heredi-

---

[1] McKenzie (1991: 41-7). Concerning v. 34, McKenzie follows a suggestion by Trebolle Barrera (1989: 129-35), who shows quite convincingly how 11:34 is the conflation of two originally separate readings, both of which are still separate in LXX[Luc]. This is a very attractive solution, which will probably become a consensus view.

[2] See e.g. Mullen (1992: 231-2).

[3] McKenzie (1991: 44-7). Perhaps the best example of this is the work of Hoffmann (1980).

[4] So e.g. Noth (1943), Seebass (1963), Plein (1966), Seebass (1976), Weippert (1983), Vanoni (1984), DeVries (1985), Ben Zvi (1993: 337-9), Toews (1993: 31-2).

[5] So e.g. Nelson (1981: 110-6), Campbell (1986: 24-30, 87-8). See also Birch (1976: 154), McCarter (1980: 18-23), O'Brien (1989: 163-5).

tary means. She compares this text with other cases where a prophet performs an act to provide a divine legitimation for someone who lacks the hereditary means to achieve the throne, such as the divine anointings of Saul (1 Sam 10:1, 7b) and Jehu (2 Kgs 9:6b), together with Hag 2:23 and 2 Sam 7. She therefore classifies this story as the 'Ätiologie des Nordreiches und seines ersten Königshauses'.[1] McKenzie has shown Weippert's association of her pre-Dtr kern with other prophetic designations of throne pretenders (1 Sam 10:1, 7b and 2 Kgs 9:6b) to be somewhat forced.[2] Nevertheless, Weippert's interpretation remains an attractive possibility.

According to the second alternative, there appears to be more solid ground for considering a historical base for vv. 29-39, since it would then rely on a (prophetic) narrative that predates Dtr. However, the flaw of this line of reasoning is just as open to criticism as was the view of McKenzie, above, although from the opposite direction. Why is this early (prophetic) story less likely to be fictive, just because Dtr did not create it?[3] The view that everything that is older in its literary formation is also more likely to be historical, is a naive and romantic view of literary history, yet apparently still very much alive in OT exegesis. Of course the opposite is just as naive, namely that whatever is formulated in typically Dtr terminology is less likely to be historical.[4]

---

[1] Weippert (1983: 370). For further on this topic of divine anointings providing usurpers to the throne with a sacral legitimation, see Viberg (1992: 89-119).

[2] McKenzie (1991). Van Seters (1983: 318, n 84) also has some serious criticism of Weippert's study.

[3] Stacey (1990: 81-2), on the contrary, provides some idiosyncratic reasons why the tearing of the mantle in twelve pieces must be regarded as unhistorical. His reasons are, first, that it is a difficult and impracticable thing to do, bordering on banal. Second, it has no significance in its context, since Israel was not divided into separate tribes. The first reason must be dismissed as a westernized form of superimposing upon the biblical texts what is likely to happen and what is not, an approach that is gratefully becoming less common. The second argument is somewhat more serious, although there is no reason why it could not have been obvious to anyone attentive to political realities in those times that the natural division would be between the 10 tribes in the north and the rest in the south. The twelve pieces are treated as a collective when they are handed over to Jeroboam, and there is no reason to suggest that the division in twelve pieces was added later by someone who tried to adapt the story to what actually happened.

[4] This has been put very clearly by Ben Zvi (1993: 350), 'the more one can discern the influence of genre requirements in prophetic stories found in the Book of Kings, the less one can accept at face value their historical-political claims concerning the centrality of the prophet." The expression 'genre requirements' appears to mean for Ben Zvi deuteronomistic language and thought.

What implications, then, do these two basic alternatives have for the symbolic act, both described and explained in vv. 30-31? First, we should note that those scholars who follow the second alternative and postulates a prophetic source used by Dtr, usually include vv. 30-31 in this source. As far as literary history is concerned, it therefore seems best to hold together the description of the act with its interpretation, as they appear in vv. 30-31.[1]

Second, what follows in vv. 32ff. is an elaboration on the basic form of the oracle in v. 31, an elaboration that is formulated in typical Dtr language. It is only then that the oracle becomes confusing, even contradicting, as it shifts its focus from Jeroboam to David and Solomon. This shift of focus does not, however, alter the understanding of the symbolic act in any substantial way.

Third, whether or not Dtr has formulated vv. 29-39 in its entirety is of no real relevance to the question of the historicity of the narrative. The connection with what precedes is difficult to evaluate, since there are no obvious tensions pointing to a secondary, construed connection. According to the present form of the text, it is because of Ahijah's oracle in favour of Jeroboam that Solomon, who just recently considered Jeroboam a גִּבּוֹר חָיִל, 'a capable man' (v. 28), now seeks to kill him. If the prophetic story in vv. 29-39 (vv. 29-31 + vv. 32-39) has been secondarily connected to what precedes, it might have been because Dtr felt a need to provide a reason for Solomon's change of attitude towards Jeroboam, as the present text will have us believe (11:40).[2] It may well be that various parts of the narrative have been used by Dtr in a context where they might not have originated, since there is some force in the argument that the expectancy awakened by the narrative prologue in 11:27-28 is hardly satisfied by what follows in vv. 29ff. As the text of 1 Kgs 11:29-40 now stands, Dtr explains the animosity of Jeroboam as yet another of Solomon's enemies, after Hadad the Edomite (vv. 14-22) and Rezon of Aram (vv. 23-25), but his animosity is meant to be caused by his divine designation by the prophet Ahijah. So although the contextual configuration of the narrative in 1 Kgs 11 may have its complex history, that is in itself no reason to rule out the historical value of vv. 29-31. Dtr is interested in highlighting what he regards as the fundamental cause behind Jeroboam, and the

---

[1] It is possible 11:31a is the work of Dtr, due to the emphasis on the guilt of Solomon and traces of deuteronomistic terminology and phraseology, so e.g. Knoppers (1993: 184-5), against e.g. Campbell (1986: 25, n 9). However, the decision is uncertain, particularly when scholars such as Campbell and Knoppers can come to diametrically opposite conclusions as to the presence of deuteronomistic language.

[2] Weippert (1983: 346, 353).

reason why he could be so successful as he indeed was, gaining power over the major part of Salomon's kingdom.

On the historical plane, one must conclude that although Dtr has edited and sometimes reworked the various traditions at his disposal, it is still clear that certain prophetic circles in the northern kingdom played a significant role in the struggle for political power.[1] Therefore, a designation by a Northern Yhwh-prophet could very well have been a decisive factor for Jeroboam in his rebellion against Solomon.[2]

Performance

As was shown above, there is a problem in 1 Sam 15:27 as to whether Saul or Samuel performs the act. It has gone quite unnoticed that there is a similar problem in 1 Kgs 11:30, although not as troublesome as the problem in 1 Sam 15:27.[3] According to 11:29a, Ahijah found Jeroboam on the road as he came out of Jerusalem, and according to v. 29b, וְהוּא מִתְכַּסֶּה בְּשַׂלְמָה חֲדָשָׁה, 'he was covered with a new mantle'. Who is referred to by הוּא, 'he', in v. 29b? It could very well be Jeroboam, since in v. 29a the literary point of view[4] is that of Ahijah, spotting[5] Jeroboam on the road from Jerusalem. This perspective could very well be continuing in v. 29b with a further description of what Ahijah saw, namely Jeroboam wearing a new mantle.[6] In v. 30 the problem seems to be resolved when Ahijah takes hold of the mantle אֲשֶׁר עָלָיו, 'which was on him', a statement which clearly means 'on himself', i.e., that it was Ahijah's mantle after all (cf. 1 Sam 18:4).[7]

---

[1] See e.g. Wilson (1980: 184-7), Blenkinsopp (1996: 56-7)

[2] So e.g. Fohrer (1977: 14).

[3] The only reference found that shows an awareness of the problem is Vanoni (1984: 222-3, n 69).

[4] For this expression, see Berlin (1983).

[5] It could very well be that we are supposed to understand וַיִּמְצָא in v. 29a as Ahijah's 'finding out" the whereabouts of Jeroboam. The whole act would then have been intentional from the very beginning, and not something the prophet decided to do when he saw Jeroboam coming.

[6] The only proponents of this view to be found is Ewald (1878: 304-5) and Godbey (1922: 101). Vanoni (1984) prefers to remain undecided on the matter, although he shows that statistically, the most probable interpretation is that Ahijah tore Jeroboam's mantle.

[7] Vanoni (1984: 222-3, n 69) suggests that אֲשֶׁר עָלָיו, 'which was on him" could have been added later in order to avoid the ambiguity of the text. There is a certain similarity between the formulation of 1 Kgs 11:30a and 1 Sam 18:4a, וַיִּתְפַּשֵּׁט יְהוֹנָתָן אֶת־הַמְּעִיל אֲשֶׁר עָלָיו, 'and Jonathan took of the mantle which was on him". No doubt both these texts form part of the

The word used (11:29, 30) for the clothing Ahijah tears apart is שַׂלְמָה, a word that usually means an outer garment. Together with its variant שִׂמְלָה, it occurs 36 times in the OT.[1]

Nevertheless, the performance of this act is clear enough; Ahijah takes his own mantle and divides it into twelve pieces, handing over ten to Jeroboam.

The Symbolism of the Act

In 1 Kgs 11:11-13 God rebukes Solomon with a particular expression, קָרֹעַ אֶקְרַע אֶת־הַמַּמְלָכָה מֵעָלֶיךָ וּנְתַתִּיהָ לְעַבְדֶּךָ, 'I will tear the kingdom from you and give it to your servant.' Later in 1 Kgs 14:8, Jeroboam is rebuked by God through Ahijah, וָאֶקְרַע אֶת־הַמַּמְלָכָה מִבֵּית דָּוִד וָאֶתְּנֶהָ לָךְ, 'I tore the kingdom from the house of David and gave it to You', alluding back to the passage in 11:31, הִנְנִי קֹרֵעַ אֶת־הַמַּמְלָכָה מִיַּד שְׁלֹמֹה וְנָתַתִּי לְךָ אֵת עֲשָׂרָה הַשְּׁבָטִים, 'I will tear the kingdom from the hand of Solomon and give the ten tribes to you.' The similarities make an intentional dependency between them hard to deny. There is also a similarity between these texts and God's harsh rebuke of Saul in 1 Sam 15:28, קָרַע יְהוָה אֶת־מַמְלְכוּת יִשְׂרָאֵל מֵעָלֶיךָ הַיּוֹם וּנְתָנָהּ לְרֵעֲךָ הַטּוֹב מִמֶּךָ, 'Yhwh has torn the kingdom of Israel from You today and given it to someone better than You.' The final allusion to the figure of the torn mantle is in 2 Kgs 17:21, which is the narrator's final speech, explaining the causes behind the downfall of the northern kingdom. According to 2 Kgs 17:21, God קָרַע יִשְׂרָאֵל מֵעַל בֵּית דָּוִד, 'tore Israel from the house of David'. Throughout all these texts there is also the obvious similarity of the mantle symbolizing the kingdom, as an indexical symbol, which associates to the person wearing it. We have to conclude that because there are references to the primary use of the phrase 'tear the hem of the mantle/mantle', the expression 'tear the kingdom from' can not be considered as a wholly idiomatic phrase. Another argument for this is that the phrase does not occur anywhere else in the OT.

Returning to the symbolic act in 1 Kgs 11:29-31, it is not possible to hold that it bears any direct allusions to a conventional symbolic act, as in 1 Sam 15:27

---

major theme used by Dtr, namely how the kingdom, symbolized by a mantle, is passed on from one to the other. For further on the symbolic act in 1 Sam 18:4, see Viberg (1992: 127-35).

[1] See Joüon, and Muraoka (1991: 74-5, § 17b). The variation is due to metathesis.

and probably also in 1 Sam 24:5.[1] The only relevant connection that can be found is the thematic unity created by the author by means of the act in 1 Kgs 11:29-31, the acts in 1 Sam 15:27; 24:5 and the expression in 1 Kgs 14:8. This cluster of various expressions and acts making use of the mantle as a symbol for the kingdom and the act of tearing or simply the verb קרע, 'tear' is created by the author to make a stylistic effect, and thus to enhance his theological point of view.[2] For the purpose of this study, however, it is important to note that the act in 1 Kgs 11:29-31 is a typical prophetic act with a symbolic significance.

The iconic symbolism of Ahijah's act of tearing his mantle in twelve pieces and handing Jeroboam ten pieces is quite clear; it symbolizes the disruption of the unified kingdom under Solomon and its division in two parts by means of analogy, imitating the split in the kingdom. One part, consisting of ten tribes, will be ruled by Jeroboam. It should be noted that the tearing of the mantle in twelve pieces does not in itself symbolize the division of the kingdom, but only the inherent tribal diversity, which had always been the case with the unified kingdom. It is when Ahijah hands over twelve pieces to Jeroboam and asks him to receive them that the division of the kingdom in two is accomplished.

As to possible indexical symbolism of the act it is as always much more difficult to be certain, since it presupposes a deeper knowledge of the culture. The associations that are brought to mind are not necessarily tied to the syntagmatic structure of the linguistic code, but can be found in all aspects of the social life. There is one possible connotative meaning that has been overlooked so far, however. The act of tearing a mantle was in the ancient Israelite society a conventional symbolic act, used to express grief, sorrow, and deep frustration and possibly also anger.[3] Is it possible for the symbolic act in 1 Kgs 11:29-31 to have been understood by the readers/viewers in its iconic symbolism without at the same time making them associate to the conventional act of tearing the mantle by means of indexical symbolism? I would hold this to be unlikely. This as-

---

[1] See e.g. Jones (1984: 243). The only possible connection would be to the act of *naḫlaptu šarāṭu*, 'tear the mantle", signifying grief or defeat. However, since there is no trace of this meaning in 1 Kgs 11:29-31, the connection is unlikely to say the least.

[2] The author also uses the mantle as a symbol for the kingdom in other contexts, such as when Elijah leaves his mantle on the ground to be taken up by Elisha (2 Kgs 2:13-15), and when Jonathan transfers his royal clothes to David (1 Sam 18:4). For the latter act as an example of the reuse of a legal symbolic act in a non-legal context, see Viberg (1992: 127-35).

[3] See e.g. TDOT 13, 175-7, Gruber (1980: 366). However, Gruber fails to note that various terms for clothing are used besides בֶּגֶד, such as מַד, כְּתֹנֶת, מְעִיל, שִׂמְלָה. The symbolic act was common enough in the ancient Near East, and the relevant phrase used in Akkadian is *naḫlapta/ṣubta šarāṭu*, see CAD, 17/2, 59.

sociative, or indexical symbolism would then provide the symbolic act with an additional character, namely that of grief and sorrow in the face of the disaster which was at hand, namely the division of the unified kingdom.

There is an emphasis on the fact that the mantle Ahijah is wearing is חֲדָשָׁה, 'new' (11:29, 30). The author emphasizes this fact by mentioning it twice. Had Ahijah a particular reason for wearing a new mantle, or, to put the question on the literary level rather than on the action level, why is the author anxious to make it clear that the prophet is wearing a new mantle? The reason normally given is that the act of the prophet Ahijah required an unused mantle in order for its inherent magical strength to be intact. Most scholars are not willing to use the concept 'magic' in this context, but their explanations are generally of that nature nevertheless.[1] Another explanation put forward is that a new mantle was more likely to draw attention to the act by the element of surprise.[2] A variant view of this is that the newness of the mantle symbolized the new and, as yet, unbroken kingdom.[3] If we concentrate on the first alternative, one has to ask for the basis for such a view, since there is no indication given in the text itself. This view is based, not so much on the analysis of this text in particular, but on the view in principle that the symbolic acts of the prophets were not communicative, symbolic acts, but attempts to accomplish what they displayed symbolically. Whether or not we use the word 'magic' is of lesser importance, since according to this view some form of mystical force or strength inherent in the acts themselves and the items used were thought by the prophets to make the symbolically displayed events come about. Since such an argument is open to the risk of circular reasoning unless it confronts the texts anew and any preconceived ideas as to the nature of these acts, we will study the question anew from the texts themselves.

Why, then, would the prophet bring a new mantle on this occasion? First, the

---

[1] So e.g. Noth (1968: 259), Würthwein (1976: 143), Fohrer (1977: 14), Nelson (1981: 111), Jones (1984: 243), Rofé (1988: 17), Stacey (1990: 80-1). The view of Gray (1970: 295) is representative, 'Based on the principle of imitative magic, the attempt to influence the power of providence by autosuggestion, it was used by the prophets to indict and emphasize the certainty of the divine intention, and so to arrest popular attention. ... According to the popular conception of acts designed to enlist the activity of the supernatural, new media were important as having had no contact with other agencies which might impair the designed effect". As to magic functions of clothing, the old article by Jirku (1917/18) is still referred to.

[2] So Dietrich (1972: 16). Amsler (1985: 11) speaks of the chocking effect the tearing of a new, and therefore valuable mantle would have had, and in that sense, the act was analogical to the tearing of the kingdom that it symbolized.

[3] So DeVries (1985), Hubbard (1991).

very fact that Ahijah did bring a new mantle to his encounter with Jeroboam implies that the meeting was intentional, and not just a casual meeting on the country road.[1] In order to understand why a new item was used, we can look at other instances in the OT where it is specifically stated that a new item is used.

1) Samson lures Delilah into believing that only new ropes will make him loose his strength, which proves to be a lie (Jud 15:13; 16:11f). Although it turns out the be a lie on Samson's behalf, the point of the statement by Samson rests on the common assumption that the newness of the rope would provide it with some extraordinary quality in terms of overcoming Samson's unusual strength.

2) When the ark is brought up from the Philistines, as well as when David brings up the ark to Jerusalem, it is specifically said that the ark is brought on a new cart (1 Sam 6:7; 2 Sam 6:3). This is a case where the ark as a cultic object calls for the cultic purity of the cart, in the sense that it should not have been used for any other purpose than carrying the ark. Only a new cart was apparently believed to possess the particular quality that was required for this particular purpose. To what extent this was a matter of conventional procedure in moving a cultic object is hard to tell.

3) David's opponent is fitted with a new sword (2 Sam 21:16). There would seem to be little reason for this to be mentioned unless there was some particular significance to the fact that the sword was not only fearful as a piece of armour, but new. Clearly this is meant to have added to the strength of Ishbi-Benob, beyond his own physical capacity (2 Sam 21:16).

4) When Elisha purifies the water of a well, throws salt in it, he requests for the salt to be brought to him in a new bowl. The only reasonable explanation to this is that Elisha, who uses the salt in a way that obviously goes beyond its natural quality and function, believes that the item connected to this salt must be new in order to bring about the supernatural quality of the salt (2 Kgs 2:20).[2]

5) When the Gibeonites try to persuade the Israelites that they have indeed come a long way, they point to the fact that their wineskins are worn, in contrast to when they were new as they left home (Josh 9:13). This has nothing to do with some extraordinary quality due to the newness of the wineskins, but is simply a way to convince the Israelites.

6) Last year's harvest will have to be removed in order to make room for the new. There is no need to see an extraordinary character here, since there is an obvious and very practical sense to what is described. Newly harvested crop is

---

[1] So e.g. Gray (1970: 295), Campbell (1986: 88, n 54), Knoppers (1993: 169, n 1).
[2] See e.g. Wright (1987: 98-9, n 14).

better than last year's harvest, not because it is new in itself, but because it is of a better quality and therefore it has priority.

7) A sacrificial animal shall be new in the sense that it has never been used for another purpose than that of sacrifice (Num 19:2; Deut 21:3).

These examples fall neatly into three categories:

1) Those instances where the fact that the item is new has a perfectly natural explanation, which is brought out by the circumstances (examples 5 and 6).

2) Those instances where the newness of an item in itself provides an added strength of supernatural character to the item itself while it is being used so that its capacity increases beyond its normal state. The item's capacity is then enhanced beyond its normal standard (examples 1 and 3).

3) Those instances where a cultic context calls for a cultic purity of the object used, in the sense that it can not be defiled by a use other than cultic. In this case it is not so much a matter of enhanced supernatural capacity as the particular requirement for using the item in a cultic context (examples 2 and 4).

Which of these categories is relevant for Ahijah's new mantle? We can easily rule out 3, the cultic use of a new item.[1] Although most scholars regard 2 as the most plausible explanation, there is nothing in the context to indicate this. On the other hand, a new mantle would in a dramatic way illustrate the wholeness of the kingdom, and enhance the chocking, contrasting effect when Ahijah tears it apart. There is also an important point in the fact that a new garment was an expensive piece of clothing, and this would also serve to enhance the chocking effect. The conclusion is therefore that the natural explanation as to why Ahijah tears a new garment is convincing, in contrast to the other alternatives.

---

[1] The common way of purifying clothes cultically was to launder them (Ex 19:10; Lev 11:25, 40; 17:15; Num 19:19 etc). It is interesting to note that LXX, in its second variant of the incident in 3 Kgdms 12:24o, adds that it was a new mantle which τὸ οὐκ εἰσεληλυθὸς εἰς ὕδωρ, 'had not come into water", i.e., it was so new that it had never been laundered. It is best, however, to take this comment as a simple common sense remark, synonymous with saying that it was new. The view of Stacey (1990: 80) that the reading of 3 Kgdms 12:24o is evidence of the belief that the water would lessen the mystic quality of a new item is without foundation.

Excursus: The alternative reading in 3 Kgdms 12:24o

The text of this very enigmatic variant in LXX, which recounts yet a second time how, a prophet tears a garment and hands Jeroboam some of the pieces is as follows;

[24o] καὶ λόγος κυρίου ἐγένετο πρὸς Σαμαιαν τὸν Ελαμι λέγων λαβὲ σεαυτῷ ἱμάτιον καινὸν τὸ οὐκ εἰσεληλυθὸς εἰς ὕδωρ καὶ ῥῆξον αὐτὸ δώδεκα ῥήγματα καὶ δώσεις τῷ Ιεροβοαμ καὶ ἐρεῖς αὐτῷ τάδε λέγει κύριος λαβὲ σεαυτῷ δέκα ῥήγματα τοῦ περιβαλέσθαι σε καὶ ἔλαβεν Ιεροβοαμ καὶ εἶπεν Σαμαιας τάδε λέγει κύριος ἐπὶ τὰς δέκα φυλὰς τοῦ Ισραηλ

And the word of the Lord came to Samaias son of Enlami, saying, 'Take to yourself a new mantle that has not been taken into water, and tear it into twelve pieces, and give to Jeroboam and say to him, 'This is what the Lord says: Take to yourself ten pieces to dress yourself with.' And Jeroboam took. And Samaias said, 'This is what the Lord says regarding the ten tribes of Israel.

This is not the place to discuss the whole issue of this much discussed variant in 3 Kgdms 12:24a-z. The issue here is to find out if there is any reason to consider the variant, first for text-critical reasons, which would mean that it would have a bearing on the reading of MT, and second, if the variant could be considered to contain a variant tradition to 1 Kgs 11:29-31, perhaps providing evidence for a pre-Dtr stage of the tradition of Elijah's calling of Elisha.

There is no scholarly consensus as to the value of the variant in 3 Kgdms 12:24a-z. It is regarded by some to be a late, midrashic treatment of MT,[1] whereas others see it as an actual variant to what is found in MT, providing some unique information to the pre-Dtr stage in the history of the traditions concerning Jeroboam.[2] What speaks against an identification of the variant as midrashic is that it is shorter than both LXX and MT. Much of the typical Dtr language is

---

[1] So e.g. Gooding (1967), Gordon (1975). Cf. also Debus (1967: 68-80), Knoppers (1987: 172-86), McKenzie (1991: 21-40), Talshir (1993).

[2] So e.g. Debus (1967), Trebolle Barrera (1980), Knoppers (1993). The view of Talshir (1992: 617-8) is similar, in that she holds that the variant is based on a source similar to Kings, but it does not witness to a pre-Dtr stage. Auld (1994: 165-7) presents his own highly original view on the composition of the Kings and Chronicles, namely that both of them made use an earlier source, what Auld calls the 'Shared Text', and subsequently added material in accordance to their respective ideologies. Since 1 Kgs 11 is a plus in Kings, i.e., it has no counterpart in Chronicles, it means for Auld that it has been added in Kings to the 'Shared Text'. The alternative reading in 3 Reigns 12:24a-z is for Auld (1994: 104, n 1) 'a first draft of the introduction to the first king of northern Israel". Auld holds it possible that the alternative reading was part of his 'Shared Text'.

missing, which could point in the direction of the variant bearing testimony to a stage in the history of traditions when there had not as yet been a thorough Dtr redaction. On the other hand, this negative evidence could just as well be the result of an author who is selective in creating his own account. Although the problem is likely to remain, the arguments put forward by McKenzie are convincing.[1] In MT, the meeting between Jeroboam and the prophet is situated just before Rehoboam goes to Shechem, whereas the variant has the meeting earlier at the division of the kingdom. Since Rehoboam had met with a prophet called Shemaiah in 1 Kgs 12:22-24, it seemed natural to the author of the variant to name the prophet in his variant story Shemaiah as well, since it describes an occurrence almost immediately after 1 Kgs 12:22-24.

If we look more closely at 3 Kgdms 12:24o, there are some indications that would substantiate McKenzie's view even further.

1) When the new mantle, which Shemaiah is told to take with him to the meeting, is said not to have come near water, it appears to be an explanation for something that has caused bewilderment in an earlier version. Since MT does not have this explanation, it would appear to be the earlier of the two.

2) When Shemaiah is told by God to tell Jeroboam to dress himself in ten pieces of what used to be a new mantle, it is hard to understand this as something else than an attempt to explain something that has caused bewilderment at an earlier stage. What was Jeroboam supposed to do with the ten pieces, readers are likely to have asked. The answer given by the variant, perhaps ironically, is that he should wear them!

3) At the end of 12:24o, Shemaiah says, 'This is what the Lord says regarding the ten tribes of Israel', but there is no record of what God is supposed to say.[2] The reason is probably that the author of the variant has abbreviated the account in MT, in order to exclude any reference to Solomon, which is why he ended up with such an anticlimactic formulation.[3]

4) MT does not say that Jeroboam takes the pieces of the mantle from the prophet, whereas the variant does. This should be understood as yet another case where the author of the variant has created a simpler and more straight-forward narrative than what he had before him.

5) In MT, the prophet Ahijah is not said to 'give' Jeroboam the pieces, which occurs only in the divine oracle in v. 31b, וְנָתַתִּי לְךָ אֵת עֲשָׂרָה הַשְּׁבָטִים, 'and I will give the ten tribes to you.' According to the variant, on the other hand, the prophet Shemaiah is told by God to δώσεις τῷ Ιεροβοαμ, 'give to Jeroboam'. This is another case where the text has been simplified in the sense that a part of

---

[1] McKenzie (1991: 91-140)

[2] Knoppers (1993: 181) holds that the statement pronounces the implications of the symbolic act, but that would have to take the verb 'say' as relating to the nonverbal act, which is quite unusual.

[3] See especially Talshir (1992: 612-3).

the oracle, which was not considered as working against the overall intention of the author, was incorporated into the narrative to make Ahijah's mission more explicit. This should be taken as a rather sure indication that the author of the variant knew of the traditional account as it appears in MT, with its Dtr redaction, however far that went.[1]

The fact that 1 Kgs 11:32-39, which is usually considered as deuteronomistic, is missing from the variant might be considered an argument in favour of that characterization, but it can also be that the author of the variant considered those verses as not in line with his purpose, which was to put the story in the time of Rehoboam, and not to connect it with the time of Solomon, a tendency not unlike that of the Chronicler.[2] The conclusion is therefore that the variant in 3 Kgdms 12:24o is of no use in rehabilitating MT, which should be considered the original account. The author of the variant account has based his story on MT, and has dealt selectively with his source in accordance with his intentions.

---

[1] This would negate the view of e.g. Knoppers (1993: 179-86), that the variant shows no awareness of Dtr redaction.

[2] Knoppers (1993: 184-5) is of course correct in noting that it is 'technically untrue' for 1 Kgs 11:31b to say that the kingdom is removed from Solomon, since it was actually removed from Rehoboam, and that this would indicate that 11:31b is from Dtr. However, this is an overly simplistic view of the matter. We have to presume that whether it is the author of an earlier narrative or Dtr we are focusing on, they are both likely to have known about these matters. The question is rather what reason the author could have had for his manner of presentation.

Summary and Conclusions

1. The symbolism inherent in the acts in 1 Sam 15:27 and 24:5 makes use of a more extensive symbolism of the hem of the mantle, namely as a symbol for the kingdom. The symbolism involved is indexical, since the mantle is used to associate to the person wearing it. Whereas these two acts are related to conventional, legal symbolic acts, the act in 1 Kgs 11:29-31 is a typical prophetic symbolic act, that makes use of the legal symbolism to communicate its message.

2. The narrative in 1 Kgs 11:29-31 goes back to a pre-Dtr tradition, describing a prophetic symbolic act. This tradition has been used by Dtr as a means of elucidating the division of the kingdom. The figurative language inherent in the description of the act has been worked into the overall theme of how the kingdom was 'torn away'.

3. The symbolic meaning of the prophetic symbolic act in 1 Kgs 11:29-31 is iconic, since it refers to the division of the kingdom by means of analogy, although in a rather abstract sense. The mantle itself can not be said to be symbolic in the indexical sense of the acts in 1 Sam 15:27 and 24:5, since it is not worn by a king or a king to be. Only some pieces of the mantle are handed over to the king to be, which makes it unlikely that we are meant to see an indexical symbolism.

4. The fact that the mantle Ahijah is wearing and subsequently tears apart is said to be new, is best explained naturally. The newness is meant to emphasize the suddenness, the unexpected event that is to happen.

5. The alternative reading in 3 Kgdms 12:24o is secondary to the Hebrew text of MT.

C. Isaiah Goes Naked (Isaiah 20)

Introduction

Is 20 is an odd narrative in several respects. It refers to Isaiah in third person and makes no claim to come from the hand of the prophet himself, it describes the only prophetic symbolic act by Isaiah in the book that bears his name, it breaks in among the collection of oracles against foreign nations, presumably after the oracle against Egypt to provide added force to that oracle (Is 19), and it refers to events taking place 714-711 concerning which we have no other explicit reference in the OT.[1] If we also take into consideration the complex grammatical structure of the first three verses of the chapter, it would appear that it stands out as something quite extraordinary in comparison to its literary context. To fully understand the prophetic symbolic act referred to in this chapter, we must try to understand the narrative at large, since this understanding will form our understanding of the symbolic act as it was performed, if indeed it was, and how it is described in the text.

The Text

בִּשְׁנַת בֹּא תַרְתָּן אַשְׁדּוֹדָה 1
בִּשְׁלֹח אֹתוֹ סַרְגוֹן מֶלֶךְ אַשּׁוּר
וַיִּלָּחֶם בְּאַשְׁדּוֹד וַיִּלְכְּדָהּ[a]
בָּעֵת הַהִיא דִּבֶּר יְהוָה בְּיַד[b] 2
יְשַׁעְיָהוּ בֶן־אָמוֹץ לֵאמֹר לֵךְ
וּפִתַּחְתָּ הַשַּׂק מֵעַל מָתְנֶיךָ
וְנַעַלְךָ[c] תַחֲלֹץ מֵעַל
רַגְלֶיךָ וַיַּעַשׂ כֵּן הָלֹךְ
עָרוֹם וְיָחֵף 3 וַיֹּאמֶר יְהוָה
כַּאֲשֶׁר הָלַךְ עַבְדִּי יְשַׁעְיָהוּ
עָרוֹם וְיָחֵף[d] שָׁלֹשׁ·

1 In the year that the commander-in-chief, who was sent by King Sargon of Assyria, came to Ashdod and fought against it and took it, 2 at that time Yhwh had spoken to Isaiah son of Amoz, saying, 'Go, and loose the sackcloth from your loins and take your sandals off your feet,' and he had done so, walking naked and barefoot. 3 Then Yhwh said, 'Just as my servant Isaiah has walked naked and barefoot for three years as a sign and a portent against

---

[1] Although some scholars prefers to see in the narrative references and allusions to other events, e.g. Clements (1980a: 174), who prefers to see the revolt in Judah 705-701 as the relevant uproar, and Kaiser (1974: 118) who prefers to see the narrative as alluding to the disaster of 587 These views will be discussed further below. The only other reference to the Assyrian attack on Ashdod is, as one would expect, in the inscriptions of Sargon II, which will be discussed below.

שָׁנִים אוֹת וּמוֹפֵת עַל־מִצְרַיִם
וְעַל־כּוּשׁ 4 כֵּן יִנְהַג
מֶלֶךְ־אַשּׁוּר אֶת־שְׁבִי
מִצְרַיִם וְאֶת־גָּלוּת כּוּשׁ
נְעָרִים וּזְקֵנִים עָרוֹם וְיָחֵף
וַחֲשׂוּפַי שֵׁת עֶרְוַת מִצְרָיִם
5 וְחַתּוּ וָבֹשׁוּ מִכּוּשׁ מַבָּטָם
וּמִן־מִצְרַיִם הָאִי הַזֶּה
תִּפְאַרְתָּם 6 וְאָמַר יֹשֵׁב
בַּיּוֹם הַהוּא הִנֵּה־כֹה מַבָּטֵנוּ
אֲשֶׁר־נַסְנוּ שָׁם לְעֶזְרָה
לְהִנָּצֵל מִפְּנֵי מֶלֶךְ אַשּׁוּר
וְאֵיךְ נִמָּלֵט אֲנָחְנוּ

Egypt and Ethiopia, 4 so shall the king of Assyria lead away the Egyptians as captives and the Ethiopians as exiles, both the young and the old, naked and barefoot, with buttocks uncovered, to the shame of Egypt. 5 And they shall be dismayed and confounded because of Ethiopia their hope and of Egypt their boast. 6 In that day the inhabitants of this coastland will say, 'See, this is what has happened to those in whom we hoped and to whom we fled for help and deliverance from the king of Assyria! And we, how shall we escape?''

Textual notes

[a] I have taken the phrase וַיִּלָּחֶם בְּאַשְׁדּוֹד וַיִּלְכְּדָהּ as part of the second temporal clause which is introduced by בִּשְׁלֹחַ, awaiting the main clause in v. 2 in the final text, but v. 3 in the original form of the text, since I hold v. 2 to be a later Dtr addition. However, it is also possible to take וַיִּלָּחֶם בְּאַשְׁדּוֹד וַיִּלְכְּדָהּ as the main clause, although it is less likely. The first temporal clause provides a more general description, which is subsequently provided with a more detailed description in the second temporal clause, providing details as to who sent him, the nature of his mission and its result. Verse 1b is therefore a specifying parenthesis in relation to v. 1a.

[b] LXX simplifies the dubious בְּיַד in MT by the more expected πρὸς, 'to'.

[c] Variants and 1QIsa[a] reads the plural instead of singular in MT. However, it is best taken as a defectively written dual, in line with the following dual רַגְלֶיךָ, 'your feet'.

[d] MT has interpreted 'three years' as belonging to the following phrase, 'as a sign and symbol' and to not the previous phrase, 'walked naked and barefoot' by putting the atnach after וְיָחֵף, 'barefoot' and not after שָׁנִים, 'years'. However, this is hardly the correct division of the text. The time marker limits the previous clause, i.e., 'Isaiah walked ... for three years'.

[e] This phrase may very well be an asyndetic apposition to what precedes, and need not be a late gloss, as suggested by BHS, Wildberger (1974), Blenkinsopp (2000: 321).

[f] MT has an irregular ending ־ִי, which is corrected, see BHS, Wildberger (1974).

[g] 1QIsa[a] has מבטחם, 'their trust' but not in v6, so Blenkinsopp (2000: 321). MT has the lectio difficilior, however.

[h] The phrase is not in LXX, which may have regarded it as awkward and superfluous.

Analysis

Structure

The interpretation of Is 20 is full of both textual and historical problems, as well as the problem of the nature of the prophetic symbolic act itself. As the text now stands, it consists of three parts;

1) v. 1		A historical reference to the time when the Tartan of Sargon II, i.e., his chief general, attacked Ashdod perhaps around 71 and conquered it in 712;[1]
2) v. 2		An oracle with a vague historical reference telling Isaiah to undress, and a subsequent note saying he did so;
3) vv. 3-6		A second oracle, consisting of three parts;
	a. v. 3	A description of Isaiah's symbolic act with a brief reference to its interpretation;
	b. v. 4	A more elaborate interpretation of the symbolic act;
	c. vv. 5-6	A description of how 'those who live on this coast' (v. 6) react to Egyptians and Ethiopians being exiled.

Historical background

To begin with, there is no need to question the dating of v. 1 as well as the fact that it was the Tartan and not Sargon II himself who led the punitive expedition against Philistia.[2] According to the inscriptions of Sargon II, he himself led an expedition westwards in 712, although this might very well be a case where the king takes credit for the accomplishments of his general. According to Tadmor's attempt to put the annalistic inscriptions of Sargon II in chronological order, Sargon stayed in Assyria in 712 when the punitive expedition against Philistia was undertaken.[3] This expedition was caused by a rebellion by Ashdod that must have started some time before 712, perhaps in 714.[4] The period 714(?)-712

---

[1] The period three years which originates from Is 20:2-3 could actually have been only 14 months long, since such a short period could have covered three years, one completely and two partly. This should be remembered below when the figure three years is given in the following below.

[2] The following summary account is based on the various inscriptions of Sargon II, see ARAB II, § 30, 62-3, 79, 193-5; ANET, 285-7. For the annals of Sargon II, see also the translation in Lie (1929).

[3] Tadmor (1958: 79); Tadmor (1966: 94, n 31). This is accepted by e.g. Spalinger (1973), Ahlström (1993: 693).

[4] As was suggested by Ahlström (1993: 692, n 7).

would then be enough to substantiate the reference in Is 20:3 that Isaiah walked naked and barefoot for three years, taking the start of the rebellion as the time at which Isaiah received his divine command to perform the symbolic act.

The rebellion was led by Aziru, the king of Ashdod. He refused to pay taxes to Assyria and tried to stir others in the nearby region to do the same, with the result that Sargon replaced him with his younger brother Aḥimetu.[1] According to Tadmor, this expedition took place in 713, but was considered to be of such a minor nature that it was not recorded in the annals as a proper expedition. Aḥimetu was subsequently overthrown by groups from within Ashdod, called 'Hittites' in Sargon's inscriptions. They replaced Aḥimetu with a person called Iadna (Yamani),[2] sometimes thought to be a Greek, but who was more probably a Philistine, even indigenous to Ashdod.[3] Iadna tried to stir others in the region to join him in his rebellion and form a coalition against Assyria. In one of Sargon's inscriptions Judah is mentioned among those who were contacted by Iadna.[4] He even sent gifts to Egypt in order to gain aid in the attack he knew would come from Sargon.

The broken prism A is at the centre of this discussion, based on Winckle's text, ll. 28-33;[5]

'To [the kings] of (the lands of) Philistia, Judah, Edom, Moab, who dwell by the sea, who pay tribute (and) tax to Assur, my lord, (they were) uttering numerous lies (and) evil things.'

The undefined plural subject is obviously the 'Hittites', as in Sargon's description of the event in his annals.[6] The attempt by Na'aman[1] to reconstruct the text,

---

[1] We learn from Sargon's correspondence that he received tribute during his reign from Ashdod, Egypt, Gaza, Judah, Moab, Ammon, Edom and Ekron, SAA 1, 29.23-4, 110.4'-13'.

[2] The two names alternate in Sargon's inscriptions, see Tadmor (1958: 80).

[3] So Tadmor (1958: 80, n. 217), Tadmor (1966: 94), Spalinger (1973: 97), Ahlström (1993).

[4] Ahlström (1993: 692-3) states that Iadna did form a coalition, but that seems to be taking the evidence too far. From what we can read in Sargon's annals, it appears that he tried to form such a coalition, but whether he succeeded or not is impossible to say. However, we can surmise that had he succeeded in doing so, the punitive expedition would certainly not have limited itself to Ashod and some other Philistine cities, but would have included Judah, Edom and Moab as well. See e.g. Donner (1986), Miller, and Hayes (1986), Laato (1988), Briquel-Chatonnet (1992: 182-3). Donner also speaks of Judah and other kingdoms as, at least initially, taking part in the rebellion, but withdrawing from it when they realized where it was taking them.

[5] Winckler (1889). ANET, 287, ARAB 1, § 195, see also CAD 6, 229b for l. 32.

[6] ARAB II, § 62.

apparently followed by Miller and Hayes,[2] makes the rulers of Ashdod and the other countries nearby the subject of the act of sending presents to the pharaoh, thus making Hezekiah more active in the rebellion against Sargon. However, Na'aman's reconstruction demands much more than the simple reconstruction proposed here. It is, on the basis of the translation favoured here, obvious from the broken prism inscription that there is no hint in the direction of an active part on Judah's behalf in the rebellion against Sargon II, but only that a coalition was sought by the leaders of Ashdod. Incidentally, Sargon's annals mention that Azuri also spread an invitation to form a coalition against Sargon.[3] We should note that only Azuri was punished for this, not any other countries nearby, such as Judah. Tadmor[4] tries to show by means of a cuneiform fragment (BM 81-3-23, 131) that Sargon's army attacked the Judean town of Azeqah after the capture of Ashdod. The damaged text speaks of an attack on *A-za-qa-a*, which can be Azeqah, but the date is very hard to specify. Tadmor has been followed by Ginsberg,[5] who sees the attack on Azeqah pictured vividly in Is 22:1-14. Na'aman,[6] however, is more persuasive in dating the text to the time of Sennacherib, close to the end of his campaign to Palestine in 701. Mattingly,[7] after an archaeological overview of the cities usually suggested to have been attacked together with Ashdod, concludes that 'the desire to include other cities (i.e., except Ashdod, Gath and Ashdod-Yam) as targets of this expedition unnecessarily exaggerates Yamani's ability and Sargon's intention.'[8]

No help came however, and in 712 the punitive expedition was sent out against Ashdod as well as other Philistine cities along the southern coastal area.[9] Iadna heard of this expedition while it was on its way and fled to Egypt, expecting asylum there from the Assyrians.[10] He found no help in Egypt, however, and continued to the territory of Kush. However, the Nubian ruler Shabako, who had

---

[1] Na'aman (1974: 32).

[2] Miller, and Hayes (1986: 352).

[3] ARAB II, § 62.

[4] Tadmor (1958: 80-4).

[5] Ginsberg (1968: 49).

[6] Na'aman (1974: 31).

[7] Mattingly (1981: 54).

[8] See particularly Kaplan (1969: 149) on the excavation and significance of Ashdod-Yam. He would also see Yamani's efforts as his own and not as part of the efforts of a coalition.

[9] For Sargon's intention of making the conquest of Ashdod the first step towards conquering the whole of Philistia, see Alt (1953: 234-41), Na'aman (1979: 71-2, n 7).

[10] The attack on Ashdod has earlier been assigned to 711, but recently the year attributed to this event has proved to be 712, see e.g. Redford (1985: 6).

recently conquered Egypt, did not want any disturbances in his delicate diplomatic relations with Assyria, so he sent Iadna in chains to Assyria.

It is not certain which Pharaoh Iadna hoped would come to his aid. The Nubian ruler Shabako possibly conquered Egypt in 716/15.[1] In his notes of revision for the second edition, however, Kitchen puts 713/12 as the latest possible date for Shabako's conquest of Egypt.[2] Iadna could have expected Bakenranef (Bocchoris) to be reigning.[3] However, he found the Nubian ruler Shabako in his place, a ruler from which he could expect no possibility of asylum. Redford holds, however, that Shabako took over Lower Egypt late in 712 or possibly in January 711.[4] According to him, this means that Shabako had not yet conquered Egypt when Iadna arrived there.[5] Iadna simply could not get any help from the pharaoh, and therefore continued further to the border between Egypt and Kush.[6]

This is the most plausible historical background to Is 20, and it is almost unanimously seen to be so among scholars.[7] However, Clements and Kaiser have each proposed different historical settings for the text, and indeed different evaluations of the symbolic act described therein.[8]

Clements argues that the symbolic act was originally intended against the Philistines, particularly the city of Ashdod at the time of the rebellion, but this was later reapplied by a redactor to suit a later time when Egypt and Kush were indeed called upon for help, and when Isaiah's prophecy of Ashdod's downfall had proved itself true. This, more suitable rebellion according to Clements, occurred in 705-701.[9] However, Clements seems more eager to rescue the prophetic character of Is 20 than is necessary. There is no reason to doubt the risk

---

[1] See Kitchen (1986: 154, 378-80).

[2] Kitchen (1986: 552).

[3] So Redford (1985: 6, n 16).

[4] Redford (1985: 9), Redford (1992a: 348).

[5] Redford (1985: 7).

[6] As in l 12 of the so-called 'Display inscription' from room 14 at Khorsabad, *ana itê Muṣri ša pât Meluḫḫa*, 'to the border of Egypt which is (contiguous) to the territory of Kush'. See CAD 7, 313, Weisbach (1918: 179), ANET, 285, ARAB II, § 79.

[7] Various other parts of the book of Isaiah have been suggested to relate to the same incident as Is 20. One of them is the oracle against Philistia in Is 14:28-32, so e.g. Fohrer (1966a: 201-2), although the chronology poses some acute problems for such a date. It would be more reasonable to date Is 14:28-32 to the death of Tiglat-Pileser in 727. Another text dated to 712 is Is 22:1-14, so e.g. Ginsberg (1968: 49), Hayes, and Irvine (1987: 277). However, that too is a highly disputable dating.

[8] Kaiser (1974: 116-8), Dietrich (1976: 135, n 103), Clements (1980a: 174-5).

[9] Hayes, and Irvine (1987: 271-2) seems to be inclined to agree with Clements.

that was felt in Palestine for the coming attacks from Sargon, especially since his attack on Egypt in 720 would still be in fresh memory among most people.[1] That Isaiah actually believed that Egypt would intervene on Ashdod's behalf and that there would be a battle between the Assyrians and Egypt/Kush is not in the least improbable, in the light of what had happened in 720.[2] The problem is that things did not turn out the way Isaiah thought they would, at least not at that time.[3] However, that should not be made into an argument for the view that the prophecy was directed against another time. Another main criticism of Clements against the traditional interpretation is that the prophecy in vv. 3ff. presupposes the downfall of Ashdod, which makes the prophecy loose much of its force. However, here Clements has failed to make the simple distinction between the date of the prophecy itself and the date of the writing of Is 20, in which the prophecy is a part.[4] There is no reason why the prophecy could not have been given shortly before the downfall of Ashdod, and then, when Is 20 was written, including the prophecy, the dating in v. 1 did not stop at the point in time where the prophecy had been given (v. 1a), but went on and described the result of the Assyrian attack on Ashdod (v. 1b).[5]

Kaiser is more radical since he considers the story about the performance of the symbolic act to be fictional. He furthermore dates the narrative to exilic times, when it became popular to tell stories of how Isaiah had warned against taking help from Egypt, which had later proved itself to be true. However, he has hardly any substantial arguments for his case. Above all, there is no reason why such stories could not have been popular in exilic times even though they had been composed earlier, and described actual events. The dating in v. 1, with its detailed reference to the Tartan would be very difficult to explain was it a fictional description from exilic times. Kaiser has rightly been criticized by other

---

[1] See ANET, 284-6; Miller, and Hayes (1986: 336-7).

[2] See Donner (1964: 115).

[3] For the whole issue of prophecies that fail to come about as the prophets thought they would, i.e., the application of 'Dissonance theory' to OT prophecy, the fundamental study is Carroll (1979).

[4] Wildberger (1974: 750) seems to make the same mistake.

[5] Clements (1980a: 174-5), as well as Wildberger (1974: 757), insists that Isaiah could not have been performing his symbolic act for two or even three years without explaining it, as v. 3 would have us believe. However, such an argument is more a case of wishing the prophet was more rational and understandable in our eyes, rather than trying to understand him in his own context, however irrational and unexplainable it may seem to be.

scholars for his hypercritical attitude to the book of Isaiah at large, and to Is 20 in particular.[1]

Literary coherence

The second half of v. 1, consisting of the second temporal clause of the verse, 'when Sargon, king of Assyria ...', seems to be a repetition of the first temporal clause, providing the first with more details as to who send the Tartan, what the purpose with the punitive expedition was and its result. Verse 2 is then introduced by the temporal marker הַהִיא בָּעֵת, 'at that time', which has a rather vague character as far as pinpointing a specific historical occurrence is concerned.[2] The temporal marker introduces an oracle, which tells Isaiah to remove his sackcloth and sandals, and go naked and barefoot. The temporal marker seems to refer to the point in time that has just been described in v. 1; when Ashdod was attacked, God spoke to Isaiah through an oracle, telling him to remove his sackcloth and sandals. It is then, in v. 3, that the problems begin to arise. Here, another oracle is presented, but this time Isaiah is presumed to have walked naked and barefoot for three years! This apparent discrepancy has forced scholars to come up with several suggestions as to how it can be resolved.

The most common solution is to consider v. 2 a later addition to the text.[3] Furthermore, it is not uncommon to consider the addition to be Dtr in its origin.[4] If v. 2 has been added later, it would eliminate the problem with the correlation with the datings in vv. 1 and 3, since the oracle in v. 3 is definitely set around the time of the conquest of Ashdod in 712, and so vv. 1 and 3 would belong together smoothly. I will come back with further reasons for the secondary nature of v. 2 below. One problem with this solution, however, is that it bereaves the text of a command to the prophet to execute his symbolic act, something that is otherwise always a part of the text that describes the performance of prophetic symbolic acts.[5] Some scholars would not consider this a price worth paying, but

---

[1] See e.g. Wildberger (1974: 751-2), Vermeylen (1977: 325, n 2).

[2] See DeVries (1975: 40-1).

[3] So e.g. Huber (1976: 107), Barth (1977b: 9, n 18), Hayes, and Irvine (1987: 270), Høgenhaven (1988: 135-6). Some would also consider v. 1b as secondary, but that is a minority view, e.g. Huber. Stacey (1990: 124) holds that only the words 'two years' were added to v. 2 in order to fit in the reference to the three years given later in v. 3. A more odd solution is to consider v. 1 as secondary instead, so Wildberger (1974: 750), but it has no convincing arguments on its side.

[4] So e.g. Dietrich (1976: 115), Vermeylen (1977: 325), Høgenhaven (1988: 135-6).

[5] It is part of the threefold schema of Fohrer (1968: 18). 1. A command to perform the prophetic symbolic act. 2. A description of the act. 3. An explanation of the act.

that would be giving the form critical analysis more authority than it can actually bear. Although a certain structure occurs quite often, there is no inherent reason why that particular structure could not be shortened, as would have been the case in Is 20, with only the description of the act and its interpretation available.

In order to try to make sense of v. 2 in its context, whether or not it has been added later, some prefer to consider it as a parenthesis or anacoluthon, breaking off from the line of argument started in v. 1 and not followed up in v. 3.[1] There are basically two ways in which v. 2 can be construed as a parenthesis. The first is to hold that the time marker at the beginning of v. 2, בָּעֵת הַהִיא, 'at that time', refers to the attack of Ashdod as mentioned in v. 1. In order to avoid the apparent discrepancy between vv. 1 and 2 it then becomes necessary to see a pluperfect in v. 2, referring to a time three years before the date in v. 1.[2] Verse 2 might then be translated, 'At that time God had (already) spoken through Isaiah ...'. The reason for this is naturally that it presents a possibility to retain v. 2 as an original part of the narrative, although some would consider v. 2 to be a later addition and still have the character of a parenthesis with a pluperfect.[3] The other alternative way of construing v. 2 as a parenthesis would be to consider the time marker at the beginning of v. 2 to be inclusive enough to include the three years mentioned in v. 3 before what is referred to in v. 1.[4] Verse 2 would then describe the command to Isaiah some time before the attack on Ashdod, and there would be no need for a pluperfect. Verse 2 might then be translated, 'Around that time, Yhwh spoke through Isaiah ...'. However, this is a most unnatural and forced interpretation of בָּעֵת הַהִיא, the most natural and obvious interpretation of which is to see it as referring to the event mentioned in v. 1. This survey can be summarized as follows;

1) Verse 2 can not be read as a straightforward continuation of v. 1 and precursor to v. 3 because of the apparent conflicts over chronological references.

2) The time marker at the beginning of v. 2 can not be used to refer to an unspecified event in time prior to what is described in v. 1, but must be taken as referring to the event referred to in v. 1, the attack on Ashdod in 712.

---

[1] So e.g. Bentzen (1944: 155), Donner (1964: 114)

[2] So e.g. Delitzsch (1879: 238), Bentzen (1944: 155). It is usually the דִּבֶּר that is considered as being in the pluperfect, but Oswalt (1986: 381) strangely considers the second verb, לֵאמֹר as pluperfect.

[3] So Duhm (1922: 148), Hoffmann (1974: 74, n 286), Kaiser (1974: 112-4). Cf. the discussion on this issue by Gray (1928: 345).

[4] So e.g. Kissane (1960: 216), Watts (1985: 264).

3) The syntax of Biblical Hebrew would not allow the clause structure of v. 2 to have one of its verb forms in pluperfect. The pluperfect only occurs when the word order is S-P, whether or not we designate that particular structure as being typical of a compound nominal clause, or allow it to be an alternative structure of a verbal clause. The following digression on syntax will explain this further.

> To characterize a nominal clause as a clause that begins with an independent subject, and a verbal clause as a clause that begins with a verbal form, has been the traditional way of characterisation by Arab grammarians.[1] This is applied by some scholars to Biblical Hebrew as well, e.g. Nyberg, Schneider, Talstra and Niccacci.[2] Some scholars do not subscribe to this view, however. According to the grammar of Gesenius-Kautzsch-Cowley, a verbal clause can have the word order S-P, although it is admitted that such a clause does not carry on the narrative with further actions, but rather describes a particular state.[3] When the verb in this case is a suffix form, this state usually belongs to the past in relation to the time of the surrounding narrative, i.e., a pluperfect sense.[4] Muraoka prefers the view that the nature of the predicate and not its place decides between nominal and verbal clauses.[5] In his study on emphasis in Biblical Hebrew, Muraoka makes no connection between the issue of the word order S-P in verbal clauses and 'Casus Pendens' in his treatment of the latter.[6] Gross prefers to speak of a 'Pendenskonstruktion', or a 'Pendenssatz', where the extraposed Pendens is imbedded in the clause, and the construction is without internal clause boundaries.[7] Waltke-O'Connor speaks of a 'Nominative absolute', the equivalent of the 'Casus pendens' that is one of the roles of the 'Nominative function'.[8] When the word order is S-P, it is usually due to a disjunctive *waw*.[9] This disjunctive *waw*, introducing parenthetical material, is the second category – besides relative, causal or temporal clauses – that can introduce a pluperfect, or, in the terminology of Waltke-O'Connor, a 'Past perfect'.[10] Waltke-O'Connor do not discuss whether we should use the category 'Compound nominal clause', or simply char-

---

[1] See e.g. Contini (1982: 11-2), Cohen (1984: 47-57).

[2] Nyberg (1952, §85), ('sammansatt nominalsats'); Schneider (1974, 44.4), 'Zusammengesetzten Nominalsatz'); Niccacci (1990, §6), ('complex noun clause'); Talstra (1978: 170) ('complex nominal clause').

[3] Gesenius (1910, §140 a-f).

[4] Gesenius (1910, §142 a-b).

[5] Muraoka (1985: 4, n 8; 32-7). See also Joüon, and Muraoka (1991: 561-3).

[6] Muraoka (1985: 93-9). There are some slight comments in this direction in Joüon, and Muraoka (1991, §153, esp. n 2; §156 e).

[7] Gross (1987: 37-8, 190).

[8] Waltke, and O'Connor (1990, §4.7 a-c, 8.3 a).

[9] Waltke, and O'Connor (1990, §8.3 a, 39.2.3).

[10] Waltke, and O'Connor (1990§30.5.2 a-b).

acterize the construction as a form of particular emphasis or casus pendens. They also prefer the expression 'Verbless clause' instead of 'Nominal clause', a distinction that takes a more neutral stand on the issue. Meyer considers the boundary to be floating between a compound nominal clause with a verbal predicate and a verbal clause with an extraposed subject.[1]

The only reasonable conclusion at this stage is to consider v. 2 to be a later addition to the narrative, a conclusion that, as was shown above, is the most commonly taken. There are several reasons for this conclusion, as well as regarding it as a Dtr addition:

1) The phrase דִּבֶּר יְהוָה בְּיַד is a typical Dtr phrase, as well as typical for P, in the typical description of how God spoke through Moses.[2]

2) The failure, intentional or not, to change בְּיַד of the favourite phrase into the more suitable אל, 'to' shows how the Dtr redactor was merely adding to the text, without the intention of fully integrating his additions with the narrative at large.

3) The phrase וְנַעַלְךָ תַחֲלֹץ מֵעַל רַגְלֶיךָ is rather close to the one in Deut 25:9, וְחָלְצָה נַעֲלוֹ מֵעַל רַגְלוֹ, 'and she removed his sandal from his foot', the only other occurrence of the verb חלץ together with the nouns נַעַל and רֶגֶל and the preposition מֵעַל. This can hardly be a coincidence, especially since the parallel is found in Deuteronomy, the terminological storehouse of the Dtr. The Dtr redactor apparently felt a need for a divine command to Isaiah to undress, and the formulation in Deut 25:9 for the removal of the sandals was close at hand.

4) The epithet בֶּן־אָמוֹץ, 'son of Amos', is otherwise given to Isaiah.[3] The references are thus found in the DtrG and its equivalent in Isaiah 37-38 and Chronicles (2Kgs 19:2, 20; 20:1; 37:2, 21; 38:1; 2 Chr 26:22; 32:20, 32), and three times in Isaiah where it forms part of various superscriptions, all referring to Isaiah in third person (Is 1:1; 2:1; 13:1). The phrase 'son of Amos' was apparently a reference given to Isaiah particularly among the Dtr tradition, and therefore its occurrence in Is 20:2 forms a strong argument for not only the secondary status of the verse, but also that the addition can be traced to a Dtr redactor.

5) The phrase at the beginning of v. 2, בָּעֵת הַהִיא, 'at that time', is also a typically Dtr phrase. It occurs 67 times in the OT, of which 15 occur in Deut, 19 in Josh-2 Kgs, 7 in Jer, 2 in Is besides 20:2 (18:7; 39:1), 10 in 1-2 Chr and the remaining 13 dispersed evenly through the rest of the OT. The phrase then occurs

---

[1] Meyer (1972, §91.2 a, 92.4 b).

[2] I Sam 28:17; I Kgs 8:53, 56; 14:18; 15:29; 16:34; 2 Kgs 9:36; 10:10; 14:25; 17:16, 23; 24:2; Jer 37:2.

[3] 2Kgs 19:2, 20; 20:1; Is 1:1; 2:1; 13:1; 37:2, 21; 38:1; 2 Chr 26:22; 32:20, 32.

mainly in Deut, in DtrG and in texts already known for their Dtr phraseology, such as Jer and Is 39.

There is always the problem that if we consider v. 2 secondary, the text is left without a divine command to Isaiah to perform the symbolic act. However, there are two alternative ways of explaining this. The lack of a command can be attributed to the unusual character of the narrative in general, e.g., being in third person and referring to Isaiah in third person. It can also be explained by postulating that the Dtr redactor replaced a command with his own version. This can of course not be shown beyond doubt, but there is always the possibility that the Dtr redactor felt it necessary to not only rephrase the description of the command, but to replace it. That v. 2 would itself be the result of an original command that has been merely worked over by a Dtr redactor is less likely because of its many similarities with Dtr phraseology, as was shown above.

There has also been a discussion concerning whether vv. 5 and 6 are parts of the original narrative, or whether one of them is secondary. Some would argue that v. 5 is secondary,[1] whilst some would choose v. 6.[2] However, I find it hard to take any of these suggestions seriously. The argument for taking v. 5 as secondary is usually that it anticipates,[3] explains[4] or is simply dependent on v. 6.[5] However, the simple fact that one part of a literary narrative anticipates another part, or explains it, or if it is dependent upon it in some form, is hardly reason enough to consider it to be secondary. We have to keep in mind that Isaiah expected a major clash between the Assyrians and the combined forces of Egypt and Kush. The Assyrians would win a major victory and remove the captured enemies in exile, as was their policy (v. 4). The Philistine cities that supported the uprising and were punished by Sargon's army would then wonder how they could be so foolish to trust in a power so weak in comparison with the Assyrians (v. 5).

The argument for taking v. 6 as secondary is usually that there is a change of subject from Judah in v. 5 to the Philistines in v. 6.[6] However, Wildberger points out correctly that it would not be unusual for an OT prophet to speak to Judah through an oracle directed against another people, in this case the Philistines.[7] However, Wildberger then still goes on to consider v. 6 to be secondary instead

---

[1] So e.g. Hoffmann (1974: 74, n 286), Huber (1976: 107, n 96), Clements (1980a: 175).
[2] So Wildberger (1974: 751), Dietrich (1976: 131).
[3] So Huber (1976: 107, n 96).
[4] So Hoffmann (1974: 74, n 286).
[5] So Clements (1980: 175).
[6] So Dietrich (1976: 131).
[7] Wildberger (1974: 751).

of v. 5. His argument, taken up from Kaiser, is that if the inhabitants of the coastal cities had fled to Egypt, they would have been caught by the Assyrians in the attack that Isaiah imagined would come. And if they only took refuge in the help they could get from Egypt, why would the Assyrians first attack Egypt (v. 4) and only then take on the Philistine cities (v. 6)?[1] Again, these scholars fail to take seriously the fact that vv. 5-6 is part of Isaiah's oracle, what he, in an inspired moment thought would happen. To Isaiah, the main enemy to Assyria was Egypt, which was no doubt a correct interpretation. Therefore, it would seem to be reasonable that the Assyrians would attack their main enemy first, and then the minor ones on the coast. It must be remembered that this is how Isaiah presented these matters in his oracle. In such a context, equal emphasis might very well have been given to the terrifying example the conquest of Egypt and Kush would be for the coastal cities, and indeed to Judah as well. That in itself might have been the reason for Isaiah to put the conquest of Egypt and Kush first.

The subject of v. 5 is not stated, but those who take it to be Judah must acknowledge that Judah plays no part whatsoever in this chapter, at least on the surface structure. The lack of a subject in v. 5 creates an anticipation, which is satisfied in v.6, where the subject is said to be 'those who live on this coast', i.e., the inhabitants of the Philistine cities on the coastal line, the apparent leader of which was Ashdod. However, although this oracle is then looking much like an oracle against foreign nations, the lack of a subject in v. 5 together with the fact that the symbolic act was naturally performed in Judah in order to convince them not to take part in the rebellion, argue for that we are supposed to see Judah as part of the actual subject of vv. 5-6.[2] The last phrase of v. 6, 'How can we escape?' can not easily be applied to Judah alone, which is why Judah should be seen as only part of the subject in vv. 5-6 and not the subject exclusively. This would suit the historical situation quite well, since Ashdod was trying to build a coalition with nearby states against Assyria, and it was against Judah taking part in this coalition that Isaiah prophesied and acted symbolically.

According to Is 20:3, Isaiah, i.e., the activity of Isaiah, has for three years been אוֹת וּמוֹפֵת, 'a sign and symbol'. There is no need to go into a detailed word study of these terms here, since it is obvious that, in the form of an hendiadys, Isaiah's activity was meant to have indicated something else and beyond the mere fact that he walked around naked.[3] There was a further, subtler meaning to

---

[1] Kaiser (1974: 117).
[2] See Huber (1976: 111-2) for a similar line of argument.
[3] For אוֹת, see TDOT 1, 167-88, esp. 186; for מוֹפֵת, see TDOT 8, 174-81, esp. 178.

the act that needed a divine oracle to be explained. However, this last phrase in v. 3bβ, אוֹת וּמוֹפֵת עַל־מִצְרַיִם וְעַל־כּוּשׁ, 'as a sign and symbol of Egypt and Cush', appears to have had a rather distinct usage in the OT. Together, in the form of a hendiadys, the terms occur 17 times.[1] The overwhelming majority of these cases come from Deut or Dtr related texts.[2] There are three basic reasons for regarding this phrase as a Dtr redactional addition to the text. First, it has already been established that the text has been exposed to Dtr redactional activity in the previous verse, and this makes it likely that there is more of the same kind to be expected in the rest of the text. Second, the phrase in v. 3bβ is rather clumsily appended to the prior clause, which itself is continued in v. 4a. Verse 3bβ appears as a parenthetical remark that seeks to make explicit what is otherwise left implicitly by vv. 3a-ba, 4. Third, as was shown above, the phrase in v. 3bβ is a familiar Dtr phrase. This would make it at least plausible that v. 3bβ was added by a Dtr redactor – probably the same that added v. 2 – in order to update the text in exilic or postexilic times.[3]

Symbolic meaning of the act

If v. 2 is to be considered secondary and therefore not reliable as description of the symbolic act of Isaiah, or at least the original description of the act, then what we know from the oracle in v. 3a is simply that he walked barefoot and naked for three years. The following points can be made to illuminate the symbolic act.

As was shown above, there is every reason to take the duration seriously from the point of view of the history of the uprising in Palestine. Since three years is probably what it took from the first sign of rebellion to the final assault by the Assyrians on Ashdod, this is likely to be the duration for the symbolic act of Isaiah, or at least to have included it.

The fact that he is said to have walked in his state of nakedness could be an indication that the symbolic act was intended to be publicly noticed and interpreted by the people at large, and not only by the king and his likes. His deliberate nakedness has caused some concern among scholars, however; would it really have been possible for Isaiah to walk around naked for three years? There are several answers to this question. On the one hand, we should not be too hasty to rationalize the behaviour of the prophet, and tone done the extreme se-

---

[1] Ex 7:3; Deut 4:34; 6:22, 7:19; 13:2,3; 26:8; 28:46; 29:2; 34:11; Is 8:18; Jer 32:20,21; Ps 78:43; 105:27; 135:9; Neh 9:10.

[2] So TDOT 1, 168.

[3] So Vermeylen (1977: 325).

riousness by which he took his mission as God's spokesman. On the other hand, it would not simply have been physically possible to be naked for even a shorter time than three years, given the climate of the region. It could very well be, that Isaiah continued with is symbolic act for this period, i.e., he persisted in displaying his symbolic act when he appeared in public. The intention was surely not to be naked as such, but to bring across a message by means of his nakedness, and therefore it would only have been relevant when the prophet appeared in public. There is also the case that it was unlikely that Isaiah appeared totally naked. This is the way the Dtr redactor of v. 2 has understood it, and perhaps it was his intention to make it clear that the prophet was not totally naked, but only without his outer mantle.

The redactor specifies in v. 2 that Isaiah was dressed in שַׂק, sackcloth. But why is stated here, and in a verse that we have already concluded is a Dtr addition? The sackcloth is usually a sign of grief (Gen 37:34; 2 Sam 21:10; 1 Kgs 21:27 etc), and that is surely the way it is supposed to be taken here as well, although we are not told of the circumstances surrounding Isaiah's display of grief. Some have suggested that the sackcloth refers to the typical dress of the prophet, but the only reference to a typical prophetic dress is 2 Kgs 1:8, where Elijah is described as a אִישׁ בַּעַל שֵׂעָר, 'hairy man', i.e., as someone wearing a hairy mantle.[1] The similarity between the ruggedness of the hairy mantle and the sackcloth is too superficial, however, for drawing the conclusion that the sackcloth in Is 20:2 was intended to be a specifically prophetic clothing. This brings us back to the question why v. 2 suddenly mentions that Isaiah has been wearing the particular mourning dress. The best solution lies in the fact that elsewhere in the book of Isaiah, when Isaiah pictures a day of grief after doom, it is mentioned that in time of mourning, sackcloth will be worn (3:24; 15:3; 22:12; 37:1; 50:3; 58:5). In order to illustrate this point more emphatically, Isaiah might very well have walked around Jerusalem wearing sackcloth, as if to remind the people of what will happen if they do not follow the word of God.

Since there is no description of such a prophetic symbolic act left in the book of Isaiah as it meets us today, I would suggest that Is 20 was once part of a larger narrative that described certain activities by Isaiah, such as symbolic acts. This would explain not only the reference to the sackcloth, but also the abruptness by which Is 20 both starts and ends. This would enforce the view that has sometimes been proposed that Is 20 was once part of a 'Denkschrift', similar to

---

[1] For this type of construction with בעל as indicating the genitive in certain idioms, see Gen 14:13; 37:19; 1 Sam 28:7; Is 41:15; 50:8; Jer 37:13; Nah 1:2, Waltke, and O'Connor (1990, §9.5.3 b).

Is 6-8, and also to 36-39.[1] Is 20 would then once have followed upon a narrative which described how Isaiah walked around dressed in sackcloth, in order to bring home to the people the message that if they were to rely on Egypt and Kush for help against Assyria, they will indeed end up grieving over their foolishness. To take this a step further, the two symbolic acts would have followed upon each other quite understandably in a logical, and chronological order. The wearing of sackcloth would have indicated the time immediately before the expected attack of the Assyrians as well as during the siege of Jerusalem, while the nakedness would have indicated what would happen after the conquest of Jerusalem, namely the exiling of prisoners (cf. Am 2:16). For this is precisely what the naked Isaiah walking around Jerusalem was meant to illustrate, namely a prisoner of war being taken away into exile, a theme not unknown from ancient Near Eastern iconography.[2]

In v. 4 the oracle suddenly takes a surprising turn, surprising at least to the modern reader who would expect the act of Isaiah to have symbolized the exiling of the people of Judah. However, the act is apparently not meant to symbolize the exiling of Judahites, but of prisoners from Egypt and Kush (vv. 3-4). So again we need to be reminded of the image Isaiah had of an impending war between Assyria and the coalition of Egypt and Kush. They would be the real casualties of war, and not primarily those petty states that looked to them for help in their rebellion against Assyria. However, they would be held accountable for their rebellion soon enough, and then there would be no Egypt or Kush to help them (v. 5), the realisation of which would make them cry out, 'How can we escape?' (v. 6).

The symbolic structure of the symbolic act

In order to describe the detailed structure of the symbolism involved in this act, we must start by asking for the act that was performed, since this is a basic requirement for it to be defined as a prophetic symbolic *act*. It may be prophetic, and it may very well be symbolic, but if nothing is performed, it is simply another example of prophetic symbolism. If we start with the obvious fact that Isaiah removed some, if not all, of his clothes, then that hardly points in itself to a symbolic act. The actual undressing receives no emphasis in the text of Is 20, as it would have had Isaiah been described as removing his clothes in public.

---

[1] So e.g. Gray (1928: 344), who thinks Is 20 once formed part of a biography of the prophet; Wildberger (1974: 751), Hayes, and Irvine (1987: 271-2). However, for a critical analysis of the notion of a 'Denkschrift', see Irvine (1992).

[2] ANEP nr. 332, 358, 365.

The crucial element is what is performed. The mere fact that Isaiah is naked is not in itself an act, although it very close to an actual performing. The act that should be understood as the symbolic act is described in v. 3, הָלַךְ עַבְדִּי יְשַׁעְיָהוּ, 'my servant Isaiah has walked'.[1]

It is therefore the walking around in the state of nakedness that is the act which, when performed, symbolized something to those standing by. Those two items together, the particular dress – or lack of it – and the act of walking around, are what make up the prophetic symbolism of this prophetic symbolic act. To be more precise, the walking around naked and barefoot makes up a symbolic meaning of iconic nature, in the sense that it imitates the behaviour of a subdued people going into exile.

Is there any form of indexical symbolism involved in this symbolic act? As a rule, indexical symbolism is harder to detect than iconic, as metonymies are harder to detect than metaphors. The analogical nature of the icon/metaphor is what makes it easier to detect, whereas the detection of index/metonymy is dependent on our knowledge of the culture and context around the performance of the act and the formulation of the description of that act. Having said that, however, there is a likely case of indexical symbolism in the fact that the act symbolizes going into exile, a threat very much real to Israel and various other smaller states in the region. However, it is not as likely that the same would have been true for Egypt and Kush. The consequence of this is that the symbolic performance of exile was meant to associate to war and defeat, and in this particular context, to the defeat of Egypt and Kush to Assyria. Isaiah then used a concrete act, well known to his people, namely going into exile, as a means of referring, not necessarily to the exile of Egypt and Kush, but by means of association to their defeat to Assyria.

There is actually a further requirement that we could add, but which has no direct support in the text, namely that is was to be performed in public. It would have been quite nonsensical for Isaiah to perform his act without an audience, as if it had some quasi-magical force in bringing about what is symbolized merely by its performance. The audience played the vital role of providing the first tentative interpretation of Isaiah's act as it was performed on the streets of Jerusalem. However, this interpretation formed only the first in a series of interpretations that can be deduced from Is 20. These various interpretations can be outlined as follows;

---

[1] The Dtr redactor repeats this in v. 2b, הָלֹךְ, 'he went'. There is, however, no mentioning in the divine commandment in v. 2a to walk around, a discrepancy which could be attributed to the redactor's sole focus on emphasising the divine command to undress.

1. The people of Jerusalem saw the symbolic act of Isaiah as it was performed on the streets of Jerusalem, and they presumably understood it as a symbol of exile. It is also likely that they associated by means of this symbolisation to war, military attack, defeat, humiliation, etc.

2. Isaiah himself interprets the act, perhaps in the light of the interpretation made initially by the people of Jerusalem, in his oracle in vv. 3-6. According to this oracle, the symbolic act symbolizes the exile of prisoners from Egypt and Ethiopia.

3. Although there is no evidence for it in the text of Is 20, we should presume that the people of Jerusalem that heard Isaiah's oracle again interpreted the symbolic act, now in the light of the explanatory oracle provided by Isaiah. How Isaiah's oracle was received is impossible to say, although we can surmise that since Judah was not involved in the rebellion, at least not enough to suffer the attacks of the punitive expedition from Assyria, and since the story was put down in writing not long after the attack on Ashdod, it is likely that Isaiah's oracle was received favourably. This would mean that people at large, and in particular Hezekiah the king, took the oracle seriously and understood the symbolic act as symbolising the possible exiling of Judah, after the defeat of Egypt and Ethiopia.

4. At a later stage, while the people still remembered what had happened to Ashdod, and the political debate in Judah between joining the rebellion or not, someone put the oracle down into writing (vv. 3a+bα-6), and prefaced it with a reference to the historical setting (v. 1). This could very well have taken place soon after 701, when Jerusalem was understood to have been miraculously saved by God from the Assyrians, and when Egypt and Ethiopia had suffered a defeat at the hands of Assyria. However, it is impossible to be certain of such a date. The symbolic act is thought to have symbolized the exiling of Egypt and Ethiopia, with the implicit inclusion of Judah as well among those expecting exile.

5. After quite some time, in exilic times, a Dtr redactor sought to bring the narrative up to date with his own time by adding vv. 2, 3bβ. Since Judah itself had now been forced to go into exile, this Dtr redactor saw the symbolic act of Isaiah as not only a symbol of exile, but above all as a symbol of prophetic authority and of the legitimate function of God's prophets to foretell the future. In order to emphasize this interpretation, the Dtr redactor added v. 2 to complete the structure of the description of the symbolic act of the prophet.

Summary and Conclusions

1. Is 20 has evidently gone through a complicated history of redaction and interpretation. However, it is clear that originally, the people of Jerusalem saw the symbolic act performed on the streets of Jerusalem by Isaiah, and they understood it as a symbol of a people going into exile.

2. The symbolic meaning of this prophetic act is iconic, in the sense that it pictures in an analogical sense how the inhabitants of a conquered people walk, humiliated because of their nakedness and lack of sandals.

3. The symbolic act is interpreted in Isaiah's oracle as picturing the defeat of the Egyptians and Kushites. Through indexical symbolism, where the act of walking as someone going into exile is meant to associate to war and defeat, this is accomplished, even though it is very unlikely that such an outcome was ever a threat to Egypt or Kush, but only to smaller states in the more nearby regions.

4. The duration of three years for the performance of this act should probably be seen as the period during which Isaiah would repeat his symbolic act, and not that he was actually naked during three years.

D. Prophetic Symbolic Acts in the Book of Jeremiah

Introduction

Next to Ezekiel, Jeremiah is the OT prophet who performed most symbolic acts, at least as far as we know. If we attempt to compare the symbolic acts of these two major prophets, we soon find that the character of Jeremiah's symbolic acts are less extreme than those of Ezekiel. Jeremiah takes a girdle and hides it, he smashes a pot, whereas Ezekiel may lie on his side for a long time, create highly elaborate models, or just sit sighing of grief. In general, then, the symbolic acts of Jeremiah are more easily understood, although the surrounding questions regarding history of redaction and genuineness are similar to those in the book of Ezekiel.

It is impossible to enter any form of scholarly study of the book of Jeremiah without also taking a stand on the issue of the redaction history of the book, regardless of how tentative that view may be. Recent studies on this particular subject have displayed an almost embarrassing diversity among scholars as to the existence of redactional layers, the nature of these layers and the possible role played by the prophet himself in this history of redaction. The discussion can be summed up in two questions; first, is the text of Jeremiah mainly a coherent whole, or the product of a process of various redactions at work on the text, and second, to what extent can these redactional layers be labelled 'deuteronomic'/'deuteronomistic'? In his recent commentary on Jeremiah, Holladay, followed by Jones and Lundbom, has attempted to show that the book is mainly a product of the prophet himself, and not the end product of a long and tedious redactional process, and so naturally he does not reckon with any substantial Dtr redaction of the book.[1] McKane on the other hand, in his recent commentary on Jeremiah 1-25, has tried to show that the product is the product of a long, slowly developing redactional process, however without any redactor having a firm grip on the nature of the development of the book.[2] This means that McKane does

---

[1] Holladay (1986), Holladay (1989). Jones (1992) does appear somewhat more moderate and cautious than the decidedly one-sidedness in Holladay's work. Lundbom (1999: 64-5) prefers to speak of the prose of the book of Jeremiah as 'the standard rhetorical prose of late seventh, early sixth century B.C.' instead of any form of 'Deuteronomic redaction'. He does recognize, however, the presence of a relatively small amount of exilic prose in the book.

[2] McKane (1986).

not favour any substantial Dtr redaction of the book. It follows naturally from this that McKane does not regard the prophet himself to have played any major part in the formation of the book. Carroll, on the other hand, takes a much more agnostic attitude to these questions in his commentary.[1] He does reckon with redactional activity, e.g., the existence of Dtr redactional activity, although he does not see the redaction history as quite as intricate and multifarious as McKane does. Carroll's agnostic attitude shows itself when it comes to consider the role of the historical prophet, a figure that Carroll seems quite confident to consider as more or less a fictional character. Carroll and Holladay are therefore on completely different wavelengths when it comes to consider the role of the historical prophet. Regarding the question of Dtr redaction, McKane and Holladay, as already mentioned, are quite hesitant to any form of pervasive Dtr redaction, a view that has been taken to its length by Weippert.[2] On the other hand, Thiel has attempted to show that there has indeed been a major Dtr redaction at work in the book of Jeremiah, a view he shares to a certain extent with Carroll.[3]

Even from this very brief and limited overview of recent studies on the redaction history of the book of Jeremiah it appears quite clear that no consensus can be said to exist among scholars. The divisions are, quite on the contrary, wider than ever before. The differences are mainly due to two factors; one, how we evaluate a text and its rugged texture as coherent or showing sings of redactions; two, how we evaluate the language that pervades the book of Jeremiah and which to a large degree appears similar to the language otherwise typical of Deuteronomy and to a certain extent also the Dtr history. If a text can be allowed to make sudden shifts in language, themes, motives, then there is no need to postulate a redaction history. And if the language of Deuteronomy and the Dtr history was known and used as a stock of theological formulas at the end of the 7th century, why not by the prophet Jeremiah himself or his secretary Baruch as e.g. Lundbom argues, then there would be no need to categorize its occurrence in the book of Jeremiah as Dtr redaction.

It would seem wise, judging from this overview of recent scholarly divisions over the book of Jeremiah, not to adhere to any particular school of thought. In-

---

[1] Carroll (1986).

[2] Weippert (1973).

[3] Thiel (1973), Thiel (1981). So also e.g. Graupner (1991).

stead, we will try to let the text speak for itself, and use these texts as 'test-cases' for what should be a suitable approach to the book of Jeremiah.[1]

---

[1] See e.g. Soggin (1989: 342), 'the relationships between Jeremiah and Deuteronomy and the Deuteronomistic school are, as we shall see, so complex that it is inadvisable to keep too closely to purely formal questions.'

1. The Hidden Girdle (Jeremiah 13:1-11)

The Text

1 כֹּה־אָמַר יְהוָה אֵלַי הָלוֹךְ
וְקָנִיתָ לְּךָ אֵזוֹר פִּשְׁתִּים
וְשַׂמְתּוֹ עַל־מָתְנֶיךָ
וּבַמַּיִם לֹא תְבִאֵהוּ 2 וָאֶקְנֶה
אֶת־הָאֵזוֹר כִּדְבַר יְהוָה וָאָשִׂם
עַל־מָתְנָי 3 וַיְהִי דְבַר־יְהוָה
אֵלַי שֵׁנִית לֵאמֹר 4 קַח
אֶת־הָאֵזוֹר אֲשֶׁר קָנִיתָ אֲשֶׁר
עַל־מָתְנֶיךָ וְקוּם לֵךְ פְּרָתָה
וְטָמְנֵהוּ שָׁם בִּנְקִיק הַסָּלַע
5 וָאֵלֵךְ וָאֶטְמְנֵהוּ בִּפְרָת[a] כַּאֲשֶׁר צִוָּה
יְהוָה אוֹתִי 6 וַיְהִי מִקֵּץ יָמִים
רַבִּים וַיֹּאמֶר יְהוָה אֵלָי
קוּם לֵךְ פְּרָתָה וְקַח מִשָּׁם
אֶת־הָאֵזוֹר אֲשֶׁר צִוִּיתִיךָ
לְטָמְנוֹ־שָׁם 7 וָאֵלֵךְ פְּרָתָה
וָאֶחְפֹּר וָאֶקַּח אֶת־הָאֵזוֹר
מִן־הַמָּקוֹם אֲשֶׁר־טְמַנְתִּיו שָׁמָּה
וְהִנֵּה נִשְׁחַת[d] הָאֵזוֹר לֹא יִצְלַח לַכֹּל
8 וַיְהִי דְבַר־יְהוָה אֵלַי לֵאמֹר
9 כֹּה אָמַר יְהוָה כָּכָה אַשְׁחִית
אֶת־גְּאוֹן יְהוּדָה וְאֶת־גְּאוֹן
יְרוּשָׁלִַם הָרָב[c] 10 הָעָם הַזֶּה
הָרָע הַמֵּאֲנִים לִשְׁמוֹעַ
אֶת־דְּבָרַי[f] הַהֹלְכִים אַחֲרֵי אֱלֹהִים
אֲחֵרִים לְעָבְדָם וּלְהִשְׁתַּחֲוֹת לָהֶם
וִיהִי כָּאֵזוֹר הַזֶּה אֲשֶׁר לֹא־יִצְלַח
לַכֹּל 11 כִּי כַּאֲשֶׁר יִדְבַּק הָאֵזוֹר
אֶל־מָתְנֵי־אִישׁ כֵּן הִדְבַּקְתִּי אֵלַי
אֶת־כָּל־בֵּית יִשְׂרָאֵל
וְאֶת־כָּל־בֵּית יְהוּדָה נְאֻם־יְהוָה
לִהְיוֹת לִי לְעָם וּלְשֵׁם וְלִתְהִלָּה
וּלְתִפְאָרֶת וְלֹא שָׁמֵעוּ

1 Thus said Yhwh to me, "Go and buy yourself a linen loincloth, and put it on your loins, but do not dip it in water." 2 So I bought a loincloth according to the word of Yhwh, and put it on my loins. 3 And the word of Yhwh came to me a second time, saying, 4 "Take the loincloth that you bought and are wearing, and go now to the Euphrates, and hide it there in a cleft of the rock." 5 So I hid it by the Euphrates, as Yhwh commanded me. 6 And after many days Yhwh said to me, "Go now to the Euphrates, and take from there the loincloth that I commanded you to hide there." 7 Then I went to the Euphrates, and dug, and I took the loincloth from the place where I had hidden it. But now it was ruined, and good for nothing. 8 Then the word of Yhwh came to me: 9 Thus says Yhwh: Just so I will ruin the pride of Judah and the great pride of Jerusalem. 10 This evil people, who refuse to hear my words, and have gone after other gods to serve them and worship them, shall be like this loincloth, which is good for nothing. 11 For as the loincloth clings to one's loins, so I made the whole house of Israel and the whole house of Judah cling to me, says Yhwh, in order that they might be for me a people, a name, a praise, and a glory. But they would not listen.

Textual notes

---

[a] In 4QJer[a], Perah has a *he-locale*, which is most likely an accommodation to the two occurrences in vv. 6-7.

[b] The phrase וָאֵלֵךְ, 'and I went', is missing in LXX, probably added in accordance with v. 4, קַ, so Janzen (1973: 40), Holladay (1986: 394).

[c] The ו is extant in several manuscripts and Syr, probably left out with the addition of הָאֵזוֹר.

[d] The word הָאֵזוֹר, 'the loincloth', is missing in LXX, probably added in accordance with v. 7a, so Janzen (1973: 40), Holladay (1986: 394).

[e] Holladay (1986: 394, 397) argues that the text is corrupt at the end of v. 9 and beginning of v. 10. However, his solution is simply to elaborate to be convincing. Indeed, so is his view that there is a problem. His only indication that something is amiss is what he considers the dubious word order of the phrase הָעָם הַזֶּה הָרָע in v. 10, noun - demonstrative pronoun - adjective, admittedly an unusual construction. However, the same construction occurs in Jer 33:12, בַּמָּקוֹם הַזֶּה הֶחָרֵב, 'in this place, that is waste', and Holladay (1989: 222) appears to have no objections to the construction this time.

[f] The phrase הַהֹלְכִים בִּשְׁרִרוּת לִבָּם, 'who stubbornly follow their own will', is missing in LXX. It is likely to be a later addition, inspired by the verb הלך, which both introduces this phrase and follows it, so Janzen (1973: 40), Holladay (1986: 394), cf. its widespread use in Jer 3:17; 7:24; 9:13; 11:8; 16:12; 18:12; 23:17; cf. also Deut 29:18; Ps 81:13.

Analysis

The problems involved in the story of Jeremiah's loincloth and the symbolic act that he performs with it, has met with an array of divergent solutions from scholars. The problems range from the structure of the text, its redaction history, to what has probably been the most difficult question of them all, the nature of the performance of the symbolic act. The problems interact with each other, but in order to present a workable solution to the text as a whole, we will begin by analysing the structure of the text and its possible redaction history, then discuss the performance of the symbolic act, and eventually analyse the symbolic value of the act.

Structure

The structure of vv. 1-11 appears to be simple enough. Jeremiah is commanded by God to buy a loincloth, wear it, and then hide it under a stone by a stream (vv. 1-5). He is later told to go and fetch the loincloth, only to find out it has been ruined (vv. 6-7). In the typical oracular form, he then provides the interpretation of the act or acts (vv. 8-11). The structure can be displayed as follows;

1 Performing symbolic acts

v. 1   Command to perform symbolic act: Phase I
v. 2   Description of the performance of the symbolic act: Phase I
v. 3-4 Command to perform symbolic act Phase: IIa
v. 5   Description of the performance of the symbolic act Phase: IIa
v. 6   Command to perform symbolic act Phase: IIb
v. 7   Description of the performance of the symbolic act Phase: IIb

2 Interpreting symbolic acts

v. 8-10 Interpretation of symbolic acts: Phase IIa+IIb
v. 11   Interpretation of symbolic act: Phase I

The structure is uniformly ordered by three rows of command followed by description of performance.[1] Of these three rows the latter two, here called phase
IIa and b, concerning the hiding and retrieving of the loincloth, are closely connected and make up a second phase of the symbolic act. The first phase is the
buying and wearing of the loincloth. Together these two phases make up the
whole of the prophetic symbolic act. It is interesting to note that the interpretation of the symbolic act in vv. 8-11 is chiastically structured in relation to the
two phases of the symbolic act in vv. 1-7. The interpretation of the second phase
in vv. 3-7 is found in vv. 8-10, whereas the interpretation of the first phase in vv.
1-2 is found in vv. 11. The structure is therefore chiastically ordered, a:b//b¹a¹.
With the exception of some minor glosses,[2] the structure of vv. 1-11 appears to
be quite coherent.

Literary coherence
Most scholars have regarded vv. 1-7 as more or less a coherent unit,[3] but there
have been some dissident voices. Clements argues that the original story about
the symbolic act has been reworked later by identifying Israel with the loincloth,
and specifying that the loincloth will be hidden by the Euphrates, something that
would then be a clear reference to the exile.[4] Schreiner has also tried to find a
later reworking in vv. 1-7 by seeing the reference to Euphrates as a later inter-

---

[1] Cf. e.g. Lundbom (1999: 666).
[2] Verse 5, וָאֵלֵךְ, v. 7, הָאֵזוֹר, v. 10, הַהֹלְכִים בִּשְׁרִרוּת לִבָּם, see the notes to the text above.
[3] Most recently, Lundbom (1999: 667).
[4] Clements (1988: 85-6).

pretation.[1] If the 'original' text is believed to go back to the prophet himself, then I can find no reason why he must be refused to make the very obvious connection between the sinful state of the people, the coming judgement, and the thought of an oncoming exile to Babylon.[2] The act of bringing back the loincloth is not to be taken symbolically for the return after the exile,[3] something that I will argue for later in relation to the symbolic value of the act at large. However, the most elaborate attempt to find evidence of redactional activity in vv. 1-7 has been made recently by Hubmann.[4] His thesis is that vv. 1-2, 11 describe one symbolic act, which is inherently positive in its attitude towards the Babylonians. This has later been supplemented by another description of a symbolic act, to be found in vv. 3-10. This latter description is merely a literary product, meant to produce a further expansion and interpretation of the earlier, original symbolic act, and it displays an inherently negative attitude towards the enemy.[5] Novel as this theory may be, there is simply no reason why the highly structured story of this symbolic act should be divided in two. One searches in vain in Hubmann's analysis for textual indications that forces us to accept his interpretation. It would appear that it has been the search for a novel interpretation itself, rather than the search for a convincing interpretation of the text that has guided Hubmann. He claims that the two acts are in no way related to each other, and that the first does not in any way contribute to the understanding of the second act. The wooden character of Hubmann' analysis is obvious when he discards the simplest of all textual indications, namely its contextual placement. There has to be more than a theoretical possibility for a redaction-critical hypothesis to be relevant; it has to be forced upon us by clear textual indications, and there are no such indications to support Hubmann's interpretation.

If we then consider vv. 1-7 to be a coherent whole,[6] we must turn to the more difficult passage of the interpretation in vv. 8-11. What has been the issue here is the apparently clear presence of Dtr language. However, as was concluded above, we do not follow any particular school of thought on the matter of Dtr redaction of the book of Jeremiah, since the issue seems to divide scholars to such a large extent. Carroll considers vv. 10-11 to be a Dtr expansion,[7] but Thiel, who has made the most extensive analysis of a possible Dtr redaction of

---

[1] Schreiner (1981: 88).

[2] See Bright (1965: 96).

[3] As was rightly emphasized by Bright (1965: 96).

[4] Hubmann (1991).

[5] Hubmann (1991: 120-1).

[6] So Thiel (1973: 169).

[7] Carroll (1986: 293), so also Nicholson (1973: 121-2).

the book of Jeremiah, considers v. 10a, except its first three words, and v. 11 to be the work of a Dtr redactor. Thiel's main argument regarding v. 11 is that it displays an allegorising interpretation of vv. 1-2.[1] Holladay is even more cautious, when he considers only v. 10aß to be a Dtr redaction.[2] McKane is of the opinion that the book of Jeremiah does not provide us with enough clear structure to suggest a thorough Dtr redaction. Instead he suggests that the language is similar to the language of Deuteronomy/Dtr history, but this is an ongoing influence during the drawn out process of growth of the text of the book. Nevertheless, McKane finds two additions to vv. 1-7, one in vv. 8-9 and one in vv. 10-11.[3] McKane appears to be alone in viewing vv. 8-9 as a later addition to vv. 1-7. Weippert fails to find any support for a Dtr redaction in vv. 1-11, mainly because the phraseology is scattered through the OT and because in Jer 13:10, it is imbedded in otherwise typical Jeremianic material.[4] The attitude chosen by Jones seems very wise, namely that the tradition from Jeremiah was preserved in circles that were highly influenced by Dtr language,[5] and I would add also that they probably were influenced by Dtr theology as well. However, there is no need to limit the influence to the bearers of the tradition, and not include the prophet himself in this circle. Jones recognizes the typical Dtr phraseology of v. 10-11, but prefers not to end up with a firm opinion.[6]

It would seem that it is v. 10 that is most critical when it comes to consider whether the text has suffered a Dtr redaction or not. Since it involves the interpretation of the symbolic act, it is necessary to take a closer look at v. 10.

10aaa	הָעָם הַזֶּה הָרָע
10aab	הַמֵּאֲנִים לִשְׁמוֹעַ אֶת־דְּבָרַי
10ab	וַיֵּלְכוּ אַחֲרֵי אֱלֹהִים אֲחֵרִים לְעָבְדָם וּלְהִשְׁתַּחֲוֹת לָהֶם
10b	וַיְהִי כָּאֵזוֹר הַזֶּה אֲשֶׁר לֹא־יִצְלַח לַכֹּל

Verse 10 contains an unusual expression, the syntax of which makes it unlikely to be used as a typical phrase. The expression used in v. 10aab only occurs, besides here, in 1 Sam 8:19; Jer 11:10; Neh 9:17, hardly enough to consider it a typical Dtr phrase. Verse 10b is not argued by anyone to contain a distinctly Dtr

---

[1] Thiel (1973: 169-72).
[2] Holladay (1986: 397).
[3] McKane (1986: 290-2).
[4] Weippert (1973: 215-8).
[5] Jones (1992: 22).
[6] Jones (1992: 197).

formula. Instead, it is v. 10ab that has been the difficult phrase to consider in any other way than as a Dtr phrase, and therefore, the result of a Dtr redaction, however small or great. The phrase is a stock phrase, and it occurs here in its fullest form, with both the verbs עבד and שחה as additional explicates of the sinful behaviour of the people. In this its fullest form, the expression occurs in Deut 8:19; Jud 2:19; Jer 16:11; 25:6. Its basic form, הלך אחרי אלהים אחרים, is found in Deut 6:14; 11:28; 13:3; 28:14 (+עבד); Jud 2:12 (+שחה); 1 Kgs 11:10; Jer 7:6, 9; 11:10 (+עבד); 35:15 (+עבד). This shows that the phrase is definitely a stock Dtr phrase, and it is therefore very likely that it has been added here in order to emphasize the corrupt character of the people, perhaps by one of the editors of the Jeremianic traditions. However, it is highly doubtful to postulate a wholesale Dtr redaction of the passage on the basis on only one phrase. It is better to take the phrase as an isolated case of a Dtr gloss, added under the pervading influence of Dtr language and theology, rather than as a wholesale redaction.[1]

When it comes to 13:11, a similar influence can be found, although it does not appear to be a stock phrase that has been used. The expression used in v. 11 is similar to Deut 26:19:

לִהְיוֹת לִי לְעָם וּלְשֵׁם וְלִתְהִלָּה וּלְתִפְאָרֶת	Jer 13:11
וּלְתִתְּךָ עֶלְיוֹן לִתְהִלָּה וּלְשֵׁם וּלְתִפְאָרֶת וְלִהְיֹתְךָ עַם־קָדֹשׁ	Deut 26:19

However, the similarity is not that of both using a stock phrase. What connects these two verses is that they are the only two where all four designations עָם, תִּפְאָרֶת, שֵׁם and תְּהִלָּה are used, although not in the same form of expression. It would appear that they have both made use of a similar form of expression that had not gained the status of a fixed formula, as we found in v. 10ab. Some other variations of this expression are לְשֵׁם וּלִתְהִלָּה (Sef 3:19, 20) and לְשֵׁם וּלְתִפְאָרֶת (1 Chr 22:5). The closest parallel is found in Jer 33:9, וְהָיְתָה לִּי לְשֵׁם שָׂשׂוֹן לִתְהִלָּה וּלְתִפְאָרֶת, which could very well be a deliberate reuse of the expression in 13:11.[2] The expression לְ + היה + לְ + [suffix]-לְ, is largely limited to late biblical Hebrew, judging from its occurrences (Gen 17:7; Lev 11:45; 25:33, 38; 26:45; Num 15:41; Deut 4:20; 7:6; 14:2; 24:4; 26:17, 18; 2 Sam 12:10; Is 56:6; Jer 34:16; Ez 27:7).

Another case of relevant influence is the use of the verb דבק, 'cling to' (Deut 4:4; 10:20; 11:22; 13:5; 30:22; Jos 22:5; 23:8; 2 Kgs 18:6; Ps 63:9; 119:31). This term has a distinct figurative sense that occurs most frequently in Deuter-

---

[1] See also Lundbom (1999: 669-70) for a similar line of argument.
[2] See Holladay (1989: 225).

onomy.[1] The people should cling to their God, which in Deuteronomy is often more or less synonymous with הלך, 'follow' (Deut 11:22; 13:4) and אהב, 'love' (Josh 22:5), both well-known terms from covenantal language.

So neither can v. 11 show us any clear evidence of the work of a redaction.[2] Instead, the language used could very well be the result of influence on the editor of the text from the phraseology commonly used in that era. Furthermore, since there is no other interpretation of the prophetic symbolic act following the description of the act itself (vv. 1-7), we must presume that either a different interpretation was replaced with vv. 8-11, which is unlikely from what we have found so far, or that vv. 8-11 do form the proper interpretation, but have been exposed to a certain amount of reformulation by later editors, due to the prevalent Dtr language en vogue in their time. We will therefore presume that there is a legitimate connection between the description of the act (vv. 1-7) and the interpretation (vv. 8-11), with a keen eye to the fact that the latter may have suffered some of its original meaning through the later adaptation to Dtr language.

Performance of the act
The most difficult problem with this text has undoubtedly been how we can imagine that Jeremiah went back and forth twice to the Euphrates, to hide and fetch the loincloth (vv. 4, 6). Various solutions to this problem has been suggested, such as that it is a vision and not a description of a prophetic symbolic act, properly performed,[3] that it is purely a literary creation,[4] or that it is not actually the river Euphrates that is referred to by פְּרָת, and therefore Jeremiah only went to a stream called Farah, near Anatoth (Jos 18:43).[5] The text has no indications whatsoever of being a vision, other than the apparently unlikely reference to Jeremiah going to the Euphrates. Quite to the contrary, the story has all the signs of a description of a typical prophetic symbolic act being performed, with the exception of an explicit reference to witnesses. It is therefore the third alternative that will have to be scrutinized further. It must be said that two trips back and forth to the Euphrates by Jeremiah can be ruled out, mainly because of the distance but also because of the fact that it would have made it impossible for

---

[1] See Lohfink (1963: 73-80), Weinfeld (1972: 83, 333), TDOT 3, 80-3.

[2] When Friebel (1999: 100, n 46) argues that there is no need to see an interpolation since what is said in vv. 10-11 is not beyond what was originally intended. However, why could not a later interpolator or redactor draw his own, quite correct conclusions from the symbolic act? That is not a relevant test as to whether we have something secondary or not.

[3] So e.g. Lindblom (1962: 131).

[4] Apparently favoured by Carroll (1986: 295).

[5] See Friebel (1999: 21-2, 106-7), and Lundbom (1999: 668-9) with further references.

Jeremiah to perform his act in front of the witnesses he needed, namely representatives of the people of Judah. Some other explanation must be found as to the use of פְּרָת. Indeed, it was suggested long ago that we should read פָּרָה with the locative ה, which would only require a slight revocalisation of פְּרָת to פָּרָת. Among the ancient versions, Aquila actually translates εἰς φαραν, 'to Parah', although the wooden literalness of his translation makes it uncertain as to which reading is followed. Bourguet has suggested, though, that we should not think of revocalising the text, but instead see the reference to the Euphrates as meant to refer to Parah, while bringing with it the association of the Babylonian river, and indexically the magical rituals performed by the Babylonians in and near by that river.[1] Although the suggestion that the association with Euphrates was meant to bring to mind the magical rites performed there should be considered without substance, the view that the spelling is deliberately פְּרָת is attractive. However, to build anything on such a weak case as a small difference in vocalisation is not recommendable. Jones has recently suggested a somewhat simpler interpretation, namely that Jeremiah went to a nearby stream where he performed his symbolic act, and referred to the stream symbolically as 'Euphrates', metonymically designating the influence of the Babylonian religion as the origin of the sins of the people (cf. Jer 7:8; 44:17-19, 25). Just as Jeremiah would have taken an ordinary loincloth and made it symbolize the people, so he would also have used an ordinary stream nearby, and have it stand metaphorically for Euphrates, which in turn would have been used as a metonym for Babylon.[2] The simplicity of Jones interpretation, with its recognition of the symbolic value of the items involved, makes it the most attractive alternative so far.

What kind of clothing was it exactly that Jeremiah bought and put around his waist, and which is called אֵזוֹר? The word occurs 14 times in the OT, and 8 of those are in Jer 13:1-11. Outside of Jeremiah it is used for a piece of clothing made of skin, most likely a loincloth, wrapped around the prophet Elijah's waist, וְאֵזוֹר עוֹר אָזוּר בְּמָתְנָיו (2 Kgs 1:8), attached closely to the waist (Is 5:27; 11:5; Job 12:18), and belted unto the waist, חֲגוֹרֵי אֵזוֹר בְּמָתְנֵיהֶם (Ez 23:15). In Ez 23:15 this piece of clothing is apparently visible, which is problematical if it is the undergarment, and this is precisely why Friebel prefers to see the אֵזוֹר as not the undergarment or loincloth, but as a waist sash, or girdle.[3] But then he misses the

---

[1] Bourguet (1987: 246, 249-57).

[2] Jones (1992: 196).

[3] Friebel (1999: 102). He goes on to argue, that if a loincloth were meant, Jeremiah would have been left naked when he removed it! However, that is taking the text in a manner that is

point of that text, since Oholibah is sexually aroused by soldiers who are not wearing as much clothes as they normally would, since they are depicted as being prepared for battle.

The אֵזוֹר formed the common undergarment for the Israelite worker and soldier, not unlike a kilt, which was usually held up with a belt, making it possible to keep items such as a knife stuck inside the belt.[1] In the relief describing Sennacherib's conquest of Lachish,[2] there are Judean soldiers described with what probably is only their אֵזוֹר, whereas the older men and women wear long, outer garments.[3] The אֵזוֹר was then a short loincloth, tightly girded round the waist (Jer 13:11), and normally held up with a belt. It is also possible that this loincloth was identified with being a 'belt' itself, although that is uncertain. When it is said that the אֵזוֹר that Jeremiah is to use is made of linen, this is no doubt an indication of good quality, as opposed to wool, and certainly skin (2 Kgs 1:8).

This symbolic act is one of several where no witnesses are mentioned. However, this should not pose a problem, since there is rarely an audience mentioned to his verbal preaching, yet this has hardly posed problems for interpreters. That an audience is not mentioned is best understood as something so obvious it only needed mentioning when the circumstances made it necessary.

Symbolic meaning of the act

When it comes to the symbolic value of this symbolic act, it is of vital importance whether vv. 8-11 are regarded as being in any way relevant as an interpretation of the act. As we saw above, there is every reason to believe that vv. 8-11 were not added as a later, separate Dtr redaction, serving its own theological stance. Rather, it should be seen as from the prophet himself, but probably reformulated by editors of the Jeremianic traditions under the influence of Dtr language, with the sole intent of bringing out the message of the prophet in an era when this particular language was en vogue.

There are certain indications in the text that need to be emphasized in order for the symbolic meaning of the act to stand out clearly. To begin with, Jeremiah

---

simply too dramatic. What is to say that Jeremiah did not go home and change? However, on p 103 Friebel himself refers to 'the clinging of the garment closely to the person'.

[1] See ABD 2, 233-4.

[2] ANEP no 371.

[3] See Wright (1955: 64-6), Weippert (1977: 187), Edwards (1992: 233), Lundbom (1999: 667-8). Edwards and Weippert both identify this piece of clothing as the אֵזוֹר.

was told to buy[1] a linen loincloth that was new, no doubt in order to emphasize the perfect quality of the item before it was ruined (v. 1). When Jeremiah took it off and put it away, it was therefore new and stainless, which served to emphasize the difference between when it was worn and when it had been ruined. This contrast seems to form the basis for the symbolic function of the act. When the people cling to their God, they are not defiling themselves with other gods, but when they depart from him, they become unsuitable as the people of God.

The loincloth is said three times to be put around the waist, an indication that would have been unnecessary had there not been a particular reason for it besides specifying how it came to be worn (vv. 1-3). The relationship between the people and their God was initiated by God, who chose the people, as one chooses to put on a loincloth. Furthermore, the point of intimacy and closeness between the person wearing the loincloth and the item itself could very well be meant to allude to the ancient understanding of the covenantal relationship between God and his people, which is also consistently said to be inaugurated on God's initiative.[2] In the following interpretation of the act in v. 11, the proper behaviour of the people in this intimate relationship is expressed by the term דבק, 'cling to', well known in this figurative sense from Deuteronomy.

The loincloth is said not to be exposed to water (v. 1), which also emphasizes the difference between the status of the item as new and without any sign of blemish, and when it was dug up by Jeremiah.[3]

The act of putting on a loincloth is used symbolically to denote a similar act, namely how God chooses his people and keeps them close (v. 11). The apparent iconic symbolism is therefore on the level of performance, although on a very abstract level. It is not the choice of a loincloth that is relevant when it comes to understanding the symbolism, but the act of putting on the loincloth, and keeping it close.

The second part of the symbolic act in vv. 4-7, the removal of the loincloth, hiding it next to a stream and bringing it back again after a lengthy period, is both different and more complex in its symbolism. Just as linen suffers from being removed from the waist and hid away for a lengthy period, so the people will suffer from not putting their trust in God. When Jeremiah brings back the loincloth, he does so in order to display its condition, and thereby completing

---

[1] The only three instances in Jer of the verb קנה are found in the descriptions of three prophetic symbolic acts, buying a loincloth (13:1-3), buying a pot (19:1), and buying a field (34:7-9).

[2] So Friebel (1999: 103), Lundbom (1999: 670-1).

[3] Similary Friebel (1999: 105).

the symbolic act. However, there is no indication in the text that the return of the loincloth should be seen as a reference of the return from exile. Indeed, not even the removal and hiding of the loincloth should be seen as symbolising the exile. It is only in v. 9, when these consequences are spelled out as God's judgement, that we come close to what could be a reference to the exile. However, the mentioning of God's judgement as the consequence is too abstract for it to be considered a clear reference. It is more likely that Jeremiah leaves it in no doubt how God will react to the sins of his people.

The symbolism involved in the latter part of this symbolic act is consistently iconic in its character as in the first part of the act, but now only when it comes to the level of use and function of the loincloth. When the loincloth is removed, it can no longer function properly. Indeed, a more emphatic symbolic meaning is achieved when the loincloth is put away, which will definitely destroy the fine linen fabric, again a vividly iconic symbolism. The comparison in this case is consistently made on the level of function and role, and not on the level of performance, as was the case in the first part of the symbolic act, the putting on and keeping the loincloth near. There is no indication that the iconic symbolism is on the level of performance, i.e., that the physical act of removing the loincloth has some relevant symbolic meaning, which also goes for the act of putting it away. Instead, it is a matter of comparing the people that is judged by their God, with the loincloth that is 'good for nothing' (vv. 7,10). The choice of the loincloth as a physical item is, on the other hand, closer to being a case of conventional symbolism, when it denotes not only closeness but also intimacy. We are somewhat at a loss as to whether Jeremiah might be making use of some conventional meaning attached to the loincloth. However, the symbolic meaning would be that the people which was once so close to their God will be destroyed, as the loincloth was destroyed when it was left 'in a cleft of a rock'.

There is no apparent symbolic meaning to the acts of purchasing or putting on the loincloth, however, even though such an interpretation could well be thought of. One could imagine that when God has 'bought'[1] his people, he joins them in an intimate, covenantal relationship. However, there is nothing in the subsequent interpretation to substantiate that any of this was intended as symbolic. The bringing back of the loincloth is also not symbolic, but only serves to illustrate the condition of the loincloth.

Instead, the act of wearing the loincloth is symbolic of the intimate, idyllic relationship between the people and their God. A problem, mostly overlooked, oc-

---

[1] E.g. Ex 15:16, where the same verb, קָנָה, is used to denote how God acquires his people through the Exodus, and also Deut 32:6.

curs when we attempt to understand the symbolic value of the act of removing the loincloth and putting it for a long time in a cleft of a rock. If this is understood as a symbol for God's punishment, where is the sin of the people being symbolized? Moreover, if the people are to be defiled by their sins by the Euphrates, where is the symbol for the punishment? The only possible solution is to follow the interpretation in v. 9, and see the removal and putting away of the loincloth as a symbol for God's punishment on the people. The actual sinful pride of the people (v. 9) is read out from between the lines in the symbolic portrayal of the idyllic state and the punishment. This brings us to the conclusion that this symbolic act serves to illustrate most vividly the stark contrast between the status of the people as they were in their heyday, and how they will become when they have suffered God's wrath.

The otherwise consistently iconic symbolism breaks down, however, if the loincloth is said to be taken to Euphrates, since that properly belongs to the semantic area of that which is being symbolized, the people being threatened by the Babylonians, and not to that of the symbol, the loincloth. As was discussed above, however, this may not after all be a reference to the Euphrates river but to a nearby stream. If so, there would not be a breakdown of the iconic symbolism.

The symbolic act clearly functions as an extension of Jeremiah's verbal preaching. He exposes the people to the very real threat of destruction, in order to convince them of the urgent need for renewed commitment and realistic action in the face of the inevitable disaster. It is not that the act in some semi-magical sense brings the disaster about, but it warns the people of the disaster, and tries in every way possible to make them understand the realism of what is to come.

Summary and Conclusions

1. The symbolic meaning of this act would be, that just as a loincloth has a specific purpose, namely to be closely attached to a person's body, so the people of
God has the specific purpose of being near their God. However, just as the loincloth becomes useless to its original purpose when it is removed and exposed to
natural forces in a cleft of a rock, so the people will be useless to their purpose
when their God has served them his punishment (v. 9).

2. The interpretation in vv. 8-11 is quite suitable to the act that is described in
vv. 1-7, even though it elaborates somewhat beyond what is symbolized in the
actual performance.[1] The reformulation and elaboration that seem to have occurred at a later time in accordance with Dtr language has not added anything
that can not be understood as a natural and relevant interpretation of the prophetic symbolic act.

3. There is nothing in either the description of the symbolic act or the interpretation that would indicate a clear reference to the exile, either going into exile in
the putting away of the loincloth, or in bringing it back.

4. The symbolism involved in the prophetic act is consistently iconic, but on two
different levels. The putting on and wearing of the loincloth stands ironically for
the idyllic relationship between the people and their God on the level of performance, however abstract. The removal and defilement of the loincloth, on the
other hand, stands ironically for the result of God's punishment on the people on
the level of function.

---

[1] Against Carroll (1986: 293).

2. The Smashed Jar (Jeremiah 19:1-2, 10-11)

The Text

כֹּה אָמַר יְהוָה הָלוֹךְ וְקָנִיתָ 1
בַּקְבֻּק יוֹצֵר[b] חָרֶשׂ וּלְקַחְתָּ[a]
מִזִּקְנֵי הָעָם וּמִזִּקְנֵי[c] הַכֹּהֲנִים
וְיָצָאתָ אֶל־גֵּיא בֶן־הִנֹּם אֲשֶׁר 2
פֶּתַח שַׁעַר הַחַרְסִית[d] וְקָרָאתָ שָׁם
אֵת־הַדְּבָרִים אֲשֶׁר־אֲדַבֵּר אֵלֶיךָ

......

וְשָׁבַרְתָּ הַבַּקְבֻּק לְעֵינֵי הָאֲנָשִׁים 10
הַהֹלְכִים אוֹתָךְ 11 וְאָמַרְתָּ אֲלֵיהֶם
כֹּה־אָמַר יְהוָה צְבָאוֹת כָּכָה אֶשְׁבֹּר
אֶת־הָעָם הַזֶּה וְאֶת־הָעִיר הַזֹּאת
כַּאֲשֶׁר יִשְׁבֹּר אֶת־כְּלִי הַיּוֹצֵר אֲשֶׁר
לֹא־יוּכַל לְהֵרָפֵה עוֹד[e]

1 Thus said Yhwh: Go and buy a jar made of clay. Take some of the elders of the people and some of the senior priests, 2 and go out to the valley of Ben-Hinnom at the entry of the Potsherd Gate, and proclaim there the words that I tell you.

......

10 Then you shall break the jar in the sight of those who go with you, 11 and shall say to them: Thus says Yhwh of hosts: So will I break this people and this city, as one breaks a potter's vessel, so it can never be mended.

Textual notes

[a] Following LXX (καὶ ἄξεις), Syr., Tg., in inserting the verb לקח after ו, so e.g. McKane (1986: 444). This emendation, together with the following note, might very well point in the direction of a physical damage of the text at some point in the textual transmission.

[b] LXX has πεπλασμένον, 'formed', which is suggested by e.g. BHS, Holladay (1986: 534), McKane (1986: 444), Rabin, et al. (1997) to translate the passive participle יְצֻר, 'a jar, made of clay', suggesting a subsequent metathesis in MT. A simpler solution that does not require a metathesis would be to postulate the reading of the Hebrew text behind LXX as יוּצַר (cf. Is 54:17, כָּל־כְּלִי יוּצַר עָלַיִךְ לֹא יִצְלָח, 'no weapon fashioned against you shall prosper'). This would then later have been wrongly vocalised as the well-known יוֹצֵר, 'potter'. This in turn created a problem with the following חֶרֶשׂ, cf. Holladay (1986: 539), which then seems superfluous after 'potter', and some take it therefore as an explanatory gloss, e.g. Syr., Lundbom (1999: 838). To prioritize the vocalised MT here before LXX, e.g. Friebel (1999: 115, n 91), Lundbom (1999: 838), is being overzealous, since LXX does read a different vocalisation that should have a higher priority.

[c] For this latter expression, see 2 Kgs 19:2//Is 37:2. In LXX[B,L] the word πρεσβυτέρων is lacking in relation to the priests, but it is most likely a case of Haplography, τῶν ... τῶν, against e.g. Janzen (1973: 41), McKane (1986: 444).

[c] See Mulder (2006: 745-6).

[d] Following the singular Qere, supported by LXX, χαρσιθ against the plural Kethib.

[e] The phrase וּבְתֹפֶת יִקְבְּרוּ מֵאֵין מָקוֹם לִקְבּוֹר is missing in LXX, and the most likely solution is that the phrase was meant to gloss v. 12 as a 'scholarly footnote' Janzen (1973: 43). For various other explanations, see McKane (1986: 446). An interesting indication of a rather late glossing activity involving this phrase is the fact that in LXX[L] the phrase is found at the end of v. 13, the very passage in vv. 12-13 it was meant to elucidate, see Janzen (1973: 205, n 17), a later accommodation to the expanded Hebrew text. The views of Thiel (1973: 223), Lundbom (1999: 841) can not be substantiated, since the glossing is all too obvious.

Analysis

Literary coherence

Scholars have recognized for some time the coherence and structure of the text as the main problems with Jer 19. The chapter begins in a way similar to Jer 13, namely with God ordering Jeremiah to perform a prophetic symbolic act (v. 1-2a), and in both instances he is told to purchase an item needed for the performance of the act.[1] However, the description is in this case interrupted by an instruction to Jeremiah from God to preach a sermon before he performs the symbolic act (vv. 2b-9). Only then are we given the continuation of the instruction regarding the prophetic symbolic act (vv. 10), together with an interpretation of the act (v. 11). Then the sermon seems to continue (vv. 12-15), with a brief description of what happened when Jeremiah came back to the temple.

The sermon shows clear marks of Dtr language, although there are examples of distinctive Jeremianic language as well.[2] However, since the description of the act as well as the interpretation are apparently left intact, we can still understand the prophetic symbolic act, although its literary context still poses a problem.

It has been considered a sure result for some time, that vv. 1-2a + 10-11a forms an authentic nucleus, going back to Jeremiah. This has then been reworked by the addition of v. 2b-9 + 11b-13. Some would regard this sermon as a typical Dtr creation, being part of a wholesale Dtr redaction of the book of

---

[1]

| Jer 13:1 | הָלוֹךְ וְקָנִיתָ אֵזוֹר פִּשְׁתִּים | 'go and buy yourself a linen loincloth ...' |
| Jer 19:1 | הָלוֹךְ וְקָנִיתָ בַקְבֻּק | 'go and buy a jar ...' |

[2] Stulman (1986: 78) estimates that in vv. 3-9 there are nine stock phrases particular to Dtr/Deuteronomy, and four peculiar to the 'Jeremianic prose sermons'.

Jeremiah.[1] Some, on the other hand, would agree that there has been later re-working of a nucleus, but refrain from describing the redactional activity as Dtr.[2] A third group would hold that the text is nevertheless coherent, showing no signs of later reworking.[3]

It is likely that a story concerning a prophetic symbolic act has been used later as an opportunity to expand in the form of a sermon on a topic that has already been entertained in Jer 7:31-2. After the command to Jeremiah to buy an earthen jar from a potter (v. 1), he is suddenly told to go to the valley of Ben-Hinnom to preach (v. 2). Verse 2 seems to have been reworked, since it is strange to refer to a valley outside the city by a reference to a gate, and a gate that is nowhere else known at that. It is therefore likely that when the sermon was inserted (vv. 3-9), the phrase אֶל־גֵּיא בֶן־הִנֹּם אֲשֶׁר was also added to v. 2 in order to accommodate the sermon to the literary context.

Jeremiah is told to bring with him some of the elders of the people and some of the 'elders' of the priests, but in his sermon he addresses not them but the kings of Judah and the inhabitants of Jerusalem (v. 3). Although this does not pose an insurmountable problem, the elders and the priests could perhaps be seen as symbolic representatives of the kings and people, it nevertheless indi-cates that the sermon has a different focus than the situation which is presented in v. 1-2*, 10-11a, and should be seen as yet another indication of the independ-ent character of the sermon. However, this is not to say that we can postulate that the sermon existed on its own prior to its insertion in Jer 19. The word וּבַקֹּתִי (v. 7) forms a word-play on בַּקְבֻּק (v. 1), which rules out any doubt as to the na-ture of the sermon as a creation made specific for this literary context. The ser-mon was meant to expand on a subject central to Dtr theologians, i.e., the sin of Topheth[4] in the valley of ben-Hinnom, linked to the cultic practice of child sac-rifice in the reign of Manasseh (2 Kgs 16:3; 21:6; 23:10; Jer 7:31-3).

On the other hand, it seems rather naive to postulate that precisely those verses in Jer 19:1-15 that go back to Jeremiah are precisely what constituted an original story concerning the symbolic act. In fact, we have no way of finding out whether later editors of the text replaced parts of the earlier text with mate-

---

[1] So e.g. Rudolph (1968: 127), Nicholson (1973: 163), Thiel (1973: 228-9), Carroll (1986: 386).

[2] So e.g. Bright (1965: 131, 133), McKane (1986: 451-4).

[3] So e.g. Holladay (1986: 536-7), Craigie, et al. (1991: 256-8). Jones (1992: 264-5) also agrees with this view, although he recognizes the possible presence of 'didactic amplifica-tions'. Friebel (1999: 117-8, 101) is reliable in his dogmatic refusal to see any possible redac-tion of the text, whereas Lundbom (1999: 836-7) argues more persuasively.

[4] See TDOT 15, 757-8.

rial of their own. It is therefore only with certain qualifications that we can speak of an early nucleus of Jer 19 going back to Jeremiah. One thing that would appear to be missing is a description of the actual carrying out of the symbolic act. However, this description is sometimes missing elsewhere (e.g. Ez 37:15-28), and there is no apparent reason why a later editor would keep the description of the command to perform the symbolic act but remove the description of how the prophet carried it out.

Performance of the act

The performance of the symbolic act is straightforward enough, with the obvious acknowledgement that the text we presume to have come down from Jeremiah is a hypothetical, although very likely, text. Jeremiah is told to go to go and buy a piece of pottery, a reference which explains some if not all of the editorial decision to place this story immediately after the story of Jeremiah's visit to the potter in Jer 18.

No doubt the reason for buying the pottery and not using something already at hand is the same as the reason behind buying the loincloth in ch. 13. The effect of smashing a brand new piece of pottery would be greater than smashing a used one, the latter probably having cracks and showing other signs of being worn. That would have involved the risk of witnesses understanding the act as the everyday act of throwing useless pieces of pottery on the heap of broken pottery. Instead, the very concrete absurdity of breaking a brand *new* piece would have made it very clear to people watching, that Jeremiah must have meant something else by his act than simply disposing of useless pottery. This could also be compared with when the prophet Ahijah performs his symbolic act in 1 Kgs 11:29-30 by tearing a mantle that is emphasized as a *new* mantle. The same explanation for this emphasis can be used in 1 Kgs 11 as in Jer 13 and 19.

Jeremiah is told to buy a בַּקְבֻּק יוֹצֵר חָרֶשׂ, 'a jar made of clay' to use in his symbolic act. It might seem superfluous to specify that a jar bought from the potter should be made of clay, but again this indication serves not so much to inform the reader of the nature of the jar, as to enhance the symbolic character of the act. The reader is meant to be left in no doubt that what Jeremiah is about to smash will certainly break in tiny pieces, as was always the case with useless pottery, thrown on the heap of rubbish. The author may also want to make certain that the reader does not think of a jar made of metal, which was likely to exist, although very rarely. The word for jar, בַּקְבֻּק, occurs only here in Jer 19 and in 1 Kgs 14:3, where it is used for a jar of honey. It is therefore likely that a בַּקְבֻּק was larger than an ordinary jug (cf. NRSV). The word is formed as a reduplication for onomatopoetic purposes,[1] its pronunciation being an imitation of the gurgling sound of pouring liquid from a jar, preferably one with long, thin neck.[2] In Iron II Palestine, the narrow-necked jar, probably used as water decanter, was quite common.[3] If such a long-necked jar was purchased by Jeremiah, the delicate form would have served well to enhance the symbolic value of smashing it to pieces.

Jeremiah is further told to bring 'elders of the people', and 'elders of the priests', presumably as witnesses to the symbolic act that he is about to perform. These two groups were no doubt selected as a form of merism for the whole of the people. Their status as witnesses are clearly brought out in v. 10, where Jeremiah is told to perform his act לְעֵינֵי הָאֲנָשִׁים, 'in front of the men', which is a rare emphasis of the role of witnesses among the texts describing prophetic symbolic acts. It might be that unambiguous reference to the performance of the act made the author feel it unnecessary to include a reference to the actual outworking of the ordered act. The use of witnesses was a vital part of the whole project of a prophetic symbolic act, and something without which the act would have been useless, as futile as any form of communication that never reached a receiver to be understood.

The point of the purchase of the jar is to smash it to pieces, and to do so in front of the representatives of the people. This act of smashing pottery has led scholars generally to associate to an Egyptian magic/religious practise. This practise either involved forming models in various materials of enemies of the state, or inscribing their names on pottery, presumably followed by the recitation

---

[1] See HAL 149, Nyberg (1952 §72.i), Blau (1955: 339).

[2] The word seems to have a dubious origin. It can be found in Syriac, Arabic, see BDB 132, and Ugaritic, *bk*, KTU[2] 1.3.I.12, where *bk rb* is used synonymously with *ks* and *krp[[m]]nm*. There is a possible occurrence in Aramaic, in the so-called Sabbat Ostraca. Dupont-Sommer (1949: 31-2), followed by Lipínski (1970: 81), holds that the letters בקלא form two words, meaning, 'no jar'. This was questioned by Milik (1967), who identifies only one word, 'malt', in accordance with Akkadian *bāqilu*, see also DNWSI 186, Grelot (1972: 370). No doubt the same word is found in the Greek βῖκος, Liddell, et al. (1996: 315), which is the translation in the LXX of Jer 19:1, its only occurrence of that word. Lipínski (1970: 81) has argued that the word originally came from Anatolia, through Ionian to western Asia and Ugaritic, his main argument being the rarity of the word among Semitic languages. However, he does not mention בַּקְבֻק in BH. Masson (1967: 78-80) has suggested the opposite direction without mentioning the Ugaritic occurrence, which strengthens his case. In *Tg. Ps-J.* Ex 12:12; Num 33:4, we find the derivative word בקיקא, 'potsherd'.

[3] See the many examples in Amiran (1970: 256-65). Kelso (1948: 17, 48) suggests some particular jars to be the בַּקְבֻק. However, it should be emphasized that the grounds for identification are imprecise and unclear.

of specific curses. These curses are extant in the so-called 'Execration texts', naming west-Asiatic states.[1] The pottery was subsequently smashed, as a vivid display of the fate that awaited the designated enemies. This act of smashing the pottery has also been associated with 'the rite of breaking the red pots'.[2] It has become customary among scholars to associate Jeremiah's symbolic act with this ancient Egyptian ritual,[3] a comparison which comes easily enough when the prophetic symbolic acts are regarded as magical rituals.[4] The similarities between the Egyptian ritual and Jeremiah's act are two; the obvious fact of the smashing of the pottery, and the identification of the pottery with a nation under some form of divine judgement, in Egypt from Pharaoh and in Jeremiah's case from God. Various other texts in the OT are then brought in as further evidence of this allusion to the Egyptian custom, such as Jer 22:28,[5] Ps 2:9[6] and Am 1:2-2:16[7]. However, in Jer 22:28 the king is rhetorically described as without any means of governing, thus figuratively illustrated as a potsherd. In Ps 2:9 there might be an allusion to the Egyptian ritual, since God is asked to crush the enemies like pottery, but the image is so well-known and collected from everyday life, that any such allusions must be made with firmer arguments. In Am 1:2-2:16 there is no mention of breaking pottery, only an enumeration of condemnations on surrounding nations. Although this list could be compared with the execration texts, the comparison with the ritual is too far-fetched. However, the most vital point of comparison that is missing in all these texts is the inscription, since it is never mentioned that the name of an enemy is inscribed on the pottery. This makes the comparison between Jeremiah's act and the Egyptian ritual highly suspect, mainly because what we are left with is the everyday custom of throwing useless pottery on the potsherd pit. This reuse of a simple act that belonged to the everyday management of the household in a secondary, prophetic

---

[1] ANET 328-9, 'The Execration of Asiatic Princes', cf. Otto (1975), see also Friebel (1999: 119-20, n 106).

[2] See Wilson (1951: 156-8), Dijk (1986: 1393), Redford (1992b: 681).

[3] So e.g. Holladay (1986: 541).

[4] It is interesting to note that Dijk (1986: 1393) has some doubts about characterising the Egyptian ritual as magical, preferring rather a more mythological interpretation, 'Although the ritual may be described in a technical sense as an act of sympathetic magic it is more likely to be interpreted as a rite of reassurance, enacted to reassure and thereby protect the participants of the ritual when they approach the dangerous borderline between the ordered world and the domain of the powers of chaos.'

[5] So Berridge (1970: 179-80, n. 354).

[6] So e.g. Kleber (1943), Berridge (1970: 179-80, n. 354), Soggin (1970: 195).

[7] So e.g. Bentzen (1950: 87), although he is keen to note that Jeremiah's act does not entail any inscription on the pottery.

symbolic act was presumably highly effective. The prophet could then make use of an act that would have been relevant to each of his listeners, thus creating recognition, while at the same time applying the smashing of the pottery to divine judgement on the people itself, which created astonishment and surprise. When he crashed a new piece, he also did so in order to make a statement that was deliberately built on the customary act, and this seemingly foolish behaviour created interest and attention from his audience. The fact that Jeremiah is told to go to the potsherd pit and perform his symbolic act there is a further indication that the allusion is to the everyday custom, and not to the Egyptian ritual. This is of course not to say that a witness to the act might very well have alluded to the ritual, but there is no reason to regard such an allusion to have been intended by Jeremiah performing the act, or whoever formulated the text as we have it.

Symbolic meaning of the act
The most profound OT symbolism involved in the figurative use of how the potter works is that of creation.[1] This is a motif that can hardly be emphasized enough as background to Jeremiah's act. The notion that God had made man out of clay was fundamental (Gen 2:7; Ps 103:14 etc) and not restricted to ancient Israel. Deutero-Isaiah brought this to bear on the nation as a whole (Is 43:7; 44:24), and Jeremiah used the image of the potter hard at work to form his vessel as a symbol of how God creates and shapes his people, and destines them for blessing or curse (Jer 18, cf. Is 64:8). The next logical step in the use of this imagery of the potter's work is to focus on the shattering of the pottery itself, as a vivid image of God's judgement, not the least in the book of Jeremiah (Ps 2:9; Eccl 12:6; Is 30:13-4; Jer 22:28; 48:12, 38). This last step can not be understood without the profound notion of God as the creator, who deals with his creation as he sees fit, as the potter controls his clay. This is the proper background to Jeremiah's act in this instance, part of the conventional figurative language used in ancient Israel to describe their view of their God. This is also the symbolism that the prophet makes use of and elaborates upon in his symbolic act.

In Lev 15:12 pottery that is touched upon by a man with discharge is to be smashed. However, here the act is used in its primary sense, and not in a figurative sense that could have any direct bearing on the prophetic act in Jer 19. The pottery is not smashed because it is unusable, but despite the fact that it is brand new. The only connection could be on the level of connotative meaning, since Jeremiah is explicitly addressing the senior priests, and they were familiar with

---

[1] TDOT 6, 259-64, with further literature.

such a procedure, although with a different meaning. Nevertheless, the mere similarity in performance was often enough to awaken recognition and thereby interest and attentiveness to the new meaning that the prophet is bringing forward through his act.

The symbolism of the act consists of a dramatic identification between the smashing of the jug on the one hand (v. 11aba), and the coming destruction of the people and in particular the city of Jerusalem on the other (v. 11aa). As mentioned above, this is based on the more profound iconic symbolism between the potter's work on his clay and God's work with his people, an iconic symbolism that is focused not on procedure but on effect and the total control that the potter has on his clay. The smashing of the jug is an example of how this total control can express itself. In this case, the identification is not made with how the potter decides on whether to keep the item he has made or start all over again with the clay. Instead, this symbolic act is based on the everyday act of smashing pottery that was of no use, except to use the small pieces that are left as ostraca. As God is conventionally symbolized as the potter, who has total control over his clay, God is also symbolized as the one who smashes the pottery. It is possible to continue to see a symbolic representation of the potter also in this symbolic act,[1] but the phrase in v. 11, כַּאֲשֶׁר יִשְׁבֹּר אֶת־כְּלִי הַיּוֹצֵר, 'as one breaks a potter's vessel', argues against such a view. Instead, the rhetorical thrust of the symbolic act, as this particular phrase from v. 11 would imply, is that everyone could identify with how one smashes useless pottery to pieces. Therefore, the prophet is primarily playing the role of an ordinary Israelite who smashes his pottery, and not in effect the role of God, a role that is logically speaking played by the 'ordinary Israelite'.[2] What makes the symbolic act work so concretely is that the jug smashed by Jeremiah actually stands ironically for the pottery that is smashed by the ordinary 'Israelite', as well as the act of smashing itself. This act by the 'Israelite', performed on a symbolic level by Jeremiah, and not on the level of actual physical performance, is then again used symbolically in a secondary iconic sense to describe how God will act with his people. God is not smashing pottery as Jeremiah does, but as everyone watching would be accustomed to do. The identification that everyone watching would have been able to make is pre-

---

[1] This would explain why the jug that Jeremiah is said to buy must be new. The potter is finished with his work, the item is ready to be used, when the potter suddenly decides that it should be smashed (cf. Is 41:25). This is part and parcel of the conventional symbolism involved in the imagery of the potter, who not only starts over with the clay when he is less than satisfied, but who also smashed pottery that is not to his satisfaction after it has been burned. This symbolism could have been used by Jeremiah, but it was not.

[2] Against e.g. Friebel (1999: 119).

cisely what Jeremiah intends, as in the symbolic use of the linen cloth in ch. 13. It could be argued that the use of a new jug was meant to cause bewilderment, since no one in his or her right mind would smash a perfectly usable jug, especially one that was brand new. However, there is not enough indication within the text to substantiate such an interpretation, and it must therefore be left open as a possibility.

Furthermore, the intent of the destruction is spelled out, namely so that it will be total and leave no room for future repair (v. 11abb). This too is an iconic symbolism with its focus on the effect, since the jug can not be repaired since it has been smashed. It also continues the use of the imagery of the Israelite who smashes his useless pottery. This iconic symbolism focuses on the effect of the act and not on the procedure, which is conventional. It could theoretically have been a symbolic use of the weaver, the blacksmith, or the carpenter, since the choice of the potter is a case of conventional symbolism of the ancient Israelite culture, whereas the symbolic use of his acts are iconic, focusing on the effect and control involved, and not on the procedure.

It could be concluded from this emphasis that the prophet in this instance did not intend to suggest that there would be a future for the people after the destruction. However, in language used to interpret symbolic acts one can expect a certain amount of hyperbolic force, due to the effort to bring out the comparison as clearly and persuasively as possible. The message seems to be, that the people has no future in the form it has when Jeremiah performs his symbolic act, and certainly not until it has suffered divine judgement.

Summary and Conclusions

1. The symbolic act of smashing a jug symbolizes ironically on two levels. First, what Jeremiah does stands for the ordinary Israelite who smashes useless pottery to pieces. Second, this ordinary and well known act stands, again ironically, for what God will do to his people.

2. The iconic symbolism involved in this symbolic act is focused on the effect of the act on the various levels, physical performance as well as symbolic levels. The choice of the potter, however, is conventional, since it is part of the Israelite culture to symbolize God's creative activity with the work of the potter. It is only on the level of the effect of the act that the symbolism involved becomes iconic.

3. An important aspect of this act is how it vividly displays, by means of iconic symbolism, the total and irreparable state of the pottery after it has been smashed to pieces. It is precisely this aspect of the act that is brought over to how God will deal with his people, who have reached a point of no return. They too will be of no use when God has had his way with them.

3. Wearing a 'Yoke-Collar' (Jeremiah 27:2-3; 28:10-11)

Introduction

Before we can start analyzing the symbolic acts in these particular texts, the matter of the textual history of Jer 27 has to be faced. This concerns the well-known problem as to why LXX is so much shorter than MT.[1] Does MT provide evidence for a later, expanded Hebrew text, and the Hebrew text behind LXX then being the shorter and more reliable, or vice versa? This problem has been tackled without any apparent solution in sight until the findings of some fragments from Jeremiah among the Qumran scrolls, namely 4QJer[a-c].[2] Of these fragments, it is apparent to most scholars that 4QJer[b,d] provide us with evidence for the shorter text of LXX, and, thus, also the Hebrew text behind LXX. The other fragments show similarities with the longer MT. The shorter text of LXX has therefore been shown not to be a later expanded text, but to rely on a Hebrew text that is at least as old and reliable as MT, if not more so. Most scholars, e.g. Janzen, Tov, and Stulman, have therefore drawn the conclusion that the shorter Hebrew text behind LXX is also the preferred one.[3] Tov uses the terminology of two editions, the Hebrew text behind LXX being edition I and the text behind MT edition II.[4] This view has been criticized by Soderlund, on the basis that internal arguments must be emphasized as well before such a conclusion can be made.[5] Although this is not the place for a full-scale analysis of such an intricate technical problem, we need nevertheless to establish which Hebrew text

---

[1] For a useful overview of the pluses in MT of Jer 27, see Stulman (1986: 86-8), Tov (1992a: 319-27). MT is 42 %, or 170 words, longer than LXX, see Stulman (1986: 86). According to the analysis of Min (1977: 255) (unavailable to me), the Hebrew text behind LXX was 1/7 shorter than MT, the reference to Min is from Stulman (1985: 1, n 2).

[22] Tov (1981a: 145-6) described them as 4QJer[a-c], but later Tov (1992b) has discriminated between the various fragments earlier assumed to make up 4QJer[b] into separate fragments, 4QJer[b,d,e], originating from different scribes. The latter article contains publications of 4QJer[b,d,e], 4QJer[c] was published in Tov (1991), and 4QJer[a] is now available in a preliminary edition by Tov (1994), except of course the recently made available microfiche edition Tov (1993).

[3] Janzen (1973), Tov (1981a), Stulman (1986).

[4] Tov (1981a), Tov (1992a: 321). See also the further bibliographic references provided by Tov.

[5] Soderlund (1984), and similarly Lundbom (1999). Soderlund's view was later questioned by Janzen (1989).

we are to follow, or, and this is Soderlund's view, that it will still be up to the individual cases which Hebrew text that is preferable. Perhaps the most interesting and useful analysis has been done by Stulman, who has compared the Dtr passages with the pluses in MT (MT+), and attempted to understand how the two fit together. His conclusion is that although MT+ show Dtr language, they prefer to imitate and develop the Dtr language already available in the text common to both LXX and MT. He has shown that the text of Jeremiah suffered a Dtr redaction before it separated into two different textual variations, or text traditions. After this separation, the Vorlage behind MT was exposed to a redaction that expanded the text.[1] Although it is hard to be dogmatic in this case, Stulman does appear to have provided a convincing case.

The question is, then, whether MT+ are to regarded a matter of textual or literary criticism. As far as MT+ can be shown to be more of a creative stage in the literary history of MT, they can hardly be a matter of textual criticism.[2] However, This is precisely what has not been convincingly shown so far. When the examples from MT+ in Jer 27:1-2; 28:10-11 are analysed, they appear to have been no more than various forms of interpolations in the Hebrew Vorlage behind MT. We will therefore treat MT+ as a phenomenon that can in certain instances be a matter of textual criticism.[3] This is not to say, of course, that there is no overall editorial strain to be found in MT+, but we have found no such strain in Jer 27:1-2; 28:10-11, or indeed in Jer 27-28 at large.[4] In the text of Jer 27:2-3; 28:10-11 below we have therefore treated M+ as a likely concern of textual criticism, and largely found the Hebrew text behind LXX to be superior to that of MT.[5]

---

[1] Stulman (1986: 89, 139-40, 145-6).

[2] So e.g. Tov (1981b: 296), Barthélemy (1986: 665-6, 670), Tov (1992a: 347).

[3] See the judicious comment by Albrektson (1994: 29). For an example of text-critical analysis where MT+ is not singled out as a literary and not text-critical issue, see McKane (1989), cf. also Holladay (1989: 115).

[4] The attempt by Stulman (1986: 146) to characterize MT+ is all too vague to be taken seriously.

[5] See Janzen (1973: 132), 'The differences between M and G are those which characterize the textual, rather than the redactoral, phase of development of a Biblical book.'

The Text

2 ²ᵇכֹּה־אָמַר יְהוָהᵃ עֲשֵׂה לְךָ מוֹסֵרוֹת
וּמֹטוֹת וּנְתַתָּם עַל־צַוָּארֶךָᶜ 3 וְשִׁלַּחְתָּם
אֶל־מֶלֶךְ אֱדוֹם וְאֶל־מֶלֶךְ מוֹאָב
וְאֶל־מֶלֶךְ בְּנֵי עַמּוֹן וְאֶל־מֶלֶךְ
צֹר וְאֶל־מֶלֶךְ צִידוֹן
וּצִידוֹן בְּיַד מַלְאָכִיםᵉ הַבָּאִיםᵈ
יְרוּשָׁלַם אֶל־צִדְקִיָּהוּ מֶלֶךְ יְהוּדָה

......

28:10 וַיִּקַּח חֲנַנְיָה ᵍ˒ʰ אֶת־הַמּוֹטָהᶠ
מֵעַל צַוַּאר יִרְמְיָה וַיִּשְׁבְּרֵהוּⁱ
11 וַיֹּאמֶר חֲנַנְיָה לְעֵינֵי
כָל־הָעָם לֵאמֹר כֹּה אָמַר
יְהוָה כָּכָה אֶשְׁבֹּר אֶת־עֹלᵏˡ
מֶלֶךְ־בָּבֶלⁱ מֵעַל־צַוַּאר
כָּל־הַגּוֹיִם וַיֵּלֶךְ יִרְמְיָה לְדַרְכּוֹ

2 Thus Yhwh said: Make yourself cords and pegs, and put them on your neck. 3 Send word to the king of Edom, the king of Moab, the king of the Ammonites, the king of Tyre, and the king of Sidon through the envoys who have come to Jerusalem, to King Zedekiah of Judah.

......

10 Then Hananiah took the collar from the neck of Jeremiah, and broke it. 11 And Hananiah spoke in the presence of the people, saying, "Thus says Yhwh: This is how I will break the yoke of the King of Babylon from the neck of all the nations." Then Jeremiah went his way.

Textual notes

ᵃ MT+ אֵלַי, probably added to strengthen the Hebrew text behind MT, see Tov (1979: 81). The text is changed, although it should be realized that this change is on the border-line between textual and literary criticism.

ᵇ MT+ v. 1. The verse is taken over from 26:1, with the addition of אֶל־יִרְמְיָה. That Jer 27 is not situated in the time of Jehoiachim is clear from vv. 3, 12. There is no need only to replace the names Jehoiachim and Zedekiah. The verse is a MT+, it is clearly taken over from 26:1, and narratives often start without an introduction such as 27:1, as in e.g. Jer 13, 16, 19, 23 etc, of which 13 and 19 both describe a prophetic symbolic act, as is the case here in Jer 27:2-3.

ᶜ MT has ם-, indicating a suffix third person masculine plural with the verb in piel. It is generally preferred to follow LXX*ᴸ ˊ⁻⁴⁴⁹* and read ךָ- with the verb vocalized as qal, without the suffix, since the 'yoke' prepared was presumably meant for Jeremiah, so BHS, Bright (1965: 199), Rudolph (1968: 176-7). The emendation could have occurred as an attempt to resolve the awkward Hebrew idiom by connecting to the items that Jeremiah has collected. However, LXX*ᴸ ˊ⁻⁴⁴⁹* remains a weak support to warrant a change in relation to MT, which makes some retain MT, e.g. Barthélemy (1986: 666-7) and similarly McKane (1996: 686). See further below, under 'Performance'.

ᵈ LXX+ εἰς ἀπάντησιν αὐτῶν, apparently overlooked by Janzen (1973: 66-7), who contributes similar LXX+ to 'scribal memory of (slightly different) parallel passages prevailing over attention to the text at hand.' Tov (1979) considers MT more original. The Greek is probably a Hebraism for לקראתם, see Jer 41:6, MT לִקְרָאתָם // LXX εἰς ἀπάντησιν αὐτοῖς, a common Hebraism throughout LXX. The Hebrew could have been interpolated in the Hebrew text behind LXX, see Tov (1981b: 133-5), but the influence from Jer 41:6, together with the suitability of the phrase, could also have been sufficient factors behind the interpolation on a Greek level, whether translation or later scribal activity.

e LXX+ αὐτῶν, probably a clarifying interpolation, see Tov (1979: 78-9, n 25), Barthélemy (1986: 667-8).

f LXX has plural τοὺς κλοιοὺς against singular in MT, so also in v. 12. In v. 13 there are two plurals in both MT and LXX. This has led some scholars to change the singular forms in 28:10, 12 into plurals, under the influence of the plurals in 27:2; 28:13 (twice), so e.g. Carroll (1986: 539), Holladay (1989: 125), but not e.g. Rudolph (1968: 178, 180), Wanke (1971: 24), Seidl (1977: 80), Jones (1992: 358). If Hananiah is said in vv. 10, 12 to have broken one yoke belonging to Jeremiah, then what is to be made of the plurality of yokes in v. 13 that Hananiah is said to have broken? Rudolph does his best by explaining these plurals as general plurals, not particularly referring to the yoke Jeremiah had been wearing. That is precisely the 'yoke' that is the issue in Jer 28, and there is no room for an abstract, general reference. Seidl explains the differences in number as 'sprachliche Varianten', the Greek plurals displaying an inner-Greek phenomenon, which is not a very satisfying explanation. Wanke considers the plurals to have been used in reference to the production of yokes, and the singular in reference to the yoke around Jeremiah's neck. Wanke is near the solution to this problem, when he distinguishes between the wearing and producing of the הַמּוֹטָה. The plural in 27:2 refers to the several pegs that Jeremiah was to use in making 'yoke-collars' for the royal messengers (27:3b). The singular forms in 28:10, 12 refer to the particular 'collar' that Jeremiah was wearing himself. The plurals in v. 13 should be understood as pegs of wood and pegs of iron, since they are used in the context of producing them, as in 27:2. See further below, regarding the figurative language used.

g MT+ הַנָּבִיא, and also the second occurrence in v. 10, and the one in v. 11, probably explicative interpolations in the Hebrew text behind MT, see Janzen (1973: 64, 69-70), who apparently overlooked the second occurrence. The same applies to the occurrences in vv. 5, 6, 9.

h LXX+ ἐν ὀφθαλμοῖς παντὸς τοῦ λαοῦ, probably interpolation, inspired by the same expression in vv. 5, 11, so Janzen (1973: 64).

i MT הּוֹ-. This suffix is singular masculine, whereas the מוֹטָה is feminine. The suffix is singular as it should be. The wrong gender can be explained by dittography of the וֹ, so BHS, Rudolph (1968: 178). The scribe mistakenly saw עֹל as the antecedent of the subject. However, Jeremiah is never described as wearing a עֹל, a word that is only used metaphorically for Nebuchadrezzar's oppression.

j M+ כָּל, probably strengthening interpolation to the Hebrew text behind MT and in accordance with כָּל־הָעָם in v. 5, see Janzen (1973: 65-7).

k M+ נְבֻכַדְנֶאצַּר, probably specifying interpolation in the Hebrew text behind MT. The spelling of the name with נ is consistently found in the eight occurrences of the name in Jer 27:6-29:3, and all eight are missing in LXX, see Janzen (1973: 64). This is a clear indication that Jer 27-29 have had a literary history of their own, cf. also Lemke (1966), Overholt (1968).

132

[1] M+ שְׁנָתַיִם יָמִים. בְּעוֹד, probably interpolated in accordance with v. 3, see Janzen (1973: 64: 48), Seidl (1977: 71). A similar MT+ is also עַתָּה מְהֵרָה in 27:16, see Malamat (1975: 137, n32).

Analysis

Literary coherence

Several indications make it quite clear that Jer 27 and 28 share a similar textual history, partly separated from the rest of the book. The subject is substantially the same, the prophetic symbolic act of carrying a collar of a yoke is used metaphorically throughout both chapters, whereas in ch. 28 the issue is more that of false prophecy than the symbolic yoke of the king of Babel. Naturally, the amount of MT+ in these chapters also sets them apart, even in the book of Jeremiah, which throughout shows this dissimilarity.[1] They both share the same historical situation, the coalition that gathered in Jerusalem to spark a rebellion against Nebuchadrezzar.

After the initial divine command to Jeremiah to perform his symbolic act (27:2-3), there follows a summary of what the royal messengers are supposed to tell their masters when they get back, a passage which is quite unique among the prophets in its emphasis on creation theology.[2] Then follows three sermon passages, directed against the people (vv. 8-11), king Zedekiah (vv. 12-15), and the priests (vv. 16-22). Throughout these sermon passages, we find numerous instances of the expressions 'bend one's neck under the yoke of the Babylonian king' (vv. 8, 11, 12) and 'serve him/the king in Babel' (vv. 6, 9, 11, 12, 13, 14, 17). In vv. 11 and 12 the two expressions occur together, making it clear that the second explains the former. Throughout this passage, the symbolic act of Jeremiah is used metaphorically in reference to the submission, or vassal hood under the rule of the king of Babel.

In Jer 28:1, we receive a precise dating, which is more reliable than the dating in 27:1, although MT shows sings of expansion in 28:1 as well. This narrative is set in the fifth month in the fourth year of the reign of Zedekiah. This places us in 594/93. We know from the end of the fragmentary Babylonian chronicle, that Nebuchadrezzar called out his army in Kislev (Dec) of 594 for another expedi-

---

[1] Smith (1908: 103) noted concerning Jer 27 that 'there are not many parts of the OT where the variations of the Greek and Hebrew are so extensive as in Jeremiah.'

[2] Cf. Lemke (1966), Overholt (1968), Lang (1983a), McKane (1989).

tion to Syria.[1] Presumably, it was to put a stop to an anti-Babylonian coalition growing in the west.[2] Two years earlier, in 596/95, the king of Elam had probably attempted to through off 'the yoke of the king in Babel', but with no avail.[3]

As is mostly the case, Jer 27:4-22 have been variously divided into an 'original nucleus' and later redactions. Nicholson sees a nucleus in 27:2-4, 8, with the rest of Jer 27 and 28 being Dtr redaction.[4] Thiel sees a nucleus in 27:2-4, 11, that has suffered a Dtr redaction to make it suit the following ch. 28, which is more or less without Dtr redaction.[5] McKane holds to a similar nucleus in 27:2-4, 11, with a subsequent addition in vv. 5-8, and yet another one in vv. 9-10, 14-18.[6] Hossfeld has a nucleus in 27:2-3, 11; 28:10-14, with a further 'Bearbeitung' in 28:1-9, 15-7, and yet another one in 27:4-10, 12-22.[7] Schreiner sees a nucleus in 27:2-4, 12; 28:2, 3a, 11a*.[8] Holladay would seem to regard both Jer 27 and 28 to stem more or less from Jeremiah,[9] whereas Carroll appears to find nothing that could be called Jeremianic in either chapter.[10] Seidl runs his own race, severely criticising the redaction-critical methodology of Thiel in particular. Seidl finds Jer 27 and 28 to be originally independent of each other, only to have been brought together at a later stage. Seidl sees a host of minor interpolations in the texts of Jer 27 and 28, but nothing that would classify as a redaction.[11]

The purpose of the very brief overview of various alternatives of doing literary criticism on Jer 27-28 above is not meant to be an analysis in itself, but a mere suggestion that some parts are more agreed upon than others. The verses that describe the symbolic act of Jeremiah (Jer 27:2-3) are apparently agreed upon by almost all scholars to be part of an original nucleus, going back to

---

[1] See Grayson (1975: 102), BM 21946, 1 25, *ina* iti*Kislîmi šàr Akkadî*ki *ummāni*me-*[šú id-ke-e-ma]* *[ana* kur*Ḥ]at-lú illik*, 'In the month Kislev the king of Akkad [mustered his] army.' See also Wiseman (1956: 37).

[2] For the particulars regarding the chronology of this event, see Malamat (1975: 135-8), Wiseman (1985: 27, 36). Apart from Jer 27, we have no other indication of this coalition in Jerusalem.

[3] See Grayson (1975: 102), BM 21946, 1 16-20, Malamat (1975: 136), Wiseman (1985: 34).

[4] Nicholson (1970: 95).

[5] Thiel (1981: 5-10).

[6] McKane (1989: 109).

[7] Hossfeld, and Meyer (1973: 90-1, 93, 99).

[8] Schreiner (1987: 5, 9). See also Schreiner (1984).

[9] Holladay (1989: 119, 127).

[10] Carroll (1986: 530, 541).

[11] Seidl (1977: 61, 86-7). Jer 27 without interpolations consists according to Seidl of vv. 1*, 2-6, 7aa, 8-9, 10aa*.ab, 11-13a, 14-16a-e, 18*, 19-20, 22a, and similarly Jer 28, vv. 1a.bc-g, f, 3aa, 4aa.ab.b, 5aa, 6b.ca-b, 7-11a-b.ca.d, 12-14a.ba.bb, 15-17.

Jeremiah. What we find in 27:2-3 is similar to what we have found earlier in descriptions of prophetic symbolic acts, except that there is no description of the actual performance. The interpretation is also difficult to pin down, since the whole of the rest of ch. 27 concerns the meaning of the symbolic act. However, most scholars appear to agree that v. 11 might be more reliably earlier than the prose sermons in which it is imbedded. Most scholars also appear to accept a nucleus around 28:10-11, where a second prophetic symbolic act is performed. Here the description is in third person, and we are, as it were, given an eyewitness account of the dramatic encounter between the two prophets, both strong believers in their cause. 28:10-11 both describes the prophetic symbolic act as well as provides the interpretation through Hananiah's oracle to the people (v. 11). The subsequent encounter between the two prophets is building its figurative language on the prophetic symbolic acts both of them have performed, which is the same relationship that exists in ch. 27 between vv. 2-3 (v. 11?) and the remaining blocks of prose sermon (vv. 4-22).

Performance of the act

The performance of the symbolic act by Jeremiah in 27:2-3 presents some difficulties, particularly as to the terminology involved in its description. Jeremiah is initially commanded to 'make' several מוֹסֵרָה and מוֹטָה and not buy them, as was the case with the jug and the linen girdle (Jer 13, 19). He is then to put them on his neck, presumably as some form of yoke.[1]

The term מוֹסֵר/מוֹסֵרָה[2] is more unequivocal in its meaning of 'band' or 'cord'. It is only used together with מוֹטָה/מוֹט in Nah 1:13 and Jer 27, but earlier in Jer 2:20; 5:5; 30:8, we find the parallelism נתק מוֹסֵרוֹת // שבר על, 'break the yoke' // 'snap the cords'.[3] It would appear be clear from this analysis, then, that מוֹסֵרוֹת should be equated with cords that, while attached to the yoke, tie the ox to the yoke.

---

[1] Friebel (1999: 140) is simply mistaken when he says that Jeremiah was 'commanded to make a yoke (עֹל)', since that word is not even used in vv. 2-3. It seems to be a case of wishful thinking on Friebel's part, who wants to understand what Jeremiah fabricates as a whole yoke, consisting of a pole and cords. When he continues to describe this yoke as 'consisting of a bar (מוטה) and bonds (מוסרות)' he is again completely wrong, since the text uses the plural מֹטוֹת.

[2] The word displays a gender variation, of which the book of Jeremiah appears to favour the feminine, also in Deut 10:6; Nah 1:13; Ps 107:14; Ps 2:3; Job 39:5. The masculine is found in Is 28:22; 58:2; Ps 116:16. The feminine seems to have been favoured in later Biblical Hebrew.

[3] A similar parallelism occurs in Ps 2:3, שלך עבתות // נתק מוֹסֵרוֹת, 'snap the cords' // through away the ropes'.

The more ambiguous term מֹוט/מֹוטָה occurs 19 times in the OT, of which 5 are in Jer 27 and 3 are irrelevant to our present analysis (Ps 55:23; 66:9; 121:3). It is sometimes used for a bearing-pole (Num 4:10, 12; 13:23; 1 Chr 15:15). In Lev 26:13 God says that וָאֶשְׁבֹּר מֹטֹת עֻלְּכֶם, 'I have broken the מֹטֹת of your yoke', presumably referring to something that is part of the yoke. Since the yoke is in singular but the מֹוטָה in plural, one yoke must have had several מֹוטָה. A similar expression can be found in Ez 34:27, אֲנִי יְהוָה בְּשִׁבְרִי אֶת־מֹטֹות עֻלָּם, 'I am Yhwh when I break the מֹטֹת of your yoke', and Ez 30:18, בְּשִׁבְרִי־שָׁם אֶת־מֹטֹות מִצְרַיִם, 'when I break the מֹטֹות of Egypt', a remarkably similar metaphorical expression to the one used in Jer 27-28 (cf. also Nah 1:13).

The word מֹוטָה is also used figuratively, which will be of importance to our present case. In Is 58:6aß, הַתֵּר אֲגֻדֹּות מֹוטָה, 'to undue the cords of the מֹוטָה', the מֹוטָה is in the singular, and is at the same time not said to be attached to a yoke but to cords. Since each מֹוטָה apparently has more than one cord, it can not simply refer to one peg. Furthermore, Is 58:6bß, וְכָל־מֹוטָה תְּנַתֵּקוּ, 'every מֹוטָה you shall snap', is quite unrepentant as to its terminology. The verb (pi) נתק generally occurs in relation to מֹוסֵרָה, 'cords', and never elsewhere with מֹוטָה/מֹוט. The reason is presumably that the emphasis in Is 58:6 lies on the release of the one tied up in bondage, which is why the verbs used earlier in the verse are פתח, 'open', (hi) נתר, 'loosen', (חפשׁי +) שׁלח, 'set free'. When we come to v. 6bß, the thought is still on the cords, and מֹוטָה is used as a synechdoche for the whole construction of two pegs, each with a cord at its end. When the ox broke free, it would involve shattering both pegs and cords, hence the use of נתק, 'snap'. These cords are apparently meant to hold the מֹוטָה in place on the neck of the ox, yet another part of the yoke.

What is then this מֹוטָה, which clearly is differentiated from the yoke, and to which the cords are attached? In descriptions of yokes used by Palestinian peasants at the end of the 19th century, there are pegs of wood driven through a bar, lying cross over the backs of the oxen.[1] The wooden pegs are on either side of the head of the ox, and each of the pegs has a cord attached to it at its lower end. These cords are then tied under the head of the ox, thus creating something that might be described as a 'collar' around the ox's head.[2] Naturally we must leave

---

[1] See Schumacher (1889:), Dalman (1933 (Repr. 1964): 93-105, nr. 29, 33, 41, 42), Turkowski (1969 :29-30, ill b), Galling, and Irwin (1977: 255), King (1993: 161, b).

[2] Note that LXX translates מֹוטָה consistently as κλοιός, 'collar' in Jer 27-28, and does so nowhere else. Holladay (1989: 120) takes this as a clue to the proper interpretation of the Hebrew term, and that may well be. But he fails to note that κλοιός is also used to translate עֹל, 'yoke' 10 times. This means that the translator might just as well have understood מֹוטָה as synonymous with עֹל, as Tg. (ניר) and Syr. (nîr) do.

room for the obvious fact that constructions may have varied and certainly developed, but the basic principles appear to suit the textual evidence.[1]

> Friebel argues that the text describes a different form of yoke, where a pole or crossbar was placed across the back of the ox, and cords were used to fasten this bar either to the horns or around the neck of the ox.[2] We will deal briefly with his arguments.[3]
>
> First, since the word מוֹטָה/מוֹט is used to describe the poles by means of which the ark as well as other items was carried (Num 4:10, 12; 13:23; 1 Chr 15:15), it must refer to a pole and not a peg. However, this is merely a matter of size and nothing else, and therefore the same word could well be used to describe both a larger pole as well as a very similar but smaller peg.
>
> Second, the singular forms of מוֹטָה (28:10, 12) must refer to a singular item, namely a pole. Nevertheless, as was shown above, the most satisfying explanation is that מוֹטָה is used as a synecdoche for the yoke-collar when it is worn. Otherwise, one is left with the insoluble problem of the plural forms, a problem that Friebel prefers to pass by. He actually says that the plural is used when more than one cross-bar is meant,[4] but then Jeremiah made several cross-bars (27:2), and why is Hananiah replacing one cross-bar of wood with several of iron?
>
> Third, Since Hananiah can break the מוֹטָה, it must have been one item and not two pegs. However, it is difficult to follow the logic of this argument. If מוֹטָה is used to describe an item consisting of two pegs, what else could be said? Furthermore, it would take much more strength to break a crossbar than two pegs, let alone carrying it around.
>
> It is obvious that Friebel' unconvincing attempt to understand Jeremiah's construction produces more problems that it solves.

The wooden pegs hold the head close to the bar, and the cords tie the head to the pegs. This 'yoke-collar' would then have been made of wood and cords, and in particular, it would have been rather thin pegs of wood, in comparison with the thick bar across the necks of the oxen. The yoke, עֹל, is then usually a term for the whole construction taken together. The bar is across the neck, the pegs on either side of each ox's head, and the cords at the end of the pegs. If we return to the parallelism שׁבר עֹל // נתק מוֹסֵרוֹת, 'break the yoke' // 'snap the cords', we note that the parallelism is grammatical as to its form (v-o//v'-o'), and synthetic as to its semantics, since it describes two consecutive actions. First, the yoke, at-

---

[1] So also Holladay (1989: 119-20).
[2] See e.g. ANEP 84, 167.
[3] Friebel (1999: 141, n 152).
[4] Friebel (1999: 142, n 155).

taching the ox to the cart or plough, is crushed, and then the cords, attaching the ox to the yoke, are snapped.

If we return to Jer 27-28, we find that in 27:2 Jeremiah is told to fabricate cords and pegs, i.e., he is supposed to make so-called yoke-collars.[1] It is important to note here that Jeremiah is never said to have either made or worn a עֹל, 'yoke', only מוֹטָה/מֹטוֹת.[2] As was concluded above, מוֹטָה could be used as a synecdoche for the whole of the yoke-collar, including the cords, in the sense of part for the whole (cf. Is 58:6, 9). However, that still does not equate the מוֹטָה used as a synecdoche with the yoke itself. The term עֹל, 'yoke', on the other hand, is only used metaphorically in Jer 27-28, in reference to oppression (Jer 27:8, 11, 12; 28:2, 4, 11, 14).[3] In the same sense the act of wearing a collar is symbolically related to submitting to suppression:

יִתֵּן אֶת־צַוָּארוֹ בְּעֹל	'he puts his neck in the yoke' (27:8)
יָבִיא אֶת־צַוָּארוֹ בְּעֹל	'it makes its neck come into the yoke' (27:11)

The expression used here, אֶת־צַוָּארוֹ בְּעֹל נתן/בוא (hiph), shows how the synecdoche works in the opposite direction of yoke to collar, when עֹל, 'yoke' is used as a synecdoche for the collar, in the sense of the whole for a part (so also Is 58:6bß, see above).[4] This leads to the conclusion, that what is actually on display in this symbolic act is not a full-blown yoke, but yoke-collars, that themselves refer synechdochically, or indexically if we speak more properly in semiotic terminology, to the whole of the yoke. The reason for this distinction between the literal collar and the metaphorical yoke was of course that it would have been very hard, if not impossible, for Jeremiah to wear a whole yoke. In addition, it would have involved some difficulties for Hananiah to break an ac-

---

[1] It is important to note here that if מוֹטָה mean 'yoke' in 27:2, it would leave the following reference to 'cords' hanging in the air, since they would obviously have been considered parts of the yoke.

[2] Fabrication: 27:2; 28:13 (2x); wearing: 28:10, 12, see further below.

[3] For the use of עֹל in this metaphorical sense of oppression in the OT and the ancient Near East, see TDOT 11, 72-6 and the further discussion below.

[4] Incidentally, in this expression, the צַוָּאר is used as a synecdoche for the head, since the bar of the yoke is to rest on the back of the neck. The act of putting a yoke on the neck, is mentioned in 28:14, עֹל בַּרְזֶל נָתַתִּי עַל־צַוַּאר, 'a yoke of iron I have put on the neck', and its opposite in 28:11, אֶשְׁבֹּר אֶת־עֹל ... מֵעַל־צַוַּאר, 'I will break (and thus remove) the yoke ... from the neck'.

tual yoke instead of the much lighter collar, hanging around the neck of Jeremiah.[1] Hence the symbolism, accomplished by means of synecdoche.

This figurative language comes to a climax in 28:13, where Jeremiah tells Hananiah that although he has broken עֵץ מוֹטֹת, 'pegs of wood',[2] he has, through his false prophecy, actually created מֹטוֹת בַּרְזֶל, 'pegs of iron' in its place. What is to be made of these plurals, in the light of the use of figurative language that has been shown above? In 27:2, where the context refers to the making (עשׂה) of collars, the plural of מוֹטָה is used in a literal sense, referring to the wooden pegs used to make of the yoke-collar. The same context appears to be relevant in 28:13, since there is a reference to Hananiah making (עשׂה) מֹטוֹת of iron. The reason for the plurals in 28:13 is therefore that מוֹטָה is again used in its literal sense of pegs, driven through the bar of the yoke, and making up the main part of the yoke-collar. The figurative language was changed in v. 13 from synecdoche (28:10, 12) to a literal sense, and from that literal sense to the provocative metaphor in 'yoke-pegs of iron'.[3] This creates a nice inclusio for Jer 27-28; in 27:2, Jeremiah makes pegs for yoke-collars of wood, but in 28:13, Hananiah makes pegs for a quite different yoke-collar, this time made of iron (cf. Deut 28:48).

A further problem that has to do with performance is the antecedent of the suffix of וְשִׁלַּחְתָּם in MT, 'and you shall send them' (27:3).[4] The most natural interpretation would be that the suffix refers to the cords and yoke-pegs mentioned in 27:2. However, most scholars have found grave difficulties with this transla-

---

[1] It is strange to find Friebel (1999: 141, n 152) arguing in the other direction, namely that it would have been easier for Jeremiah to carry a yoke on his neck than a collar made of pegs and cords. It becomes even more unbelievable when he suggests that Jeremiah could actually have made six yokes and carried them all on his neck Friebel (1999: 142)! In the end, however, he at least opens up for the more realistic view that the suffix ם- in Jer 27:3 is secondary, and that Jeremiah only made one yoke, consisting of a pole and cords attached to it Friebel (1999: 140-3). However, the problem he does not deal with then is the plural מֹטוֹת in 27:2. If מוֹטָה refers to a yoke-pole, and Jeremiah only makes one yoke, why then the plural?

[2] Friebel (1999: 142, n 154) wishes to revocalize מֹטֹת into a singular construct, since otherwise only the second holem is written plene. However, the word nowhere else occurs in singular construct, only plural. Furthermore, if Hananiah has broken only one מוֹטָה, what about the ones of iron that Jeremiah says he has replaced them with? And finally, and most severely, what should we make of the statement in v. 13, that Hananiah has made מוֹטָה of iron תַּחְתֵּיהֶן, 'instead of *them*'? Friebel attempts desperately to understand מוֹטָה as a yoke-pole, and therefore each plural form becomes an acute problem. The strange plene-writing is best understood as a later scribal mistake in the form of a hyper-plene writing, not something that would require a revocalisation to a singular form.

[3] For the contemporary associations connected with 'iron', see Sawyer (1983).

[4] See Textual note c.

tion, mostly because they have translated מוֹטָה as yoke-bar or even yoke. As we have shown above, however, 27:2 does not intend to refer to a yoke but a yoke-collar, so the cords and pegs could very well be the antecedent of the suffix. Jeremiah is also told in v. 2 to put the cords and pegs on his neck, using a formulation that will reoccur later in 28:14, וּנְתַתָּם עַל־צַוָּארֶךָ, 'and you shall put them on your neck'. A more serious difficulty appears, though, if we are to understand that Jeremiah only made one yoke-collar for himself. Then we would be forced to understand v. 3 as dispersing the various parts he had used to make the yoke-collar among the royal messengers. Even if he did this, however, he would be without a yoke-collar himself, and that would make 28:10 quite difficult to understand since it clearly presupposes a Jeremiah wearing a yoke-collar in public. We would have to force the interpretation that Jeremiah actually made a new yoke-collar for himself, or even several collars, one for each of the envoys. Yet another alternative would be to see the reference to the royal messengers and the handing over of the cords and pegs to them as a symbolic gesture only. It is impossible to understand, due to the brevity of the text in v. 2-3, if this was something that was performed as a proper prophetic symbolic act or if it was only a symbolic expression, denoting that the threat of the Babylonian yoke was upon all countries in the area, not just Judah. If Jeremiah did go to these royal messengers, he might well have preached something similar to what we have in 27:5-7, and perhaps further until v. 11, although vv. 8f displays traces of Dtr expansions, behind the M+. As far as we know, prophets were not an unfamiliar phenomenon in this cultural context, and it would presumably have been considered the responsibility of the Judahites and Zedekiah in particular to deal with an opposing prophet.

Even though the text-critical issue is a difficult one, the best solution remains to see the suffix as secondary. It was presumably added as an attempt to on the one hand simplify the rather awkward Hebrew expression, and on the other to explain what came of the pegs and cords that Jeremiah put on his neck. What was lacking, and therefore caused this suffix to be added, was the understanding that the pegs and cords together made up a yoke-collar. They were not merely a collection of items that Jeremiah gathered, but the materials out of which he fabricated a collar around his neck. Furthermore, since the text clearly indicates that this collar was to be put around Jeremiah's neck, it would be strange to immediately afterwards state that the parts by means of which the collar was made should be distributed among several envoys. It is therefore better to see an example of the rather common expression PN שלח אל, 'send (a message) to PN', as e.g., Gen 38:25, וְהִיא שָׁלְחָה אֶל־חָמִיהָ, 'she sent (word) to her father-in-law'.[1] However, this also requires revocalising the verb into qal,[2] since there are no examples of this use with the verb in piel. Apparently, the enforced transitivity that belonged to the piel stem required the message to be made more explicit, as in e.g. Mal 2:4, שִׁלַּחְתִּי אֲלֵיכֶם אֵת הַמִּצְוָה הַזֹּאת, 'I have sent this command to you'.

Jeremiah's intention was then to have the envoys deliver the message he was delivering to their respective king, a message they may very well have received both verbally as well as nonverbally.

Symbolic meaning of the act
We have already seen how this symbolic act was understood to symbolize the submission to the Babylonian king, and presumably the cessation of any plans of collective rebellion. We do not have a clear case of an interpretation of the symbolic act as is usually the case, something which must be attributed to the many elaborations that the text has suffered, presumably additions as well as removals, both at an early literary level of Dtr redaction, and later, exemplified by the size of M+ in Jer 27. However, v. 11 seems remarkably unattached to its surrounding context, which might indicate that interpolations have been made between the description of the symbolic act in vv. 2-3 and its interpretation in v. 11. The content of v. 11 seems to be directed to the foreign nations, and so it would be natural to consider this to be at least part of the oracle that Jeremiah delivered to the royal messengers. To succumb to the king of Babel would be a sensible thing to do, since to serve him would be to serve God (v. 6-7). This is in line with the earlier use of the metaphor of breaking the one's yoke (Jer 2:20; 5:5). In these texts the rebellion of the people of old is described as breaking the yoke that God had laid upon them, consisting of the command to serve him as the only true God, and seek his will (cf. Sir 51:26; Matt 11:29-30).[3] This metaphorical use of wearing, submitting to and breaking a yoke is well known from various regions and ages of the ancient Near East.

---

[1] Further examples are Num 22:10, 22:37, Jos 11:1, 1 Sam 20:12, 2 Sam 11:6 etc. It is also found in Jer (23:38, 29:28).

[2] So e.g. HAL 1401.

[3] This dual perspective in the metaphorical use of the yoke, being the obedience to God as the great king, and the oppressive force of a foreign king, persists through time and in later Jewish traditions, see Deutsch (1987: 115-35).

In a late Assyrian fragment of the Atraḫasis epic,[1] we find the following expression; ...] *i ni-iš-bi-ir ni-ra*, 'let us break the yoke!' The corresponding Akkadian expression to the Hebrew is used, *šebēru nîra* // שבר על.

The annals of the Assyrian kings leave ample evidence of the well established expressions 'throw off the yoke of the king', 'bear/submit to the yoke of the king', 'impose a heavy yoke on a people' etc.[2]

In EA 296:39, we read the following declaration; *ni-ri/ḫu-ul-lu*[3] *šarri bêli-ia a-na kišâdi-ia ù ub-ba-lu-šu*, 'I have set the front of the yoke of the king, my lord, on my neck and carry it' (see also 257:15).

In the 'Babylonian Theodicy', we find the following saying; *ša-di-id ni-ir ili lu-ú ba-ḫi sa-di-ir a-kal-šú*, 'He that bears his god's yoke never lacks food, though it be sparse.'[4]

We saw earlier that on the literary level, the yoke-collar was referred to by means of metonymy, or more precisely, synecdoche. This mirrored what was accomplished on the level of performance through the use of indexical symbolism. The yoke-collar symbolized indexically the whole of the yoke, mainly for practical reasons, since Jeremiah could hardly have carried a whole yoke on his shoulders. Being caught in a yoke was then used symbolically in an iconic sense on the level of performance, since it vividly dramatised how the ox was tied to his yoke. The more abstract use of being in someone's yoke as a symbol of being under oppression is iconic with a focus on the effect of the act, i.e., one is totally under someone else's authority and without any ability to act on one's own. There is also a certain amount of conventional force involved in the choice of the image of being in someone's yoke, since we can imagine other similar items of that particular culture that could have carried a similar meaning, e.g. slavery. As a matter of fact, the figurative expression of bringing the neck under the yoke under the Babylonian king is used synonymously in 27:12 with וְעִבְדוּ אֹתוֹ, lit. 'slave for him'. This symbolism must have had the very clear and obvious referential meaning of the threatening oppression of the Babylonian king, whose yoke Jeremiah was referring to by means of his symbolic act.

We have found earlier in Jeremiah's symbolic acts, that there is an element by means of which he breaks the conventional pattern and expectations that are associated with the symbolism involved. The loincloth should be new when he buried it, although one usually would dispose of an item of clothing only when it

---

[1] Lambert, and Millard (1969: 44), l 2. The parallelism in l 1, 'let us kill [him]' leaves no one in doubt as to the meaning of the figurative expression.

[2] CAD N II, 262-3.

[3] Cf. CAD Ḫ, 230, *ḫullu* B.

[4] Lambert (1960: 84), l 240.

142

had been worn out, and the jug was brand new when he smashed it, although one usually would smash pottery that no longer was of any use. Both of these digressions from the expected conventional behaviour must have created a sense of bewilderment in the mind of the viewer. This sense of bewilderment was deliberately manufactured by the prophet in order to pave the way for the new and disturbing message that the prophet meant to communicate by means of his act.

In the case of this act of carrying a yoke-collar, the digression consisted not only in the physical performance of carrying a yoke-collar by a human, which in itself must have been bewildering, although strange acts was expected from a prophet. What was most disturbing, and which is the precise point that Jeremiah is trying to communicate, is the fact that he is under a yoke without being forced into it. The fact that Jeremiah does so willingly is the very item of the symbolic act that must have made the audience react most strongly. Even though we know of no custom, which consisted of forcing a human into something similar to a yoke, one would still easily associate to the ox, which hardly would walk under the yoke of its own free will. On the symbolic level this created the shocking message from Jeremiah that they should willingly bow themselves under the Babylonian king, who is also stated clearly in the interpretation that follows, הָבִיאוּ אֶת־צַוְּארֵיכֶם בְּעֹל מֶלֶךְ־בָּבֶל, 'Bring your necks under the yoke of the king of Babylon' (27:12). One was generally aware of the conventional, figurative language that spoke of 'being under someone's yoke', an expression that might very well have come close to being an idiom, i.e., totally opaque semantically and only used in a primary sense. However, when this quite opaque, yet figurative expression was dramatized by Jeremiah, the expression was revitalized in its secondary, figurative sense by the bewildering act of putting a yoke-collar on a human instead of an ox, and who does so willingly. Jeremiah's intention was to make his audience realize with a new and more intense concreteness what the future would bring for them. More importantly, he wanted them to realize that on the one hand they were unavoidable headed for the yoke of the Babylonian king. On the other hand, though, they could themselves have an impact on how the future would appear, with total destruction or with life, albeit in exile (27:12).[1] Had Jeremiah only settled with using the conventional phraseology of 'being under someone's yoke', he would hardly have managed to create this new and provocative realisation of what submission could mean.

---

[1] Friebel (1999: 141, n 150) is surely incorrect when he argues that Jeremiah thought that the exilic captivity would be avoided if they 'wore the yoke'. Jeremiah saw the exile as unavoidable, but life could be spared if they accepted their fate.

If there is anything to be learned from the earlier overview of various attempts to recover some form of nucleus and later 'Bearbeitungen', it is that it is a highly subjective enterprise. Beyond what we have considered to be reasonably sure Jeremianic or relying on his traditions, i.e., 27:2-3; 28:10-11, there is nothing more we need to know concerning the symbolic meaning of the prophetic act, even if there might be more relevant Jeremianic traditions in ch. 27-28.

The second prophetic symbolic act in this context is performed by a prophet called Hananiah (28:10). Although the description is in the form of an eye-witness report, it is still clear that what we have described here is a prophetic symbolic act, although not performed by a prophet that has achieved canonical status, but one that fell short in the struggle with Jeremiah, or at least that is what Jer 28 asks us to believe. Apparently searching fore something more drastic than words, and knowing that Jeremiah has already been performing his symbolic act, Hananiah decides to perform a prophetic symbolic act of his own. There is no need to question that this was behaviour as natural to Hananiah as it was to Jeremiah. However the distinction between a true and false prophet was thought to have been made in Judah at the time,[1] there is no need to imagine that this also involved a distinction in the use and interpretation of prophetic symbolic acts.[2] Hananiah takes hold of the yoke-collar around Jeremiah's neck and breaks it (v. 10). He then follows the normal procedure in such a case, i.e., he provides the interpretation of the prophetic symbolic act in the form of an oracle from God (v. 11). There is no need to question the tradition regarding this prophetic symbolic act. It is simple, realistic, and may be showing us the cause for the highly developed metaphorical language in Jer 27-28 regarding the submission to the yoke of the king versus breaking it, a metaphorical cluster of expressions that we already have seen were quite well known in other parts of the ancient Near East, besides Judah.[3]

---

[1] It is interesting to see how Jer 28:6-9 applies the deuteronomic law regarding true and false prophets selectively to only oracles of peace, but apparently not to oracles of doom. Whether this should be seen as interpretation or application is a moot point, but it does seem that application more appropriately describes the argument that is being made, see Carroll (1986: 544).

[2] We will not go into the problem of how to understand 28:11b, where Jeremiah is said to simply leave the scene, as if he gave up the struggle in the face of the opposing oracle and symbolic act from Hananiah. For the more general question of true and false prophets and how such a distinction was made, its relation to the cessation of prophecy in postexilic times and its relation to the issue of canonical authority, see Osswald (1962), Zimmerli (1963), Overholt (1970), Crenshaw (1971), Hossfeld, and Meyer (1973), Meyer (1977), Wilson (1980: 249-51), Childs (1985: 133-44), Sanders (1987: 107-15), Sheppard (1988), Coggins (1993).

[3] See TDOT 11, 72-6.

Summary and Conclusions

1. The procedure of the symbolic act consisted for Jeremiah in fabricating a yoke-collar out of pegs and cords, which he was to put around his neck like an ox. This yoke-collar was only part of the conventional form of yoke that is referred to, since the bar through which the pegs were supposed to be driven had to be imagined. As this worked on the literary level through the means of synecdoche, it was accomplished on the level of performance by means of association inherent in indexical symbolism.

2. The act of wearing a yoke-collar symbolized ironically with a focus on the effect how a weaker part submits to a stronger part. In the concrete situation in which Jeremiah performed his act, it clearly symbolized how the people should submit to the Babylonian king, if they were to survive. This was all based on the conventional use of this particular symbolism of wearing, submitting to and breaking a yoke. It is this conventional language that Jeremiah then elaborates upon both verbally as well as nonverbally, in order to come across with his disruptive message.

3. When a human wore an ox's yoke-collar, the oddness of the act lies on the freedom by which the human enters into submission, in opposition to the ox. Jeremiah's message was precisely this, that the people should willingly submit, without a struggle that would cost lives needlessly.

4. Buying a Piece of Land (Jeremiah 32:6-15)

The Text

6 וַיְהִי דְּבַר־יְהוָה אֵל יִרְמִיָהוּ[a]
לֵאמֹר 7 הִנֵּה חֲנַמְאֵל בֶּן־שַׁלֻּם
דֹּדְךָ בָּא אֵלֶיךָ לֵאמֹר קְנֵה לְךָ
אֶת־שָׂדִי אֲשֶׁר בַּעֲנָתוֹת כִּי לְךָ
מִשְׁפַּט הַגְּאֻלָּה לִקְנוֹת 8 וַיָּבֹא
אֵלַי אֶת־שָׂדִי חֲנַמְאֵל בֶּן־דֹּדִי[b]
אֶל־חֲצַר הַמַּטָּרָה וַיֹּאמֶר
אֵלַי קְנֵה נָא אֶת־שָׂדִי[c]
אֲשֶׁר־בַּעֲנָתוֹת אֲשֶׁר
בְּאֶרֶץ בִּנְיָמִין[c] כִּי־לְךָ
מִשְׁפַּט הַיְרֻשָּׁה[d] וּלְךָ הַגְּאֻלָּה
קְנֵה־לָךְ וָאֵדַע כִּי דְבַר־יְהוָה
הוּא 9 וָאֶקְנֶה אֶת־הַשָּׂדֶה
מֵאֵת חֲנַמְאֵל בֶּן־דֹּדִי
וָאֶשְׁקֲלָה־לּוֹ[f] אֶת־הַכֶּסֶף שִׁבְעָה שְׁקָלִים
וַעֲשָׂרָה הַכָּסֶף 10 וָאֶכְתֹּב
בַּסֵּפֶר וָאֶחְתֹּם וָאָעֵד עֵדִים
וָאֶשְׁקֹל הַכֶּסֶף בְּמֹאזְנָיִם
11 וָאֶקַּח אֶת־סֵפֶר הַמִּקְנָה
אֶת־הֶחָתוּם[h] וְאֶת־הַגָּלוּי 12 וָאֶתֵּן[g]
אֶל־בָּרוּךְ בֶּן־נֵרִיָּה בֶּן־מַחְסֵיָה לְעֵינֵי
חֲנַמְאֵל[i] בֶּן־דֹּדִי וּלְעֵינֵי הָעֵדִים
הַכֹּתְבִים בְּסֵפֶר הַמִּקְנָה לְעֵינֵי
הַיְּהוּדִים[k] בַּחֲצַר הַמַּטָּרָה[j]
13 וָאֲצַוֶּה אֶת־בָּרוּךְ לְעֵינֵיהֶם
לֵאמֹר 14 כֹּה־אָמַר יְהוָה צְבָאוֹת[l]
לָקוֹחַ[m] אֵת הַסְּפָרִים הָאֵלֶּה[p] אֵת סֵפֶר הַמִּקְנָה
הַזֶּה[p] אֵת הֶחָתוּם וְאֵת[o] הַגָּלוּי[n]
וּנְתַתָּם[s] בִּכְלִי־חָרֶשׂ לְמַעַן יַעַמְדוּ[q]
יָמִים רַבִּים 15 כִּי כֹה אָמַר
יְהוָה[s] עוֹד יִקָּנוּ בָתִּים וְשָׂדוֹת
וּכְרָמִים[t] בָּאָרֶץ הַזֹּאת

6 The word of Yhwh came to Jeremiah: 7 Hanamel son of your uncle Shallum is coming to say to you, "Buy for yourself my field that is at Anathoth, for the right of redemption by purchase is yours." 8 Then my cousin Hanamel came to me in the court of the guard, and said to me, "Buy my field that is at Anathoth in the land of Benjamin, for the right of possession and redemption is yours; buy it for yourself." I knew this was the word of Yhwh, 9 so I bought the field from my cousin Hanamel, and weighed out to him seventeen shekels of silver. 10 I signed the deed, sealed it, got witnesses, and weighed the money on scales. 11 I took the deed of purchase, the sealed part and the open part, 12 and gave to Baruch, son of Neriah, son of Mahseiah, in the presence of my cousin Hanamel, in the presence of the witnesses who signed the deed of purchase, and in the presence of the Judeans who were in the court of the guard. 13 In their presence I charged Baruch, saying, 14 Thus says Yhwh of hosts: Take this deed of purchase, the sealed part and the open part, and put it in an earthenware jar, so that it may last for a long time. 15 For thus says Yhwh: Houses and fields and vineyards shall again be bought in this land.

Textual notes

[a] MT has been redactionally adapted to suit the new context of having a prelude in vv. 1-5. The accusation by Zedekiah is given an answer from the prophet, thus creating a hinge between vv. 1-5 and the earlier tradition in vv. 6-15. LXX provides the earlier and more reliable text, καὶ λόγος κυρίου ἐγενήθη πρὸς Ιερεμιαν, where no such adaptation has taken place. This is therefore more a case of literary, i.e., redactional history of the text, rather than textual criticism, in the form of MT+. Again, we see how difficult it is to differentiate between the two in the study of the history of the text of Jeremiah.

[b] MT+ כִּדְבַר יְהוָה, emphasising the fulfilment of what God has said previously in v. 7.

[c] LXX has the reverse order Benjamin-Anathoth. However, there seems to be little or no reason to alter MT by taking אֲשֶׁר בְּאֶרֶץ בִּנְיָמִין as a later addition, a 'Randglosse', as is done by e.g. Bright (1965: 235), Rudolph (1968: 208), Janzen (1973: 133), Migsch (1996: 65). This should then have made its way into the text before the two variants made their appearance, probably to foreshadow v. 44. Holladay (1989: 203, 210) suggests the opposite, since 'in Anathoth' has already occurred in v. 7, and is clearly secondary in v. 9, see below. However, the curious variation in order in v. 8 can be attributed to mechanical transmission, and the variation in length between vv. 7 and 8 is probably stylistic. The same variation in length between vv. 7 and 8 can be seen in that v. 7 has only לְךָ מִשְׁפַּט הַגְּאֻלָּה, but v. 8 the more developed and probably also formal language of לְךָ מִשְׁפַּט הַיְרֻשָׁה וּלְךָ הַגְּאֻלָּה. The uncle is apparently given a slightly varied diction from what is found in v. 7. A similar lengthening of 'field', this time due to emphasis, is found in v. 15.

[d] LXX surprisingly interprets, probably correctly, the phrase וּלְךָ הַגְּאֻלָּה as καὶ σὺ πρεσβύτερος, 'and you are old(est)'. The lack of the article, necessary for the superlative, makes it possible that the Hebrew text behind LXX read something like וְאַתָּה זקן, so Migsch (1996: 283-6). There is no doubt, however, that MT is preferable, see Wanke (1989: 267, n 29). Holladay (1989: 210) prefers to view וּלְךָ הַגְּאֻלָּה as a later scribal addition between the lines, and so scarcely readable by the Greek translator. This makes it possible for Holladay to place the following קְנֵה־לָּךְ at the end of v. 7, as the apparently missing divine command to perform the symbolic act. However, this only begs the question whether such a command should be considered obligatory. The question remains why LXX omits קְנֵה־לָּךְ. This could be seen as a MT+, clarifying what the intention of more technical terminology in the previous phrases. However, the formal structure of the whole verse argues against this view, see below on the structure of these verses. The most likely solution is that the decision by the translator to surrender every attempt to translate the previous phrase and instead insert a simplifying interpretation rubbed off on the following phrase as well.

[e] MT+ אֲשֶׁר בַּעֲנָתוֹת, an attempt to conform v. 9 to what has been said in vv. 6-8, so e.g. Janzen (1973: 49), Migsch (1996: 65).

[f] MT+ אֶת־הַכֶּסֶף, a clarifying interpolation.

[g] MT+ אֶת־הַסֵּפֶר הַמִּקְנָה. LXX αὐτό represents an earlier אתו in the Hebrew text behind LXX. This MT+ is therefore taken as an attempt to conform v. 12 to v. 11. This can best be seen from the fact that this expansion created an irregular Hebrew, corrected in Q^{Or},

where the Nomen regens has the article, which is not possible in a construct position. In v. 11, however, the correct form is used.

[h] MT+ הַמִּצְוָה וְהַחֻקִּים, an attempt to emphasize the legal character of the document. The scribe could well have been thinking of Deut 31:26, לָקֹחַ אֵת סֵפֶר הַתּוֹרָה הַזֶּה, 'take this book of the law', and thus added these terms, commonly used for 'commandments', cf. Wacholder (1986), who relates these two texts to *Dam. Doc.* 5.1-6, esp. 1 2, ודויד לא קרא בספר התורה החתום, 'and David did not read the sealed book of the Torah', Charlesworth (1995: 20-1). To relegate the terms to the end of v. 10, so Rudolph (1968: 208), is needless and without support. See Migsch (1996: 66, n 48) for various other explanations.

[i] MT has lost בֶּן־, LXX υἱοῦ, see vv. 6, 9. So e.g. Bright (1965: 236), Holladay (1989: 204). Barthélemy (1986: 694-6) argues strangely in favour for MT, which only goes to show the absurdity of the principle of never allowing for correction of an obviously damaged text. For a needed critique of Barthélemy's text-critical methodology, see Albrektson (1994).

[j] MT+ הַיֹּשְׁבִים, explanatory interpolation.

[k] MT+ כָּל־, emphasising expansion, common to MT+, see Janzen (1973: 66).

[l] MT+ אֱלֹהֵי יִשְׂרָאֵל, filling out to a standard expression, see 25:27, see Janzen (1973: 15), Holladay (1989: 204), Wanke (1989: 269). It is common to regard the full expression as a doublet of what is supposed to come only in v. 15a, so e.g. Bright (1965: 236), Rudolph (1968: 208), Schreiner (1984: 192, n 10). Wanke (1989: 268-9) rejects the possibility of mechanical error because the 'Botenformel' occurs in LXX as well. On the other hand, Wanke regards v. 15 to be an 'interpretierende Fortschreibung' (275) of the original story, but then the argument has turned from textual criticism to literary criticism, see therefore below.

[m] MT+ אֶת־הַסְּפָרִים הָאֵלֶּה, an attempt to clarify that it concerns two documents.

[n] MT+ הַזֶּה, an attempt to harmonize with the earlier expression in v. 14.

[o] MT סֵפֶר, LXX τὸ βιβλίον. Quite early in the transmission of the text a mistake was made in thinking that there were two documents involved, and not a hidden and an open part of the same document, so Janzen (1973: 15), Holladay (1989: 215). For a thorough discussion, see also Porten (1968: 198-9, 213). This mistake is found in both MT and LXX, so the erroneous interpretation must have occurred at an earlier stage than MT+ in the transmission of the text. That סֵפֶר was added later can be seen from the fact that it should be considered part of an attributive phrase, but then it should have been construed with an article, since the following participle is so construed, הֶגָּלוּי. This goes to show that סֵפֶר was added rather mechanically in resemblance to the earlier occurrence of the word in v. 14.

[p] MT וְ. It is likely that this was felt necessary to be added by a later scribe after the addition of סֵפֶר in v. 14, since that lead to the idea of two documents and thus made it necessary for a modal וְ, so Migsch (1996: 68, 168, 249), or possibly 'both ... and' together with the second וְ, so Rudolph (1968: 208). These two additions are methodologically to be found in the grey zone between textual criticism and literary/redaction criticism.

[q] MT+ וְ(יַעֲמְדוּ), another example of the attempt to see two documents, The Greek δια-μείνῃ can be understood as a collective singular, since the subject consists of two ob-

jects in the neuter. Migsch (1996: 72) is strangely inconsistent when he takes this explanation further in seeing the plural to be the only form that existed in Hebrew, while maintaining that there was originally no plural object to the verb וּנְתַן, earlier in v. 14. If the change from singular to plural is allowed by some later scribe in the one case, why not in the other?

ʳ MT+ ם ,-, another expansion with the attempt to clarify that there were two documents. The object is spelled out as the singular αὐτὸ in LXX^{B,L}, giving a different interpretation that the plural in MT, but not necessarily relying on the same in its Hebrew Vorlage. This αὐτὸ is therefore relegated to the apparatus by Ziegler (1957: 369). The plural form is found in LXX^{I} and Syh^{mg}, clearly accommodating MT.

ˢ MT+ צְבָאוֹת אֱלֹהֵי יִשְׂרָאֵל, added in order to comply with the standard phrase. For similar expansions, see e.g. 5:14; 6:6, 9; 7:3, 20, 21; 9:6, 14, 16.

ᵗ LXX has the three words in a different order, ἀγροὶ καὶ οἰκίαι καὶ ἀμπελῶνες. Based on this variation, Holladay (1989: 204) argues that only שָׂדוֹת, 'fields' is original, since that has been the issue so far in ch. 32, and nothing has been said of houses or vineyards. However, this is too weak support to change a text that does not seem to originate with MT+. The mentioning of houses and vineyards on top of fields can simply be a case of expansive language at the climax of the story. The variation in order can easily be attributed to mechanical error.

Analysis

Introduction

Jer 32 has attracted much scholarly attention, due to its apparently complicated history, its mixture of narratives in both first and third person, and its relation to chapters 30-31 and 33, the rest of the 'book of comfort'. We will limit our study to the story of the purchase of the field in vv. 6-15, and so not go into the apparently impossible question whether the following prayer in vv. 16 goes back to Jeremiah or at least his time, or whether it is a Dtr composition from start to finish. In general, scholars seem to agree, however, that the story in vv. 6-15 is authentic in that it describes an incident that occurred and, more particularly, a prophetic symbolic act that Jeremiah performed.

There are of course some scholars who question this assumption, and one in particular is Carroll, who regards the story not as a description of a historical event but 'a paradigmatic account of how the future was secured by Jeremiah the prophet'.[1] There is the obvious problem of the contextual configuration, where the story in vv. 6-15 is prefaced with vv. 1-5, saying that the city is under siege (v. 2). But if the city was under siege, how could Hanamel manage to

---

[1] Carroll (1986: 621).

come into Jerusalem with his offer to Jeremiah? Most scholars prefer to solve this by concluding that the story of the purchase of land has been put in this contextual setting secondarily, and that it actually belongs to a period when there was no siege, or at least when the siege was temporarily lifted. To Carroll, however, this will not do, for two reasons. First, since the story is a positive statement about the future, it belongs to the additions to ch. 30-31. But that in itself provides no reason why the story does not describe an historical incident, only that it was put to use secondarily when positive utterances by the prophet regarding the future were added, if indeed they were. Second, Carroll notes a contrast between the constricted circumstances of the prophet in vv. 1-5, and the freedom by which he 'manipulates the future so as to secure it for the nation'.[1] However, again Carroll refuses to see a qualitative difference between the possible historicity of the story behind the present text, and how it was later put to use in the redaction of ch. 30-33. Carroll goes on to add that since Jeremiah had been on unfriendly terms with the men of Anathoth earlier (11:21-23), it would have been unlikely for him to purchase a field there, to which he would never be able to return. Suddenly the story in ch. 11 is to be taken at face value. More importantly, how much do we know of the prophet's intention with his act, whether it was ever meant to be anything other than purely symbolic? Furthermore, is it possible to rationalize to such an extent that we think we can construe a logical coherence between these two texts that are situated in a book that is admittedly one of the most delicately redacted books in the OT? It would seem that Carroll's reading of vv. 6-15 are very much his own, a result of his highly idiosyncratic reading of the book.[2]

Structure and literary coherence

The common structure of presenting a prophetic symbolic act, *command to perform – performance – oracular interpretation*,[3] does not seem to apply very well to this text. Although this is not a structure of presentation that is always used, it does seem to have been a standardized way of describing these symbolic acts, and perhaps therefore an indication of their particular status and even genre.

The structure of vv. 6-15 is as follows:

1) v. 6   The word of God to Jeremiah, describing the message that Hanamel is bringing.

---

[1] Carroll (1986: 621)

[2] Carroll (1986: 621)

[3] Fohrer (1968).

2) vv7-8	A description by Jeremiah of the meeting between Hanamel and himself.
3) vv. 9-12	A detailed description of the technical procedure of purchasing a piece of land.
4) vv. 13-15	Jeremiah provides the interpretation of the symbolic act as a word of God.

However, the common structure can be found in this text as well, although not as obvious to us as is most often the case. Vv. 9-12 describe the performance of the act, and vv. 13-15 describe the interpretation that Jeremiah provides, as a prophetic utterance. The problem lies with the command to perform the act, since what is given in v. 6 is only a message from God to Jeremiah, saying that Hanamel is coming. The only command at hand is the command by Hanamel, for Jeremiah to buy the piece of land, and it is here that most scholars have failed to see the more nuanced version of the common structure of presenting a prophetic symbolic act. What Hanamel says to Jeremiah in vv. 7-8 leads Jeremiah to remark, as a form of afterthought in v. 8bβ, that this was indeed the word of God. The reason for this was evidently that what was given to Jeremiah in v. 6 occurs later in vv. 7-8. Through the connection between the word of God in v. 6, telling Jeremiah of the coming of Hanamel, and his coming in v. 7, also elevates Hanamel's urging of Jeremiah to buy the land to the status of a divine command.

The phrase at the end of v. 8, וָאֵדַע כִּי דְבַר־יְהוָה הוּא, is meant to be understood as the realisation on Jeremiah's part that Hanamel came as God had told Jeremiah, and therefore Hanamel's message is also a message from God. This realisation can be made clearer by making the phrase subordinated to the following clause, וָאֶקְנֶה אֶת־הַשָּׂדֶה, 'I knew this was the word of Yhwh, so I bought the field ...'.[1] Jeremiah's decision to act in accordance with Hanamel's wish is thereby made explicitly dependent upon his realisation of the divine origin of the exhortation to buy the piece of land.

Legal terminology

In the divine command to Jeremiah (v. 7), as well as in Jeremiah's description of Hanamel's speech (v. 8), there is technical legal terminology and phraseology

---

[1] The ו is conjunctive, specifying a consequence that consists in a different act from that of the previous phrase.

involved, and it is interesting to note that it is substantially the same message in both instances;

1) Exhortation to by the field in Anathoth

2) That Jeremiah should buy the field because
   he is in the particular socio-juridical position
   where he is expected to buy the land.

However, there are nevertheless some interesting variations. The two formulations can be compared as follows:

v 7   כִּי לְךָ מִשְׁפַּט הַגְּאֻלָּה לִקְנוֹת   קְנֵה לְךָ אֶת־שָׂדִי אֲשֶׁר בַּעֲנָתוֹת

v 8   קְנֵה נָא אֶת־שָׂדִי אֲשֶׁר־בַּעֲנָתוֹת אֲשֶׁר בְּאֶרֶץ בִּנְיָמִין כִּי־לְךָ מִשְׁפַּט הַיְרֻשָּׁה וּלְךָ הַגְּאֻלָּה קְנֵה־לָךְ

It is clear from the comparison that Hanamel's own words are more developed and technical than is the more summary version that is given in the form of a divine command to Jeremiah. This is indicated in Hanamel's formulation by the provision of more details, such as the specification of Anathoth being in the land of Benjamin, the more detailed explication of the legal character of the transaction, and the repetition of the exhortation at the end. The regional specification and the repetition of the imperative are examples of a more delicate rhetorical strategy in the composition of the utterance. However, the more detailed legal terminology deserves some further comments.

It is clear from the comparison between the two statements, that the phrases כִּי־לְךָ מִשְׁפַּט הַיְרֻשָּׁה וּלְךָ הַגְּאֻלָּה קְנֵה־לָךְ (v. 6) and כִּי לְךָ מִשְׁפַּט הַגְּאֻלָּה לִקְנוֹת (v. 8) are intended to be more or less equivalent, whether or not they are synonymous remains to be seen.[1] Two things stand out when these phrases are compared. First, the second phrase makes use of יְרֻשָּׁה, 'possession',[2] in the syntactical position where the first phrase has גְּאֻלָּה לִקְנוֹת, namely as a specification to

---

[1] The view of Lohfink (TDOT 6, 376), that since both the terms יְרֻשָּׁה and גְּאֻלָּה occur, they can not have the same meaning, is, apart from being naive, also misleading, since it rules out in advance any possibility of word variation for stylistic reasons.

[2] For the abstract *qĕṭullâ*-form of יְרֻשָּׁה, see Nyberg (1952: 214), and its particular use in legal vocabulary in exilic times, see Mettinger (1971: 11-4). It seems to have escaped scholars how functionally similar this term is to אֲחֻזָּה, 'property'. In an analysis of the canonical distribution of the two terms, we find that whereas אֲחֻזָּה usually in priestly traditions, יְרֻשָּׁה occurs Dtr-traditions. The use of the terms is therefore not based so much on their semantic difference, as on their respective connotations, inherent in the various theological traditions in which the terms have been favoured.

כִּי־לְךָ מִשְׁפָּט, 'For yours is the right of ...'. What is significant is the lack of the verb קנה, 'buy'. This is compensated in the second phrase by the addition of yet another specification, וּלְךָ הַגְּאֻלָּה, 'i.e., yours is the right of redemption'.[1] Second, the first phrase further specifies כִּי־לְךָ מִשְׁפָּט with לִקְנוֹת, 'in order to purchase'. This comparison between the two phrases shows that what is added in Hanamel's case, namely that it is a matter of right of possession, is semantically equivalent with what is specified in God's word to Jeremiah, namely that it is a matter of purchase. But why, then, is the in phraseology different? It is likely that the legal setting, and the conventions governing the customary law surrounding the proceedings in such a case as this, required the particular imperative command, קְנֵה־לָךְ, 'buy for yourself', to function as a climax, and therefore be put at the end of the statement. It had to be specified, nevertheless, that it was a matter of a particular application of the *geullah*-regulation, namely that of ownership rights.

The more extended version from the mouth of Hanamel in v. 8 can best be explained as due to its contextual placement. It is the statement to which the exhortation in v. 6 is pointing to, and is therefore the more important of the two, due to its formal character as part of the proper legal procedure. This emphasis suits the rhetorical function of Hanamel, but would not have been necessary in the divine command, the only purpose of which was to provide a summary of the later exhortation.

The rhetorical structure of Hanamel's exhortation can be compared with a similar phrase in a similar context in Ruth 4. Here Boaz exhorts the unnamed relative of Naomi to קְנֵה, 'buy' Ruth and the land that goes with her (4:4). If he does not, he should notify this publicly. The relative does precisely this when he exhorts Boaz in return to קְנֵה־לָךְ, 'buy for yourself'. I have noted earlier that we find a mingling of two speech forms in Ruth 4, one more formal, using the verb קנה, 'buy', and one less formal, using the verb גאל, 'redeem'.[2] Boaz begins his public confrontation with the relative by using the more formal language, exhorting him to 'buy' (v. 4a). The following discussion then switches between the two forms of speech; an informal acceptance on the relative's part to act as redeemer (v. 4b), a formal specification of the legal circumstances by Boaz whereby he clarifies that should the relative 'buy' Ruth, he must also buy the piece of land (v. 5), an informal dismissal by the relative to act as redeemer un-

---

[1] The ו is disjunctive in specifying what precedes, see Waltke, and O'Connor (1990: 650-1, 652-3). It could even be epexegetical, but the overall analysis would argue against it as creating an all too close semantic equivalence between the two terms.

[2] Viberg (1992: 149-51).

der such circumstances (v. 6), a formal exhortation to Boaz to perform the legal duty instead (v. 8) and a formal acceptance by Boaz to 'buy' (vv. 9-10). The only legally binding phrase that occurs in the text is therefore made by Boaz, using the performative perfect of קנה, קָנִיתִי, 'I hereby buy'.[1] The relative almost never used anything but the less formal speech of 'redeem' in relation to himself, thus not committing himself to any legally binding agreement. The exception is his use of קנה when he waives his right to purchase and hands the right over to Boaz (v. 8), an act that clearly has some legal repercussions.

In Jer 32, we find a similar compound of speech forms, where the formal speech, using קנה, is found in the exhortations, and the informal, using גאל, is found in the specifications of the reason why Jeremiah ought to perform this legal deed. Two things can be deduced from this; first, this only goes to show how deeply rooted the language of Jer 32:6-15 is in the conventional legal procedures of the customary law of ancient Israel. Second, the elaborations in the version by Hanamel was not primarily caused by the need for stylistic variation, although that purpose probably had an effect on the literary composition, but more likely for reasons of adhering to proper procedures of legal formulae. The formal declaration, coming from the mouth of Hanamel, had, on the literary level, as its intended effect to convince the reader of the genuineness of the legal act. This originated from the fact that the utterance functioned in the particular situation of transference of ownership of land in ancient Israel. Through the use of this formal utterance, the author made it possible to associate the prophetic symbolic act with a forceful and conventional utterance, and in that process of association, some of the force of the legal utterance would 'rub off' on the prophetic symbolic act, thus adding to its rhetorical persuasiveness. This associative function of the use of the legal act for the purpose of furthering and strengthening the effectiveness of the prophetic symbolic act can be said to constitute an indexical symbolism inherent in the prophetic symbolic act.

An application of speech-act analysis

The analysis of the force of the formal language can be taken further in applying to it certain categories of speech act theory, namely illocutionary and perlocutionary acts, and with them the terminology that is usually accompanied such an analysis.[2] The distinction between illocutionary and perlocutionary acts and the various forces used to accomplish these acts can fruitfully be applied to the

---

[1] See Campbell (1975: 151), Witzenrath (1975: 255), Waltke, and O'Connor (1990: 488-9).

[2] See e.g. Searle (1969), Austin (1975), Searle (1979), Searle, et al. (1980), Searle, and Vanderveken (1985), Tambiah (1985), Schaller (1988), Houston (1993), Downing (1995).

variation between the force behind the legal act in Jer 32, as well as the force behind the prophetic symbolic act. The illocutionary act is a speech act that consists in the attempt to create a certain conviction, or belief, in the hearer. The illocutionary force is the force, or authority, that is used in order to achieve that conviction in the mind of the hearer. The perlocutionary act, on the other hand, is a speech act that creates certain behaviour, 'perlocutionary effect', on the part of the hearer. The perlocutionary force is the force, or authority, necessary in order to accomplish this perlocutionary act.

If this analysis is applied to this particular nonverbal act of Jeremiah, we can say that the illocutionary act that is accomplished by means of Jeremiah's legal act consists in the fact that his hearers are convinced that he is now the rightful owner of the piece of land, and will be treated as such in the future. The illocutionary act is inherently conventional, since it rests on social conventions, in this case legal conventions in the form of customary law, in order to achieve its aim. The act Jeremiah has performed, by uttering the explicit performative statement 'I hereby buy', is therefore an illocutionary act. The force or authority behind this act is the legal conventions inherent in the customary law concerning transference of ownership of property in ancient Israel.

The symbolic act, on the other hand, has no such force or authority behind itself, and can therefore not be termed illocutionary. Since it can not rely on social conventions in order to achieve its aim, i.e., it can not accomplish an interpersonal, social reality, it has to limit itself to achieving its aim on the individual level, as an intrapersonal reality. On the other hand, the persuasiveness that lies inherent in the symbolic act comes from the association with the legal act. The symbolic act therefore seeks to convince the hearers of its message, but it is not possible to speak of the symbolic act as an illocutionary act, even with a questionable felicitousness,[1] or success. Jeremiah had no conventional authority behind him in performing his symbolic act, which is why he sought instead to create in his hearers an association between the symbolic act and the legal act, since the latter is thoroughly conventional in its legal function. We could even describe the symbolic act as a parasite on the strength of the conventions of the legal act, the strength being above all in its capacity to create a social reality. It is through this association to conventional force, and not through the use of any inherent force of its own, that the symbolic act tries to succeed in its attempt to convince. However, it can never reach beyond the sphere of the prophet himself, consisting of a promise, albeit a divine one. The prophetic symbolic act can therefore be termed a perlocutionary act, with questionable success.

---

[1] A technical term in the area of speech act analysis, see Lyons (1977: 733).

What is apparently missing in Jer 32, is the formal, performative utterance[1] on Jeremiah's behalf, expressing his formal purchase of the piece of land, as in Ruth 4:10, קָנִיתִי, 'I hereby buy'. There seem to be two reasons for this apparent irregularity.

First, the text as we have it in the book of Jeremiah is not a proper legal text, and as such, it need not fulfil the particular requirements demanded by that genre. Instead, it constitutes a dramatic description of a symbolic reuse of a legal act, and in that reuse the prophet, as well as the author on the literary level, can allow himself any amount of freedom in relation to the requirements of the particular genre of legal transactions.

Second, the dramatic description allows for a different and more colourful way of providing the information of the actual purchase. Instead of the formal utterance by Jeremiah, we therefore have the description of the technical manoeuvres in all their details. It is precisely here, in this choice of a dramatic description of the action instead of the formal expression, that we will find the clue to the intention of this prophetic symbolic act. The interpretative principle that we thereby use is to find the marked or deviating items in the language used.

Performance and symbolic meaning of the act
There is no reason to doubt that Jeremiah fulfilled the requirements of the legal act by pronouncing the formal declaration of purchasing the land. However, this appeared so self-evident to the author and his conception of the original, intended reader, that it could be left implicit and replaced with the description of the act instead. This could be accomplished, since the requirements on this text were not those belonging to the genre of legal texts, but those of dramatic and persuasive prophetic discourse. And in this particular genre, there is a particular fondness for dramatic descriptions of symbolic acts performed by the prophets.

In the description of the procedure of the legal act, there are three issues that are particularly emphasized. These three themes are used ironically, or metaphorically on the literary level, for certain central theological themes:

Item in performance		Iconicity symbolized in theology
1) ownership of a piece of land	⇒	1) God's ownership of the land

---

[1] Friebel (1999: 320) speaks of the act of property transfer as a 'performative act'. However, the whole point of a verbal statement being a speech act is that it actually does not accomplish anything, except as a social reality. A physical act, on the other hand, by its very definition accomplishes something. It may be interpreted in its primary or possibly in its secondary sense, but that is another matter.

| 2) removal of evidence of this ownership | ⇒ | 2) the exile as an act of God |
| 3) the return to the land | ⇒ | 3) God's promise of a return to the land |

In order to bring across this message, Jeremiah must have realized how admirably well the legal act served, both in its overall function of securing land, but also in its three basic parts. In his fervour to get his message across to his fellow Judahites, Jeremiah must have seen how close this symbolism resembled the everyday life of his audience. Whoever owns a piece of land strives to use it, and should it be made impossible for a time, the memory of that land and its possibilities would nevertheless be remembered. What could have been considered as breaking the logical argument is the exile. But the beauty of the image of the symbolic act is the fact that the act of putting the scroll out of sight belonged integrally to the performance of the legal act. The act of hiding the scroll was not added by the prophet in a desperate attempt to accommodate his theological intention with the conventional procedure of the legal act, since that would have added little or nothing to the symbolic value and persuasiveness of the prophetic act. The fact that hiding the scroll was inherently part of the conventional act made it possible to use it convincingly in the symbolism of the prophetic act. This is another example of how the prophet seizes upon an everyday conventional act, recognized by all in his audience, and makes use of it in order to bring his message across. We have found the same phenomenon earlier in relation to Jeremiah's acts with the loincloth, the jug and the yoke-collar (Jer 13, 19, 27-28). The conventional is used in order to make the unconventional understood and, more importantly, believed. It is here, in the rhetorical function of the prophetic symbolic act, that we find the most important reason why the prophets made so much use of conventional, legal symbols. These conventions are associated with strong convictions of right and wrong, and behind that, as the guardian of all practise of law in ancient Israel, the God of Israel.

It was not enough for Jeremiah to argue that his word was a word from God, in order to gain the necessary authority, because the social setting was not such that it would have been enough. Doubtless Jeremiah had his devout followers, who needed no such associations with conventional, legal acts to be persuaded of the point in Jeremiah's argument. The prophetic status of Jeremiah as the spokesman of God was to them inherently sufficient to achieve the necessary effect. However, Jeremiah was addressing a context where he could not rely on such a belief in his prophetic status, and had to rely on the possible force that could be gained from the association with the legal symbolic act.

The symbolism involved in this act is basically iconic, since it is meant to pre-figure how the people will once again come back to their land. The iconicity is focused on the procedure as well as the result of the act, namely ownership and separation from one's own land. This prophetic symbolic act stands out in the sense that what is made use of is not a dramatised version of a conventional act, but that very conventional act itself. The piece of land is actually offered to Jeremiah, and his purchase is legitimately his own after the transaction is complete. There is an indexical symbolism involved when the piece of land is meant to stand for the whole of land that will flourish in the future, not only Jeremiah's but also the land at large (v. 15). As has been emphasized above, the act of purchasing the piece of land is thoroughly conventional, both in procedure as well as in the relevant formulations. But for all this conventional status of the act, we again find something odd that does not belong there, and that is when Jeremiah puts away the deed of purchase. It may very well have been understandable as a cautionary act under those circumstances to those who believed Jeremiah, but it was certainly not conventional. It was that part of the symbolic act that broke the conventional pattern and made the audience troubled and opened their minds to the message Jeremiah had prepared for them.

Summary and Conclusions

1. The act of purchasing a piece of land is thoroughly conventional, even at the hands of Jeremiah and also when he performs it as a prophetic symbolic act.

2. The act remains a conventional act of purchasing a piece of land, while at the same time being theologically daring and suggestive when Jeremiah breaks the pattern of the conventional behaviour by putting away the deed of purchase. By this odd behaviour, Jeremiah indicates to his audience that his act is not merely conventional. He, as a prophet, is making use of the conventional act in order to create a symbolism that certainly was nothing near conventional.

3. The symbolism involved in the act is basically iconic, between the purchase of the land by Jeremiah and the future purchases that will be done by returning Judahites. There is also a basic indexical symbolism involved, since the piece of land that Jeremiah purchased stands for all the land, 'houses and fields and vineyards' (v. 15) that will be purchased again in the land.

5. Putting Stones in the Clay (Jeremiah 43:8-10)

The Text

<table>
<tr>
<td>

8 וַיְהִי דְבַר־יְהוָה אֶל־יִרְמְיָהוּ
בְּתַחְפַּנְחֵס לֵאמֹר 9 קַח בְּיָדְךָ
אֲבָנִים גְּדֹלוֹת וּטְמַנְתָּם
בַּמֶּלֶט[a] בַּמַּלְבֵּן אֲשֶׁר בְּפֶתַח
בֵּית־פַּרְעֹה בְּתַחְפַּנְחֵס לְעֵינֵי
אֲנָשִׁים יְהוּדִים 10 וְאָמַרְתָּ[c]
כֹּה־אָמַר יְהוָה[d] הִנְנִי שֹׁלֵחַ וְלָקַחְתִּי
אֶת־נְבוּכַדְרֶאצַּר מֶלֶךְ־בָּבֶל[e] וְשַׂמְתִּי
כִסְאוֹ מִמַּעַל לָאֲבָנִים הָאֵלֶּה אֲשֶׁר
טָמַנְתִּי וְנָטָה אֶת־שַׁפְרִירוֹ[f] עֲלֵיהֶם

</td>
<td>

8 The word of Yhwh came to Jeremiah in Tahpanhes: 9 Take some large stones in your hand, and bury them in the clay pavement at the entrance to Pharaoh's palace in Tahpanhes, in front of the Judeans. 10 Say, 'Thus says Yhwh: I will send for King Nebuchadrezzar of Babylon, and set his throne above these stones that I have buried, and he will spread his awning over them.'

</td>
</tr>
</table>

Textual notes

[a] The word בַּמַּלְבֵּן has usually been considered a doublet or gloss in relation to בַּמֶּלֶט, see e.g. Holladay (1989: 276), McKane (1996: 1054-6). LXX has κατάκρυψον αὐτοὺς ἐν προθύροις ἐν πύλῃ τῆς οἰκίας, leaving out both words. This could be seen as evidence of a MT+, but such a conclusion becomes unlikely for two reasons. First, the Greek text may have suffered a haplography, וּטְמַנְתָּם (בַּמֶּלֶט בַּמַּלְבֵּן אֲשֶׁר) בְּפֶתַח, second, the fragment 4QJer[b], which is commonly considered to adhere to the shorter Hebrew text behind LXX, contains a lacuna at this place that is large enough to have included both words. It is therefore most likely that haplography is the explanation for the minus in LXX, and MT should be retained.

4Qjer[d] I 8 has some further peculiarities in v. 9;

<table>
<tr>
<td>4Qjer[d]:</td>
<td>אשר בפתח בתחפכנחס לעיני</td>
<td>[at least four words]</td>
</tr>
<tr>
<td>MT:</td>
<td colspan="2">בַּמַּלְבֵּן בְּפֶתַח אֲשֶׁר בֵּית־פַּרְעֹה בְּתַחְפַּנְחֵס לְעֵינֵי</td>
</tr>
<tr>
<td>LXX:</td>
<td colspan="2">ἐν προθύροις [ἐν πύλῃ] τῆς οἰκίας Φαραω</td>
</tr>
</table>

The text of 4Qjer[d] seems inverted in relation to MT, since the size of the lacuna suggests that it contains the words בית־פרעה as well as במלבן. The text of 4Qjer[d] appears to have suffered haplography at some stage, בפתח, בתחפנחס (בית־פרעה) and בית־פרעה was added later, but then earlier on the line, thus explaining the size of the lacuna. The preference for MT over 4Qjer[d] is also supported by LXX, although the specification ἐν πύλῃ might very well have been added later, so Ziegler (1957: 432), on the basis that it is omitted in LXX[O,L]. במלבן would then be an explanatory apposition, specifying the clay construction of the floor, possibly with bricks. Together, the two words would then mean 'clay pavement'.

This solution is to be preferred to that of Janzen (1973), who suggests the lacuna contained במלט במלבן בשער בית פרעה, which creates a rather dubious and unlikely text, stating that Jeremiah's act was performed 'at the gate of Pharaoh's house, which was (!) at the entrance in Tahpanhes', see Tov (1992b: 540).

[b] The word מֶלֶט is a hapax legomenon of dubious origin. However, Syr has *mĕlātā*, mortar, clay mixed with sand, see KB, 458, Holladay (1989: 301), and see also above regarding במלבן.

[c] MT+אֲלֵיהֶם, clarifying the addressee of the speech. It is strange that neither Holladay (1989) nor Rudolph (1968) takes any note of this, cf. also McKane (1996: 1050-1).

[d] MT+ צְבָאוֹת אֱלֹהֵי יִשְׂרָאֵל, common expansion to the full form of the expression.

[e] LXX has καὶ θήσει, which could represent ושם את־, preferred by most scholars, e.g. Rudolph (1968: 258), Pohlmann (1978: 160), Holladay (1989: 277), McKane (1996: 1056-7). The same problem occurs later in v. 10, where MT has טָמַנְתִּי, 'I have buried', but LXX has κατέκρυψας, 'you have hidden', cf. Thompson (1980: 670, n 3). If we consider MT to be preferable in both cases, there is a problem with the logic of טָמַנְתִּי, since it is God speaking to the Judeans standing by, yet the verb being in first person suggests that it is Jeremiah speaking. However, LXX is just as problematic, since it has God speaking suddenly to Jeremiah, 'which you (i.e. Jeremiah) have buried'. In the choice between the two, MT would seem preferable. Since LXX can not be relied upon in the second instance, doubts are cast upon its reliability in the first instance as well. There is nothing inherently problematic with MT וְשַׂמְתִּי, and that it would have been created out of ושם את is possible, but in no way necessary. It would be easier to explain how the translator behind LXX preferred to have the verb with the Babylonian king as subject, possibly in line with the later נָטָה, referring to his conquest directly, rather than to explain how the Text behind MT came to have the verb in the first person. The parallelism with the preceding sentence is intact with the first person, 'I will send and take King Nebuchadrezzar ... and I will set his throne above these stones that I have buried.'

[f] MT+ עַבְדִּי, most likely an interpolation as in Jer 27:6, see Janzen (1973: 54-7), Holladay (1989: 276), McKane (1996: 688). On the issue of Nebuchadrezzar as the 'servant of God', see Lemke (1966), Overholt (1968), McKane (1989).

[g] Qere שַׁפְרִירוֹ, hapax legomenon. The Qere is probably created in analogy with Biblical Aramaic שַׁפִּיר, 'beautiful' (Dan 4:9, 18). For a further analysis, se below.

Analysis

Structure and literary coherence

The structure of this story of a prophetic symbolic act is incomplete, in that we only have the command to perform the act (vv. 8-9) and the subsequent oracular interpretation (v. 10). Although this is a deviation from the normal pattern, it is not unusual. What makes it clear that we are supposed to interpret this as another instance of a prophetic symbolic act is the command to perform the act in front of the Judeans (v. 9), the necessary audience to any prophetic symbolic act. What follows in vv. 11ff is a further elaboration in the form of a judgement oracle against Egypt, referring to the oncoming assault by Nebuchadrezzar.

Procedure of the act

The symbolic act is said to be performed by Jeremiah while in Egypt, after he has been forced to emigrate there with rebellious groups from Judah (43:6). His message is clear, though: Egypt will not provide a hiding-place for them, since Nebuchadrezzar will be brought by God himself to Egypt, to conquer the land in his might.

Jeremiah is told to take some large stones, and bury them in the clay pavement at the entrance to Pharaoh's house in Tahpanhes. Since it is highly unlikely that Pharaoh kept a palace so close to the border, the 'house' more probably refers to some form of fort.[1] This would not have presented any difficulties to Jeremiah, since the fort symbolized clearly enough the might and power of Pharaoh, and that was all that was needed for the symbolism of his act to come across. The verb used in describing the act with the stones, טמן, usually means 'hide', and that meaning is probably intended here as well.[2] Jeremiah is to take the large stones and hide them in the soft ground at the entrance to the fort, and we could probably understand the act as burying the stones in the ground. That is what constitutes the prophetic symbolic act, and the following oracular interpretation actually does not explicitly define the symbolic act, but builds on it to describe what is to happen on these stones. It is only in understanding this oracle that we have any possibility of understanding the symbolism involved in the actual symbolic act of burying the large stones.

Symbolic meaning of the act

God declares that he will bring Nebuchadrezzar, and put his throne on top of the large stones (v. 10). The stones have then been understood in various ways, namely as a foundation or pedestal for the throne of the Babylonian king,[3] or simply as a marker for the arrival of Nebuchadrezzar.[4] Since there seem to be no consensus as to what this act is supposed to symbolize, and since there is no

---

[1] See ABD VI, 308-9, Friebel (1999: 351-2, n 615)).
[2] The verb is also used in the description of the symbolic act of hiding the linen cloth in Jer 13:4-7.
[3] So e.g. Buzy (1923: 153), Thompson (1980: 670), Holladay (1989: 302), Stacey (1990: 166), Keown, et al. (1995: 257), McKane (1996: 1055).
[4] So Jones (1992: 480), Friebel (1999: 356-7).

clear interpretation of the act that follows, we will have to focus closely on the text in order to find any clues as to what form of symbolic meaning the act was meant to convey.

To begin with, we have to ask what the stones are meant to convey in terms of being parts of a symbolic act, i.e., what do they symbolize, if anything? Friebel has recently argued that the stones are merely meant to be taken as markers for the place where the throne would be erected. His arguments are, first, that the stones are concealed in the ground, and not erected above ground as a form of visible structure, and the only meaning these concealed stones could have had is that of markers of the site. Second, there is no symbolism involved in the stones themselves, nor to the ground in which they are hidden. Third, there is no symbolism involved in the act of burying the stones. The only relevant symbolism involved is the designation of the specific locale. [1] We will have to deal with these arguments at some length, since they go to the heart of the act itself, whether it is symbolic or not.

First, are the stones merely to be taken as markers of the place where the throne is to be placed? It does seem that Friebel is contradicting himself, since on the one hand he argues that were the stones visible they could have been meant to construe some form of structure, but how can they mark a particular place if they are not visible? In addition, if they can mark a place although invisible since they are buried, why can they not also be part of some form of construction? Also, there is no indication whatsoever in the text to indicate that the stones are meant to mark the place. Second, there is no reason why an act can not be symbolic although the parts that make up the act are not, and I would agree that the stones are meant to be nothing else than stones. Third, it is in the symbolic use of the act of burying the stones that we might find the clue to this prophetic symbolic act.

In ancient Palestine, buildings were erected a foundation buried deep into the ground.[2] Before a wall could be erected, a firm foundation trench had to be dug out, and filled with rough fieldstones. The precise nature of the trench could vary somewhat, but the basic principle was the same, rough stones thrown down into a trench, upon which a wall was subsequently built (see fig. 1, 2).[3] In the light of the practise, we can easily understand what Jeremiah is portraying symbolically by his act.

---

[1] Friebel (1999: 356-7).

[2] Netzer (1992: 17-21).

[3] In 1 Kgs 5:31, 7:10 we have this practise described as part of the description of the building of the temple.

By burying the stones in the ground, he is symbolising the filling of a foundation trench, and from this practise we also learn that the rough fieldstones were not visible, only the bricks of the wall above were, hence the command to 'bury' the stones. The fact that he is told to use 'large' stones can also be seen as part of this symbolism, since a foundation trench was to be filled with larger stones

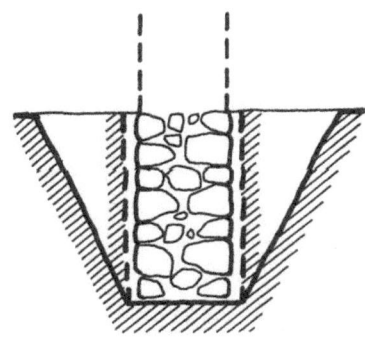

Fig. 1. See Netzer (1992: 19, no 5).

that would remain in place despite the pressure from the wall that would be erected above it. Also, when it is said that Jeremiah buries the large stones in the ground it could well have been understood as mere markers. However, when the stones also appear in the symbolic universe, consisting of the throne that will be set above 'these stones' and the awning that will be spread over 'them' (43:10), it becomes clear that the stones themselves are symbolical, not for some other sub-

stance, but for a particular kind of stones, namely stones that are used to fill up a foundation trench. Upon this symbolically portrayed foundation trench, the

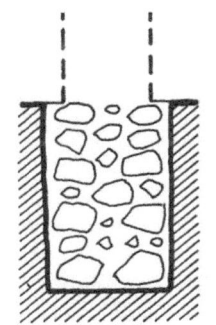

Fig. 2, see Netzer (1992: 19, no 6).

throne was symbolically pictured as residing in a secure and firm fashion, not sinking into the ground but remaining fast. This interpretation, then, eliminates the understanding of the stones as mere markers, and provides a highly relevant and needed symbolism of both the stones as well as the act itself. It is also important to note the idiomatic expression שׂים כסא that is used here, as it occurs with the prepositions ממעל/מעל only here in Jer 43:10 and in Est 3:1, וַיָּשֶׂם אֶת־כִּסְאוֹ מֵעַל כָּל־הַשָּׂרִים, 'and he set his seat over all the officials'.[1] In Jer 49:38 the expression is used with the preposition ב instead of

מעל, although with a similar meaning, וְשַׂמְתִּי כִסְאִי בְעֵילָם, 'I will put my throne in Elam', with the following consequence that 'I will destroy their king and officials, says Yhwh'. A relevant text is also Ps 89:30, וְכִסְאוֹ כִּימֵי שָׁמָיִם · וְשַׂמְתִּי, 'I will establish ... his throne (as long as) the days of heaven'. The idiom clearly

---

[1] There are some variants to this idiom, e.g. הקים כסא על (2 Sam 3:10; 1 Kgs 9:5), הקין הסא על (1 Chr 22:10), and possibly נתן כסא על (2 Kgs 25:28).

denotes a hostile activity against the party upon which the throne is placed, and this suits the present context of Jer 43 very well.

In the following statement (v. 10ba), the stones are referred to as 'the stones which *I* have buried (טְמַנְתִּי)', a choice of person for the verb which has caused some concern, evidently for the Greek translator as well, since LXX has the verb in second person, κατέκρυψας. But that is even more illogical, since God, while addressing the Judeans, would suddenly start to speak directly to Jeremiah. It would therefore be best to retain the first person of MT, and consider this to be a case where not only the words of the prophet are considered to be those of God, but the symbolic acts of the prophets as well. However, it does let us in on yet another part of the symbolic universe of the symbolic act, namely that Jeremiah, in burying the stones, are playing the role of God, who is actively engaged in bringing Nebuchadrezzar to Egypt.[1]

The next statement (v. 10bb) is considerably harder to understand, but since it stands in a parallel relationship to the previous statement, we can find some interpretative help. God now declares that Nebuchadrezzar will 'spread out his שַׁפְרוּר over them', i.e., over the large stones. The word שַׁפְרוּר is a hapax legomenon, and we can only speculate as to its meaning. However, because of the relationship to the prior statement, we can conclude at least that this statement as well must have a hostile sense, probably signifying conquest and rule.

> We can compare with שִׁפְרָה, 'beauty' (Job 26:13), Biblical Aramaic שַׁפִּיר, 'beautiful' (Dan 4:9, 18),[2] and Northwest Semitic *špr*, 'be beautiful', 'radiant', 'glowing'.[3] This can also be traced to Jewish Aramaic צְפַר, 'morning',[4] and Biblical Aramaic (Dan 6:20) שַׁפַרְפָּר, 'dawn',[5] with a reduplication of the last two radicals.[6] The Hebrew term in question has a reduplication of the third radical.[7] Earlier suggestions for this hapax are 1) 'sceptre' < Akkadian *šibirru*, 2) 'throne-carpet', or 3) 'magnificent tent'.[8] What provides the most plausible starting-point is the Akkadian words *šuparruru*, 'spread out' (verbal adjective)/*šuparruru*, 'to spread out'.[9]

---

[1] Against e.g. Friebel (1999: 357).

[2] HAL 1794-5.

[3] HAL 1509, DNWSI 1184-5.

[4] DNWSI 973, ṣpr4.

[5] HAL 1795.

[6] Bauer, and Leander (1927: 193).

[7] Gesenius (1910, §84bm).

[8] HAL 1510.

[9] AHw 1278.

The dawn, beautiful and shining, was apparently seen metaphorically as a covering, or awning,[1] stretched out over the land. Through that metaphorization the covering itself came to stand for the beautiful light of the dawn, and subsequently radiance and beauty.

In order to come closer to the meaning of שַׁפְרוּר in the precise context we must, however, leave etymology behind and look at similar expressions to עֵל [noun] נטה within the OT.

1. The most common is the hostile idiom נטה יד על, 'to stretch out the hand against' (Ex 7:5; Is 7:25; Zeph 1:4 etc). This idiom is used literally in the common description of Moses stretching out his hand/staff, נטה מטה/יד על, as in וַיֵּט מֹשֶׁה אֶת־מַטֵּהוּ עַל־אֶרֶץ מִצְרַיִם, 'and Moses stretched out his staff over the land of Egypt' (Ex 10:13 etc), וַיֹּאמֶר יְהוָה אֶל־מֹשֶׁה נְטֵה יָדְךָ עַל־אֶרֶץ מִצְרַיִם, 'and Yhwh said to Moses, 'stretch out your hand over the land of Egypt'' (Ex 10:12).[2]

2. There is also the expression, although with only one occurrence, נטה אהל על, 'pitch a tent upon' (2 Sam 16:22).

3. An expression with definite mythological allusions to a 'Chaoskampf' is נטה שמים, 'stretch out the heavens' (Jer 10:12; 51:15; Is 44:24; Zech 12:1; Job 9:8 etc). Normally this expression does not have the preposition עַל, but it does occur in the variant נֹטֶה צָפוֹן עַל־תֹּהוּ, 'who stretches out Zaphon[3] over the void' (Job 26:7, cf. Ez 1:22). This expression is based on the literal 'pitch a tent', since the skies were seen metaphorically as an awning, stretched out over the land by God in creation, or even as a net, spread out over the beast in the primeval ocean.[4]

---

[1] This is the choice of McKane (1996: 1057).

[2] The use of יָד in the command and מַטֶּה in the description shows how interchangeable, even synonymous, these variant expressions are bordering on being idiomatic.

[3] For Zaphon, see Pope (1973: 183).

[4] It is interesting that it may very well be the same root in Akkadian s/šaparru, 'net', 'throw-net', CAD S, 161-2, even used for sunrise (p. 162, b.2.c), AHw 1026, '(Götter-)Netz', sa-par nakirî, 'the net for the enemy'. Cf. Enuma Elish IV 41, where Marduk makes a net, sa-pa-ru, to catch Tiamat in. Pope (1973: 185), attempts to see this s/šaparru behind another hapax legomenon of the same root, namely שִׁפְרָה (Job 26:13), but this is highly doubtful, as well as the suggestion by Gordis (1969), Habel (1985: 365), that it should be related to Akkadian šuparruru, 'to spread out'. The meaning of 'net' in Jer 43:10 is out of the question, since spreading a net is otherwise consistently described with פרש in Biblical Hebrew (eg Ez 12:13; Hos 5:1; Ps 140:6).

4. A very different, and highly metaphorical, expression is נטה על NN קו, 'stretch a measuring line upon NN' (2 Kgs 21:13; Is 34:11; Zech 1:16; Job 38:5; Lam 2:8 [no על], cf. also the literal form Is 44:13).

Of these alternatives, 1 and 3 are supported by the comparative material, and 2 indirectly in relation to 3. Alternative 4 lacks any comparative support, and is not in any way relevant in this context.

No 1, stretching out the royal sceptre, would imply the exercising of Nebuchadrezzar's royal authority over this particular dominion, as is implied in the earlier phrase, putting the throne upon the stones. However, the problem with this interpretation is that this expression entails a definite hostile attitude towards the object of the act, in this case the large stones, which would seem unreasonable in this particular instance. There is also the problem with why this apparently very rare word was chosen, instead of the common מַטֶּה (e.g. Ps 110:2).

The problem with 3 is that there are no examples in the OT of that phrase being used in relation to a definite, concrete object, such as the large stones buried by Jeremiah. This could be remedied if the more literal phrase 'pitch a tent' is correct, since Nebuchadrezzar could be expected to set up his royal tent, containing his throne, on the stone foundation that has been prepared by the prophet. This would make a suitable parallel to the prior expression of putting the throne on the stones. Once the throne is in place, it is covered with a tent, or perhaps simply an awning, to make it suitable for the great king. The most likely translation of שַׁפְרוּר, although still speculative, would therefore be 'awning'.

The symbolic value of the prophetic symbolic act is then to form part of a larger drama, involving the arrival of Nebuchadrezzar, and the judgement he is about to implement upon Egypt. As mentioned earlier, the large stones, buried in the ground, are likely to symbolize a firm foundation trench for the throne, which can be termed the iconic symbolism of the large stones. The stones themselves symbolize ironically the rough stones normally used in such an enterprise. The fact that Jeremiah is burying stones denotes the strength and irresistibility that is implied in the arrival of Nebuchadrezzar. Whether this is to be seen in contrast to the surrounding soft ground in which Jeremiah buries his stones is uncertain, since nothing is emphasized in the text to substantiate such a conclusion, however attractive it may be. The soft ground is more likely nothing but a practical reference to where the burying is to take place.

We can also speak of an indexical symbolism of the buried stones, in the sense that the forming of a stone foundation associates to that which is to rest on that foundation, namely the throne, and through that association, further on to the purpose of Nebuchadrezzar's arrival and subsequent judgement on Egypt. It is this indexical symbolism that is the heart of this prophetic symbolic act. Indeed, the overall symbolic drama of preparing a stone foundation, the arrival of the throne and the setting up of the awning, gives rise to indexical symbolism, since it associates to the result or consequence that this preparation will lead to, namely Nebuchadrezzar's judgement on Egypt, which is later spelled out (vv. 11-13). The iconic symbolism involved therefore only serves to enhance the indexical symbolism. That is the overall message of the prophetic symbolic act, the fierce association it brings to mind, without ever referring to it.

A similar case of subtle, yet highly important indexical symbolism can be found in Ex 24:10. When Moses and his followers actually see God, אֵת אֱלֹהֵי יִשְׂרָאֵל וַיִּרְאוּ, 'and they saw the God of Israel', we are suddenly met with a description of the beauty of what God is standing on, 'under his feet there was something like a pavement of sapphire stone, like the very heaven for clearness.' The reason is simply that since the beauty of God could not be described in an iconic sense, that is, through the description of something that could be understood to be an image of God, we are instead given a description of the beauty of God that is based on indexical symbolism. What God is standing upon is associated with God in a very physical sense, and by describing the beauty of that which is near God, God could also be described, although in an indexical sense. As always, a symbolism based on indexical signification is subtler since it requires more of cultural and linguistic competence.

Summary and Conclusions

1. The act of burying large stones in the clay pavement should be understood as a prophetic symbolic act, with a complex symbolic universe that is created by both indexical as well as iconic symbolism.

2. By burying the large stones, Jeremiah is symbolising ironically the building of a foundation trench, as it was conventionally done in ancient Palestine, being able to support the pressure of a large building.

3. The act of burying the stones also functions symbolically in an indexical sense, in that it associates to that which is said to arrive and settle on the foundation, namely the throne of Nebuchadrezzar.

4. This symbolic universe, where Nebuchadrezzar erects his throne on the buried stones, serves further to symbolize indexically the coming attack of Nebuchadrezzar on Egypt, with the consent of God. It is on this, more abstract level of the symbolism of the act that Jeremiah can be said to play the role of God.

6. Sinking the Scroll in the River (Jeremiah 51:59-64)

The Text

59 הַדָּבָר^a אֲשֶׁר־צִוָּה יִרְמְיָהוּ
הַנָּבִיא אֶת־שְׂרָיָה בֶן־נֵרִיָּה
בֶּן־מַחְסֵיָה בְּלֶכְתּוֹ מֵאֵת־צִדְקִיָּהוּ^{a-a}
מֶלֶךְ־יְהוּדָה בָּבֶל בִּשְׁנַת הָרְבִעִית
לְמָלְכוֹ וּשְׂרָיָה שַׂר מְנוּחָה^b
60 וַיִּכְתֹּב יִרְמְיָהוּ אֵת כָּל־הָרָעָה
אֶל־בָּבֶל אֶל־סֵפֶר אֶחָד
אֵת אֲשֶׁר־תָּבוֹא כָּל־הַדְּבָרִים
הָאֵלֶּה הַכְּתֻבִים אֶל־בָּבֶל
61 וַיֹּאמֶר יִרְמְיָהוּ אֶל־שְׂרָיָה
כְּבֹאֲךָ בָבֶל ^cוְרָאִיתָ וְקָרָאתָ^c אֵת
כָּל־הַדְּבָרִים הָאֵלֶּה וְאָמַרְתָּ
62 יְהוָה אַתָּה דִבַּרְתָּ אֶל־הַמָּקוֹם
הַזֶּה לְהַכְרִיתוֹ לְבִלְתִּי הֱיוֹת־בּוֹ
יוֹשֵׁב לְמֵאָדָם וְעַד־בְּהֵמָה
כִּי־שִׁמְמוֹת^d עוֹלָם תִּהְיֶה 63 וְהָיָה
כְּכַלֹּתְךָ לִקְרֹא אֶת־הַסֵּפֶר הַזֶּה
תִּקְשֹׁר עָלָיו אֶבֶן וְהִשְׁלַכְתּוֹ
אֶל־תּוֹךְ פְּרָת 64 וְאָמַרְתָּ כָּכָה
תִּשְׁקַע בָּבֶל וְלֹא־תָקוּם מִפְּנֵי
הָרָעָה אֲשֶׁר אָנֹכִי מֵבִיא עָלֶיהָ^e

59 The word that the prophet Jeremiah commanded to Seraiah son of Neriah son of Mahseiah, as he went from King Zedekiah of Judah to Babylon, in the fourth year of his reign, Seraiah being the tribute-master. 60 Jeremiah wrote in one scroll about all the disasters that would come on Babylon, all these words that are written concerning Babylon. 61 And Jeremiah said to Seraiah: "When you come to Babylon, be sure to read aloud all these words, 62 and say, 'O Yhwh, you yourself threatened to destroy this place so that neither human beings nor animals shall live in it, and it shall be desolate forever.' 63 When you have finished reading this scroll, tie a stone to it, and throw it into the middle of the Euhrates, 64 and say, 'Thus shall Babylon sink, to rise no more, because of the disaster I am bringing on her.'"

Textual notes

a-a MT הַדָּבָר אֲשֶׁר־צִוָּה יִרְמְיָהוּ הַנָּבִיא אֶת־שְׂרָיָה ... בְּלֶכְתּוֹ אֶת־צִדְקִיָּהוּ, 'The word that Jeremiah the prophet commanded Seraiah ... when he went to Zedekiah'. LXX has a somewhat different text, marked by certain pluses, ὁ λόγος ὃν ἐνετείλατο κύριος Ιερεμια τῷ προφήτῃ εἰπεῖν τῷ Σαραια ... ὅτε ἐπορεύετο παρὰ Σεδεκιου, 'The word that the Lord commanded Jeremiah the prophet to speak to Seraiah ... when he went from Zedekiah'. Most scholars would prefer the shorter MT, and consider LXX to be an attempt to mould the account into the more typical form of narrative that describes a prophetic symbolic act, and provide Jeremiah with added divine authorization, see e.g. McKane (1996: 1350f). An interesting case has been made for LXX by Holladay (1989: 432-3), cf. also Keown, et al. (1995: 372). Holladay notes correctly that LXX+ is not to be treated in the book of Jeremiah lightly, and certainly not on the same level as MT+.

He tries to show how the text has been damaged on both sides of a column, affecting two lines of the column;

... הדבר אשר צוה

יהוה את ירמיהו הנביא לאמר אל

שריה בן נריה בן מחסיה בלכתו מ

... את צדקיהו

The text would have suffered damage and made Jeremiah the subject, and the preposition from מאת into את. A damaged text would also solve the problem of finding a convincing reason for the variations between MT and LXX, particularly between the prepositions. However, what finally decides against the reading of MT is the obscure Hebrew formulation that would have to be reconstructed, since the verb צוה is never used with a second object, in the sense of 'command PN to VERB ...', so Stipp (1994: 163). The standard formulation can be found in e.g. Jer 36:5.

As for MT ־אֶת, 'with', LXX παρά, 'from', it should be noted that the historical sources in the OT are silent as to a journey by Zedekiah to Babylon, presumably shortly after the collapse of the anti-Babylonian coalition (cf.Jer 27), and the Babylonian chronicle is not available for this period. It is more likely that a מ has been lost in the transmission of the text which we have already concluded has been complex, and the preposition ־אל was read instead. LXX therefore has the preferable reading, so e.g. Rudolph (1968: 316), Holladay (1989: 432), Keown, et al. (1995: 357).

[b] MT מְנוּחָה, 'resting place', a title otherwise unheard of; LXX δώρων (מנחות), 'tribute', so also Tg. תוקרבא, which makes more sense in the context. The mistake of reading מנוחה instead of מנחות occurred after the mistake of reading את instead of מאת, since then the task for Seraiah was thought to have been related to his task of accompanying Zedekiah in person. The words could easily have been read wrongly if they had been written defective. LXX is preferable, in describing Seraiah as 'head of tribute', and it was in that role that he was sent by Zedekiah to Babylon to pay the outstanding tribute, so Rudolph (1968: 316), Holladay (1989: 432), Keown, et al. (1995: 357), Friebel (1999f: 154-5, n 182).

[c] An unusual idiom, with ראה as an added emphasis to קרא, lit. 'See (to it that) you read aloud ...', cf. Ex 25:40, וּרְאֵה וַעֲשֵׂה, lit 'see (to it that) you make ...'.

[d] LXX ἀφανισμὸς. The word שְׁמָמוֹת also occurs in Jer 25:12; 51:26; Ez 35:9. All four occurrences are described as עוֹלָם, they are all treated as singulars by LXX, and so the 'plurals' are sometimes amended into the singular שְׁמָמָה, e.g. Holladay (1989: 432). However, both the Greek and the Hebrew are correct, since שְׁמָמוֹת is most likely an intensive use of the feminine plural of the noun שְׁמָמָה, Gesenius (1910, §124a, d-e). A less likely, but still possible explanation is that שְׁמָמוֹת is an abstract nominalization of the adjective שָׁמֵם, in order to express deeds characterized by that adjective, Nyberg (1952: 202) §73z, see Thompson (1980: 770, n 3).

[e] MT+ וְיָעֵפוּ עַד־הֵנָּה דִּבְרֵי יִרְמְיָהוּ, a late redactional comment. There is a possible indication here that the oracles against Babylon (50:1-51:58) ended with this phrase in the Hebrew tradition, since 51:58 ends with וְיָעֵפוּ. The lack of this accommodative phrase in LXX, together with another structural placing of the oracles against Babylon (27:1-28:58), indicate, however, that the Greek tradition preserves a more genuine, or at least older, structure of the book. Bogaert (1981: 170) and Reimer (1993: 250-1) argue simi-

larly that v. 64b was added after the restructuring of the oracles, but they fail to provide any explanation as to why this would have been done. It would seem, however, to be more explainable to see this redactional comment as an end to the original collection of oracles against the nations in its original position at the beginning of the book, thus as the counterpart to the introductory phrase דִּבְרֵי יִרְמְיָהוּ (Jer 1:1). Then, when the oracles were moved away from this position, the phrase lost its function as part of an inclusio, so Huwyler (1997: 380). The problem as to the apparent continuation of the description of the oracle to be delivered by Seraiah in v. 64b is best seen as a redactional attempt to accommodate the new ending with the end of the description of the act.

Analysis

This brief narrative, at the end of the oracles against Babylon, describes, according to the textual tradition behind MT, the last saying of Jeremiah in the book. It is surprising to find the narrative here, somewhat similar to the narrative concerning Amos at Bethel (Amos 7:10-17). It is clearly a redactional attempt to connect the story about the oracle of doom that Jeremiah sent to Babylon with the extensive oracles in 50:1-51:58.

Structure and literary coherence
The structure of this story is as follows;

> 1) v. 59; Summary introduction, setting the stage and describing the participants.
> 2) v. 60; Parenthetical comment, relating the story to the preceding oracles against Babylon (50:1-51:58).
> 3) vv. 61-64; Jeremiah's instructions to Seraiah
>   a) v. 61; Jeremiah's instruction to Seraiah to read his oracles against Babylon
>   b) v. 62; Jeremiah provides Seraiah with a suitable prayer, to introduce the prophetic symbolic act.
>   c) v. 63; Jeremiah describes the performance of the act Seraiah is to perform after having read the scroll.
>   d) v. 64; Jeremiah provides Seraiah with the interpretation his is to utter in the form of an oracle.[1]

There are three questions that are clearly on the agenda when dealing with Jer 51:59-64. First, what is the state of the literary coherence of the text? Second,

---

[1] As was mentioned above in the *Textual notes*, v. 64b is best taken as a later, redactional comment, marking the canonical, if not chronological, end to the words of Jeremiah in the textual tradition behind MT.

does the story go back to Jeremiah and a command that he actually gave Seraiah, and third, how does this negative evaluation of Babylon square with the positive attitude earlier in the book (e.g. 29:4-23).

When it comes to literary coherence, we note that according to v. 60, Jeremiah wrote down all the misfortunes that would befall Babylon אֶל־סֵפֶר אֶחָד, 'in one scroll'. The reason for the emphasis in v. 60 on אֶחָד, 'one', scroll is unclear, however. Does it mean 'one particular' in a specifying sense, as in e.g. 1 Sam 1:1, וַיְהִי אִישׁ אֶחָד, 'there was *a certain* man', or 'only one' in the limitative sense of 'not several', as in e.g. 1 Kgs 4:19, וּנְצִיב אֶחָד אֲשֶׁר בָּאָרֶץ, 'there was *only one* official in the land'?[1] The latter could be understood in the sense of relating to the preceding oracles, and saying that there was only one scroll that Jeremiah handed over to Seraiah, as if the oracles would have been expected to demand several scrolls, and perhaps it would have been unlikely that they would all have been sunk by one stone. However, this interpretation appears rather strained. It is simpler to see a reference to *a certain* scroll, namely the scroll that Jeremiah later was to hand over to Seraiah. This particular scroll is said to have contained a description of all the disasters that would come upon Babylon (v. 60a). This reference forward is natural, since bringing the scroll to Babylon and performing the prophetic symbolic act is the thrust of this whole story.

It is likely that later, when this story was attached to the oracles against Babylon (50:1-51:58), the editor behind this redaction attempted to connect the scroll written by Jeremiah with the preceding oracles, by means of adding v. 60b.[2] A further argument for the secondary status of v. 60b is the formulation הַכְּתֻבִים, 'had been written'. This passive construction is significant, and displays the redactor's awareness that the earlier oracles had a separate origin, at least as a final collection, than the story in 51:59-64. Otherwise, it would have been quite easy to simply say, 'all the words which Jeremiah spoke ...'. If the reference to

---

[1] In the specifying sense אֶחָד functions as an attributive adjective, marking an indefinite noun, Waltke, and O'Connor (1990: 251, 273-4). For the limitative sense, see Waltke, and O'Connor (1990: 274).

[2] So e.g. Bright (1965: 210), and McKane (1996: 1353-4) with further references. Despite his thorough review of scholarship, however, McKane still provides no convincing arguments for his own position, that 51:59-64 is not historical, but a late 'midrash'. Holladay (1989: 433-4) argues that v. 60b is authentic, although he fails to explain how this could have been accomplished on one singe scroll. However, it is not correct to label v. 60b a 'gloss', since it does form an integrated part of the redacted whole as we now have it. It is not a comment in the marginal, but serves to connect 50:1-51:58 with 51:59-64, and this is too much for a gloss. It is therefore not a matter of textual criticism but of redaction history, which makes one wonder why McKane (1996: 1350) deletes it from his translation of the passage. This redactor could well have stood in a deuteronomistic tradition.

כָּל־הַדְּבָרִים הָאֵלֶּה, 'all these words' is secondary in v. 60b, what about its use in v. 61, which in the present text clearly refers to what has been mentioned earlier in v. 60b? In v. 60a, Jeremiah is said to have written in a סֵפֶר, 'scroll', and that is also the case in v. 63, when Seraiah is told what to do when he has finished reading אֶת־הַסֵּפֶר הַזֶּה, 'this scroll'. It is possible that the redactor behind v. 60b also changed a reference to אֶת־הַסֵּפֶר in v. 61 into a terminology of his own, כָּל־הַדְּבָרִים הָאֵלֶּה, thus clarifying the connection both between vv. 60 and 61, as well as to the preceding oracles.

This would strengthen the view that the story in 51:59-64 had an independent history, as far as its present literary context is concerned. If this story had been created de novo to fit the collection of oracles, there would have been no need to make this rather forced accommodation to the preceding oracles.

Does the description of the act go back to a command from Jeremiah to Seraiah? Since we are not told in this story whether Seraiah actually performed the act, all we can ask is whether it could have been possible, or indeed reasonable, for Jeremiah to require such a thing from him. What Jeremiah asks Seraiah to do, is to bring a scroll with him to Babylon, proclaim what appears to be a summary oracle against Babylon, tie a stone to the scroll, and throw it into the Euphrates, while uttering yet another summary oracle, more specifically related to the symbolism of the act. As has been argued in the *Textual notes* above, the best reading of the text is to follow LXX, and not see a reference to a visit by king Zedekiah to Babylon, but that Seraiah acted as part of a group sent by the king. Seraiah had the office of 'tribute-master', i.e., he was in charge of the tribute to the imperial king. Since Seraiah is said to be the son of Neriah,[1] probably the father of Jeremiah's scribe Baruch as well (Jer 32:12 etc), Jeremiah is entrusting the task of performing the prophetic symbolic act to the brother of his personal scribe. It is also likely that Seraiah himself was a scribe, since this was often a family tradition.[2] There is nothing inherently improbable about this arrangement, and McKane's view, that it would have been unsuitable for a man in that position to start prophesying and performing a prophetic symbolic act, is anachronistic, to say the least. The truth is that we know nothing of what Seraiah could or could not have been expected to do while in Babylon, and as to what would have been considered suitable, it might be that both Jeremiah and Seraiah would have been excluded from modern day diplomatic circles, but that is not a

---

[1] This is probably confirmed by a bulla of unknown origin, dated to the 7th century B.C.; לשׁריהו נריהו, 'belonging to Seraiah, (son of) Neriah', Davies (1991: 230), 100.781; Avigad (1978).

[2] See Lundbom (1986: 102) with further references, and Dearman (1990).

relevant argument.[1] As far as redaction history is concerned, we can note that the somewhat awkward placing of the story is not original at the end of the book, since LXX has it as the end of the oracles against Babylon in the middle of the book.[2] As the story stands today, it serves the function of providing closure to the book as a whole. However, it is inconceivable that Jeremiah would have ended his office as prophet already in 594 BC. The canonical concerns have thereby been seen to weigh more heavily that the chronological coherency of the story of the book at large.[3]

The third issue is subtler. Is it possible for us to see 51:59-64 as going back to a prophet, who emphasized so strongly that Babylon was the instrument of God, and therefore not to be resisted by Judah (29:4-23)?[4] Behind the view that this could not be the case, lies a misunderstanding of the rhetorical or strategic purpose behind Jeremiah's emphasis on the role of Babylon in God's plan regarding Judah. There is no question regarding Jeremiah's view as to the final downfall of Babylon (25:12-4; 27:7; 29:10).[5] But for the sake of being able to convince those who have been taken in exile, that it has been in accordance with God's will, Jeremiah is emphasising the role of Babylon as a role written by

---

[1] McKane (1996: 1355), '... a statesman who was Zedekiah's adviser or one of his coterie of advisers at a crucial confrontation in a foreign land could hardly afford the luxury of the prophetic diversion which is attributed to him.' It is deplorable that McKane can rely on such superficial argumentation. If those scholars who advocate the historicity of the story display their tendency in saying that the oracle was pronounced in private by Seraiah, so as not to disturb his official function, then McKane is displaying an equally strong tendency by relying on such weak arguments for his dismissal of the historicity of the story, McKane (1996: 1356).

[2] See Gosse (1986), who notes correctly that the later redactional activity behind MT, as opposed to the Hebrew text behind LXX, emphasizes the oracles of doom directed against Babylon, since this had by that time come true. Whether oracles against Judah were later transformed into oracles against Babylon is, however, to take this beyond plausibility. See also Gosse (1994), Gosse (1996). A similar line of arguing, and even less likely, can be found in Paterson (1984). There is simply no reason to postulate that the act was originally intended as the opposite to what we now have in our text, namely an act directed against the prophets who opposed Babylon.

[3] See Brueggemann (1991: 281).

[4] Scholars answering no are e.g. Carroll (1986: 816), McKane (1996: 1358), those answering yes are e.g. Bright (1965: 212), Thompson (1980: 770-1), Jones (1992: 546), and, perhaps most forcefully, Holladay (1989: 434).

[5] It is worth noting how the short reference to the future downfall of the kingdom in 25:12-3[LXX] is expanded in MT with unambiguous references to the king being the Babylonian king, as v. 9 was clarified with a reference to the Babylonian king Nebuchadnezzar. This is clearly part of the redactional process, which made MT something of a second edition of the Hebrew text behind LXX.

God, as well as it provides him with a strong condemnation of those who insists on remaining in Judah (29:15-23). It should not be taken as a statement in a non-contextualised sense on how Jeremiah viewed Babylon, but in the highly limited context of attempting to provide arguments for his rhetorical strategy.[1] Put simply, just because God makes Babylon do something right, does not mean the empire is altogether good. The oracles against Babylon (50:1-51:58), that have been edited and expanded in successive stages, could very well go back in some microcosmic form to Jeremiah, who would then have declared his more profound view of the empire, regardless of what was required of him in a particular historical situation. It is likely that most of these oracles are the products of a later, exilic 'Jeremiah-school', which tried to contextualise the message of Jeremiah in a later day. Even then, it would make no sense if these oracles did not in some way originate with Jeremiah himself. There is thus nothing inherently improbable concerning this apparent inconsistency on behalf of the prophet.[2] It should also be noted, that Jeremiah is not proclaiming this on the streets of Jerusalem, which definitely would have created the problems that McKane and Carroll discuss. Instead, he is sending this oracle in a diplomatic pouch, to be pronounced in summary in Babylon, which is a quite different context with a different audience, requiring a message particular to that audience and situation.

Performance of the act

Of the three standard parts of a story that relates a prophetic symbolic act, namely divine command to perform the act, descriptions of the performance, and an interpretation of the act in the form of an oracle, we only find the first (v. 63) and the third (v. 64). There is no reference to the actual performance of the act, so we are left completely in the dark as to whether the act was actually performed by Seraiah in Babylon, or even if the story itself intends to say that it was performed. However, it appears reasonable, based on the story itself, that the act was intended to be performed, and its performance is reasonable enough to be accomplished. As far as the question why the description of the perform-

---

[1] See Keown, et al. (1995: 364).

[2] Scholars who deny the prophet anything more than one view regardless of the historical setting displays a deplorable rationalistic and reductionistic attitude. This could also be called anachronistic, since it would make sense in modern book writing, but hardly in the ancient times, since the very concept of 'book' is anachronistic. Since the redaction of the book of Jeremiah as we now have it is the product of a long process of redaction in various stages, some doubtless going back to the time of Jeremiah and some not, the fact that the final text can display apparently different views becomes quite probable.

ance is not given, we can only speculate. It might be as simple as that the story was kept and written down in Judah, and no information was received as to whether the act had been performed or not. It could also be for economical reasons, i.e., it was felt unnecessary to include a description of the act both in the command section as well as in a section describing the actual performance of the act.

Something that also complicates the identification of a prophetic symbolic act in this story is the lack of any reference to an audience. One could conclude that by implication Babylon stands for the community of exiled Judahites living there, but there is no way of verifying such a hypothesis. The reading of the summaries provided by Jeremiah is not prescribed to be done by Seraiah in the presence of any form of audience. The only possible indication of an audience is the emphasis on the act of reading, both before the act (v. 61-2), as well as simultaneous with the nonverbal act. It is also emphasized that Seraiah is to make perfectly sure that the scroll was read aloud because of the choice of the verb קרא, 'call' or 'shout', וְרָאִיתָ וְקָרָאתָ, 'be sure to read aloud'. In the end, we can only conclude that this is another factor which complicates the interpretation of this story, and which casts some suspicion on the character of the act as a prophetic symbolic act.

Symbolic meaning of the act

Seraiah is told to tie the scroll to a stone after reading it, and to throw it into the Euphrates. The description of the act seems clear enough, and its interpretation equally so (51:64). The sinking seems to symbolize the fall of the Babylonian kingdom, and the definite destruction of the kingdom, וְלֹא־תָקוּם, 'to rise no more', is as sure as that the stone will not float up to the surface of the Euphrates. The reason for the downfall of the kingdom as given in the interpretation, is that it suffers from the disaster brought upon it by God. However, if the stone is meant to symbolize the kingdom, then the symbolism of the cause for the downfall is contrary to the interpretation, since the stone draws the scroll with the oracles of doom to the bottom, and not vice versa. We must conclude, therefore, that there does not seem to be any clear iconic or indexical symbolism related to the stone. Whether there is any conventional symbolism related to the stone is something we will return to below.

But what about the scroll? Friebel has recently argued that the scroll stood figuratively for Babylon, and the sinking for the fate of the city.[1] Indeed, if we work a priori on the assumption that the scroll, or the stone, must symbolize

---

[1] Friebel (1999: 160).

something by itself, then of course Babylon is the obvious choice. However, the problem is that the text does not support such a simple and straightforward interpretation. The text simply states, that כָּכָה תִּשְׁקַע בָּבֶל, 'thus shall Babylon sink', which only draws the analogy between the sinking as an event and the demise of Babylon. Friebel also notes this quite correctly, but he fails to find support for his notion that not only the act, but also the scroll thrown into the water is symbolically relevant.[1] If anything, it is the stone tied to the scroll that would make the best candidate for being a symbol for Babylon, but this is ruled out by Friebel. However, in v. 64 it says clearly that Babylon will sink because of the disaster that God will bring on her, and these disasters are described by Jeremiah in the scroll (v. 60).

There is an interesting parallel phrase in 2 Kgs 22:16, where it is also a matter of a scroll that contains the words of Jeremiah but has been read by someone else, this time by the king of Judah. The prophetess Huldah declares;

כֹּה אָמַר יְהוָה הִנְנִי מֵבִיא רָעָה	Thus says Yhwh, I will bring disaster[2] on
אֶל־הַמָּקוֹם הַזֶּה וְעַל־יֹשְׁבָיו	this place and on its inhabitants, *according*
אֵת כָּל־דִּבְרֵי הַסֵּפֶר אֲשֶׁר	*to* all the words of the book that the king
קָרָא מֶלֶךְ יְהוּדָה	of Judah has read.

The phrase אֵת כָּל־דִּבְרֵי הַסֵּפֶר defines the bringing of רָעָה as what is described in the scroll. The object marker אֵת functions here in an unusual adverbial sense of limitation or specification.[3] This bears a striking similarity with Jer 51:64, and we can use the similar phraseology to conclude that the רָעָה in v. 64 is described and to some extent made synonymous with the scroll. This is also brought out by a similar use of the object marker in v. 60, וַיִּכְתֹּב יִרְמְיָהוּ אֵת כָּל־הָרָעָה .. אֶל־סֵפֶר, Jeremiah wrote in a scroll *about* all the disasters ... in a scroll'.

There is, therefore, a case of indexical symbolism related to the scroll, in the sense that the message it contains relates by means of association to the disaster that the message describes. However, this indexical symbolism is subtle, and subordinate to the symbolism of the act itself.[4]

---

[1] Friebel (1999: 159-61).

[2] See Jer 51:64 for the phrase הֵבִיא רָעָה אֶל, so typical of the Deuteronomistic phraseology in the book of Jeremiah, 2 Sam 17:14, 1 Kgs 9:9, 14:10, 21:1 et al.

[3] See Waltke, and O'Connor (1990: 181).

[4] On the literary level, this is a case of metonymy.

Besides trying to find a rather peripheral symbolic meaning to the particular items, we should expect the very act of throwing a stone into the deep waters to carry some important symbolic meaning. In addition, the background in tradi- tional Israelite imagery to this act is to be found in Ex 15:4-5. It is surprising that scholars have usually not taken this text into consideration when they have sought for the symbolic value of this prophetic symbolic act. In Ex 15, we find the victory song of the Israelites, after the safe passage through the dangerous waters. The enemies, on the other hand, have been יָרָה בַיָּם, 'thrown into the sea', טֻבְּעוּ בְיַם־סוּף, 'sunk in the sea of reeds' (v. 4), and, more particularly in relation to Jer 51:63-4, יָרְדוּ בִמְצוֹלֹת כְּמוֹ־אָבֶן, 'they went down into the depths *like a stone*' (v. 5). It is likely that the imagery behind the prophetic symbolic act in this case is based on the formulation regarding the divine wrath shown upon the Egyptians. God is said to 'throw' the Egyptians into the sea, and they are said to sink 'like a stone', a simile which forms an intertextual link to Jer 51:63-4 that is hard to overlook. One possible objection would be that whereas Jer 51:63 uses the verb שלך (hiph) for 'throw', Ex 15:4 uses יָרָה. However, it is noteworthy that we find yet another reference to the downfall of the Egyptians in Neh 9:11, וְאֶת־רֹדְפֵיהֶם הִשְׁלַכְתָּ בִמְצוֹלֹת כְּמוֹ־אֶבֶן, 'You threw their persecutors into the depths *like a stone*', a reference apparently unnoticed so far.[1] Both Jer 51:63 and Neh 9:11 display the prevalence for שלך (hiph) for 'throw', instead of יָרָה,[2] which is likely to mean that the formulation of the old tradition had gone through a ter- minological transformation. This shows that the imagery behind the act is the tradition regarding the divine wrath upon the Egyptians, as told in Ex 15:4-5, and in particular the simile, כְּמוֹ־אֶבֶן, 'as a stone'.

In trying to explain the various forms of symbolism that are involved in the description of the symbolic act more systematically, we must pursue the relation between Jer 51:63-4 and the tradition in Ex 15. This is yet another example of how the prophet uses well-known traditions and symbols in his rhetorical strat- egy, searching for his much needed authority and persuasiveness. This process of symbolization can be divided into the following stages;

1. The persuasive strength, or illocutionary force, of the nonverbal act is founded on a particular conventional imagery, namely that God throws his ene- mies into waters as stones (Ex 15:4-5). The choice of 'stone' is arbitrary, as it is

---

[1] Williamson (1985: 313) describes Neh 9:9-11 as 'almost a pastiche of quotations from the Exodus account'. Brueggemann (1991: 283, n 87), who notes the allusion to Ex 15:4-10 and the different verbs, fails to take Neh 9:11 into account.

[2] The verb ירה does not occur in either Jeremiah or Ezekiel.

chosen simply because of its weight, and because most people would be able to identify with how inevitable it is that the stone will sink. This conventional imagery is based on an iconic symbolism, or simile, 'as a stone'.

2. This conventional imagery is meant to be brought to mind by the use of the iconic symbolism of the act in Jer 51:63-4, an iconic symbolism that points backwards. An analogy is thereby drawn between the simile in Ex 15:5 and the act of Seraiah, by acting out the simile. The iconic symbolism of the symbolic act is meant to trigger the conventional imagery in Ex 15, and subsequently one would be reminded of the theological message, that God destroys the enemies of his people.

3. This is then applied to a second level of iconic symbolism, where the sinking is made analogous to the demise of Babylon. This time, the iconic symbolism points forward. The tradition from Ex 15 that has been brought to mind by means of the first iconic symbolism is thereby made analogous to the destiny of Babylon. The text does not emphasize any particular symbolic meaning of either the stone or the scroll, because the whole thrust of the prophetic symbolic act is to create an analogy, not between the items and Babylon, but between Egypt and Babylon. Also, the indexical symbolic message of the scroll, whereby the physical scroll associates to the disaster that is described in the text on that scroll, plays a subordinate role here. It provides an explanation for the disaster on Babylon, but the main focus is on the very downfall itself.

A related question is why a scroll had to be brought to Babylon at all, in addition to the utterances made by Seraiah? The text emphasizes that Jeremiah wrote the contents of the scroll himself (51:60a), most likely because he will not be the one who delivers the oracles. The problem this creates is both theological as well as practical in nature. Could Seraiah be considered a prophet, so that he could utter an oracle from God? There is nothing in the text that would indicate this, instead it is emphasized that he simply recites (קרא, vv. 61, 63) the words of Jeremiah from the scroll. Seraiah is merely a means of extending Jeremiah's prophetic activity into a land where the prophet could not go. The scroll is therefore needed as a means of ensuring that the prophetic activity of Jeremiah is intact, even though it is extended through the use of Seraiah. However, when it comes to performing the symbolic act, the authority of Jeremiah is behind it, ensuring its prophetic character when Jeremiah prescribes the performance of the act. Scholars have been puzzled by the fact that here Jeremiah describes the performance in first person and not in the form of an oracle. This unusual manner becomes understandable, however, when we recognize the need for a legitimation of the symbolic act as an act, if not performed by Jeremiah, so at least as one laid out in advance, planned and ordered by him. The intention behind these particular emphases in the text is clearly that the utterances and the act of Seraiah are to be regarded as if they were made by Jeremiah.[1]

---

[1] So e.g. Schmidt (1982: 217), who describes Seraiah's task as a 'prophetic delegation'.

Summary and Conclusions

1. The symbolism of this prophetic symbolic act is based on the tradition of how the Egyptians, as the enemies of God and his people, are thrown into the sea 'as a stone' (Ex 15:4). There is no relevant symbolism related to the choice of a stone. It is the act of throwing something into the waters that is symbolically relevant, not the choice of the particular object.

2. The prophetic act receives an iconic symbolism through the analogical relationship between the act of Seraiah and the Exodus tradition, more particularly the simile 'sink as a stone'. The intention of this iconic symbolism is to awaken the awareness of the theological message of the Exodus tradition, namely that God punishes the enemies of his people.

3. By means of a second iconic symbolism, now between the act of Seraiah and the future demise of Babylon, the enemy of God and his people is again 'thrown into the waters', i.e., subdued. This attempt to transfer conventional authority and belief from an older, well-known tradition to a new message through a creative act is attempted by means of illocutionary force.

4. What this prophetic symbolic act lacks as far as the traditional ingredients of prophetic symbolic acts in the Old Testament are concerned, is performance by the undisputable prophet. An attempt has been made to overcome this by attaching a scroll with a prophetic oracle to the stone, thus creating a connection between the prophet and the performance of the act.

E. Prophetic Symbolic Acts in the Book of Ezekiel

1. Building a Siege (Ezekiel 4:1-3)

Ezekiel is given instructions through a vision to perform certain symbolic acts, which all make up one overall symbolic description of the city of Jerusalem under siege. The instructions easily into three parts, vv. 1-3, 4-8 and 9-17. In the first part, Ezekiel is told to take a brick, put it in front of him and then inscribe a picture of a city on the brick. He is then told to construct various siege appliances, to take an iron plate and put it between himself and the city, and keep his face turned towards the city. In the second part, the prophet is said to lie on his left side for a certain amount of days, and in the third part he is to prepare food for himself suited for a siege situation. We will consider these parts individually, while not forgetting that they form parts of a description of one single performance.

The Text

<table>
<tr>
<td>

1 וְאַתָּה בֶן־אָדָם קַח־לְךָ
לְבֵנָה וְנָתַתָּה אוֹתָהּ לְפָנֶיךָ וְחַקּוֹתָ
עָלֶיהָ עִיר אֶת־יְרוּשָׁלָם 2 וְנָתַתָּה
עָלֶיהָ מָצוֹר וּבָנִיתָ עָלֶיהָ דָּיֵק וְשָׁפַכְתָּ
עָלֶיהָ סֹלְלָה וְנָתַתָּה עָלֶיהָ מַחֲנוֹת
וְשִׂים־עָלֶיהָ^a כָּרִים סָבִיב 3 וְאַתָּה
קַח־לְךָ מַחֲבַת בַּרְזֶל וְנָתַתָּה אוֹתָהּ
קִיר בַּרְזֶל בֵּינְךָ וּבֵין הָעִיר וַהֲכִינֹתָה
אֶת־פָּנֶיךָ אֵלֶיהָ וְהָיְתָה בַמָּצוֹר וְצַרְתָּ
עָלֶיהָ אוֹת הִיא לְבֵית יִשְׂרָאֵל

</td>
<td>

1 And you, O mortal, take a brick and set it before you. On it portray a city, Jerusalem; 2 and put siegeworks against it; build a siege-wall against it, cast up a ramp against it, set camps against it, and plant battering rams against it all around. 3 Then take an iron plate and place it as an iron wall between you and the city; set your face toward it, and let it be in a state of siege, and press the siege against it. This is a sign for the house of Israel.

</td>
</tr>
</table>

Textual notes

[a] This fifth עָלֶיהָ is not recognized in LXX. Whether this is due to a slip in the transmission of the Hebrew text or an attempt to construe a nice three-part structure in the Greek translation is impossible to say.

Analysis

Performance of the act

An extensive analysis of the prophetic symbolic acts in Ez 4-5 has recently made by Uehlinger, particularly in relation to iconographic material.[1] He specifically asks whether the portrayal of the city on the brick should be seen in terms of a ground plan (e.g. ANEP 260, Nippur), or a drawing on a vertical plane (e.g. ANEP 366, Assyrian victory relief). Again, the fact that the siege equipment is to be erected against the city speaks in favour of a drawing on a vertical plane. The brick would then be erected and the siege equipment standing next to it, together displaying a miniature siege.[2]

Regarding the performance of this act, the question that remains is how much of what is described in vv. 1-2 is actually meant to be inscribed on the brick. More specifically, the question is what the pronouns in v. 2 refer to, the brick or the city. The most natural conclusion is to take them as referring to the city, portrayed on the brick. This could mean, then, that these siege equipment were also portrayed on the brick. However, the fact that the city is explicitly said to be portrayed on the brick, whereas the siege works are said to be 'put against'/'built against'/'cast up against'/'set against it'/'planted against' it, does seem to make a significant distinction between the portrayal of the city and the setting up of the siege equipment. There is also the fact that a clay brick from this time would hardly be large enough to contain the whole of this description.[3] There is also the indication that the verb for 'set', נתן, is used in relation to the brick (וְנָתַתָּה אוֹתָהּ לְפָנֶיךָ, v. 1) as well as in relation to the siege equipment (וְנָתַתָּה עָלֶיהָ מָצוֹר, v. 2). Conversely, the verb for 'inscribe', חקק, used in describing the mode of portraying the city on the brick (וְחַקּוֹתָ עָלֶיהָ, v. 1) is not used in relation to the construction of the various forms of siege equipment. It is therefore likely that the portrayal was made separately from the construction of the siege.[4] It might well be that the siege equipment was also portrayed on bricks, which were then put next to the brick showing the city. However, since the language used in the command to Ezekiel to produce the siege works is metaphorically used from the actual construction of battle rams and various other siege works, we can not reach a firm conclusion as to how this was meant to be done. However, it does seem likely that bricks were used in these instances as well.

---

[1] Uehlinger (1987).

[2] For details as to how a siege was conducted at this time, see Yadin (1963: 313-28).

[3] So Wevers (1969: 60), Allen (1994: 64).

[4] So also Uehlinger (1987: 150-2), Allen (1994: 64).

The various siege works referred to in this text are known from the ancient Near East, and more particularly from the Assyrian empire.[1] From there, they were inherited by the neo-Babylonian kingdom, which is how they came to be described by Ezekiel, who foresaw a siege of Jerusalem by the Babylonians. The first word, מָצוֹר, 'siege', is here used as an introductory description, to be followed by concrete examples of siege works. Although מָצוֹר can be used for a rampart, we should note that it is used in connection with the verb נתן. Although it is never used elsewhere in the OT in connection with this verb, it does occur as the object of the rather closely related verb שׂים in Mich 4:14, 'מָצוֹר שָׂם עָלֵינוּ', 'siege is laid against us' (cf. Also v. 2f, וְשַׂמְתָּ־עָלֶיהָ). This is also born out by the fact that the two occurrences of מָצוֹר in vv. 2 and 3 form an inclusio, both referring to the siege in general, within which are found the various concrete references to siege-works.[2]

The word דָּיֵק has been understood in different ways. Some hold it to stand for a siege-wall, whereas others see it as referring to a siege-tower.[3] However, no clear and unambiguous indications can be found that could substantiate the translation 'siege-tower', a translation that seems to go back to a comparison with the Akkadian equivalent *dāiqu* in an inscription of Asarhaddon. This suggestion, however, does not seem to stand up in the light of the most recent edition of this text;[4]

ammu ul iṣ[bat ...] dūršu	'(the fire) did not ignite the siege ramp but
iqmūma ušēme ditalliš [...]	burned his own fortification wall and re-
e-piš qabli u tāḫazi da-a-a-i-qu	duced it to ashes, [my troops?] climbed
ibbalkituni	over the siege wall [to do] battle'.

---

[1] See e.g. Ussishkin (1983), Eph'al (1984).

[2] So Uehlinger (1987: 179).

[3] So Driver (1954: 147-8), Driver (1960: 157), Yadin (1963: 315), Allen (1994: 65). It is likely that Driver's study is the source behind Allen and Yadin. Driver himself relies on Bauer (1928-9: 240-1, 253, n 31) for the comparison with the Akkadian *dāiqu*, although Bauer translates 'Belagerungsmauer'.

[4] Borger (1956: 104), §68.II.8, CAD D, 27. Uehlinger (1987: 176, n. 254) does not recognize the alternative 'siege-tower', but prefers 'Belagerungswall'. He also refers to some representations in the iconography of that time.

[5] HALOT 1, 220-1.

Apparently, the translation 'tower' arose from an earlier reading of this text by Bauer, who wanted to translate the text as saying that the soldiers climbed *into* the *dāiqu*, whereas they are actually said to climb, or even better, run, *over* it. Thus, it can not be translated as 'siege tower', and a translation along the lines of 'siege wall' or 'bulwark'[5] is therefore more likely. A further argument against translating דָּיֵק as 'tower' is the fact that in 2 Kgs 25:1 it is said to have been built around the city, וַיִּבְנוּ עָלֶיהָ דָּיֵק סָבִיב, something which conclusively excludes 'tower' as a relevant translation.[1] The סֹלְלָה is commonly taken as 'ramp', i.e., earth piled up (שָׁפַךְ, lit. 'pour out') against the wall so that the כָּרִים, 'battering-rams', could overcome the steepness and penetrate the wall of the city.[2] The מַחֲנוֹת is the military camp of the besieging army, which in this case could not have been mistaken for the neo-Babylonians.

The last item Ezekiel is to prepare is an iron plate, מַחֲבַת בַּרְזֶל (v. 3). The word מַחֲבַת stands for a cooking plate, which as far as we know was used at least for the cultic purpose of cooking sacrificial meals on over the fire.[3] The plate was to be set up between the prophet himself and 'the city', and it is explicitly said that it is to be an 'iron wall', which suggests that this plate should also be seen as an instrument of siege.[4] However, we do not have any examples of iron walls being used in this way, the closest thing we know of is the use of large shields against the arrows from the defenders of the city.

Symbolic meaning of the act

The final statement of vv. 1-3 is that this is to be an אוֹת, sign or symbol, to the house of Israel, which introduces the question of what Ezekiel's acts symbolizes. The brick with the portrayal of the city and the various siege attributes naturally stand for what they imitate in a miniature way, and together they make up a situation that could hardly have been missed by one who observed what Ezekiel had accomplished. In this sense, the various symbols are iconic in nature, since they seek to portray and imitate. However, Ezekiel did not only produce various symbols, but he also symbolized the siege itself, since he is told to *put* siege attributes, *build* a siege-wall, *cast up* a ramp, *set* camp, and *plant* battering rams around the city. The verbs do not primarily refer to the acts Ezekiel

---

[1] HWAT 2, 249. The only modern lexicon that apparently fails to see through the suggestion by Driver is DCH 2, 435, which provides both translations and refers to Driver's article (p. 627).

[2] See Yadin (1963: 315, 408, 422-3, 425).

[3] See Lev 2:5; 6:21; 7:9; 1 Chr 23:29, and Kelso (1948: 23).

[4] So Uehlinger (1987: 180).

were to perform in constructing the miniature models, but to that which these models symbolized, the construction of actual siege attributes, that is, the verbs are used metaphorically. This shows that the act is then also iconic in its symbolic nature, since it seeks to imitate the conventional technique used in building siege works.

It is only when we come to the last item, the iron plate, that this can hardly be said to apply. This is probably linked to the fact that the iron plate can not be easily identified with a conventional item used in a siege situation. What, then, could the iron plate symbolize? Jewish tradition has interpreted it in various ways, mostly theologically motivated, such as the sins of the people that hinder their God from being near.[1] However, a more convincing function of the iron plate can be found by seeing it as a symbol of strength and protection, a means of shutting out more than shutting in. In this sense, the prophet is symbolising not God but the Babylonian army, constantly gazing (וַהֲכִינֹתָה אֶת־פָּנֶיךָ אֵלֶיהָ) towards the city to see whether it will withstand the pressures of the siege (וְהָיִיתָה בְמָצוֹר וְצַרְתָּ עָלֶיהָ). An argument against this would be that the prophet is told to 'set his face towards' the city, an expression commonly used when the prophet is to prophecy against the people.[2] However, this argument is not so simple at it first may seem. In Ez 4:3, 7 the verb used in the expression is כון, fix', whereas the verb otherwise used in the book of Ezekiel is שׂים.[3] The verb שׂים is also followed by the verb נבא, 'to prophecy'. These variations between the two expressions makes it possible that in this particular instance, when the prophet seems to be using his acts in a symbolic way, another form of the otherwise common expression is deliberately used. The reason for this would be to differentiate this instance from the more common form of expression, so that the reader would not understand the prophet as playing his usual role, but instead that of the oppressing army. Furthermore, after the prophet is told to set his face toward the city, his told to 'press the siege against it', an act which is clearly to be understood as yet another imitating, iconic symbolism, and he can only be imitating the Babylonian army. What, then, is the iron plate supposed to symbolize? It is quite common to see Ezekiel as symbolising God, who is firmly determined not to come to the city's rescue, but to let the siege have its course.[4]

---

[1] See Is 59:2, and Bokser (1983).

[2] For this expression, see Zimmerli (1976: 182-3), Brownlee (1983), Layton (1986: 172-3).

[3] 6:2; 13:17; 21:2, 7; 25:2; 28:21; 29:2; 35:2; 38:2.

[4] E.g. Greenberg (1983: 104), Allen (1994: 65), Block (1997: 173-4), Friebel (1999: 204-9).

However, this interpretation has no indications from within the text, and relies wholly on what appears to be a suitable theological interpretation. It also presumes that the symbolic act in 4:1-3 must be interpreted in accordance with the following symbolic acts in vv. 4ff, but there is no inherent reason why Ezekiel must remain with a particular symbolism of himself in the different symbolic acts. Instead, the simplest understanding of the plate is to see it as a shield or siege wall, separating the city from its attacker, since that is the only meaning that has any support in the text. Both shield and siege wall are items used in this particular form of war, and it is hard to choose between the two, especially since the text leaves us with very little indications. That the plate is made of iron should then be seen as a means of symbolising the strength of the shield/wall, as a conscious exaggeration, while at the same time being conscious of what is actually being used to construct the miniature siege situation. This iron plate should not be seen at denoting the strength of the city, but that of the army outside the city, since it occurs in a context of various descriptions of siege equipment and is followed by an instruction to keep the city under siege.[1] Otherwise, the text does not in any way refer to the quality of the city's defence, and there is no reason to see such a reference in the symbolism of the iron plate either. It stands for the strength and protection of the attacking army, and its imagery is probably built on the knowledge of the use of metallic shields to protect soldiers, but the possibility remains that it can refer to a siege wall. The symbolism of this iron plate is less certain, since Ezekiel is not told to construe a shield/wall, i.e., what it is supposed to symbolize, but to take an iron plate, i.e., that which is meant to symbolize. It stands, nevertheless, for a strong separation between the attacking army and the city. Although the symbolic meaning of the iron plate is less certain that the other siege items, it is iconic in its capacity to symbolize a shield/wall, but conventional in denoting strength by being made of iron.

At the end of this first part of the larger description of the symbolic act of Ezekiel, we have one of the few instances were symbolic act is explicitly said to have been intended to be understood as a אוֹת, 'sign' or 'symbol',[2] i.e., as signifying something else but the obvious primary meaning of the physical perform-

---

[1] See e.g. Iwry (1961: 29-30). Cf. also Kruger (1989: 128), who sees Ezekiel depicting God, but still sees the iron plate as a form of shield.

[2] The only other instance is Is 20:3, where Isaiah's symbolic act is described as a אוֹת וּמוֹפֵת, 'sign and portent'.

[3] See TDOT, 1, 167-88, esp. 186 regarding symbolic acts.

ance of the act.[3] The clause where this is stated is a nominal clause, and it seems most reasonable to take the tense of the clause as present. The symbolic act would then be saying that it is a sign to Ezekiel's people that symbolizes that a siege is immanent, and presumably the nature of the enemy did not take too much imagination to unveil. This symbolic meaning is iconic in nature, imitating the conventional behaviour in construing a siege.

Summary and Conclusions

1. Ezekiel is told to portray an image of Jerusalem on a plate, and it is likely that he portrays various other siege equipments on other plates as well, although that will have to remain uncertain.

2. The imitation of the city and the various items involved in construing a siege are imitated by Ezekiel in order to picture the known procedure for such an enterprise. The symbolic meaning inherent in this miniature work is therefore iconic.

3. The exception is the iron plate, which does not receive the same explicit symbolic meaning as the other items of siege. However, the most probable symbolic meaning of the iron plate is iconic, as that of a shield or siege wall that stands for the strength of the Babylonian army. The fact that it is said to be made of iron is a case of conventional symbolism, denoting strength.

2. Laying on One Side (Ezekiel 4:4-8)

The Text

4 וְאַתָּה. שְׁכַב עַל־צִדְּךָ
הַשְּׂמָאלִי וְשַׂמְתָּ אֶת־עֲוֹן
בֵּית־יִשְׂרָאֵל עָלָיו[a] מִסְפַּר הַיָּמִים[b]
אֲשֶׁר תִּשְׁכַּב עָלָיו תִּשָּׂא אֶת־עֲוֹנָם
5 וַאֲנִי נָתַתִּי לְךָ אֶת־שְׁנֵי עֲוֹנָם
לְמִסְפַּר יָמִים. שְׁלֹשׁ־מֵאוֹת וְתִשְׁעִים
יוֹם וְנָשָׂאתָ עֲוֹן בֵּית־יִשְׂרָאֵל
6 וְכִלִּיתָ אֶת־אֵלֶּה וְשָׁכַבְתָּ
עַל־צִדְּךָ הַיְמִינִי[d] שֵׁנִית[c] וְנָשָׂאתָ
אֶת־עֲוֹן בֵּית־יְהוּדָה אַרְבָּעִים יוֹם
יוֹם לַשָּׁנָה יוֹם לַשָּׁנָה נְתַתִּיו לָךְ
7 וְאֶל־מְצוֹר יְרוּשָׁלַם תָּכִין פָּנֶיךָ
וּזְרֹעֲךָ חֲשׂוּפָה וְנִבֵּאתָ עָלֶיהָ
8 וְהִנֵּה נָתַתִּי עָלֶיךָ עֲבוֹתִים
וְלֹא־תֵהָפֵךְ מִצִּדְּךָ אֶל־צִדֶּךָ
עַד־כַּלּוֹתְךָ יְמֵי מְצוּרֶךָ

4 Then lie on your left side, and place the punishment of the house of Israel upon it; you shall bear their punishment for the number of the days that you lie there. 5 For I assign to you a number of days, three hundred ninety days, equal to the number of the years of their punishment; and so you shall bear the punishment of the house of Israel. 6 When you have completed these, you shall lie down a second time, but on your right side, and bear the punishment of the house of Judah; forty days I assign you, one day for each year. 7 You shall set your face toward the siege of Jerusalem, and with your arm bared you shall prophesy against it. 8 See, I am putting cords on you so that you cannot turn from one side to the other until you have completed the days of your siege.

Textual notes

[a] There is no reason to follow the harmonistic attempt in BHS, going back to Wellhausen, and read ושמתי and עליך, since it would disregard the very symbolism the text is trying to convey. The suggestion by Zimmerli (1976 148), following older commentaries, is to read ונשאת instead of וְשַׂמְתָּ and delete the following עָלָיו is equally unconvincing, since it attempts to create a more suitable and understandable symbolic act. However, the whole point of Ezekiel's symbolic acts are to be precisely chocking and even offending.

[b] LXX inserts πεντήκοντα καὶ ἑκατόν, 150. Together with reading 190 days in v. 5 instead of 390 in MT, the translator apparently sought to make sense of the calculations, since the 190 days is the sum of 150 days on the left side, and 40 days on the right side in v. 6. This is not done in order to answer the question 'How long?', but to make sense of the time spans.

[c] שֵׁנִית is lacking in LXX* and Syr, and may very well be a clarifying gloss, so e.g. Zimmerli (1976: 148). But its awkward sense, 'lie on your left side a second time', makes it more reliable, and probably why it was deleted in the versions, so e.g. Greenberg (1983: 105), Allen (1994: 50), Block (1997: 175, n 50).

ᵈ The Kethib הימוני is an apparent scribal error for הימיני, and Qere is based on the variant יְמָנִי, which is less likely since it can not explain the ו.

Analysis

Much can be said about this text and its allusions, particularly to the priestly phraseology that is used. However, we will have to focus on the symbolic acts and their symbolic meanings, and the main difficulty here is not so much the symbolic meanings of the symbolic acts, but deciding as to whether certain expressions are merely figurative, or actually referring to symbolic acts.

To begin with, it is not immediately clear what connection vv. 4-8 have with vv. 1-3. However, according to v. 7 Ezekiel is said to make use of his bared arm in prophesying against Jerusalem. This is only understandable if the prophet is lying down on his left side with only his right arm free to use, and the laying down is understandable in the light of the miniatures that has been described earlier. Now Ezekiel begins to play a part himself in the siege against the city. The reference to Jerusalem under siege in v. 7 ensures the connection with what precedes.

However, it is clear that this text includes a later addition creating certain inconsistencies. The term Israel has up till now been used for Judah, but in v. 6 the name Judah is being used instead, implicitly limiting Israel to the northern kingdom. In v. 8 Ezekiel is said to be tied up so that he can not turn over, but in v. 6 he is told to turn over on his left side. Finally, the matter of siege suddenly resides to the background in v. 6. The conclusion is that v. 6 has been added later, in a situation when the exile was no longer a threat but instead a matter of the past.[1] This change of focus can be illustrated by the double use of the expression נשׂא עון; 1) 'bear guilt' (v. 4), suitable in the situation of the textual world of this text, and 2) 'bear punishment' (v. 6), suitable to an exilic or postexilic time, when what had happened must be explained in order to be understood and ac-

---

[1] So Allen (1994: 68) Zimmerli sees v. 6 as only part of a larger expansive process at work, Zimmerli (1976: 166-7). The attempt by Block (1997: 179-80) seems almost doctrinally defensive of MT, to the point of sounding idiosyncratic, and similarly Friebel (1999: 216).
[2] So Allen (1994: 68).

cepted.[2] In the following, we will therefore not take v. 6 into consideration when it comes to understanding the performance and meaning of the symbolic act.[1]

Ezekiel is told to lie down on his left side, presumably to free his right hand, which is to be used in a symbolic gesture (v. 7). Ezekiel is now playing himself in this miniature drama. In this position he is said to וְשַׂמְתָּ אֶת־עֲוֹן בֵּית־יִשְׂרָאֵל עָלָיו, 'place the punishment of the house of Israel upon it (i.e. his left side)' (4:4). If this was meant to be worked out in any way is not clear, but since the instructions so far in Ez 4 have been rather detailed and quite physical, it would seem consistent to consider this statement, lacking any such detailed description, as a figurative statement. However, arguing from silence is hazardous, so we must remain uncertain.

The expression 'PN שִׂים עֲוֹן עַל', with its only occurrence here in v. 4, serves the purpose of bridging the gap between on the one hand the concrete situation where the prophet is laying on the ground on his left side, and on the other the use of the technical, idiomatic priestly formula, 'נשׂא עֲוֹן', lit. 'bear the sin' (v. 4).[2] This bridge is accomplished by saying that Ezekiel is to 'place' the punishments of the people 'on his left side'. This also revives the frozen metaphor 'נשׂא עֲוֹן' into a more active one, which makes the reader think of an actual carrying, namely what Ezekiel is performing in his symbolic act, visibly or not.

That the otherwise technical expression 'נשׂא עֲוֹן' is not used here in its conventional, idiomatic form confirms to the reader that it is only used symbolically, without any suffering or punishment being inflicted on the prophet. That is only the case in the symbolic world, which is ironically dramatized by Ezekiel through his act. When the conventional use of the expression 'נשׂא עֲוֹן' is no longer relevant, the phrase has to be reused in a non-conventional way by awakening the metaphor upon which the expression relies. This has to be done in order to make use of the connotations that are connected with the conventional use

---

[1] Some scholars feel, perhaps rightly, that there is no need to go beyond Ezekiel himself as being behind this addition, as well as v. 13, se below, since his prophetic ministry stretched well into the future, see Allen (1994: 79).

[2] For this phrase, see Zimmerli (1976: 164-5), TDOT 10, 31-7, esp. 33 in regard to Ez 4. It is rare that the technical phrase is used in relation to the sins of the people, but it does occur in Ex 28:38; Ps 85:3. The expression is used in a different sense in v. 6, a later addition from exilic or postexilic times, as noted above.

of the phrase in priestly theology.[1] Through this process of re-metaphorizing, or awakening of a frozen metaphor, a new meaning is created, but with all the valuable connotations associated with the conventional use of the frozen metaphor still intact.[2] That new meaning is the symbolic meaning of Ezekiel's symbolic act of carrying, which is iconic as far as its relation to the figurative description of the people by means of the frozen metaphor. This symbolic meaning can hardly be called iconic, unless some physical object was put on Ezekiel to play the part of the suffering. It must therefore be categorized as a conventional symbolic meaning, which relies heavily on the verbal interpretation to convey its meaning.

In v. 5 Ezekiel is told to lie down for 390 days, one day for each year of punishment for the people.[3] This is one of the main reasons why some scholars in the past considered these descriptions of symbolic acts in the book of Ezekiel to be fictitious, since the prophet could hardly have been laying on the ground, on his side, for over a year. However, it is not necessarily the case that Ezekiel should have had to perform this act for a major part of each day, or even every day during this period of 390 days. It may well have been that it was part of prophetic ministry, and only required him to perform his act every now and then to uphold the impression of a long period. The miniature constructions would then have been there for everyone to see during this period, as a constant reminder of Ezekiel's message, but not necessarily Ezekiel himself.[4]

Lying down, and figuratively having the punishments of the people upon himself, Ezekiel is told in v. 7 to direct his face (תָּכִין פָּנֶיךָ) and his outstretched arm (וּזְרֹעֲךָ חֲשׂוּפָה), presumably towards the city, and prophecy against it. The first phrase has already been investigated above (4:3), and seen as a unique vari-

---

[1] A similar use of the technical expression has been made in the so-called suffering servant song in Is 53:4-5, 7, 11-2, see Zimmerli (1976: 165), Blenkinsopp (1990: 35).

[2] For a similar case where a conventional metaphor, stemming from the cultic sphere, is awakened into a new and innovative use in a prophetic context, see Viberg (1994).

[3] The figure 390 refers to the period of the first temple, during which Israel accumulated its sins according to e.g. the deuteronomistic historian, which is to lie heavily on Ezekiel, see Zimmerli (1976: 165-7), Allen (1994: 66-7). The number would then have to be a rather round figure, something which is hard to avoid in any alternative view on this matter.

[4] So e.g. Allen (1994: 67), Block (1997: 179), Friebel (1999: 222).

ant of an otherwise well-known idiom. The same is very much the case with the second expression. The common phrase בְּזְרוֹעַ נְטוּיָה, 'with an outstretched arm', usually stands metonymically for God's strength and capacity to save his people,[1] and it also occurs in the book of Ezekiel (Ez 20:33). The precise formulation used here, however, וּזְרֹעֲךָ חֲשׂוּפָה, does not occur elsewhere. Apparently, great care has been taken to avoid the standard expression, while still keeping a general similarity to it, so as to ensure that the metaphor is taken in a revived sense and not in its traditional, frozen state.

The two traditional phrases then shows that Ezekiel is ironically symbolising God, in the sense that he resembles God as he figures in the revived figurative language of the two phrases. The phrases are slightly changed in order to revive these frozen metaphors, since otherwise they may not have awakened the figurative imagery that was needed to make the analogy to Ezekiel's act.

Ezekiel is also said to וְנִבֵּאתָ עָלֶיהָ, 'prophecy against it (the city)', which is best taken in its primary sense of a command to speak God's word against the city, without any relevant symbolic meaning.

Then, in v. 8, Ezekiel's role shifts again. He is said to have cords put on him until the end of the siege to keep him from turning away.[2] It is very hard to understand whether this is meant to be taken figuratively as a restraining by God on his prophet, so that Ezekiel does not deviate from his duty as a prophet, or as a symbolic act, where actual cords were put on Ezekiel to symbolize that same restraining. However, since there is no command to put these cords on Ezekiel or any other indication that it stands for an actual performance, it is best to understand the statement as a metaphor,[3] vividly describing God's intention of not letting Ezekiel escape his symbolical siege, as the people will not escape their actual siege.[4] Verse 8 is therefore not relevant as far as the symbolic acts in this text are concerned.

---

[1] See Ex 6:5; Deut 4:34; 1 Kgs 8:42; Jer 27:5, etc.

[2] Although Ezekiel is said to be bound by cords also in 3:25, the two texts are not related, against e.g. Zimmerli (1976: 165), Block (1997: 180-1). In 3:25, Ezekiel is restrained by other exiles, whereas what is imposed on him in 4:8, figuratively or not, is done so by God.

[3] Tg. understands it similarly and clarifies by a simile, כאיסור גדילן, 'like twisted cords'.

[4] So Greenberg (1983: 106), Allen (1994: 67), Friebel (1999: 223). Aside from their literal meaning, cords can also be used figuratively, see Ps 2:3, 129:4; Hos 11:4; Is 5:18.

Summary and Conclusions

1. Ezekiel's act of lying on his left side is a symbolic act, which focuses on the act of carrying. Through indexical symbolism that associates to the figurative meaning of certain priestly phrases, the act of carrying symbolizes more or less conventionally the carrying of sins on behalf of the people. Since nothing is said as to whether any physical object is actually placed on Ezekiel's side, the symbolism is dependent on the conventional symbolism inherent in the priestly theological phraseology. The people have carried their sins almost throughout the monarchical period, and it is about to reach its climax.

2. When Ezekiel is told to *gaze* at the city and prophesy with his *arm bared*, he is ironically symbolising God as portrayed within the figurative language of these phrases. He symbolizes the strength of God in opposition to the city.

3. Verse 4:8 does not describe a symbolic act, but only a metaphorical statement, that God will not let Ezekiel refrain from his task until the siege has reached an end.

3. Preparing a Meal (Ezekiel 4:9-12)

The Text

וְאַתָּה קַח־לְךָ חִטִּין[a] וּשְׂעֹרִים 9
וּפוֹל וַעֲדָשִׁים וְדֹחַן וְכֻסְּמִים וְנָתַתָּה
אוֹתָם בִּכְלִי אֶחָד וְעָשִׂיתָ אוֹתָם[b] לְךָ
לְלֶחֶם מִסְפַּר הַיָּמִים אֲשֶׁר־אַתָּה שׁוֹכֵב
עַל־צִדְּךָ שְׁלֹשׁ־מֵאוֹת וְתִשְׁעִים יוֹם
תֹּאכֲלֶנּוּ 10 וּמַאֲכָלְךָ אֲשֶׁר תֹּאכֲלֶנּוּ
בְּמִשְׁקוֹל עֶשְׂרִים שֶׁקֶל לַיּוֹם מֵעֵת
עַד־עֵת תֹּאכֲלֶנּוּ 11 וּמַיִם בִּמְשׂוּרָה
תִשְׁתֶּה שִׁשִּׁית הַהִין מֵעֵת עַד־עֵת
תִּשְׁתֶּה 12 וְעֻגַת שְׂעֹרִים[c] תֹּאכֲלֶנָּה וְהִיא
בְּגֶלְלֵי צֵאת[d] הָאָדָם תְּעֻגֶנָה לְעֵינֵיהֶם

9 And you, take wheat and barley, beans and lentils, millet and spelt; put them into one vessel, and make bread for yourself. During the number of days that you lie on your side, three hundred ninety days, you shall eat it. 10 The food that you eat shall be twenty shekels a day by weight; at fixed times you shall eat it. 11 And you shall drink water by measure, one-sixth of a hin; at fixed times you shall drink. 12 You shall eat it as a barley-cake, baking it in their sight on human dung.

Textual notes

[a] The plural is an Aramaism of חִטִּים, 'wheat', see Wagner (1966: 135), Gesenius (1910: §87e).

[b] To understand this as a prepositional expression, 'with them', so Block (1997: 181, n 78) is unnecessary and strange, since it makes the ingredients instrumental.

[c] This could be a casus pendens, as is clearly the following וְהִיא, so Greenberg (1983: 107), Block (1997: 181, n 83, 185). However, it does not follow that a new topic is begun, as Greenberg and Block believe. The topic is still the bread from v. 10, although now in v. 12 a feminine synonym is used, which determines the gender of the verbal suffix, see Allen (1994: 51). The nominal phrase וְעֻגַת שְׂעֹרִים is appositional, and specifies in what form or shape the bread is to be eaten. There is therefore no need for revocalising שְׂעֹרִים into שֵׂעֹרִים, 'rotten', (cf.Jer 29:17) as Görg (1982) suggests, although the alliteration could have created an association in that direction.

[d] Since the word does not occur again in v. 15, it has been regarded as a gloss by Fohrer (1955), Freedy (1970: 136). However, to require such a minute correspondence from any author, and deny any possibility of variation is simply not warranted, similarly Allen (1994: 51).

Analysis

In this act, the focus shifts from the siege outside the city to the situation inside the city. Ezekiel is told to prepare food and water particular to a siege situation, with particular estimates so that the food and water will last for everyone according to rations. In v. 12 he is told to prepare the food[1] by means of human dung.

Verse 13, as well as v. 6 (se above), is a later addition to the text, made from an exilic or postexilic context in order to update the interpretation of the symbolic act. It shifts the focus from accusation to punishment, meaningful in a later time, but not while the siege is imminent, when Ezekiel has another pressing message to proclaim, namely that the people must learn to bear their guilt.

We then get an interlude in vv. 14-15, where Ezekiel protests against the instruction in v. 12, apparently reacting to what he regards as something beyond the limit of what even God could expect from one of his prophets. His protest is based on his observance of dietary laws. If he was to use human dung as fuel, the meat would be defiled, and therefore unfit to eat, and especially to a priest such as Ezekiel. When God retracts, and allows Ezekiel to use animal dung instead, we should understand this to have a more overarching purpose than simply allowing Ezekiel to perform a less dramatic act. This has been the reason why many scholars have seen an exilic perspective not only in v. 13 but the whole of vv. 12-15, providing a divine acceptance of something that would have been inevitable in a gentile context. However, this is not necessarily so. We can also see this lowering of the dramatic effect of the symbolic act as a limitation to the prophet himself, while still making it clear that the horror of the oncoming siege would transcend any notions of normal living conditions (cf. 5:10). The narrative closes with a further description by God of how there will be a shortage of food and water in the city, and how starvation will begin, all because of their sin (vv. 16-7).

The symbolic meaning of the act is quite clear. The act of preparing the food and water by someone who is already symbolically put under siege simply continues that iconic symbolic picture of a Judahite inside the walls of Jerusalem while under siege. Indeed, what is performed according to this description is the act of baking bread, not only symbolically but also in a concrete manner, since it is supposed to be the food and water for Ezekiel while lying down (v. 9). The eating of the bread is of course also symbolic for how the people under siege will have to eat. There is no symbolic relevance indicated by the text as to how either the preparation of the bread, or the eating of it is to be performed, merely that fact that it is done. The selection of various ingredients, however, resembles

---

[1] There is no need to see a new topic in v. 12ff, describing a new symbolic act, so Greenberg (1983: 107), Block (1997: 185), since the noun-phrase וְעֻגַת שְׂעֹרִים specifies the shape of the bread, not another bread from the one made earlier.

the desperate need to survive in a situation where one has to pick the scraps out of the almost empty storage jars in the kitchen, baking bread that would normally not have been fit to eat.

We have no description of the actual performance, but there is a clear indication that this symbolic act is to be performed לְעֵינֵיהֶם, 'in public' (v. 12). As in other cases, the description of the actual performance of the symbolic act is left out, presumably because it is considered to be superfluous and simply taken for granted. Also related to the performance is the strange length in time of this symbolic act. The food prepared is meant to be sufficient for Ezekiel for a period of 390 days (v. 5). Whether any form of symbolism is involved here as well is impossible to say. It would seem almost impossible to endure such a hardship for Ezekiel, but we must separate what we would regard as suitable or acceptable, and simply understand the fervour and passion the prophet his God.

Summary and Conclusions

1. The meals that Ezekiel is commanded to prepare are ordinary meals, although symbolically relevant, and they are meant to be Ezekiel's regular meals while he endures his symbolic act.

2. The symbolic meaning of these meals and their preparation is iconic, since they aim to resemble the meals that are prepared inside the walls of Jerusalem. This is indicated by assembling several items of food in the same bowl, since there is only very little of each food, and that various items of food normally not used are collected in order to display the desperation that would be spreading inside the walls.

4. Splitting Hairs (Ezekiel 5:1-4)

The Text

וְאַתָּה בֶן־אָדָם קַח־לְךָ 1
חֶרֶב חַדָּה תַּעַר הַגַּלָּבִים תִּקָּחֶנָּה
לְךָ וְהַעֲבַרְתָּ עַל־רֹאשְׁךָ
וְעַל־זְקָנֶךָ וְלָקַחְתָּ לְךָ מֹאזְנֵי
מִשְׁקָל וְחִלַּקְתָּם. 2 שְׁלִשִׁית בָּאוּר
תַּבְעִיר בְּתוֹךְ הָעִיר כִּמְלֹאת יְמֵי
הַמָּצוֹר ᵃהַשְּׁלִשִׁית תַּכֶּה
בַחֶרֶב סְבִיבוֹתֶיהָ וְהַשְּׁלִשִׁית תִּזְרֶה
לָרוּחַ וְחֶרֶב אָרִיק אַחֲרֵיהֶם
3 וְלָקַחְתָּ מִשָּׁם מְעַט בְּמִסְפָּר וְצַרְתָּ
אוֹתָם בִּכְנָפֶיךָᵇ 4 וּמֵהֶם עוֹד תִּקָּח
וְהִשְׁלַכְתָּ אוֹתָם אֶל־תּוֹךְ הָאֵשׁ
וְשָׂרַפְתָּ אֹתָם בָּאֵשׁ מִמֶּנּוּᵈ ᶜᵈתֵצֵא־אֵשׁ
אֶל־כָּל־בֵּית יִשְׂרָאֵל

1 And you, O mortal, take a sharp sword; use it as a barber's razor and run it over your head and your beard; then take balances for weighing, and divide the hair. 2 One third of the hair you shall burn in the fire inside the city, when the days of the siege are completed; one third you shall strike with the sword all around the city; and one third you shall scatter to the wind, and I will unsheathe the sword after them. 3 Then you shall take from these a small number, and bind them in the skirts of your robe. 4 From these, again, you shall take some, throw them into the fire and burn them up; from there a fire will come out against all the house of Israel.

Textual notes

ᵃ The phrase וְלָקַחְתָּ אֶת is uniformly regarded as a later adaptation to vv. 1 and 3, as it destroys the symmetry of v. 2, and makes תַּכֶּה cry out for a conjunction (so Syr, a later accommodation), or else it is a strange case of asyndeton, so e.g. Zimmerli (1976: 150), Allen (1994: 52). Greenberg (1983: 108-9), followed by suggests that MT has not arisen due to a conflation of two alternative readings, but since none of those are extant, it remains hypothetical.

ᵇ This could be a mistaken plene-writing, since e.g. LXX has singular, as most versions, so e.g. Zimmerli (1976: 151), Allen (1994: 52). But they understand כנף as 'mantle', whereas it actually stands for the corners of the mantle (see TDOT 8, 231), and so the plural may be correct.

ᶜ The antecedent of the masculine suffix is no doubt אֵשׁ, even though it is feminine.

ᵈ BHS takes the mistake in the masculine suffix as an indication that the whole phrase is a later gloss, and follows LXX in reading ואמרת instead, but it is hard to understand how the phrase would have been formed secondarily. LXX has a different punctuation, where v. 4b begins v. 5.

Analysis

This symbolic act follows logically from the acts that have been studied in chapter 4, and it seems to presuppose that the miniature built earlier is still intact. This symbolic act is said to be performed 'when the days of the siege are completed' (v. 2), i.e., when Ezekiel's earlier symbolic act has run its course, regardless of how long it actually took to perform it.

Ezekiel is told to shave off his hair, but the expression is unusual.[1] First, no verb for shaving is used, and instead he is given a description of how he is to perform the shaving. He is to take a חֶרֶב, 'sword', and use it as 'a barber's knife' and slide it across his head and cheek. He is to use the sword again when he strikes at the second pile of hair outside the city (v. 2). This unusual procedure is due to the fact that the sword appears later and now figuratively as the sword of judgement in the hand of God (vv. 12, 17). The continuity between the description of the physical performance of the act and its interpretation is secured by means of the unusual use of the sword in the act. We will return to the use of 'sword' below.

He is then told to use a scale to divide the hair into three equal piles. The first is to be burned 'inside the city', the second Ezekiel is to strike outside the city with a sword in the midst of the miniature enemy camp,[2] and the third he shall scatter to the wind, but the sword will go after them nevertheless. From the third group, a few hairs are to be bound in the hem of the mantle, presumably Ezekiel's, but even from these few some will be taken and thrown into the fire.

The fire that is presumed from the first pile of hair to the last few, is a fire in the city, which could mean that Ezekiel is to set his miniature city on fire, and throw the first pile of hair on that fire. It could also have been the fire Ezekiel used to cook his food on the iron plate, but there would hardly have been room on the brick for a fire and an iron plate.

It is noteworthy that the act of taking a few hairs out of the last pile and again taking a few and throwing them into the fire (v. 3-4a), does not receive an interpretation, something which argues for that this again is a case of later application. However, this is not as clear-cut at was the case with 4:6, 13, where the exilic background was shining throw. Here in 5:3-4a, the setting is not clearly

---

[1] For various ways in which shaving was used in the ancient Near East, see Friebel (1999: 235, n 253).

[2] Note in v. 2, סְבִיבוֹתֶיהָ, 'around it (i.e. the city)', and in 4:2, the battering rams are to be put סָבִיב, 'around (the city).

the exile, but most that of the failure of hope in rescue from the catastrophe about to come on the city.

Close to Ezekiel's act of shaving the head stands Is 7:20, a possible example of intertextual dependency.[1] Isaiah spoke of the king of Assyria, who would be hired in by God himself to separate the people from its land as a razor separates hair from skin. The image in Ez 5:1 is substantially the same, although much more is woven into the symbolism here, as will be shown below.

The shaved head also receives its symbolic value in the following interpretation, 'I will make you a desolation and an object of mocking among the nations around you, in the sight of all that pass by' (v. 14). Baldness was a shameful state, unless it was accomplished under proper circumstances, such as when a nazir had been defiled or was about to end his Nazirite period (Num 6:9, 18-19), cultic cleansing (Lev 14:8-9) or sorrow and lament (Is 7:20; 15:20; Jer 7:29; 48:37; Ez 7:18; Mi 1:16). Since none of these would suit Ezekiel's context, he would unavoidably suffer shame and humiliation, which was to symbolize the shame of the people, who succumbed to the enemy despite of its mighty God.[2] And in Ezekiel's case this would have been even more so since shaving was forbidden for priests (Lev 19:27; 21:5), something which can be found in the book of Ezekiel itself, וְרֹאשָׁם לֹא יְגַלֵּחוּ, 'they shall not shave their heads' (Ez 44:20). What made it possible for Ezekiel to break this rule was the symbolic connection that was made between his symbolic act and the priestly regulation regarding the shaving of the head of the nazir (Num 6:18-19).

Even though Ezekiel was in no way a nazir, it is still the description of the nazir in Num 6 that is the most profound background to this prophetic symbolic act. Levine has recently suggested that Ez 5:1-3 could be understood as a literary dramatization of the nazir's sacrifice' of his hair (Num 6:18-19):[3]

18 וְגִלַּח הַנָּזִיר פֶּתַח אֹהֶל מוֹעֵד אֶת־רֹאשׁ נִזְרוֹ וְלָקַח אֶת־שְׂעַר רֹאשׁ נִזְרוֹ וְנָתַן עַל־הָאֵשׁ אֲשֶׁר־תַּחַת זֶבַח הַשְּׁלָמִים 19 וְלָקַח הַכֹּהֵן אֶת־הַזְּרֹעַ בְּשֵׁלָה מִן־הָאַיִל וְחַלַּת מַצָּה אַחַת מִן־הַסַּל	18 Then the nazirites shall shave the consecrated head at the entrance of the tent of meeting, and shall take the hair from the consecrated head and put it on the fire under the sacrifice of well-being. 19 The priest shall take the shoulder of the ram, when it is boiled, and one unleavened cake out of the basket, and one unleavened wafer, and shall put

---

[1] So e.g. Amsler (1985: 28).

[2] This is a common interpretation, so e.g. Zimmerli (1976: 172), Allen (1994: 71), Block (1997: 192), Friebel (1999: 236).

[3] Levine (1993: 233-4).

וּרְקִיק מַצָּה אֶחָד וְנָתַן עַל־כַּפֵּי   them in the palms of the nazirites, after they have
הַנָּזִיר אַחַר הִתְגַּלְּחוֹ אֶת־נִזְרוֹ   shaved the consecrated head.

It is strange that earlier scholarship has not noted the similarities between the description of the symbolic act of Ezekiel and what the nazir is said to have to do when he ends his state as a nazir. We will therefore focus on this particular relationship in order to display the depth of the symbolism involved in Ezekiel's act.

The nazir cuts his hair and puts it into the fire, which is the only instance except Ez 5:1 where such an act is mentioned. Coupled with the fact that Ezekiel was a prophet, and that the institution of the nazir was closely tied to the priestly institution, makes it likely that we should take Num 6 into consideration when we try to understand the symbolic value of the act in Ez 5:1. As a matter of fact, we can strengthen this comparison suggested by Levine by relating to yet another text, namely Jer 7:29;

גָּזִּי נִזְרֵךְ וְהַשְׁלִיכִי וּשְׂאִי   Cut off your hair and throw it away;
עַל־שְׁפָיִם קִינָה   raise a lamentation on the bare heights.

In this text, it is a matter of a symbolic act of lamentation, and the performance of the act is not used symbolically. This is the opposite to Is 7:20, where the procedure is used symbolically but where there is no reference to the shaving as an act of lamentation. What unites these three texts is that they all, in various ways, convey a notion of shame through the act of shaving off the hair.

What makes Jer 7:29 of particular interest in relation to Num 6:19 and also to Ez 5, is the word נִזְרֵךְ.[1] The word נֵזֶר is used in Num 6 as a designative of the head of the nazir; גלח (שְׂעַר) רֹאשׁ נִזְרוֹ, lit. 'shave the head of his consecration' (vv. 18, 19), or better, 'shave his consecrated head', and טמא רֹאשׁ נִזְרוֹ, 'defile the consecrated head' (v. 9). However, both of these expressions also occur in the same chapter in a more contracted form, גלח אֶת־נִזְרוֹ, 'shave his consecration' (v. 19) and טמא נִזְרוֹ, 'defile his consecration' (v. 12). What is referred to in this more contracted expression is the hair that part of the body, which for the nazir was consecrated, lit. 'restricted' from ordinary trimming. His hair was an outward sign of his state as a nazir, and therefore the term denoting the state of being a nazir was transferred by metonymy to that which outwardly signified that state, namely the hair. It is for that reason that Jeremiah, himself the son of a priest (Jer 1:1), used the word נֵזֶר for hair, גָּזִּי נִזְרֵךְ, 'Cut off your hair'. The rea-

---

[1] Holladay (1986: 266).

son why Jeremiah does this is to make his readers associate to the hair as an item of great value and esteem, as was the hair of the nazir, and it is that part which is to be removed.

What we have done so far is that we have established a connection between a prophet's symbolic use of shaving and the description of the nazir. When we then come back to Ez 5:1-3, it is nothing new to say that the prophet's symbolic use of the shaving of the head makes an iconic connection with the description of the nazir, and a conventional connection with the meaning of the shaving of the nazir.

There are also some striking similarities that argue strongly for a deliberate connection between Num 6 and Ez 5;

Num 6:5	כָּל־יְמֵי נֶדֶר נִזְרוֹ תַּעַר לֹא־יַעֲבֹר עַל־רֹאשׁוֹ
Ez 5:1	תַּעַר הַגַּלָּבִים תִּקָּחֶנָּה לָּךְ וְהַעֲבַרְתָּ עַל־רֹאשְׁךָ

The similarities between the two expressions are the word תַּעַר, 'razor',[1] and the expression עבר עַל־רֹאשׁ, 'pass over the head', the latter occurring in only these two instances in MT.

The sum of all this must be that the description that Ezekiel receives in Ez 5:1-3 is deliberately formed on the basis of the description of how the nazir would end his state of being a nazir. It is in this context that we must seek the symbolic value of this comparison between the prophetic symbolic act and the cultic act of deconsecrating a nazir. I would suggest that we find the basic clue in Num 6:8, כֹּל יְמֵי נִזְרוֹ קָדֹשׁ הוּא לַיהוָה, 'All their days as Nazirites they are holy to Yhwh'. Israel was supposed to be God's pride among other nations, his holy people. However, they turned away and worshipped other gods, and they must therefore loose their status of being holy and consecrated, within the protective sphere of God's presence. We should also note, that there is no indication in the text that we should find a symbolic role to Ezekiel personally. It is the very act of shaving that is symbolically relevant here, nothing else.[2]

---

[1] Cf. KTU² 1.5.VI.17-19, (17) *mizrtm . gr . b abn* (18) *ydy . psltm . b yʿr* (19) *yhdy*, 'they scratch the skin with a stone, they scratch with a flint as a razor'. However, it remains uncertain whether this refers to shaving of hair.

[2] Against e.g. Friebel (1999: 236), who takes Ezekiel as a representative of the people as the one being shaved, and as a representative for God as the one who shaves. This is without any support in the text, and creates a very complicated symbolism indeed. Friebel fails to note the very elaborate literary connections to the theme of the nazir, as does most commentators, with the exception of Levine (1993), as described above.

Another text that is clearly related to Ez 5 is Lev 26, the ending of the holiness code with blessings and curses. It is particularly the image of the roaming sword as divine judgement that constitutes the link between these two texts;[1]

Leviticus 26		Ezekiel 5	
(v. 2)	וְחֶרֶב לֹא־תַעֲבֹר בְּאַרְצְכֶם	(v. 1)	קַח־לְךָ חֶרֶב ... וְהַעֲבַרְתָּ עַל־רֹאשֶׁךָ
(v. 25)	וְהֵבֵאתִי עֲלֵיכֶם חֶרֶב	(v. 17)	וְחֶרֶב אָבִיא עָלָיִךְ
(v. 33)	וַהֲרִיקֹתִי אַחֲרֵיכֶם חָרֶב	(v. 2)	וְחֶרֶב אָרִיק אַחֲרֵיהֶם

Scholars have debated the direction of dependence between the two, or if there might be a mutual dependence on a common tradition.[2] The strong relationship between Lev 26 and Ez can also be extended to include Jer,[3] which makes it all the more likely that Ezekiel at least made use of an already well-known, conventional phraseology in formulating chapter 5.

When Ezekiel is done shaving, he is told to weigh the hair, and divide it, and from vv. 2-4 we understand that it will be divided into three piles. There is no indication that this act of weighing should be understood symbolically. Instead, the weighing is merely a preparation for the acts that follow in vv. 2-4.[4]

The acts whereby Ezekiel is said to disperse with the hair are representative of the fates of the people after the city has fallen. In these acts, Ezekiel plays the role of God, and the hair stands conventionally for the people. There is no relation regarding this symbolic use of the hair and the hair that has been shaved off in the preceding act. Instead, the various acts in vv. 2-4 make a fresh start with a new symbolic meaning of the hair.

One third of the hair is to be burned inside the city, ironically symbolising those who fall when the enemies enter. However, the fire itself may very well be used throughout this text be used as a conventional symbol for the fate of the people at the hands of the Babylonians, which is also described as the punishment by God.

---

[1] In both Lev 26:33 and Ez 5:2, the expression in question is preceded with an expression that is similar in boths instances, תִּזְרֶה לָרוּחַ (Lev 26:33a), אֱזָרֶה בְּגוֹיִם (Ez 5:2a). In both instances it is Israel that is to be swept away by the wind. This even further strengthens the ties between these two texts.

[2] Levine (1987: 29-30) argues that although they both emanate from the same literary circles, Lev 26 echoes Ez 5, see also Levine (1989: 280-1). Kilian (1963: 161-2) sees a disciple of Ezekiel as the likely author, and Hartley (1992: 460-2) dates Lev 26 earlier that Ez 5.

[3] See the collection of similar items between Jer, Ez and Lev 26 in Levine (1987: 29-30).

[4] Against e.g. Block (1997: 193), Friebel (1999: 237), who both make their exposition of this act without claiming any textual support.

One third of the hair Ezekiel is told to strike with the sword outside the city, ironically symbolising those who fall while trying to escape after the city has fallen.

One third will be 'scattered to the wind', presumably blown away by Ezekiel as a symbol that would seem to be more conventional than iconic. When it is said that God 'will unsheathe my sword after them', it remains uncertain if this refers to some further symbolic act on Ezekiel's part, or simply a figurative reference to the fact that even those who seem to escape will eventually be caught up.

Ezekiel is then to take from the third pile of hair a small part, and bind[1] them into the corners of his mantle, symbolising in a conventional way the notion of rescue and safety with those who would seem convinced that they have been convinced of their safety. This might also stand, as a conventional symbol, for the theological belief that there will be a rescue by God from the Babylonians, but this must remain uncertain.

Finally, Ezekiel is to take from the hair in his mantle a small part and throw into the fire, as a conventional symbolism for the fate of those who would seem convinced that they have escaped to security.[2] This may very well refer to complacent exiles,[3] but is very hard to find any sure indications in that direction. The act of hiding in the corners of the mantle is conventional, since those who are referred to have presumably escaped, and the act of burning them does not function in an iconic sense of representing an analogy. Instead, it symbolizes in a conventional sense that even from those who escape, many will eventually perish. If the act of tying into the mantle stands for a theological understanding, this act then stands conventionally for a denouncing of this belief, saying that there will be no safe haven with God and that any such belief is futile.

---

[1] The word וְצַרְתָּ may very well carry with it a deliberate association to its previous occurrence in 4:3, where it is used in its more technical sense of 'besiege', but it is hard to see any significance to that wordplay, if indeed it is intentional. A more fruitful reference has been made by Block (1997: 195), to a figurative use of a similar phrase, מִי צָרַר־מַיִם בַּשִּׂמְלָה, 'who has wrapped up waters in the mantle'. See also Malul (1986), Viberg (1992: 137).

[2] Friebel (1999: 241) holds that this last small part of the hair was not taken from the hair in the mantle, but from the hair that was scattered, making vv. 3 and 4 parallel in this regard. But this breaks the structure whereby the whole thrust of the message in vv. 2-4 relies, namely that regardless of how much the inhabitants will try to escape, and even believe they have done so, it will be futile.

[3] So Block (1997: 195) and similarly Friebel (1999: 242).

Summary and Conclusions

1. The symbolic act of shaving the head is based on the iconic symbolism of a nazir being shaven. The further meaning of the symbolic act relies, however, on the conventional symbolism, which is achieved by means of relating to the meaning of the shaving of a nazir. The changed state of the nazir is then used as a conventional symbol for the people, as they are no longer God's protected people.

2. The weighing of the hair does not receive any symbolic meaning, as it is merely a preparation for the symbolic acts that follow.

2. In the following acts, the hair is used conventionally for the people, and this has no relation as far as its symbolic meaning is concerned with the preceding act.

3. In the briefly described acts in vv. 2-4, various forms of both iconic and conventional symbolism is used in order to describe the fates of those who inhabited the city, now conquered. Regardless of whether they perish inside the city or while trying to flee, they will not succeed.

5. Preparing to Leave (Ezekiel 12:3-7)

The Text

3 וְאַתָּה בֶן־אָדָם עֲשֵׂה לְךָ כְּלֵי
גוֹלָה וּגְלֵהⁿ יוֹמָם לְעֵינֵיהֶם
וְגָלִיתָ מִמְּקוֹמְךָ אֶל־מָקוֹם
אַחֵר לְעֵינֵיהֶם אוּלַי יִרְאוּ כִּי
בֵית מְרִי הֵמָּה 4 וְהוֹצֵאתָ
כֵלֶיךָ כִּכְלֵי גוֹלָה יוֹמָם
לְעֵינֵיהֶם וְאַתָּה תֵּצֵא בָעֶרֶב
לְעֵינֵיהֶם כְּמוֹצָאֵי גוֹלָה
5 לְעֵינֵיהֶם חֲתָר־לְךָ בַקִּיר
וְיָצֵאתָᵇ בּוֹ 6 לְעֵינֵיהֶם
עַל־כָּתֵף תִּשָּׂא בָּעֲלָטָה תֵצֵאᵇ
פָּנֶיךָ תְכַסֶּה וְלֹא תִרְאֶה
אֶת־הָאָרֶץ כִּי־מוֹפֵת נְתַתִּיךָ
לְבֵית יִשְׂרָאֵל 7 וָאַעַשׂ כֵּן
כַּאֲשֶׁר צֻוֵּיתִי כֵּלַי הוֹצֵאתִי
כִּכְלֵי גוֹלָה יוֹמָם וּבָעֶרֶב
חָתַרְתִּי־לִי בַקִּיר בְּיָד בָּעֲלָטָה
יָצֵאתִיᵇ עַל־כָּתֵף נָשָׂאתִי לְעֵינֵיהֶם

3 Therefore, mortal, prepare for yourself an exile's baggage, and go into exile by day in their sight; you shall go like an exile from your place to another place in their sight. Perhaps they will understand, though they are a rebellious house. 4 You shall bring out your baggage by day in their sight, as baggage for exile; and you shall go out yourself at evening in their sight, as those do who go into exile. 5 Dig through the wall in their sight, and go out through it. 6 In their sight you shall lift the baggage on your shoulder, and walk out in the dark; you shall cover your face, so that you may not see the land; for I have made you a sign for the house of Israel. 7 I did as I was commanded. I brought out my baggage by day, as baggage for exile, and in the evening I dug through the wall with my own hands; I went out in the dark, lifting it up on my shoulder in their sight.

Textual notes

ⁿ It has been common to regard this as a dittography, since it is missing in LXX, Vulg, Syr and appears to anticipate the later וְגָלִיתָ, so, e.g., Cooke (1936: 134), Zimmerli (1976). This would change the translation into 'make your items for exile during the day'. However, it would be original if Driver were right in that the following sentence is conditional Driver (1954: 150). Allen (1994: 171) argues correctly that the הלג motif is used generally in v. 3a, whereas it is divided in the following into two phases, one where the items are brought out of the house and one where the prophet goes through the hole in the wall. The minus in LXX would then be a case of haplography.

ᵇ MT has hiphil וְהוֹצֵאתָ, as well as in v. 6a and 7b. However, these verbs should be understood as qal forms, otherwise the story becomes unintelligible. The change has strong support in the versions, see BHS. If Ezekiel has already brought out his baggage for exile in the first phase during the day (vv. 4a, 7a), he would not have to bring it with him the second time, in the evening, so e.g. Allen (1994: 171). Allen prefers not to change the hiphil in v. 12, translating it as 'in order to bring him (i.e. Zedekiah) out'. However, this is inconsistent and unnecessary in view of how the earlier hiphil forms in that very same expression have been changed. Some would retain MT, but at the cost of creating a very complicated text, e.g. Zimmerli (1976: 265), Laato (1992: 150), Block (1997: 362, 370-1), Friebel (1999: 264-5, 418).

Analysis

This time Ezekiel is told to perform a more elaborate symbolic act. After a summary description of the whole of the act in v. 3, the following verses describe it as taking place in two stages (vv. 4-7).[1] In the first phase Ezekiel is to gather together items needed when going into exile and bring out the items (v. 4a), after which he is to leave himself in the evening (v. 4b). He is to make a hole in the wall,[2] presumably of his house, exit that way himself, pick up his baggage and leave for another place (v. 5-6a). He is also said to leave with his face covered (v. 6b). In v. 7 the prophet then describes in a summary fashion how he performed the act.

The fact that the major part of the symbolic act is performed in public receives a major emphasis through the five occurrences of the expression לְעֵינֵיהֶם, 'in their sight' in vv. 1-7. If we look carefully at how these occurrences are used, we find that Ezekiel performs four acts that receive this particular emphasis; bringing out the baggage, making a whole in the wall, lifting up the baggage on the shoulder, and walking away. In contrast, the arranging of the items to be brought along in exile is not said explicitly to be done publicly, however, which could mean that it should be interpreted as a preparatory measure only and not part of the symbolic act. Although this might be the case, there is the fact that God explicitly says that Ezekiel is to compose what is needed for exile (v. 3), which would imply that the prophet did perform such an act, which in turn would be of symbolic value. The rest of the act is emphasized as being performed in public because it is the actual departure from the city that is the mark of exile, together with picking up the baggage. The act of covering the face while walking away shares certain characteristics with the packing of the luggage. Neither of the acts is said to be performed in public, and neither is mentioned when the prophet recounts his performance in first person (v. 7). Since

---

[1] So Allen (1994: 179).

[2] This formulation strongly alludes to Ezekiel 8:8, where the prophet is told to enlarge a hole in a wall of the temple, חֲתָר־נָא בַקִּיר וָאֶחְתֹּר בַּקִּיר, '"dig through the wall"; and I dug through the wall'.

there is no reason to question the symbolic value of the covering of the face, in spite of these apparent lacunas, the conclusion must be that the symbolic value of both the packing as well as the covering of the face is supplementary, hence the lack of emphasis on public performance. They are supportive to the more relevant and emphasized acts of picking up the baggage and leaving the city, and it is through them that they receive their connection with public performance and symbolic value.

Again we find the hinge between the description of the prophetic symbolic act (vv. 3-6) and its interpretation (vv. 11b-16) to be a concluding statement, that declares the prophet, and by implication his act as well, to be a sign(vv. 6, 11a). In between the two occurrences of Ezekiel being described as a 'sign', we find his own description of his act. This time the word for sign is מוֹפֵת, whereas in Ez 4:3 its synonym אוֹת was used.[1] Later in v. 11, when Ezekiel is told what to answer his fellow exiles when they ask him for the meaning of his act, his is to tell them that 'I am a מוֹפֵת to you: as I have done, so shall it be done to them; they shall go into exile, into captivity.' This seems to make it crystal clear how the act is to be understood; Ezekiel symbolizes the people who are forced into exile, only allowed to bring a small pack of personal items, itself a conventional symbol for exile. It is interesting to note how this baggage works as a rather complex symbol, since it also stands indexically for travel by means of association, and ironically for the type of baggage that were used by exiles.[2]

The people flee out through the broken wall when the city is stormed. The only exception is when Ezekiel digs a hole in the wall, which stands for the Babylonian army.[3] We have met with similar sudden shifts in what Ezekiel symbolizes in his symbolic acts before in Ez 4-5. The symbolic character of the act also comes through by the use of the preposition כְּ in a repeated simile, גּוֹלָה כִּכְלֵי, 'as the baggage of exile' (vv. 4, 7).

The symbolism of the act is focused on the verb גלה, 'go into exile' (v. 3) and its derivative noun גּוֹלָה, 'exile' (vv. 3, 4, 7), something that is also emphasized in the interpretation (v. 11).

The act receives an extended interpretation (vv. 8-16), which creates an unexpected problem by emphasising Zedekiah as part of or even representative for

---

[1] Each term occurs four times in Ezekiel, מוֹפֵת in 12:6, 11; 24:24, 27, and אוֹת in 4:3; 14:8; 20:12; 20:20.

[2] See ANEP 10, 366, 373. The small pack with personal items seems to have been a simple yet effective way to signify prisoners in the iconography of that day, cf. Jer 46:19. What Jeremiah only used figuratively, Ezekiel performed as a symbolic act.

[3] So e.g. Uehlinger (1987: 138), Allen (1994: 179), Block (1997: 370).

the exiled population of Jerusalem (v. 10b, 12-14).[1] Apparently, a later scribe or
redactor could not help but make a connection between Zedekiah's attempted
escape from Jerusalem (v. 12; 2 Kgs 25:4; Jer 39:4; 52:7) and his blindness, inflicted upon him later by the Babylonians (2 Kgs 25:7; Jer 39:7; 52:11). This
was accomplished by inserting וְאוֹתָהּ לֹא־יִרְאֶה, 'yet he shall not see it' in v. 13,
with a reference to the land of Babylonia.[2] The later scribe evidently interpreted
the veiled head of Zedekiah (v. 12) as a reference to his pierced eyes. However,
in order to make his intrusion understandable in the context he had to change the
reference of the 'land', which can not be seen due to the veil over the head (vv.
6, 12), from Judah to Babylon. This is the clearest argument for this phrase being a later adaptation.[3]

This prophetic symbolic act then symbolizes ironically how the people of Jerusalem are forced into exile by the Babylonians. This is brought home very
concretely by the packing of the typical baggage for exile. When Ezekiel symbolizes the destruction of the wall, he is suddenly not to be understood to imitate
the people but their enemies. The veiled head stands out among the acts performed by Ezekiel here because it is not likely to have been something that was
actually done to exiles. Therefore, what Ezekiel is performing does not have a
reference to a particular act but an idea, namely that they will not be able to see
their land anymore (cf. Jer 22:12).[4] This is also made clear by our reading of v.
12b, namely that Zedekiah will not be able to see with the eyes.[5] Yet, there is
another indication as to why this is emphasized. As was noted above, it is said
five times that what Ezekiel performs is done in public, לְעֵינֵיהֶם, lit. 'unto their
eyes' (vv. 3, 4, 5, 6, 7). Here we should also mention again the twice repeated
statement that Ezekiel and his act is to be a sign to the people (vv. 6, 11). In a
sharp contrast to this public display of the will of God, the people will be forced
to hide their eyes (vv. 6, 12). This is actually the narrative form of what is stated
in the introduction to the description of this prophetic symbolic act, namely that

---

[1] See Lang (1978: 21), Duguid (1994: 43-4), Friebel (1999: 272).

[2] So Lang (1978: 19, 21-3), Lang (1981a: 56), Allen (1994: 175-7). Greenberg (1983: 217-21)
has a very similar view, so also Laato (1992: 152-3). The attempts by Friebel (1999: 261-71)
and Block (1997: 372-5) to retain the text of MT only creates a most strained and unconvincing text. Allen's survey of this redactional problem is so far the most thorough and reliable.

[3] A change has also been made in v. 12, by adding הוּא אֶת־הָאָרֶץ as a gloss, in accordance with
v. 6, so Lang (1978: 19, 21-3), Lang (1981a: 56).

[4] So Greenberg (1983: 211), Allen (1994: 180), Block (1997: 375-6), Friebel (1999: 274).

[5] לֹא־יִרְאֶה לַעַיִן, lit. 'So that he can not see with the eye'. The construction with לְ is unusual,
the only occurrence with a similar meaning is 1 Sam 16:7, הָאָדָם יִרְאֶה לַעֵינַיִם, 'man sees (only)
according to the eyes'.

the people עֵינַיִם לָהֶם לִרְאוֹת וְלֹא רָאוּ, 'have eyes to see but do not see' (v. 2). The point seems to be, that if the people shut their eyes to what God has to say through his prophet, he will leave them nothing left to see.[1]

---

[1] See Krüger (1989: 405-6), who speaks of 'die Unwilligheit der Adressaten der prophetischen Kritik an der Politik Zedekias, ... zu "sehen"', and further, 'Das Publikum des Propheten ist so "blind", daß es nichteinmal seine eigene Deportation richtig wahrnehmen würde!'.

Summary and Conclusions

1. This extended and dramatized act is performed by Ezekiel in order to display how the survivors of the siege of Jerusalem will go into exile.

2. Ezekiel, as well as his act, symbolizes by means of iconic symbolism, in that he represents the behaviour of the future exiles.

3. The baggage that Ezekiel carries out of his house stands ironically for the baggage that exiles would carry with them into exile by means of similarity, indexically for travel by means of association, and as a conventional symbol for travel into exile.

6. Acts of Emotions (Ezekiel 12:17-20; 21:11-2, 17, 19)

The Text

12:17 וַיְהִי דְבַר־יְהוָה אֵלַי
18 לֵאמֹר בֶּן־אָדָם לַחְמְךָ בְּרַעַשׁ
תֹּאכֵל וּמֵימֶיךָ בְּרָגְזָה וּבִדְאָגָה
תִּשְׁתֶּה 19 וְאָמַרְתָּ אֶל־עַם הָאָרֶץ
כֹּה־אָמַר אֲדֹנָי יְהוִה לְיוֹשְׁבֵי
יְרוּשָׁלַ͏ִם אֶל־אַדְמַת יִשְׂרָאֵל לַחְמָם
בִּדְאָגָה יֹאכֵלוּ וּמֵימֵיהֶם בְּשִׁמָּמוֹן
יִשְׁתּוּ לְמַעַן תֵּשַׁם אַרְצָהּ[a]
מִמְּלֹאָהּ מֵחֲמַס כָּל־הַיֹּשְׁבִים בָּהּ
20 וְהֶעָרִים הַנּוֹשָׁבוֹת תֶּחֱרַבְנָה
וְהָאָרֶץ שְׁמָמָה תִהְיֶה וִידַעְתֶּם
כִּי־אֲנִי יְהוָה
...

21:11 וְאַתָּה בֶן־אָדָם הֵאָנַח
בְּשִׁבְרוֹן מָתְנַיִם וּבִמְרִירוּת תֵּאָנַח
לְעֵינֵיהֶם 12 וְהָיָה כִּי־יֹאמְרוּ אֵלֶיךָ
עַל־מָה אַתָּה נֶאֱנָח וְאָמַרְתָּ
אֶל־שְׁמוּעָה כִּי־בָאָה וְנָמֵס כָּל־לֵב
וְרָפוּ כָל־יָדַיִם וְכִהֲתָה כָל־רוּחַ
וְכָל־בִּרְכַּיִם תֵּלַכְנָה מַּיִם הִנֵּה בָאָה
וְנִהְיָתָה נְאֻם אֲדֹנָי יְהוִה
...

17 זְעַק וְהֵילֵל בֶּן־אָדָם
כִּי־הִיא הָיְתָה בְעַמִּי הִיא
בְּכָל־נְשִׂיאֵי יִשְׂרָאֵל מְגוּרֵי אֶל־חֶרֶב
הָיוּ אֶת־עַמִּי לָכֵן סְפֹק אֶל־יָרֵךְ
...

19 וְאַתָּה בֶן־אָדָם הִנָּבֵא
וְהַךְ כַּף אֶל־כָּף וְתִכָּפֵל חֶרֶב
שְׁלִישִׁתָה[c] חֶרֶב חֲלָלִים הִיא ...

12:17 The word of Yhwh came to me: 18 Mortal, eat your bread with quaking, and drink your water with trembling and fear; 19 say to the people of the land, Thus says the Lord Yhwh concerning the inhabitants of Jerusalem in the land of Israel: They shall eat their bread with fear, and drink their water in dismay, because its land shall be stripped of all it contains, because of the violence of all those who live in it. 20 The inhabited cities shall be laid waste, the land shall become a desolation; and you shall know that I am Yhwh.

21:6 Moan therefore, mortal; moan with breaking heart and bitter grief before their eyes. 7 And when they say to you, "Why do you moan?" you shall say, "Because of the news that has come. Every heart will melt and all hands will be feeble, every spirit will faint and every man will wet himself. See, it comes and it will be fulfilled," says the Lord Yhwh.

...

12 Cry and wail, O mortal, for it is against my people; it is against all Israel's princes; they are thrown to the sword, together with my people. Ah! Strike the thigh!

...

14 You, mortal, prophesy; Clap your hands. Let the sword fall twice, thrice; it is a sword for killing. ...

Textual notes

[a] 'Its (ie, Jerusalem's) region', so e.g. Allen (1994: 174). There is no reason to change into the easier reading of some manuscripts, ארצם, 'their land' or even simply 'land' as in the versions, see BHS.

b Lit. 'Every knee will run with water', which does not seem to make any sense here. The Akkadian *birku* is commonly used as a euphemism for male or female genitals, CAD B, 257, and it has been suggested that the same would apply for בֶּרֶךְ here, Driver (1953: 260), followed by Hillers (1965: 87, n. 7). This has the external support of LXX, Sym, Vulg and Syr. The same expression occurs in Ez 7:17. The euphemistic meaning can be substantiated by taking Joel 4:18 into consideration, וְכָל־אֲפִיקֵי יְהוּדָה יֵלְכוּ מָיִם, where the expression הלך מים definitely means 'to flow with water', 'and all the stream-beds of Judah shall flow with water'. In 1QHᵃ the expression has been transformed into a simile, 1QHᵃ IV 33, וילכו ברכי כמים מוגרים במורד, 'and my knees slide away *as* water that flows down a slope', and 1QHᵃ VIII 34, וילכו כמים ברכי, 'my knees slide *as* water', cf. Holm-Nielsen (1960: 78, 86, n. 86). This can also be found in the Tg. to Ez 21:12, וכל רכוביא יתאשדן כמיא, 'and every knee shall flow *as* water'. It is interesting to note that in 2 Kgs 18:27 (= Is 36:12), שֵׁינֵיהֶם (Kethib) 'their urine' has been corrected with the euphemism מֵימֵי רַגְלֵיהֶם (Qere).

c The emendation to pual is not convincing, see BHS commentaries, since it does not explain MT as well as LXX, ἡ τρίτη, 'the third'. The form שְׁלִשָׁתָה could be spelled defectively (Num 28:14; Deut 26:12), either with a feminine suffix, 'its third (time)', or as a slight misspelling of the variant feminine form שְׁלִישִׁיָה. (Is 19:24).

Analysis

This is a collection of various symbolic acts that Ezekiel performs, that all share the character of displaying strong emotions, mainly those of sorrow and despair.

The problem of differentiating between a symbolic act performed by Ezekiel and genuine expressions of his own feelings becomes acute in these texts. This is why we will have to pay particular attention to the contextual indications, since they are the only way to secure an understanding of an expression as not only an expression of an emotion, but also as an expression of a symbolic act, performed by the prophet.

In 12:18, a meal is used as the setting for the symbolic act of displaying fear and dismay over the impending disaster. Since the act is ordered by God, and since it receives an interpretation immediately afterwards, there is no question concerning the status of the act as a prophetic symbolic act.

Ezekiel is to eat and drink with trembling hands, and it is likely that this would show itself in other ways as well, but we are not given any more indications. The symbolic act is thereafter given its interpretation (v. 19), where the people are said to be the ones who are to eat and drink with fear, due to the catastrophe that is about to fall on their land and its cities (v. 20). The symbolism of the acts in vv. 11-12 works by means of iconic symbolism, as Ezekiel imitates how the people in the city will soon be eating their meals with fear.

Before we go into the details of the symbolic acts of Ez 21, we must pause and analyse the structure of vv. 6-22. Various attempts to structure these verses together with the rest of ch. 21 have been done, but no clear consensus seems to have been reached. One possible reason is that an originally clear structure has been overworked by later editors and glossators, so that what we now have is a conglomerate without any consistent structure. However, no consensus has been reached regarding later editing and glossing in vv. 6-22, so we should make an attempt at finding a structure that does make sense and help us in understanding the symbolic acts more thoroughly.[1]

Verses 6-22 can be divided into the following five parts;

Theme	Mission
1. 6-10 God draws his sword on his people I	Prophecy
2. 11-12 The prophet mourns the fall of Judah	Sigh
3. 13-16 God draws his sword on his people I	Prophecy
4. 17-18 The prophet mourns his stricken people	Cry, wail, strike thigh
5. 19-22 God draws his sword on his people III	Prophecy, clap hands

After the introductory part of vv. 1-5, the focus shifts no less than four times in 17 verses, as can be seen from the table above. Three of the five parts (1, 3, 5) deal with the fall of Jerusalem and Judah from the divine perspective, symbolized by a sword that is to come down on the land. It is none other than God himself who is holding the sword, the emphasis on which serves the purpose of preventing a split between forces behind the fall of Jerusalem and belief in God. To Ezekiel, the challenge is to hold them both together, which is why God must be seen as the one who swings the sword aloof. However, in between these very strong condemnatory speeches we find two passages that present the same events, but from a different perspective (2, 4). A simple sign of recognising this structure is the introductory command to the prophet, 'prophecy' in parts 1, 3 and 5, and various symbolic acts in 2 and 4. The structure is complicated in part 5, when the prophet is told both to 'prophecy' and to perform a symbolic act, 'clap your hands' (v. 19). This should be seen as a suitable climax to the struc-

---

[1] The only corrections to the text of vv. 1-22 that I would propose is what Allen has shown quite convincingly, namely that vv. 15b and 18a, both commonly regarded as suspect, were notes in the margin that mistakenly came to be inserted into the main text, Allen (1989), Allen (1990: 19-20).

ture, where the prophetic symbolic act is used to clarify the divine perspective as well.

In 21:11, the prophet is again told to use strong emotional display as a symbolic means of getting through to his people with a message they apparently had a hard time understanding, and they grew frustrated with the complicated imagery, saying, הֲלֹא מְמַשֵּׁל מְשָׁלִים הוּא, 'Is he not a maker of allegories?' (21:5). The content of the apparently difficult message from the prophet (21:1-4) is then repeated in a less abstract way, supposedly meant to be more easily understood (21:6-10). It is significant that it is in that context that we find the exhortation to the prophet to perform a symbolic act, presumably because such an act would convince more readily than highly strung imagery would. Again we find in v. 11 that the symbolic act is to be performed לְעֵינֵיהֶם, 'before their eyes', i.e., the emphasis is on the public performance of the prophetic symbolic act, and hence on its communicative function.

The symbolic act in v. 11 is a display of dismay, grief and pain. He is to אנח (niph), 'sigh', and to do so in front of the people. His sigh of pain should be so thoroughly deep and convincing that it would make people think he was falling apart, הֵאָנַח בְּשִׁבְרוֹן מָתְנַיִם, lit. 'Sigh at the breaking of thighs'.[1] The interpretation comes immediately afterwards, saying that the reason for such an emotional turmoil will be a message that will make all people experience this dismay. The event that will cause such an emotional storm is the fall of Jerusalem, and it is the divine judgement on that city, symbolized by the sword, that constitutes the theme of the following vv. 13-17. In v. 17a we again encounter an exhortation to the prophet to display strong emotions such as shouting and howling because the people are (about to be) in distress.

These strong feelings are not, however, to be considered as something new and innovative on the part of the prophet, and neither in relation to the viewers. Neither are they to be considered as evidences of the prophetic ecstasy.[2] Instead, they should be seen as a conventional form of displaying grief, sorrow and pain in response to bad news, as Hillers has amply shown.[3] Again, we find that the prophet uses conventional forms in his attempts to communicate to and persuade

---

[1] See Viberg (1992: 45). There is an interesting parallel in KTU[2] 1.3.III.33, where Anat looses control of herself, *b ʿdn . ksl . ttbr*, 'she burst hips all around', see Hillers (1965: 86-7), who attempts to show that 'in biblical Hebrew literature there is a widespread literary convention depicting the reaction to bad news, conceptually similar to that in the Canaanite poems'.

[2] So Hillers (1965: 87).

[3] Hillers (1965).

his people, something that all the more substantiate the thesis that the prophetic symbolic acts are inherently communicative.

The symbolic act that Ezekiel is told to perform in v. 17b, סְפֹק אֶל־יָרֵךְ, 'strike the thigh', is evidently of the same nature as those in vv. 11 and 17a, although it is of a more complicated nature. The act to strike the thigh is an act of grief and sorrow, which can more clearly be seen from its other occurrence in Jer 31:19. The act is also known throughout various ancient cultures.[1]

> The act occurs several times in Akkadian. It is found in 'The descent of Ishtar', where Ereshkigal reacts by striking her thigh (*imḫaṣ pēnša*) and biting her finger, because she can not comply with the simplest of wishes.[2] Sargon II writes in the account of his eighth campaign that his enemies, when they heard what Sargon's armies had performed, lamented (*iqbū*) and struck their thighs (*imḫaṣū šapar-šun*).[3] The act is also referred to in Gilgamesh VII.iv.2-4 (*im]ḫaṣ šaparšu*).[4]
>
> The act occurs twice in Homeric Literature. In the Iliad XVI.125, Odysseus strikes his thighs (μηρὼ πληξάμενος) when his boat is on fire and enemies are sighted. In the Odyssey XIII.198, he can not recognize his own country, and so he strikes his thighs with his hand (πεπλήγετο μηρὼ χερσὶ) and speaks mournfully.

These acts of grief are all to be seen as performed from the perspective of the people of Judah, experiencing the disaster of the Babylonian army raiding through its cities and destroying in its way. The question and answer form[5] found in v. 12 indicates that the nonverbal communication was accompanied by verbal as well. The acts therefore symbolize the reaction of the people of Judah by means of iconic symbolism. As performed by the people, inside the symbolic world of the symbolic acts, these acts are conventional forms of nonverbal communication, displaying grief and sorrow.

When we come to the symbolic act that Ezekiel is told to perform in v. 19, the focus has shifted. In vv. 11 and 17, the symbolic acts displayed grief and despair, whereas here in v. 19, the act of clapping hands is evidently an act of defiance and display of strength, both physical as well as mental. It is here that we are aided by our display of the structure of vv. 6-22, since v. 19 is part of a description that is seen from the divine perspective, emphasising the surety with

---

[1] Cf. Lipinski (1970), Viberg (1992: 50).
[2] Borger (1979: 101), Gruber (1980: 380-1).
[3] Mayer (1983) l. 213, see Gruber (1980: 381-2).
[4] Thompson (1930: 46), cf. VI.63, see Gruber (1980: 382).
[5] See Long (1971).

which the sword will come upon the land, and the passion with which this is to be brought about. The symbolic act is clearly meant to emphasize this impression, as is also clear from v. 22, where God proclaims his intention to perform this act and pour out his anger, אַכֶּה כַפִּי אֶל־כַּפִּי וַהֲנִחֹתִי חֲמָתִי. There is no possibility that this act of striking hands could be understood as yet another act symbolising distress and grief. Instead, it should be seen as yet another example of how the prophet makes use of conventional means to express himself.

The act is that of clapping hands, which receives no less than four different expressions; (1) ספק כף (על) (2) מכא כף (3) נכה (ב)כף/(כף אל כף) (4) תקע כף. The various examples of these expressions can be summarised as follows;

1. Rejoicing
   - a. Rejoicing in acclamation   2 Kgs 11:12 (2); Ps 47:2 (1)
   - b. Rejoicing in disaster   Ez 25:6 (3); Nah 3:19 (1); Lam 2:15 (4); Job 27:23 (4)
2. Hostility
   - a. Active display of hostility   Num 24:10 (4); Ez 21:19 (2), 22 (2); 22:13 (2)
   - b. Passive display of hostility   Ez 6:11 (2)

It is clear from this overview that there was not one distinct idiom in biblical Hebrew for clapping hands, since at least four verbs could be used in describing the same act. However, in some texts the idiomatic character appears to be stronger by not having a genitive suffix on יד/כף. This makes the expression less semantically transparent, for example וַיַּכּוּ־כָף, lit. 'and they struck hand' (2 Kgs 11:12), as opposed to הַכֵּה בְכַפְּךָ, lit. 'strike with your hand' (Ez 6:11). Indeed, the expression used in Ez 21:19, 22 is even more transparent, since it describes more clearly how one hand was used to strike the other, נכה כַּף אֶל־כָּף, lit. 'strike hand to hand'.

There is a subtle emphasis in vv. 6-22 on 'hand'. There is the *hand* of God, which pulls out the sword from its sheath (vv. 3, 5) and puts it into the *hand* of a slayer (vv. 16a, 16b), and the *hands* of the prophet (v. 17), clapping as God's own *hands* do (v. 22). The emphasis on 'hand' also works metonymically as an emphasis on the sword of God's judgement, the main theme in vv. 6-22.[1] One could imagine that when Ezekiel strikes one hand against the other, an imaginary sword is in his hands, by means of an indexical symbolism that was made

---

[1] Scholars have often talked about an ancient 'song of the sword' laying behind the present text of Ez 21, so, e.g., Guthrie (1962: 280), who argued for an original song being later edited into a union with a collection of descriptions of symbolic acts.

relevant by mentioning how Ezekiel will let the sword fall repeatedly.[1] Then, in v. 22, it all becomes understandable when God himself is said to perform this act, since he is the agent behind the sword that will strike Judah. Therefore, we could choose to translate v. 22ba epexegetically in relation to v. 22a, 'Even I will clap my hands, *and so* put out my anger'. The quite conventional symbolic act is then used by the prophet to stand for something more than it conventionally did in the symbolic world of the act, by means of iconic symbolism as being performed by God. The prophet takes what is understandable and uses it to say something that is partly old, partly new. The symbolic act still stood for its conventional meaning, but together with the integrated theme of the divine sword, the act was given a new and innovative meaning. The act was in its conventional use associated with hostility, which it was used to encourage. Through indexical symbolism, it came to be used not only to encourage hostility, but also to actually symbolize the outpouring of that anger and hostility.

---

[1] Terrien (1996) argues that Ezekiel performs a sword dance, dancing and juggling with the naked blade of a sword, 'The Dance of the Sword is, in effect, a mimetic portrait of the deity' (p. 131). Although this remains a very remote possibility, it strains the power of imagination since the text is certainly not describing anything of the kind.

Summary and Conclusions

1. The meal that is prepared with fear symbolizes ironically the meals that will be prepared inside the besieged city.

2. The various displays of grief, pain and sorrow that Ezekiel performs symbolizes ironically the emotions of the exiles when they hear of the fall of Jerusalem. Within the symbolic world of the acts, the performances are conventional forms of nonverbal communication.

3. The act of clapping hands is used ironically for how God would clap his hands to display his strength and defiance. In the symbolic world of the act, it is a conventional act of nonverbal communication. Together with the reference to a drawn sword, the act would symbolize indexically how the hands are clasped round a sword.

7. Not Mourning for a Wife (Ezekiel 24:15-24)

The Text

15 וַיְהִי דְבַר־יְהוָה אֵלַי
לֵאמֹר 16 בֶּן־אָדָם הִנְנִי לֹקֵחַ מִמְּךָ
אֶת־מַחְמַד עֵינֶיךָ בְּמַגֵּפָה וְלֹא
תִסְפֹּד וְלֹא תִבְכֶּה וְלֹוא תָבוֹא
דִּמְעָתֶךָ[b] 17 הֵאָנֵק דֹּם מֵתִים אֵבֶל[a]
לֹא־תַעֲשֶׂה פְּאֵרְךָ חֲבוֹשׁ עָלֶיךָ
וּנְעָלֶיךָ תָּשִׂים בְּרַגְלֶיךָ וְלֹא תַעְטֶה
עַל־שָׂפָם וְלֶחֶם אֲנָשִׁים[c] לֹא תֹאכֵל
18 וָאֲדַבֵּר אֶל־הָעָם בַּבֹּקֶר[d]
וַתָּמָת אִשְׁתִּי בָּעָרֶב וָאַעַשׂ בַּבֹּקֶר
כַּאֲשֶׁר צֻוֵּיתִי 19 וַיֹּאמְרוּ אֵלַי הָעָם
הֲלֹא־תַגִּיד לָנוּ מָה־אֵלֶּה לָּנוּ כִּי
אַתָּה עֹשֶׂה 20 וָאֹמַר אֲלֵיהֶם
דְּבַר־יְהוָה הָיָה אֵלַי לֵאמֹר
21 אֱמֹר לְבֵית יִשְׂרָאֵל כֹּה־אָמַר אֲדֹנָי
יְהוִה הִנְנִי מְחַלֵּל אֶת־מִקְדָּשִׁי גְּאוֹן
עֻזְּכֶם מַחְמַד עֵינֵיכֶם וּמַחְמַל
נַפְשְׁכֶם וּבְנֵיכֶם וּבְנוֹתֵיכֶם אֲשֶׁר
עֲזַבְתֶּם בַּחֶרֶב יִפֹּלוּ 22 וַעֲשִׂיתֶם
כַּאֲשֶׁר עָשִׂיתִי עַל־שָׂפָם לֹא תַעְטוּ
וְלֶחֶם אֲנָשִׁים[e] לֹא תֹאכֵלוּ
23 וּפְאֵרֵכֶם[f] עַל־רָאשֵׁיכֶם וְנַעֲלֵיכֶם
בְּרַגְלֵיכֶם לֹא תִסְפְּדוּ וְלֹא תִבְכּוּ
וּנְמַקֹּתֶם בַּעֲוֺנֹתֵיכֶם וּנְהַמְתֶּם אִישׁ
אֶל־אָחִיו 24 וְהָיָה יְחֶזְקֵאל לָכֶם
לְמוֹפֵת כְּכֹל אֲשֶׁר־עָשָׂה תַּעֲשׂוּ
בְּבֹאָהּ וִידַעְתֶּם כִּי אֲנִי אֲדֹנָי יְהוִה

15 The word of Yhwh came to me: 16 Mortal, with one blow I will take away from you the delight of your eyes; yet you shall not mourn or weep, you shall not cry. 17 Groan silenty for the dead, for you may not make a mourning ritual. Bind on your turban, and put your sandals on your feet; do not cover your upper lip or eat the bread of mourners. 18 In the evening my wife died, and on the next morning I did as I was commanded. 19 The people said to me, "Will you not tell us what these things mean, that you are acting this way?" 20 Then I said to them: The word of Yhwh came to me: 21 Say to the house of Israel, Thus says the Lord Yhwh: I will profane my sanctuary, the pride of your power, the delight of your eyes, your heart's desire; your sons and daughters whom you left behind shall fall by the sword. 22 You shall do as I have done; you shall not cover your upper lip or eat the bread of mourners. 23 Your turbans shall be on your heads and your sandals on your feet; you shall not mourn or weep, but you shall pine away in your iniquities and groan to one another. 24 Thus Ezekiel shall be a sign to you; you shall do just as he has done. When this comes, then you shall know that I am the Lord Yhwh.

Textual notes

[a] The phrase מֵתִים אֵבֶל, 'the dead, a lament', is grammatically irregular, and could at the most be taken as an attribution, 'lament for the dead', although that would be extremely unusual. Some would prefer to transpose the two words into a more understandable form with אֵבֶל in construct state, so Fohrer (1955: 141), Eichrodt (1970: 340), Allen (1990: 55), with Fohrer also deleting הֵאָנֵק דֹּם. Zimmerli (1976: 502) understands the preceding דֹּם as meaning 'motionless', and in construct state to the following מֵתִים,

'deathly stiffness'. Accordingly, אֵבֶל is taken as the object of the following, 'make no lamentation', so Greenberg (1997: 508-9). However, that מֵתִים would be part of an idiom and not refer to the dead that can not be properly lamented is highly unlikely in the context of Ez 24:15ff. Driver (1954) transposes the first two words of v. 17, 'cease, be silent in respect to groaning', but that is not necessary, see Allen (1990: 55). Bauer (1957) sees in דם a homonym, related to Akkadian *damāmu*, Ugaritic *dmm*, 'wail', 'Stöhne, klag still über die Tote, Trauertage (aber) halte nicht', cf. Dahood (1960: 400-4), Westhuizen (1986), BDB 199, HAL 217, DCH II, 451. However, Bauer must construe the 'still' himself, which makes the interpretation dubious, since the homonym is usually taken to mean 'mourn', KTU² 1.16 I.25-6, *bn . al . tbkn . al tdm . ly*, 'son, do not weap, do not mourn for me', cf. Moor (1987: 212). Nevertheless, the emphasis in the context on abstaining from the conventional forms of lamentation makes דמם, 'be silent' the most suitable verb behind דם, thus 'groan silenty'. Since מֵתִים אֵבֶל is such an awkward expression grammatically, it is preferable to see מֵתִים as the object of הֵאָנֵק דם, 'groan silently (for) the dead', see Jer 51:52, יֵאֱנֹק חָלָל, 'groan for the slain'. For a construction similar to הֵאָנֵק דם מֵתִים, see Is 23:16, נַגֵּן הַרְבִּי־שִׁיר, 'sing many songs'.

[b] The phrase וְלוֹא תָבוֹא דִמְעָתֶךָ is missing in LXX, and slows down the staccato tempo of the text. The plene spelling of the negation preceded by ו only occurs here and in Ez 16:56. However, there does not seem to be a satisfying explanation for how it came into the text, cf. Cooke (1936: 270), Zimmerli (1976), Allen (1990: 55). Only Allen makes a serious attempt to explain how the addition might have been made. Greenberg (1997: 508) proposes a haplography in the Hebrew text behind LXX, דמעתהבאהאנק ... תבכה, which would seem reasonable enough for the phrase to be retained.

[c] MT אֲנָשִׁים is hardly a correct vocalisation. More relevant would be אֲנֻשִׁים, 'unfortunate', so Allen (1990: 56). Some follow Tg. אבילין, which suggests אוֹנִים, 'mourners', cf. לֶחֶם אוֹנִים, 'bread for mourning' (Hos 9:4). The defence for MT by Greenberg (1997: 509) is strained.

[d] The phrase וָאֲדַבֵּר אֶל־הָעָם בַּבֹּקֶר, 'and I spoke to the people in the morning', does not make much sense in this context. Some see it as a gloss Zimmerli (1976: 503), but perhaps it is due to misplacement during transmission of the text. It is possible that it once stood at the end of v. 18, although this would create an unlikely doubling of בַּבֹּקֶר in v. 18, between vv. 19 and 20, so Allen (1990: 56). Pohlmann (1992: 14-5) sees the addition as more a matter of literary criticism, added in order to strengthen the dating of the subsequent prophetic oracle. However, since the phrase has full support in the versions, and since there is no obvious reason for it to be deleted, it will be retained.

[e] Omitted in LXX, Syr, Vulg. Some take it as a mistake in MT, possibly dittography, so Zimmerli (1976: 503), Allen (1990: 56), BHS, whereas Block (1997: 784), Greenberg (1997: 510) takes the omission to be erroneous. Greenberg explains the repetition as an emphasis on the interest of the audience, which is reasonable enough, more so than a case of addition, mistakenly or not. The omission may be stylistic.

[f] The form of פְאֵר is singular but the sense is plural, against Block (1997: 784).

Analysis

In this symbolic act, we encounter a motif that appears also with Hosea and Jeremiah, namely how the motif of a wife is used to symbolize the fate of the nation (Hos 1-3; Jer 16).[1] However, in contrast to the story in Hos 1-3, it is not a question of adultery on the part of Ezekiel's wife that makes her suitable for prophetic symbolism, but the sad fact that she is taken away from him. Something from real life is used as a symbol, a מֹפֵת (v. 27), in order to be realistic and convincing.

Ezekiel is told that his wife is about to die suddenly (v. 16a), but he is not to perform the conventional mourning rituals of weeping, covering the lower part of his face and keeping to the funeral diet (vv. 16b, 17c). The only sign of his grief he will be allowed to express is a virtually silent groan (v. 17). Instead, he is told to act as though nothing had happened, putting on his turban and sandals (v. 17a-b, cf. 2 Sam 15:20; Is 20:2). The symbolic act thus consists of the almost silent groaning together with the extremely common practise of dressing for an ordinary day.

The description of how the act is to be performed in vv. 16-17 is followed by a summary statement, saying that his wife died quite suddenly in the evening (v. 18a). On the following morning, Ezekiel sets out to do what he has been told (v. 18b). It is at this stage that we again encounter the explicit question from the people, 'Will you not tell us what these things mean for us, that you are acting this way?' (v. 19, cf. 12:8; 21:12). The answer from Ezekiel then comes in the form of a divine oracle, concerning the meaning of the symbolic act (vv. 21-23) and the role of the prophet (vv. 23-24a). However, in v. 22 Ezekiel deviates from the pattern of speaking about himself in third person when be says that 'you shall do as I have done; you shall not cover your upper lip or eat the bread of mourners.' This is more likely a case of where the prophet so identifies himself with the divine command that what God says melts together with what the prophet himself says. This may be because Ezekiel's oracles mostly have a literary origin, without much of an oral stage.

The interpretation of the prophetic symbolic act in vv. 21-23 centres on the identification of the wife as the temple that is about to be destroyed, as well as the children of the exiles left behind in Jerusalem, who are about to be cut down

---

[1] The argument of Garscha (1974: 82-3), that the story of the death of Ezekiel's wife is without any historical foundation because this is a motif already found in the earlier prophets Hosea and Jeremiah, is hypercritical and unconvincing. That Ezekiel 24:15-27 should be dependent on Jer 16 for its story of the death of Ezekiel's wife is equally unconvincing.

by the sword (v. 21). Although God is not presented as the agent of the destruction of the children in v. 21, we are left in no doubt as to who is behind the sword, and it also becomes explicit later in v. 25 (cf. 21:3-5).

It is apparent that the point of comparison between the wife and the temple/children is that which is dearest and most loved to the people in exile, and that is precisely what God will bring down, 'I will profane my sanctuary, the pride of your power ...' (v. 21).[1] This is brought out most clearly by means of a repeated phrase, מַחְמַד עֵינֶיךָ, 'the pride of your eyes' referring to Ezekiel's wife (v. 16), and מַחְמַד עֵינֵיכֶם, referring to the city/temple/children (vv. 21, 25). That the emphasis is on the removal of that which is dearest to the people can also be seen from the five occurrences of the third person plural suffix in v. 21, emphasising the fact that it is their pride and longing that is broken down. This is repeated later in v. 25 with six similar suffixes. But before anything is attributed to the people, no mistake is made as to whose temple is being destroyed, 'I will profane my sanctuary' (v. 21). It rightfully belongs to God, and all that is destroyed that belonged to the people is their love and longing for it. This shows most clearly Ezekiel's strong antipathy towards Zion theology as it evidently came to expression in Jerusalem, putting all trust in the presence and indestructibility of the sanctuary and therefore of the city as well.

The major problem with understanding this prophetic symbolic act is why the people will not perform the traditional ritual acts in their time of mourning, which is the main emphasis in the divine oracle (vv. 22-3). It has been customary to regard vv. 22-3 as secondary, due to the sudden shift from the description of the judgement in v. 21 to the statement that the people will then behave like Ezekiel, as well as the change from third to first person discourse.[2] However, there does not seem to be any compelling reason to consider these verses to be secondary, except to say that the roughness can be due to the redactional nature of the narrative at large. Nevertheless, that would hardly need to go beyond Ezekiel himself.

Several answers to the question of why the people should not display their grief have been put forward.[3] The most common interpretation is that the people

---

[1] So Fuhs (1986: 276), 'Die Wegnahme dessen, was man liebt, ist also die eigentliche Analogie zur Ankündigung der Vernichtung des Tempels. Nur insoweit ist der Tod der Frau zeichenhaft.'

[2] So, e.g., Zimmerli (1976: 508), Stroete (1977: 169, 175). Pohlmann (1992: 14-5) also includes v. 21b with vv. 22-3 in his 'golaorientierte Redaktion', with the intention of emphasising the exilic character of the addressees. However, this is hardly enough to excise these verses as redactional, since Ezekiel was surely familiar with his addressees being in exile.

[3] For a complete inventory of suggested interpretations, see Stroete (1977: 164-6, 174-5).

will be so paralyzed by sorrow and despair that they will not have the strength to perform the usual rituals.[1] Although this is a very attractive alternative, it does have its problems. If the people are to be so paralyzed, why is it emphasized that they are to keep the turbans and shoes on, and why are they not to cry, since crying can hardly be said to be nothing but a mourning ritual (v. 23)? Other, less likely interpretations are as follows. 1. The exiles will continue in their indifference,[2] which can hardly be taken as the divinely prescribed behaviour. 2. The overwhelming realisation of their sins make them forget to perform the mourning rituals,[3] although the added fervour in mourning would have been much more understandable. 3. They are not allowed to mourn due to their sins,[4] something that would be understandable had it some textual basis. 4. It was God who was supposed to be the one who did not mourn,[5] a most idiosyncratic view, to say the least. 5. The people was to learn that such a defiled city was not worth mourning,[6] again something which could be understandable had it some relation to the text. 6. That the people lived under oppression made it impossible for them to show any signs of grief for a city that the oppressing power had itself brought down,[7] again an interpretation that relies far too much on instinct rather than analysis. 7. Mourning would be out of place because a new era has dawned with Jerusalem's fall. This was made explicit through the cessation of Ezekiel's dumbness,[8] which requires the secondary status of vv. 22-3, and even then it seems overtly complicated.

The simple fact is that the text does not provide us with any external indication as to why the people are not to mourn. However, there are several indications in the text that could be made useful, if we are to find our way through the number of options available.

The point of comparison has already been said to be that both the wife of Ezekiel and the temple/city/children are loved and cherished. In Ezekiel's case it

---

[1] So Fohrer (1955: 142), Eichrodt (1970: 350), Zimmerli (1976: 508).

[2] So Hitzig (1847: 184).

[3] So Keil (1876: 350), who bases himself on v. 23b, 'you shall pine away in your iniquities and groan to one another'.

[4] So Noordtzij (1932: 261f).

[5] So Hempel (1933).

[6] So Born (1947: 75f).

[7] So Bauer (1957), Hals (1989: 176).

[8] So Stroete (1977: 174), who considers vv. 22-3 to be secondary. He relies on Wilson (1972) in understanding the dumbness of Ezekiel not to be a complete silence but the absence of mediation on the part of the prophet between God and his people. This was about to change with the fall of Jerusalem (v. 27), which meant that Ezekiel could again start with a more optimistic tune in his preaching.

is meant to be understood to be an act of absurdity not to mourn his wife, and the same would apply to the people if they were not to mourn, if their affection for the temple/city/children was proper and according to God's instructions. However, it is precisely here that we find the point of deviance between the two; the affection the people have for their temple/city/children is seen as abominable due to the defilement, and therefore it would be proper for the people not to mourn. However, if they do not recognize the state the city is in, they naturally wonder at the thought of not mourning it and their children, as much as they wonder at Ezekiel's behaviour.

We must also keep in mind that the prophet is not spelling out what will happen in the future, nor is he trying to accomplish this future by his words. Instead, he tries hard to convince the people of the deplorable state the city of Jerusalem is in at the present, and how just the judgement will be. He is not trying to make the people do something, only to make them understand. Through arguing for not mourning the city and their children, the prophet is accomplishing his task, namely to make them understand how God sees his own city, and his own people. Therefore, the non-mourning is nothing but an argument the prophet is using in his constant strife to make the people understand his message, and that is all he can accomplish. The problem scholars have had in not being able to come to an agreement on the most suitable interpretation depends on the fact that they have been asking the wrong question. They have been asking why the people should not mourn, when they should have asked what the prophet is trying to say by means of this comparison between his reaction to his wife's death and the people's reaction to the destruction of Jerusalem. However, since emotions can not be neglected, they are to display their grief quietly, as Ezekiel was allowed, with an almost silent groaning, almost as if nothing has happened.

In terms of symbolism, the acts of Ezekiel to bind on his turban and put on his sandals, as he would have any other day, was a case of iconic symbolism. These acts imitated the proper behaviour of the people in relation to the deplorable state of the city and its temple, and ultimately their destruction and ill fate on the children still in the city. These acts as they are symbolized as being performed by the people, symbolizes also indexically the proper attitude to the temple and the city, as corresponding to God's own attitude.

228

Summary and Conclusions

1. The symbolic act in this text is not so much Ezekiel's neglect of performing a particular mourning ritual after his wife's death, but instead his going about his life as if nothing had happened.

2. The symbolic act works by means of iconic symbolism, in that it imitates the behaviour of the people had they understood the deplorable state the city and its temple is in, as God sees it. Inside this symbolic world of the act, the exemplary behaviour of the people symbolizes indexically, by means of association, the proper view of the city.

3. The reference to the fate of the children in the city takes the symbolism into the future, symbolising how wrong the view is that takes the exiles as the unfortunate and those that remain in Jerusalem as the fortunate. Instead, Ezekiel's fellow exiles should not be surprised at the fate of the children that remain, since they are regarded by God as part of the sinfulness of the city.

8. Joining two Pieces of Wood (Ezekiel 37:15-22)

The Text

15 וַיְהִי דְבַר־יְהוָה אֵלַי
לֵאמֹר 16 וְאַתָּה בֶן־אָדָם קַח־לְךָ
עֵץ אֶחָד וּכְתֹב עָלָיו לִיהוּדָה
וְלִבְנֵי יִשְׂרָאֵל חֲבֵרוֹ וּלְקַחֹ א עֵץ
אֶחָד וּכְתוֹב עָלָיו לְיוֹסֵף ᵈ עֵץ כָּל־בֵּית
יִשְׂרָאֵל חֲבֵרוֹ 17 וְקָרַב אֹתָם
אֶחָד אֶל־אֶחָד לְךָ לְעֵץ אֶחָד וְהָיוּ
לַאֲחָדִים בְּיָדֶךָ 18 וְכַאֲשֶׁר יֹאמְרוּ
אֵלֶיךָ בְּנֵי עַמְּךָ לֵאמֹר הֲלוֹא־תַגִּיד
לָנוּ מָה־אֵלֶּה לָךְ 19 דַּבֵּר אֲלֵהֶם
כֹּה־אָמַר אֲדֹנָי יְהוָה הִנֵּה אֲנִי לֹקֵחַ
אֶת־עֵץ יוֹסֵף ᵉ וְשִׁבְטֵי יִשְׂרָאֵל חֲבֵרוֹ ᵇ
וְנָתַתִּי ᶠ עָלָיו אֶת־עֵץ יְהוּדָה
וַעֲשִׂיתִם לְעֵץ אֶחָד וְהָיוּ אֶחָד בְּיָדִי
20 וְהָיוּ הָעֵצִים אֲשֶׁר־תִּכְתֹּב
עֲלֵיהֶם בְּיָדְךָ לְעֵינֵיהֶם 21 וְדַבֵּר
אֲלֵיהֶם כֹּה־אָמַר אֲדֹנָי יְהוָה הִנֵּה
אֲנִי לֹקֵחַ אֶת־בְּנֵי יִשְׂרָאֵל מִבֵּין
הַגּוֹיִם אֲשֶׁר הָלְכוּ־שָׁם וְקִבַּצְתִּי
אֹתָם מִסָּבִיב וְהֵבֵאתִי אוֹתָם
אֶל־אַדְמָתָם 22 וְעָשִׂיתִי אֹתָם לְגוֹי
אֶחָד בָּאָרֶץ בְּהָרֵי יִשְׂרָאֵל וּמֶלֶךְ
אֶחָד יִהְיֶה לְכֻלָּם לְמֶלֶךְ וְלֹא יהיו ᵍ
עוֹד לִשְׁנֵי גוֹיִם וְלֹא יֵחָצוּ
עוֹד לִשְׁתֵּי מַמְלָכוֹת ʰ

15 The word of Yhwh came to me: 16 Mortal, take a piece of wood and write on it, "Judah, and the Israelites associated with it"; then take another piece and write on it, "Joseph and all the house of Israel associated with it"; 17 and join them together into one piece, so that they may become one in your hand. 18 And when your people say to you, "Will you not show us what you mean by these?" 19 say to them, Thus says the Lord Yhwh: I am about to take the wood of Joseph and the tribes of Israel associated with it; and I will put the wood of Judah upon it, and make them one piece of wood, in order that they may be one in my hand. 20 When the pieces on which you write are in your hand before their eyes, 21 then say to them, Thus says the Lord Yhwh: I will take the people of Israel from the nations among which they have gone, and will gather them from every quarter, and bring them to their own land. 22 I will make them one nation in the land, on the mountains of Israel; and one king shall be king over them all. Never again shall they be two nations, and never again shall they be divided into two kingdoms.

Textual notes

ᵃ The strong form of לקח in the imperative is highly unusual, but does occur, see Ex 29:1; 1 Kgs 17:11; Prov 20:6. Most scholars prefer to change to either what occurs earlier in the verse, קַח־לְךָ, so Fohrer (1955: 209), or to an infinitive absolute, וְלָקוֹחַ, so Zimmerli (1983: 267-8), Allen (1990: 190), although they both appear to be uncertain. However, if קַח־לְךָ is correct, then we have no way of explaining why LXX varied itself in its translations, λαβὲ for קַח־לְךָ and λήμψῃ for this expression. In Ez 5:1, LXX has the same variation and MT has קַח־לְךָ and וְלָקַחְתָּ לְךָ (cf.1 Sam 21:10). The infinitive absolute does not fit in either, since the preceding ו requires a preceding finite verb that the infinitive then would continue, see Nyberg (1952 §91.m). Cornill (1886) postulates וּלְקַחַת, but that form leaves no room for לְךָ, which must have been there since LXX has σεαυτῷ. Since the unusual strong imperative form is highly unlikely in such a close proximity to the weak form, the best solution is to postulate an original וְתִקַח לְךָ, where ה has been misread for ל.

^b In both cases (vv. 16, 19) this should probably not be altered to חֲבֵרָיו, but be considered a defective spelling, so Andersen, and Forbes (1986: 323-8), Allen (1990: 220).

^c MT and versions have עֵץ אֶפְרַיִם, 'the stick of Ephraim'. However, it disturbs the parallelism between the two pieces of wood, it misunderstands the lamedh inscriptionis as a lamedh of possession, and is apparently a later gloss, attempting to explain 'Joseph' as signifying the northern kingdom, so Zimmerli (1983: 68), Allen (1990: 190). Retaining it as explanatory, as done by Block (1997: 396), can only be explained on dogmatic grounds.

^d This ל is usually explained as a lamedh inscriptionis, signifying the content of some form of inscription, see Gesenius (1910 §119u), Zimmerli (1976: 274), Allen (1990: 190).

^e MT and the versions add אֲשֶׁר בְּיַד־אֶפְרַיִם, 'which is in the hand of Ephraim', probably a gloss of similar origin as the gloss in v. 16, or even presupposing the earlier gloss. Retaining it creates more problems that it solves, contra Block (1997: 397).

^f MT adds אוֹתָם, an apparent gloss or amplification of the later וַעֲשִׂיתָם.

^g K יהיה is mistakenly still referring to the king, which is corrected in Q.

^h MT has here עוֹד, which is superfluous and is not found in LXX or Vulg. It attests the practice of sometimes putting the עוֹד in a later position than immediately after the verb (Ez 19:9; 39:7), which is the usual position in Ezekiel, see Allen (1990: 190).

Analysis

This is one of the more straightforward of Ezekiel's prophetic symbolic acts, although it does have some problems. Ezekiel is told in the usual instruction from God that he is to take two עֵץ. These are usually understood to be pieces of wood of some sort, although we prefer to refer to pieces of wood, because of the problems of understanding its reference. The word עֵץ often denotes pieces of wood meant for burning (1 Kgs 17:12; Qoh 10:9; Zech 12:6 et al.), but it can also be used for pieces of wood in general (2 Kgs 6:6). The two pieces Ezekiel uses in his symbolic act were probably pieces readily available, meant for keeping a fire burning. The must have been reasonably small, since he was to hold them both in one hand (v. 17).

Ezekiel is told to write different names on the pieces, denoting not ownership but what the pieces symbolized. On one he writes 'Judah, and the Israelites associated with it', and on the other, 'Joseph and all the house of Israel associated

with it'. Judah naturally stood for the southern state, and those among the Israelite tribes that had associated them more closely with Judah. The other stick,
however, was inscribed with the more unusual name Joseph for the northern
kingdom (cf. Amos 5:6, 15; 6:6; Ez 47:13; 48:32). This was later attempted to
be clarified by the following gloss עֵץ אֶפְרַיִם, as is also the case in v. 19 with the
gloss אֲשֶׁר בְּיַד־אֶפְרַיִם. He was then to take the two pieces of wood and hold them
both in one hand, so that they would appear to be only one stick (v. 17). Presumably, this would mean holding the two pieces at their respective ends in one
hand, making it look as it was only one stick, twice as long.

Strictly speaking, v. 17 does not only describe how the act was to be performed, but it also reveals something about the symbolic value of the act. When
it is said that Ezekiel is to 'join them together into one stick, so that they may
become one in your hand', it is not a mere description of the physical act, since
that would not actually accomplish this; it is a description of how the act was to
be perceived by the people around Ezekiel. But even more than that, it says
something about how the act is to be interpreted symbolically; two items are not
only to be perceived as being one, but they are to be one, and they are not only
supposed to be perceived as being joined together, but actually joined into one.
So already in the description of the act its symbolic meaning has began to be revealed.

The use of the verb קרב, 'draw together' is deliberately used because of the
preceding vision narrative, the revivification of the dry bones (vv. 1-14). According to 37:7, the bones came together (וַתִּקְרְבוּ), representing the future reuni-
fication of the people. This meaning is also relevant for the symbolic act in vv.
15-19, which is secured by means of קרב as a 'Stitchwort'.[1] The two pieces of
wood, representing the two former nations, are two arise and be united into one
nation. Barth has rightly emphasized the continuity between the vision narrative
in vv. 1-14 and the narrative concerning the symbolic act in vv. 15-27, the latter
including some later additions. Barth has especially noted that a narrative concerning a symbolic act in Ezekiel often follows upon a vision narrative;[2]

Vision		Symbolic act
1:1-3:15	⇒	3:22-5:17
8:1-11:25	⇒	12:1-20

---

[1] So Krüger (1989: 439), cf. Barth (1977a: 48).

[2] Barth (1977a: 43). However, Barth goes too far in his emphasis on the relationship between
the two parts of ch. 37, when he claims that vv. 20-24 is a reinterpretation of the vision in vv.
1-14, and has nothing to do with the symbolic act (p. 51). Zimmerli (1983: 275) also tends in
this direction, although not as strongly as Barth.

		21:11-19
-		24:15-27
37:1-14	⇒	37:15-27

However, there does seem to be some irregularity when it comes to the interpretation of the symbolic act. What appears to be an interpretation in v. 19, especially since it follows on the quite common direct question from the people (v. 18, cf. 12:9; 21:5, 12; 24:19), can at closer analysis hardly be called anything of the sort.[1] It has more the character of a further development of the description of the symbolic act in 17. Indeed, we are not told in v. 19 what the two pieces of wood stand for, but only that now it is God himself that plays the role of uniting the two pieces in his hand. Although we are not yet given a full interpretation of the symbolic act, we are here given an introduction to that symbolic meaning, when we learn that Ezekiel is playing the role of God. Whatever the symbolic meaning of his act may be, it is supposed to be something that God does. This is hardly something an audience could have understood, either by means of iconic, indexical or conventional symbolism, hence the need for the verbal explanation in v. 19. The symbolic meaning of Ezekiel's act can therefore be said to be iconic in its relation to the verbal announcement in v. 19.

If v. 19 can not be called the interpretation of the symbolic act, then we are left with two alternatives, judging from the scholarly discussion. Either the following vv. 20-22 constitute the original interpretation of the symbolic act, forming a literary unit with the preceding vv. 15-19,[2] or there is no original interpretation available, but only one added later, in the attempt to clarify the symbolic act.[3] The basic reason why some scholars have been reluctant to consider vv. 20-22 an original interpretation of the symbolic act is that the focus shifts from the motif of uniting the two former nations to the theme of bringing

---

[1] So Zimmerli (1983: 275), who prefers to call v. 19 a divine promise instead, Allen (1990: 193), who calls it a divine metaphor, and apparently Block (1995: 177), Block (1997: 404), who calls vv. 21-28 the 'interpretation proper'. Garscha (1974: 224-5) obviously feels the need for an original interpretation of the symbolic act, describing v. 19 as a 'nur fragmentarisch erhaltenen Deutung der Symbolhandlung'. He therefore considers v. 22 to form a part of the original narrative (vv. 15-19.22) as the proper interpretation of the symbolic act. He thereby considers vv. 20-21 to be 'eine spätere Umdeutung und Aktualisierung der Symbolhandlung'. Still, many scholars make the mistake of categorising v. 19 as an interpretation of the symbolic act, so Hals (1989: 273). Baltzer (1986: 178) also sees an interpretation in v. 19, although he acknowledges that it 'wiederholt nur die göttliche Handlungsanweisung (vv. 16f.).'

[2] So Herrmann (1965: 273f), Eichrodt (1970: 359f), Allen (1990: 191), Block (1997: 408-9).

[3] So e.g. Zimmerli (1983: 275).

the people out of their present habitations among other nations. However, this can hardly constitute a convincing reason why these verses should be relocated to the status of not having an original connection with the symbolic act itself.[1] It is hardly difficult to consider that the author, in his description of the interpretation of the symbolic act, also included the prerequisite for a unification of the two kingdoms, namely the act of bringing them out of there present situations. This added comment hardly needs to be relegated to a later redactor, who saw it fit to update the original story, and had a redactor wanted to reinterpret the symbolic act, then why was v. 22 left untouched? That the book of Ezekiel displays numerous examples of having a complex redaction history is evident, but, as Zimmerli has pointed out, and which seems to stand the test of time, this often does not have to go beyond the prophet himself, or the 'school' of followers that Zimmerli presumed lay behind a large part of the book. That the theme appears to shift is only an example of the fact that the interpretation of a symbolic act can not always be extracted from the act itself. The interpretation can sometimes be allowed to move beyond what we might regard as the reasonable symbolic meaning of an act, i.e., a move from iconic or indexical symbolism to conventional symbolism. Admittedly, the following vv. 23-27 clearly provide indications of a process that has gone beyond the immediate interpretation of the symbolic act, and at least vv. 24b-27, with its clear shift in terminology and thematic emphasis,[2] should be considered a later, possibly Dtr,[3] reworking of the basic theme of the eschatological expectation of the coming, unified Davidic monarchy.[4]

Returning now to the symbolism of the act, we have noted that the merging of the two pieces of wood symbolizes the merging of the two former nations by means of iconic symbolism, and the writing of the names of the nations on the pieces indicate what they symbolize by means of indexical symbolism. The indexical symbolism is logically prior; when, and only when, the pieces have been

---

[1] Garscha (1974) in particular argues that vv. 20-21 are secondary, due to the shift in motif.

[2] Hos 2:2, לָהֶם רֹאשׁ אֶחָד וְעָלוּ מִן־הָאָרֶץ וְנִקְבְּצוּ בְּנֵי־יְהוּדָה וּבְנֵי־יִשְׂרָאֵל יַחְדָּו וְשָׂמוּ, 'The people of Judah and the people of Israel shall be gathered together, and they shall appoint for themselves one head; and they shall come up from the land'. This text appears to receive a reinterpretation in v. 23-4, where the theme of leaving the land is interpreted as the exiles leaving there countries, and not as the Exodus, which is the most probable interpretation of Hos 2:2.

[3] For the possibility of a Dtr redaction of Ez 37, see Herrmann (1965: 241ff).

[4] See Hals (1989: 274), Krüger (1989: 438), Laato (1992: 186). Vv. 23-24a also appears to share the shifts clearly noted in vv. 24b-27. However, Laato rightly stresses the difficulties involved in trying to unravel the redactional history behind vv. 15-27.

given their indexical symbolic meaning of the two nations by means of their writings, can the symbolism inherent in bringing them together be iconic.

However, it remains to ask whether there is a deeper symbolism involved in the choice of wood in this symbolic act. Several alternatives have been suggested as to the reference of עֵץ, e.g. trees,[1] ruler's sceptres,[2] and writing tablets.[3] However, none of these alternatives can be substantiated by indications in the text itself. There is therefore no reason why we should now regard the reference to that of two ordinary pieces of wood.[4]

The fact that the pieces of wood are written upon recalls Num 17:16-28, where every tribe were to put a מַטֶּה, 'staff', in the tabernacle with their name on it, and the staff that sprouted would indicate which tribe God had chosen. The parallelism is striking; a piece of wood is representing a tribe of Israel, and the name is written upon it, and most of all, God does something extraordinary with that piece of wood. Again, we find that Ezekiel's priestly background provides him with valuable material to be used in his symbolic acts. However, the problem with establishing this parallelism is that in Ez 37 it is only a עֵץ, a piece of wood, whereas in Num 17 it is a מַטֶּה, a staff. However, this seems to be the interpretation lying behind LXX, when it translates עֵץ in Ez 37 with ῥάβδος, 'staff', as was also the case with מַטֶּה in Num 17. We should also look at Ez 19:11, from a song of lamentation, where the vine, symbolising the royal Davidic house, grows מַטּוֹת עֹז, 'strong branches', translated by LXX as ῥάβδος ἰσχύος. These 'strong branches' are then described as שִׁבְטֵי מֹשְׁלִים, 'sceptres of rulers'.[5]

It is clear, then, that to Ezekiel himself, a piece of wood could be taken to symbolize the royal sceptre, and in a further sense, the king himself.[6] Since the

---

[1] Barnes (1938).

[2] So LXX, Zimmerli (1976: 273-4). Block (1997: 398) is wrong in attributing this view to Eichrodt (1970: 512), Friebel (1989: 844), Friebel (1999: 363-4), who regard it a an ordinary piece of wood that symbolizes a ruler's rod. Block seems to have totally misunderstood this view, and attributed it wrongly to some modern scholars.

[3] So Driver (1971: 549-50). Tg. has סב לך לוחא חד, which probably was an interpretation because the pieces of wood are inscribed upon (cf. Is 8:1). Block (1997: 399-405) propounds this view extensively, but he fails to provide any substantial textual evidence. It remains an imaginative interpretation by the targumic author.

[4] So e.g. Eichrodt (1970: 512), Allen (1990: 192-3), Friebel (1999: 363-4).

[5] We can find no convincing reason why the plurals of 19:11a must be converted into singular forms, see Laato (1992: 166).

[6] A smaller but yet significant argument is that in God's virtual retelling of Ezekiel's words in v. 19, the word שֵׁבֶט is used for the tribes of Israel, whereas in Ezekiel's own words in v. 16, the expressions used are כָּל־בֵּית יִשְׂרָאֵל and בְּנֵי יִשְׂרָאֵל.

whole thrust of vv. 22-28 is that the unified people shall have *one* Davidic king, it can hardly be a coincidence that wood is chosen to symbolize the nations. In a further sense, the wooden pieces therefore symbolize the royal houses, carrying the potential of becoming something new, through the extraordinary work of God, וַעֲשִׂיתִם לְעֵץ אֶחָד וְהָיוּ אֶחָד בְּיָדִי, 'I will make them one stick, in order that they may be one in my hand.'

Summary and Conclusions

1. The choice of wood for these objects are meant to ironically symbolize the royal sceptres of the north and the south, not by resemblance in any other way, as far as we know, but the material, namely wood.

2. Once the iconic symbolism of the choice of wood is established, it works indexically by letting the 'sceptres' associate to the kingdoms as a whole. Writing the names of the nations on the pieces of wood indicates what they symbolize by means of an indexical symbolism. This indexical symbolism is logically dependent on the iconic symbolism inherent in the choice of wood; when the pieces have been given their indexical symbolic meaning of the two nations by means of their writings, the symbolism inherent in bringing them together can be understood as a case of iconic symbolism.

3. The joining of the two pieces of wood is, on the basis on the symbolic interpretation of the pieces themselves, a second iconic symbolism that stands for the unification of the two nations into one. This iconic symbolism is logically dependent on the indexical symbolism, as it presumes that they stand for the kingdoms at large.

F. The Marriage of Hosea (Hosea 1:2-3; 3:1-4)

Introduction

The marriage of Hosea is one of the most discussed problems in OT interpretation, and there seems to be no end to the scholarly discussion. The suggestions
regarding the interpretation of these chapters are numerous, and so are the summaries of past research.[1] It is worth emphasising, however, that even though the
actual performances of the prophetic symbolic acts in Hos 1, 3 are very much in
the dark, the symbolic understanding of them are not.[2] There are, however, a few
items that scholars tend to agree upon regarding this text.

1. Hos 1-3 describes the actual performance of prophetic symbolic acts. Past
research were much more inclined to understand the chapters allegorically or visionary. However, the indications of actual performance are clear, and there is
nothing inherently improbable regarding the symbolic use of an actual marriage.

2. The variety of textual character and genre in Hos 1-3 indicate that these
chapters form a composition of various different traditions that are likely to have
been composed individually. Only secondarily were these traditions brought together to form a unified discourse on the issue of the prophetic use of the marriage of Hosea. Whether Hosea had a part in this or whether it is the hand of
later redactors and/or disciples of Hosea is a point of discussion, as is the
amount of redactional activity and number of redactional layers. However, it is
clear to most scholars today, that the heterogeneous character of Hos 1-3, both
literary as well as historically, must be taken seriously before any attempt is
made at an overall understanding.

3. These chapters are primarily intended to impute a prophetic understanding
to its audience, and any biographical intention is highly redundant. This has
been the problem throughout earlier attempts of understanding, and it may be a
hint that scholars ask the wrong questions to the text. Nevertheless, the biographical information is very small, which leaves us very much in the dark as to
the actual performance.

4. It has become clear that earlier scholarship, preferably male, has been largely misguided in their attempts to rescue the good reputation of the prophet

---

[1] See e.g. Rowley (1963: 66-97), Davies (1993: 79-92), Macintosh (1997: 113-26). See Bitter
(1975) for a thorough inventory of views on Hosea's marriage in ancient and precritical times.
[2] See Jeremias (1983: 26).

from questionable deeds, such as marrying a prostitute (ch 1) in order for her to give birth to his children, or a woman who has been divorced (ch 3). Various analyses from a feministic angle have been successful in pointing this out, although one would have expected these analyses to be somewhat more constructive in providing answers of their own to the old questions in Hos 1-3.[1]

Beyond these more or less consensus views, there is a fundamental disagreement as to whether Gomer from ch. 1 is the woman in ch. 3, and whether Gomer was a 'woman of whoredom' when Hosea married her. From the standpoint of our analysis of the text as a description of prophetic symbolic act, this is a useful beginning.

In Hos 1, there is a description in third person of how Hosea receives a command from God to take a 'woman of whoredom', and to have 'children of whoredom' with her, together with an interpretation of that symbolic act. Subsequently, we are told that Hosea took a woman called Gomer, and how she gave birth to three children, each of which were given symbolic names by Hosea on God's command.

Hos 2 is a collection of prophetic oracles regarding the relationship between God and the people of Israel, with constant allusions, direct and indirect, to the symbols of marriage, adultery, and how the adulterous woman was treated in that time. However, there is nothing in ch. 2 that illuminates what can safely be described Hosea's prophetic symbolic act, and therefore we will leave out ch. 2 in the following analysis.

Hos 3 is a first person account of how Hosea is told by God to 'love' an adulterous woman. He then describes in detail how he buys her back and isolates her from her former lovers, all done as a means of showing his love. This is then given an interpretation, where God is given the role of Hosea, and the people that of the woman.

The first problem we encounter is when Hosea is told to take, i.e., to marry, a אֵשֶׁת זְנוּנִים, 'woman of whoredom'. It has often been noted that the abstract plural is used here, instead of the more common term זוֹנָה, 'whore', 'prostitute', 'adulteress'.[2] The reason could be, that what is emphasized is more the character of the woman and less her precise position in society. This in itself could be an indication of the symbolic use of this description, since the focus is turned from the behaviour of the woman to her character, which is easier to use symbolically in relation to the character of the people towards its God. The question is, then,

---

[1] See e.g. Weems (1989), Graetz (1995), Keefe (1995), Sherwood (1995), Sherwood (1996), Törnkvist (1998).
[2] See TDOT 4, 99-104. See also the Excursus below.

whether Hosea actually received a divine command to take a prostitute as his wife, or whether the command in 1:2bß is the result of a symbolic understanding of Hosea's marriage made retrospectively, by one of his disciples or a much later redactor. This involves either the attempt to find an early, probably Hosean stratum in ch. 1, where it said merely in 1:2b, 'And Yhwh said to Hosea, "Go and take a woman and have children"',[1] or that ch. 1 was composed as a whole retrospectively.[2] The difference between these two variants is relevant as far as it might make us aware of a redactional activity that may have involved ch. 3 as well. It is hard, perhaps even impossible to have a clear position on this issue, and we must be aware that the social conventions are very much in the dark to us, and the prophets were capable to perform very odd things under the conviction that it was all commanded by God. So marrying a prostitute can not be said to have been impossible for Hosea. Indeed, the shocking effect might have been just what was intended, since if an audience expressed its disgust to Hosea for marrying a prostitute, his reply could have been, that they themselves were a people זָנֹה תִזְנֶה מֵאַחֲרֵי יְהוָה, 'whoring away from Yhwh' (1:2bγ).

However, the scholars who side with a retrospective understanding of ch. 1 fail to provide convincing arguments.[3] One of Seifert's basic arguments is that apart from the epithet זְנוּנִים, Gomer is nowhere else in ch. 1 described as unfaithful. That is only a relevant argument if the point of ch. 1 is to say something about Gomer, but that is precisely where the misunderstanding resides. Chapter 1 is about the people being unfaithful to their God through their worship of other gods. The people are referred to symbolically through the descriptions of Gomer and the three children, and it is only as such that the children are meaningfully referred to as זְנוּנִים. It might be, that with better insight into the personal life of Hosea we would know that his wife earned the description זְנוּנִים only after being married to Hosea. However, as long as this further insight fail us, we are left

---

[1] So e.g. Rudolph (1966: 48), Ruppert (1982a), Ruppert (1982b), Jeremias (1983: 26-7), Seifert (1996: 124-6). Schreiner (1977: 173-4) prefers to retain the description of Gomer as 'whoredom', whereas he removes it from the earliest account in reference to the children. In order to allow this, he is forced to employ some very unusual strictures on the languages used, which all seems very unlikely. Some argue that the phrase זָנֹה תִזְנֶה הָאָרֶץ מֵאַחֲרֵי יְהוָה, 'the land is whoring away from Yhwh', reveals deuteronomistic redactional activities, because of the similarity with the common Dtr phrase הלך אחרי, 'go after', so e.g. Jeremias (1983: 26-7). However, it must be noted that the phrase זנה מאחרי occurs only here in Hos 1:2. There is an obvious similarity with the expressions so typical of the Dtr style, but the difference is just as important.

[2] So e.g. Andersen, and Freedman (1980: 165-7), Macintosh (1997: 119-20).

[3] The arguments put forward by Rudolph (1966) have been sufficiently answered by Davies (1993: 80-7), and need not be repeated here.

with the very few facts that the text leaves us with, and they do not provide a convincing case for a retrospective understanding of 1:2.

Davies is one of the few who does not favour a retrospective understanding of ch. 1, but that leads him to the conclusion that Hosea, in marrying a prostitute, actually plays the symbolic role of Baal, and not God.[1] But that is only true on the premise that everything in the procedure of a prophetic symbolic act is symbolically relevant, something which Davies himself, interestingly enough, criticizes Rudolph for, when he argues that Hos 1 would be the only description of a prophetic symbolic act that does not refer to the future. Davies argues that there is no need to see a complete correspondence between the sign and the thing signified, a conclusion that makes it unnecessary to strain the imagination with having Hosea representing Baal.

As far as being a possible description of a prophetic symbolic act, an early literary stratum without any references to either the mother or the children being זְנוּנִים, would be difficult to understand as a description of a prophetic symbolic act. The mere command to marry or only enter a relationship with a woman would hardly suffice as a description of a symbolic act, especially since the explanation of the act, and the symbolic understanding of the act in general, would have been added only later, under the influence of later events in Hosea's family life. An early form of ch. 1 without any references to זְנוּנִים would therefore not qualify as a meaningful prophetic symbolic act.[2]

In Hos 3, we encounter a narrative similar to ch. 1 in that it describes what appears to be a marriage relation between Hosea and a woman. The main differences are that no children are mentioned, the woman is now referred to as מְנָאָפֶת, an adulteress and not by the more polyvalent זְנוּנִים, and the narrative is in first person. These are all indications of the fact that this narrative has a different history than ch. 1, to which it has been related at a later, redactional stage.

The symbolic intention of the narrative is also different from ch. 1. Whereas in ch. 1 the relationship between Hosea and the woman and her children were symbolically representing the depraved state in which the people were in their relationship to their God, ch. 3 means something different. The crucial point of the narrative in ch. 3 is found in 3:1, where Hosea is told, not to 'take' a woman

---

[1] Davies (1992: 108), Davies (1993: 87-92).

[2] This is also the conclusion drawn by Rudolph (1996), who holds that an early account where Hosea was simply told by God to marry and have children was later mistakenly interpreted symbolically to represent the relationship between the people and their God. Schreiner (1977: 177-8) argues similarly that the marriage between Hosea and Gomer is an introduction and presupposition to the following triad of prophetic symbolism, i.e., the naming of the children, and does not in itself form the content of a prophetic symbolic act.

as in ch. 1, but to 'love' an adulterous woman who has other lovers, as God loves Israel. Whereas ch. 1 is about God's judgement on the wayward people, ch. 3 is about God's love for a people who does not want his love.[1] This particular difference between ch. 1 and 3 does not necessarily indicate a difference in origin, but more a complementary relationship. It is likely that it is this complementary function, judgement and guilt on the one hand, and God's love on the other, that appealed to the redactor behind ch. 1-3, and led to the present text.

The main question that has been asked is whether the woman in ch. 3 is Gomer or someone else. Those who argue for a retrospective reading of ch. 1 are divided on this issue. Rudolph argues that it is a second woman, on the grounds that had it been Gomer, the text would have had every opportunity to say so.[2] Most scholars, however, argue that what makes best sense is to see Gomer as an adulteress, to whom Hosea returns in ch. 3.[3]

In ch. 3 there are no clear indications that Gomer from ch. 1 is being referred to, and this is a strong argument for a second woman. However, this argument is weakened by the fact that it is only relevant as far as the narrative in ch. 3 was composed with ch. 1 in mind, something that the differences between the two narratives have shown to be unlikely. We can only speculate as to the original setting of 3:1-4, but a likely setting would have been a public appearance made by the prophet, perhaps in response to the questions that had been raised regarding the highly dubious circumstances that Hosea had chosen for himself by marrying a prostitute. The present constellation with ch. 3 following ch. 1-2 is a redactional arrangement, which must be held separate from the understanding of ch. 3 as a first-hand account from Hosea. We must therefore seek for further possible indications that would connect Gomer with the woman in ch. 3.

In 3:1, the woman Hosea is to show his love to is referred to indeterminately, אִשָּׁה, 'a woman', which is highly unusual if an already known woman was intended. When Hosea then describes how he performs this prophetic symbolic act in 3:2, he refers to the woman determinately, וָאֶכְּרֶהָ, 'I bought her'. This suffix pronoun seems to refer to the earlier אִשָּׁה in 3:1, and it need not be taken as a reference to an already known woman outside of the narrative in ch. 3. This could also be described as a rare case of an indeterminate use of the suffix pro-

---

[1] This is also emphasized by e.g. Seifert (1996: 137-8).

[2] Davies (1993: 88) partly follows Rudolph in his analysis of ch. 3, in that he recognizes a second woman. However, he does not follow Rudolph in his more idiosyncratic views that the woman was a mistress, and the use of 'love' in the command to Hosea is used ironically.

[3] So e.g. Andersen, and Freedman (1980: 296), Seifert (1996: 130-1), Macintosh (1997: 113-4).

noun.[1] These two literary indicators seem to point in opposite directions, and it would seem that the indeterminate reference to 'a woman' is stronger than the apparent determinate use of the suffix pronoun. The conclusion is therefore that there are no indications in ch. 3 that Hosea returned to Gomer, and previous scholarship have failed to provide any convincing arguments for such a conclusion.[2]

Beside the suffix pronoun in 3:2, one is left with the rather disappointing argument, brought forward by e.g. Seifert, that 'Das Gebot, eine solche Frau zu lieben, ist nur sinnvoll, wenn sie dem Propheten selbst die Treue gebrochen hat.'[3] That may very well be true, and it may very well have been a better prophetic symbolic act. However, that brings us back to the criticism brought against Davies above, namely that not every item described in a symbolic relation must be symbolically relevant. It may be that the prophetic symbolic act would have been more effective if Hosea had been divorced from Gomer, and then went back to her, but there are simply no indications whatsoever in the text to substantiate such a conclusion. Indeed, the conclusion may actually be correct, but until we know more, we have to abide with the text at hand, even though we are tempted to make it more imaginative than it would seem to be.

---

[1] Rudolph tries to show this to be the case with examples such as Is 46:7b, Lam 3:34, 36, apparently followed by Davies (1992: 101).

[22] So e.g. Nyberg (1940: 38), who argues that it is a matter of polygamy since Hosea took a second wife, similarly Buzy (1923: 88).

[3] Seifert (1996: 130). Similarly Jeremias (1983: 53), who prefers to emphasize that as far as the message of ch. 3 is concerned, there is not much difference between the two views.

The Text

אֿ תְּחִלַּת דִּבֶּר־יְהוָה בְּהוֹשֵׁעַ 1:2
וַיֹּאמֶר יְהוָה אֶל־הוֹשֵׁעַ לֵךְ
קַח־לְךָ אֵשֶׁת זְנוּנִים וְיַלְדֵי זְנוּנִים
כִּי־זָנֹה תִזְנֶה הָאָרֶץ מֵאַחֲרֵי יְהוָה
3 וַיֵּלֶךְ וַיִּקַּח אֶת־גֹּמֶר בַּת־דִּבְלָיִם
וַתַּהַר וַתֵּלֶד־לוֹ בֵּן

......

וַיֹּאמֶר יְהוָה אֵלַי עוֹדᵇ לֵךְ 3:1
אֱהַב־אִשָּׁה אֲהֻבַת רֵעᶜ ᶜᵈוּמְנָאָפֶת
כְּאַהֲבַת יְהוָה אֶת־בְּנֵי יִשְׂרָאֵל וְהֵם
פֹּנִים אֶל־אֱלֹהִים אֲחֵרִים וְאֹהֲבֵי
אֲשִׁישֵׁי עֲנָבִים 2 וָאֶכְּרֶהָ לִי
בַּחֲמִשָּׁה עָשָׂר כָּסֶף וְחֹמֶר שְׂעֹרִים
וְלֵתֶךְ שְׂעֹרִים 3 וָאֹמַר אֵלֶיהָ יָמִים
רַבִּים תֵּשְׁבִי לִי לֹא תִזְנִי וְלֹא תִהְיִי
לְאִישׁ וְגַם־אֲנִי אֵלָיִךְ 4 כִּי יָמִים
רַבִּים יֵשְׁבוּ בְּנֵי יִשְׂרָאֵל אֵין מֶלֶךְ
וְאֵין שָׂר וְאֵין זֶבַח וְאֵין מַצֵּבָה
וְאֵין אֵפוֹד וּתְרָפִים

1:2 The beginning of Yhwh's talk through Hosea. Yhwh said to Hosea, "Go, take for yourself a wife of whoredom and have children of whoredom, for the land commits great whoredom by forsaking Yhwh." 3 So he went and took Gomer daughter of Diblaim, and she conceived and bore him a son.

......

3:1 Yhwh said to me again, "Go, love a woman who is loved by another, and hence an adulteress, just as Yhwh loves the people of Israel, though they turn to other gods and love raisin cakes." 2 So I bought her for fifteen shekels of silver and a homer of barley and a measure of wine. 3 And I said to her, "You must remain as mine for many days; you shall not play the whore, you shall not have intercourse with a man, nor I with you." 4 For the Israelites shall remain many days without king or prince, without sacrifice or pillar, without ephod or teraphim.

Textual notes

ᵃ The expression is dubious. It is usually taken as a circumstantial clause in relation to the following main clause, but we would expect an initial וַיְהִי, as in 2 Kgs 17:25, וַיְהִי בִּתְחִלַּת שִׁבְתָּם, 'When they first settled there …'. It is best taken as a title, 'The beginning of God's talk through Hosea'.

ᵇ This particle can refer to what precedes, 'The Lord spoke to me again', or to what follows, 'go again'. It is impossible to be certain since both possibilities are legitimate; the former is possible in view of the fact that ch. 1 has already spoken of how God speaks to Hosea, but the latter is also suitable since Hosea has already been told to go and take a woman in ch. 1. The difference between the two is not of any greater significance, however, for the understanding of the narrative.

ᶜ The ו is understood here as explicative, in the sense of drawing out the logical conclusion of the fact that the woman is loved by another man, i.e., that she is thereby to be characterized as an adulteress. The alternative would be that the ו introduces something new in the description of the woman, but this is less likely, see below for an explanation.

ᵈ LXX has πονηρά, reflecting the homograph רַע, 'evil', followed by e.g. Stuart (1987: 62-3). This also involves reading the preceding participle as active. However, the reading of MT has the advantage of reflecting the focus of the prophetic symbolic act. First, The emphasis is on the woman/the people being loved by Hosea/God, and not on the woman acting out her love. Second, she is loved by another man, which is in line with the next participle, which designates her as an adulteress, and the focus on other partners attracting the attention of the woman/the people.

[e] LXX and Syr. have an active participle as in v. 3b, followed by e.g. Wolff (1974: 56), Jeremias (1983: 52). However, MT is clearly the more difficult and, in this case, preferable reading, so e.g. Andersen, and Freedman (1980: 296), Davies (1992: 99), Macintosh (1997: 93-4), although Andersen-Freedman has a mistake in their argumentation. For a decisive argumentation from the context, see above, note d. MT is presupposed in Aq, Symm ηγαπημενην, and Tg. דרחימא.

[f] The dagesh is highly irregular. It can not be explained as a dagesh forte dirimens as is done by e.g. Gesenius (1910: 73), Wolff (1974: 56), since the shewa should be silent if the verb is כרה, and there is no phonological explanation that would legitimate a stop sound, see Andersen, and Freedman (1980: 298-9), Vogels (1988: 412-3). A doubling is possible if the verb is נכר, but this verb is not known elsewhere to have the meaning 'buy', which is the required meaning here because of the beth pretii in בַּחֲמִשָּׁה. The only way of making sense of the dagesh is to postulate a variant נכר to כרה, 'buy', so HAL 661, or at least that the Masoretes understood it to be a form of נכר.

Analysis

What we are left with are two narratives that describe two prophetic symbolic acts. Hos 1 describes how Hosea marries a prostitute called Gomer, who later gives birth to three children. The children are described as 'children of whoredom' as is the mother, wholly due to the fact that they are her offspring, and not due to their own behaviour. The children are also given symbolic names that illustrate the message of the narrative. This name giving, however, does not form part of the prophetic symbolic act, but is a prophetic symbolism that works complementary to the prophetic symbolic act.

Hos 3 describes how Hosea marries another woman, who is described as an adulteress, and who is apparently trapped in some form of slavery, since Hosea has to pay a price to perform his prophetic symbolic act (3:2). It may very well be that we are supposed to understand the reference in 3:1 to the רֵעַ, lit. 'friend', of the woman, as the part to which Hosea has to pay for the woman. It is an important note to make, that the woman is said to be אֲהֻבַת, 'loved', by this 'friend', and Hosea is commanded by God, not to 'go and take' a woman as in ch. 1, but to לֵךְ אֱהַב־אִשָּׁה, 'go (and) love a woman'. This theme receives an explicit counterpart in the interpretation, when Hosea is told to love the woman as God אֹהֲבַת, 'loves', the people. Apparently, the command to 'love' an adulteress must have implied a payment for the woman. It remains unclear as to the situation in which the woman lived, but it is likely that since she had been recognized as an adulteress she had been sent away from her former husband, and was now living in a slave-like situation with another man.

As to the structure of these descriptions, they appear quite normal when compared to other prophetic symbolic acts. They contain the normal tripartite structure of 1) divine command to perform a prophetic symbolic act, 2) the description of the performance of that act, and 3) the symbolic interpretation of that act. The two narratives divide as follows in these three parts;

	Ch 1	*Ch 3*
1. Command	1:2bα-β	3:1a
2. Description	1:3 (4-9)	3:2-3
3. Interpretation	1:2bγ (4-9)[1]	3:1, 4

Both narratives deviate from the normal structure in that the command follows closely by an interpretation, in what could be described as a disputational style. However, it is clear from this that the narratives do follow the normal pattern of describing a prophetic symbolic act, and there should be no hesitation as to the intention behind these texts to describe acts that were performed.

It is clear that the two prophetic symbolic acts are different as to their symbolic interpretation. The act in ch. 1, together with the symbolic naming of the children,[2] serves to emphasize the fact that as the woman is characterized by having sexual relationships with other men but her husband, the people is characterized by serving other gods besides their own. The key theme here is the unfaithfulness/apostasy of the people and, subsequently, the divine judgement invoked through the interpretations of the symbolic names of the children. It is therefore not the entrance into marriage that serves any symbolic purpose, but the marriage as such, once it has been entered into. The woman is a prostitute when she enters her marriage to Hosea, but whether she is faithful to Hosea while married is not revealed, and there is no emphasis in the narrative that

---

[1] In vv. 4-9 the symbolic names are given, and their symbolism described. This name giving is not treated here as a prophetic symbolic act, but of course it is intimately connected to the prophetic symbolic act as a very similar form of prophetic symbolism.

[2] Jeremias (1983: 26) is correct in noting, that 1:2 does not describe a prophetic symbolic act in its entirety, since the symbolic naming of the children must be taken into account. From this does not follow, however, as it appears to do for Jeremias, that 1:2 existed in an earlier form without the reference to the woman being זְנוּנִים, 'a prostitute'.

would point to such a conclusion. Indeed, there is no emphasis on Gomer's behaviour while married at all. It is the characterisation of the woman as a prostitute, founded on her behaviour previous to her marriage to Hosea, that forms the basis for naming her a אֵשֶׁת זְנוּנִים, 'woman of whoredom', and not, as far as we can tell, her behaviour after her marriage to Hosea. The children stand to the mother as the members of the people stand to the people at large, as individual members of the collective, and thus they symbolize the apostasy of the people through their origin with the whoring mother/apostate people.[1]

The noun זְנוּנִים occurs 12 times in the OT, out of which 6 are in Hosea.[2] It is not the ordinary word for 'prostitute', which is זֹנָה. There is also a particular word for 'cult prostitute', קְדֵשָׁה that could have been used, had that been what the author intended (cf. Hos 4:14; 2 Kgs 23:7). The question is therefore why זְנוּנִים has been chosen as a description of the woman in 1:2. The plural form is best explained as a plural of abstraction, which signifies an habitual behaviour as an abstract characteristic of the person in question, rather than a more or less institutionalised behaviour, since the latter would more suitable have been expressed with the common זֹנָה.[3] The closest parallel to the expression in Hos 1:2 is 2 Kgs 9:22, זְנוּנֵי אִיזֶבֶל, 'the whoring of Jezebel', where the same figurative use of the noun occurs which can be found later in Hosea (2:4, 6; 4:12; 5:4). The 'whoring of Jezebel' refers to the foreign cult that she is said to have imported to Israel, and so we have a similar figurative, symbolic use of 'whoring' for apostasy in worshipping other gods beside Yhwh (cf. Ex 20:3). The story of Jezebel may have been a well-known story in the north, maybe even part of the national heritage as it described the rise of Jehu, and may have been the origin of the figurative use of זנה and the influence behind the use of the term in Hosea.[4] There is also a more distant parallel in Nah 3:4, where the figurative use is extended to Nineveh's international politics, described as the זְנוּנֵי זֹנָה, 'whoring of the whore' (cf. also Is 23:17).

---

[1] The salvation oracle in 2:1-3, which is most likely later than the surrounding context, interprets in 2:3 the children as the collective, which is best understood as an interpretation of the prophetic symbolic act in a later time, when the question regarding the symbolic meaning of the children had already been asked.

[2] See TDOT 4, 99-104.

[3] See Waltke, and O'Connor (1990: 121).

[4] Kruger (1983: 18-9) makes a point out of a comparison between 2 Kgs 9 and Hos 1-2. Whether that aids in understanding Hos 1:2, due to the difficulties in dating the narratives in 2 Kgs, is uncertain.

When we attempt to categorize the symbolism involved in the description of the prophetic symbolic act in ch. 1, we note an obvious iconic relation between the marital relationship between Hosea and Gomer on the one hand, and God and the people on the other. This has generally been misinterpreted as implying that the relationship between God and people describes a marriage by means of metaphor, with all the implications of a comparison with 'hieros gamos' that is implied therewith.[1] However, Hos 1 as well as ch. 3 does not put any emphasis on the marriage motif as such. Indeed, it can even be argued, not very convincingly but nevertheless, that there were no marriages involved whatsoever, since there are only two rather vague commands to 'take' a woman to have children with her and to 'love' her, respectively. Both descriptions lack any emphasis on the precise character of the relationship between Hosea and Gomer. It is likely that this was done in order to focus on the one point of contact between the signifier (Hosea and Gomer) and that which is signified (God and people), namely זנה, 'whoring'. This is the character of habitually being with more than one, which is why the woman is described with the noun זְנוּנִים, 'whoredom'.

There is also a subtle indexical symbolism involved in the use of the expression כִּי־זָנֹה תִזְנֶה הָאָרֶץ מֵאַחֲרֵי יְהוָה, lit. 'for the land is truly whoring away from Yhwh'. The phrase מֵאַחֲרֵי יְהוָה is sometimes considered to be an indication of Dtr redaction, or at least to be an influence from such an origin.[2] However, it is important to note that the phrase מֵאַחֲרֵי יְהוָה occurs only in Hos 1:2. On the other hand, the phrase is clearly alluding to what later came to be a typical Dtr phrase (הלך אחרי (אלהים אחרים, which functions as an indexical symbolism.[3] This stereotypical Dtr phrase has been revitalised, or revivified,[4] through a more figurative use when the verb has been replaced with זנה, while the figurative use of the verb as such is very unlikely to have been the creation of Hosea himself. What the prophet has done is that he has taken a well-known idiomatic phrase, which clearly denoted apostasy, and connected that phrase with something which would clearly create an association to aberrant behaviour, namely the verb זנה. These two items, the idiomatic phrase and the verb, were, each by itself, conventional in its symbolic status. However, through combining these two items, the prophet revitalised their symbolic value to be indexical, i.e., they now

---

[1] So particularly Wolff (1974: 13-6). See also Ringgren (1987), Hugenberger (1994).

[2] E.g. Jeremias (1983: 26-7), see above n. 1.

[3] See Weinfeld (1972: 320-1).

[4] For making idioms or more or less dead metaphors become more like active, less transparent or living metaphors, see e.g. Kittay (1987: 298-9). For an example of this in Mal 1:11, see Viberg (1994).

referred to something else by means of the associations they stirred. In this way, Hosea was given the opportunity to say something daringly new, namely that this well-known behaviour, which was considered clearly worth condemnation by his intended audience, were in fact their own! He thereby turns what they already acknowledged to be wrong against themselves, and unknowingly they would then bring down their condemnation on themselves.

In ch. 3, we find the same basic iconic symbolism as in ch. 1, in which the marital relationship between Hosea and the adulterous woman relates analogically to the relationship between God and the people. However, whereas the focus of the prophetic symbolic act in ch. 1 was the characteristic of not being with only one, the focus of the act in ch. 3 takes the argumentation a step further. This woman, who has not stayed with her husband but has been found to be adulterous, i.e., who is characterized by not staying with only one, is still to be loved by Hosea. The focus of ch. 3 is therefore on loving someone who does not stay with only one. Hosea is given the command to אֱהַב־אִשָּׁה אֲהֻבַת רֵעַ וּמְנָאָפֶת, 'love a woman who is loved by another, hence[1] an adulteress'. It is significant to note the double focus of this command. First, she is loved by another, i.e., Hosea must take her away from someone else with whom she is involved, in order to show her his love. Second, the conclusion is drawn from what has been described, that she is characterized as an adulteress, i.e., as someone who does not stay with only one. As Gomer in ch. 1 was characterized as someone performing whoredom, the woman in ch. 3 is characterized as someone committing adultery. But it has to be remembered that she is an adulteress only as far as the symbolic interpretation is concerned, and that is all the text attempts to describe. The woman is characterized as living with another man, and given the fact that Hosea marries her, she symbolizes an adulterous woman, regardless of whether or not she actually continued to be with other men after her marriage to Hosea.

The interpretation of the act in 3:1b makes the iconic symbolism clear, in the emphasis on how the people turn to other gods, i.e., how they can not stay with only one God, as the woman is characterized as a woman who does not stay with only one man. The symbolic value therefore does not rest on whether the woman is actually acting adulterously against Hosea or not, but on the characteristics of her previous behaviour together with her being married to Hosea. When Hosea is married to the woman, the stage is set and all the necessary ingredients for the symbolic interpretation are available.

---

[1] The ו is understood as explicative, see above note c.

Summary and Conclusions

1. Hos 1 and 3 are most likely describing two different narratives, Hosea's relationship with Gomer in ch. 1, and with an unnamed woman in ch. 3. Their relationship is more due to redaction than literary formation.

2. Although the procedure is very much in the dark to us, it is likely that in ch. Hosea marries a prostitute, and in ch. 3 he marries an adulterous woman as a form of purchase from another man with whom the woman is living.

3. In both ch. 1 and 3, the symbolic meaning of the prophetic act is iconic, in the sense that it is construed based on an analogy between the relationship between Hosea-Gomer/unnamed woman, and God-people. As Hosea's first relation symbolizes ironically the people's failure to 'stay with only one' God, his second relationship symbolizes ironically God's love for a people who does not stay with only one God.

4. The iconic symbolism is based on the characteristics of the women in ch. 1 and 3, but not, as far as we can tell, on their behaviour in relation to Hosea.

5. There is nothing to substantiate the view that marriage as such is being imbued with any particular symbolic meaning in these symbolic acts.

6. Through the use of the phrase 'whoring away' the author has created a subtle indexical symbolism, which associates Hosea's symbolic act to the apostate behaviour of the people.

G. Crowning a High Priest (Zechariah 6:9-15)[1]

Introduction

Zech 6:9-16 would seem on the surface to be a rather straight forward narrative. It describes the divine command to the prophet to collect silver and gold from exiles from Babylon. He is to make a crown, and put it on the head of Joshua the high priest. He is then given an oracle concerning a future leader, called 'Branch', which he is to speak to Joshua, presumably in connection with the symbolic act. The crown is then to be deposited in the temple as a remembrance.

However, this appendix to the night visions in the book of Zechariah has proved to be a veritable crux in past attempts to unravel its meaning,[2] and not only in relation to the possible prophetic symbolic act described therein. The exegete is inevitably drawn into questions regarding messianic expectations in post-exilic Jehud, the role of the priesthood and indeed the high-priest in that time,[3] together with the possible emergence of a hierocracy already during Persian rule, and the apparent disappearance of Zerubbabel. And in past attempts we find various redaction critical methods being applied, as well as being criticized. These are vast issues that can not be solved in a narrow exegetical study such as this. However, a close examination of Zech 6:9-15 will reveal that earlier scholarship may have looked too much to the overall views and taken too much for granted as 'established results', and neglected to do a close analysis of the very text at hand. Since this text also contains some difficult discursive moments and shifts, it is only natural that scholars have become entrenched in the two well-known categories; either the text is the result of redaction work at a later time than the original composition of some of its parts, or the text is understandable as it is.[4] It follows, therefore, that what has been at the forefront of discussion regarding this text has not been the function of the symbolic act, but various exegetical problems dealing with post-exilic religious expectations, lan-

---

[1] See also my earlier study Viberg (2000).

[2] E.g. Grabbe (1992: 78). Coggins (1987: 47) even goes as far as to say that 'there is clearly no agreement as yet concerning the interpretation of this passage, nor of its relation to the visions which precede it.'

[3] See the recent treatment by Rooke (2000).

[4] So e.g. Rignell (1950: 218-42), Eichrodt (1957), Meyers, and Meyers (1987: 367), Woude (1988).

guage, redaction history and the political rule of Jehud. These technical issues have lead scholars in various directions, and we will have to deal with them in order to properly understand the prophetic symbolic act.

We are accustomed to a certain form for narratives that deals with prophetic symbolic acts. They usually contain a divine order to perform, a description of the performance of the act, and an interpretation, normally in oracular form. Here, however, we find only the order to perform the act, neither a description of its performance nor an interpretation.[1] However, this tripartite form is not always found, which is why there is no reason to suspect on this particular ground that we are not dealing with a prophetic symbolic act.

Finally, most of the discussions regarding this passage spring from a few but very central questions, and they will be returned to in various places in the following analysis. They are as follows;

1) Why is the word for 'crown' used in the plural in MT (vv. 11, 14)?
2) Why is the high-priest and not a throne pretendent said to be crowned, e.g. the davidide Zerubbabel?
3) If the 'Branch'[2] is said to be he who will build the temple, how then can the crown be commanded to be stored in the temple that is yet to be constructed?
4) Who are the elusive characters 'a priest' and the 'Branch', and in what temple is the crown to be stored?

The Text

9 וַיְהִי דְבַר־יְהֹוָה אֵלַי לֵאמֹר
10 לָקוֹחַᵃ מֵאֵת הַגּוֹלָה

9 The word of Yhwh came to me: 10 Collect
from the exiles - from Heldai, Tobijah, and

---

[1] Fohrer (1968: 18), Woude (1988: 150) are too simplistic in describing the subsequent oracle as an interpretation of the symbolic act. Woude (1988: 149-50) must resort to a very strained and unconvincing interpretation of the phrase שִׂים ב ראשׁ as idiomatic, 'put at someone's disposal', but even then, the oracle is hard to understand as interpretative.

[2] The literary pun on the noun צֶמַח is obvious, and the wordplay might explain the difficulty in understanding what is meant by the phrase 'branch out in his place'. Perhaps the pun was more literary motivated than the phrase itself. There is also a clear dependence on Jer 33:15, אַצְמִיחַ לְדָוִד צֶמַח צְדָקָה, 'I will raise up for David a righteous Branch', and the phrase in Zech might be seen as some form of commentary on the Jeremiah text, see Meyers, and Meyers (1987: 355-6), Nurmela (1996: 64-5). There is also a thematic link between the double reference earlier that he will build the temple and that he will 'sprout', both indicating some form of growth.

מֵחֶלְדַּי וּמֵאֵת טוֹבִיָּה וּמֵאֵת
יְדַעְיָה וּבָאתָ אַתָּה בַּיּוֹם
הַהוּא וּבָאתָ בֵּית יֹאשִׁיָּה
בֶן־צְפַנְיָה אֲשֶׁר־בָּאוּ מִבָּבֶל
11 וְלָקַחְתָּ כֶסֶף־וְזָהָב וְעָשִׂיתָ
עֲטָרוֹת וְשַׂמְתָּ בְּרֹאשׁ יְהוֹשֻׁעַ
בֶּן־יְהוֹצָדָק הַכֹּהֵן הַגָּדוֹל
12 וְאָמַרְתָּ אֵלָיו לֵאמֹר כֹּה
אָמַר יְהוָה צְבָאוֹת לֵאמֹר
הִנֵּה־אִישׁ צֶמַח שְׁמוֹ וּמִתַּחְתָּיו
יִצְמָח [c]וּבָנָה אֶת־הֵיכַל יְהוָה[c]
13 וְהוּא יִבְנֶה אֶת־הֵיכַל יְהוָה
וְהוּא־יִשָּׂא הוֹד וְיָשַׁב וּמָשַׁל
עַל־כִּסְאוֹ וְהָיָה כֹהֵן עַל־כִּסְאוֹ[d]
וַעֲצַת שָׁלוֹם תִּהְיֶה בֵּין שְׁנֵיהֶם
14 וְהָעֲטָרֹת[f] תִּהְיֶה [e]לְחֵלֶם
וּלְטוֹבִיָּה וְלִידַעְיָה וּלְחֵן בֶּן־צְפַנְיָה
לְזִכָּרוֹן בְּהֵיכַל יְהוָה 15 וּרְחוֹקִים יָבֹאוּ
וּבָנוּ בְּהֵיכַל יְהוָה וִידַעְתֶּם
כִּי־יְהוָה צְבָאוֹת שְׁלָחַנִי וְהָיָה
אֲלֵיכֶם אִם־שָׁמוֹעַ תִּשְׁמְעוּן
בְּקוֹל יְהוָה אֱלֹהֵיכֶם

Jedaiah - who have arrived from Babylon; and go that day to the house of Josiah son of Zephaniah. 11 Take silver and gold, and make a large crown, set it on the head of the high priest Joshua son of Jehozadak, 12 and say to him: Thus says Yhwh of hosts: Look, a man whose name is 'Branch': for he shall branch out in his place, and he shall build the temple of Yhwh. 13 It is he that shall build the temple of Yhwh; he shall bear royal honor, and shall sit and rule on his throne. There shall be a priest by his throne, with peaceful understanding between the two of them. 14 And the crown shall be in the care of Heldai, Tobijah, Jedaiah, and Josiah son of Zephaniah, as a memorial in the temple of Yhwh. 15 Those who are far off shall come and help to build the temple of Yhwh; and you shall know that Yhwh of hosts has sent me to you. This will happen if you diligently obey the voice of Yhwh your God.

Textual notes

[a] The use of לקח in the sense of 'collect' and without an apparent object is strange, and some conclude that the text is corrupt and should read a verbal adjective, so e.g. Ackroyd (1968: 194, 79, 195), Rudolph (1976: 127). BHS even suggests changing מֵאֵת into משאת or מתנת, 'gifts', in order to provide an object. However, at the beginning of v. 11, after the persons from whom the silver and gold will be collected have been introduced, the verb לקח occurs again, now in finite form and followed by the object in a straightforward manner. The delay in providing the object is clearly for literary purposes, so e.g. Meyers, and Meyers (1987: 337-8), and could well be described as an anacoluthon. Meyers, and Meyers (1987: 338) also make the interesting parallel with the priestly expression לקח מאת (Ex 25:2; Num 18:26-8; Lev 7:34) for taking offerings, and which even occurs without an explicit object (Lev 7:34) which can be detected from the context, as in this text.

[b] The form is morphologically plural, so LXX, but semantically singular, as witnessed by LXX[Luc], Syr, and the more elaborate interpretation in Tg., כליל רב, 'large crown'. However, this does not mean that the Hebrew Text behind Tg. read a singular, but precisely the opposite. That the form עֲטָרֹת is meant to refer to one crown can be seen from the singular form of the verb in the second instance of the word in v. 14, וְהָעֲטָרֹת תִּהְיֶה. There is nothing in the context that would indicate the use of more than one crown, and had the intention been to command the making of two crowns for Zerubbabel and

Joshua, a dual form would have been expected. On the other hand, there is no basis for changing the text to a singular form. This plural with a singular sense also occurs in Job 31:36, אֶעֶנְדֶנּוּ עֲטָרוֹת לִי, 'I would bind it on me like a (large) crown'. This has been explained as a variant singular form under Phoenician influence, so Albright (1955: 8), Ceresko (1980: 184-5), cf. DNWSI 838, but that is unlikely. It is better to follow the interpretation of the Tg. and see the plural as emphatic, 'a large crown', probably also in Job 31:36. See also note b.

[c-c] BHS app suggests that this is a variant reading to the near doublet, which follows in v. 13. This appears to be supported by LXX, which has the first expression in v. 12 without the independent personal pronoun. It is more likely that LXX has simplified its text by removing what must have appeared as an unnecessary doublet. Scholars who consider either of the expressions as secondary are e.g. Wellhausen (1898: 185), Chary (1969: 112). A more literary explanation would be that the iteration is meant to enforce that it is 'Branch' and no one else who is to build the temple, thus the added emphasis through וְהוּא, 'yes, he (and no one else) ...' (v. 13aα), so Rudolph (1976: 129), Petersen (1984: 276-7), Meyers, and Meyers (1987: 358), Rose (1997: 158-9). Syr only has the second phrase in v. 13a, which would argue for that both variants had at their disposals a text that contained both phrases, so Rignell (1950: 229), Petitjean (1969: 289).

[d] Some argue that the reading of LXX is preferable here, καὶ ἔσται ὁ ἱερεὺς ἐκ δεξιῶν αὐτοῦ, 'and the priest will be on his right side', but Tg. has עַל כּוּרסוֹהי, 'on his throne' in both instances in v. 13. LXX has apparently attempted to avoid the double reference to 'sit on his throne' in order to avoid any misunderstanding. A more sensitive reading of the Hebrew text discloses that the word כסא, 'throne', functions as a literary hinge between the monarchical rule of the 'Branch' in v. 13aγ and the priest next to the royal throne in v. 13bα. It links the monarch and the priest, and as the priest is physically associated closely with the throne, so he is meant to be understood symbolically as being associated with leadership and authority by Zechariah.

[e] LXX misinterprets the names as qualities, and the phrase לְזִכְּרוֹן is understood as εἰς ψαλμὸν, a rather desperate attempt to make sense of the verse. Tg. follows MT.

[f] If this form was originally plural, as in v. 11, why is it spelled defectively here in v. 14, but plene in v. 11? A likely explanation would be that an original singular form in v. 14, supported by LXX, was later accommodated to the plural form in v. 11 by an act of revocalisation, but without adding the ו to the consonantal text. This should therefore not be considered a matter of redaction but of accommodation of language in the later process of transmission. The exegetical implications of this will be dealt with below.

Analysis

The structure of the text

The symbolism involved in this passage consists of two parts; the symbolic act of crowning the high priest (vv. 10-11), and depositing the crown in the temple as a symbol for remembrance (v. 14). Since the crown has been part of the earlier symbolic act, it would be hard to see a sudden non-symbolic use of that item in v. 14. Instead, we can see how these two parts functions as an inclusio (vv. 10-11; 14) around the oracle (vv. 12-13):

1 9: Introduction
2 10-15: Command to perform the act and the accompanied oracle
  a 10-11: *The act*
    1) 10: Collecting silver and gold
    2) 11a: Fabricate a crown
    3) 11b: 'Coronation'
  b 12-15: *The oracle*
    1) 12a: Introduction
    2) 12b-13: Description of 'Branch'
      a 12bα: Designation of 'Branch'
      b 12bβ: Naming of 'Branch'
      c 12bγ: The task for 'Branch'
      d 12bδ: The 'Branch' will build the temple
      e 13aα: The 'Branch' will build, no one else
      f 13aβ: The reward of 'Branch'
      g 13aγ: The competent rule of 'Branch'
      h 13bα: A priest next to his throne
      i 13bβ: Their peaceful relationship
3 14: The crown to be deposited in the temple
4 15: Conclusion
  a 15aα: Aid in building the temple
  b 15aβ: Divine reassurance
  c 15b: Conditions

A problem that has been noted regarding the structure of the passage is to determine precisely when the oracle is finished, and the angel resumes his speech to Zechariah. The usual boundary has been set between vv. 13 and 14, since the repetition at the end of v. 12 and the beginning of v. 13 would argue in favour of those two verses being closely connected. Van der Woude has recently argued that the oracle ended with v. 12.[1] The repetition in v. 13a is then part of the following interpretation of the oracle in v. 12 to Zechariah. However, it is very hard to find any indications in the text that would substantiate this view. The beginning of the oracle to the 'Branch' is clearly marked by the phrase הִנֵּה־אִישׁ and the shift from second to third person, and the only marking in the text that could

---

[1] Woude (1988: 145). Hanhart (1991: 410) seems to argue along similar lines.

indicate the end of the oracle is the shift from third person to second in v. 14a.[1]

The composition of Zech 6:9-15 has been much discussed and the suggestions are many. It is rather common to regard the text as containing secondary material of some form. Proponents of this view have viewed the text as either the result of a fusion of two originally distinct layers, or an original oracle that has suffered later, redactional adaptation,[2] although it would seem to be hard to draw an all too fine line between these two alternatives. In order not to get involved too much in the details of this discussion, it would be helpful to outline the major differences in the case of two originally separate layers that are supposed to have been combined;[3]

Original	Secondary
11, 14-15	12-13[4]
11a, 14-15	11b-13[5]
11-12	13-15[6]
11-13	14-15[7]

It is clear from this that scholars in the past have had great problems in accepting that the description of the symbolic act (vv. 11, 14) can actually have formed part of the same original text as the oracle (vv. 12-13).

When it comes to the view that an oracle has been reshaped, Rose again provides us with a helpful overview, with three alternatives;

1) There was a crown, but originally there was no command to put it on a head.[1]

---

[1] The argument of Rose (1997: 159) that an oracle consisting of only v. 12 would hardly have been understood does not seem to bear much weight, since v. 13 does not explain v. 12, but adds further material to the narrative.

[2] See Laato (1992: 249), Redditt (1992: 252-3).

[3] The table is from Rose (1975: 149). His analysis of the composition of Zech 6:9-15 is excellent and I refer to it for a more details.

[4] So e.g. Wallis (1972), who sees the oracles in 1) vv. 9, 10a.bβ, 11, 14; 2) vv. 10bα, 12-13, 15, thus roughly dividing between the symbolic act and the oracle regarding the 'Branch'. Petersen (1984: 273) sees the two earlier oracles in 1) vv. 10-11, 14; 2) vv. 12-13; 3) v. 15, which makes the similar distinction between the act and the oracle regarding the 'Branch'.

[5] Redditt (1992: 253). Even the command to perform the symbolic is then part of the secondary material.

[6] Rignell (1950: 241), who sees vv. 13-14 as a commentary on the oracle, made by Zechariah himself, Petitjean (1969: 289), Amsler, et al. (1988: 106-7).

[7] So e.g. Horst (1964: 238), Elliger (1967: 130-1).

2) A crown was at one time put on the head of Zerubbabel, but it was later changed to Joshua the high priest.[2]

3) Two crowns were originally meant to be put on the heads of both Joshua and Zerubbabel, but later the reference to Zerubbabel was removed.[3]

It would seem embarrassingly clear that scholars have not been able to agree regarding a merge of different layers or a later redaction.[4]

What has caused scholars to take such drastic steps are the various problems they believe to have found in the text. However, the failure to come to any form of consensus indicates that it is not the proposed solutions that need reconsideration as much as the way scholars detect problems in the text. Although this is a methodological issue far beyond the scope of this study, it will still be shown below what can be achieved by a more sensitive attitude to how a text might be construed.[5] Since these are matters not only related to the possible redaction history of the text, we will deal with them in depth below. We will also attempt to look at the text anew, and try to find textual indications that can lead us to a proper understanding of the text, however it has come about. To focus again on the text and less on preconceived ideas as to how a text may or may not have come about, may very well be the best lesson to learn from earlier scholarship.

The performance of the symbolic act

The lack of any description of the actual performance of the act can be because it was never performed. All that can aid us in answering the question whether the act was ever performed or not is the practical nature of the act. There is nothing about the description of the act that makes it unlikely to have been performed, unlike the clothing of Joshua in Zech ch. 3, where it is ordered by an angle who is standing by when he is being furnished with fresh clothes. This

---

[1] So e.g. Wellhausen (1898: 43, 185). This view has not had many proponents in recent times, although it appears to be the view of Laato (1992: 248-52), but one looks in vain for a reason why v. 11b should be considered as secondary.

[2] This has clearly been the most popular solution, e.g. Horst (1964: 237-8), Elliger (1967: 128-9), Fohrer (1968: 70-1), Amsler, et al. (1988: 105), Deissler (1988: 286), Redditt (1992: 257). Blenkinsopp (1996: 207-8) seems sure, but is more uncertain in Blenkinsopp (1995: 176, n 37). See Rose (1997: 163, nn 57-9) for further references.

[3] So e.g. Carroll (1979: 167), Hanson (1979: 256), Hanson (1986: 265ß), Soggin (1989: 389-90).

[4] Rose (1997: 165-70) is again to be commended for a fine critique of the basic methodology behind these various attempts to reshape the text to their liking.

[5] For a similar approach, see Rose (1997: 172), Rooke (2000: 147).

dressing ceremony is more likely to be understood as symbolical only, the clean clothes symbolising the forgiveness of sins (3:4).

The elements of performance are straightforward in the divine command (v. 11). Zechariah is to take the silver and gold he has collected, make a crown, and put it on the head of Joshua the high priest. However, there are some problems with this description. Why is Zechariah told to take both silver and gold? The expression כֶּסֶף וְזָהָב, 'silver and gold' is quite common as a hendiadys, denoting wealth and riches, both in the having and in the giving (1 Kgs 15:9; 2 Kgs 7:8; Is 2:7; Ez 38:13 etc). Here, Zechariah has been told to collect riches from the גּוֹלָה, 'the exiles', presumably as part of the gifts for the reestablishment of the temple (cf. Ezra 1:6, 7:15f). Furthermore, the exodus tradition tells of how the people left Egypt with various riches as a spoiling, כְּלֵי־כֶסֶף וּכְלֵי זָהָב, 'jewellery of silver and gold' (Ex 12:35-36), וַיּוֹצִיאֵם בְּכֶסֶף וְזָהָב וְאֵין, 'he brought Israel out with silver and gold' (Ps 105:37). The exodus tradition, with its later elaborations, may very well have influenced the language used here in Zech 6:11.[1] The reason for the use of the phrase 'gold and silver' is therefore more due to its ability to associate with riches that have been collected from the exiles, than to the precise materials that are to be used in the fabrication of the crown.

As in any form of idiomatic language, the parts that make up the idiom should not be interpreted as having any semantic value on their own, and that is the mistake that scholars have sometimes made in this case.[2] The view of Meyers & Meyers that the two metals were meant to be made into two crowns, one in silver for the high priest and one in gold for 'the Branch', is reading much into the text that is not there, at the same time as it ignores the linguistic indications that are there.[3] They claim that because jewellery was preferably made of gold instead of silver, although the latter was scarcer, it follows that two crowns were made, one of silver and one of gold![4] There is no reason why both metals, if indeed we are to understand the expression as denoting two metals and not just as a hendiadys, could not have been used in the making of one single crown. A similar case can be found in 1 Kgs 15:19, were king Asa is sending a bribe to Ben-hadad that consists of both silver and gold, שֹׁחַד כֶּסֶף וְזָהָב. Whether this means that a particular item was furnished out of both silver and gold is hard to say, and it is just as likely that the expression 'silver and gold' is explicative of the contents of the bribe. The same vagueness should be allowed for here in

---

[1] See Ackroyd (1968: 195).
[2] The elaborate discussion by Meyers, and Meyers (1987: 346-8) is perhaps the best example.
[3] Meyers, and Meyers (1987: 349).
[4] Meyers, and Meyers (1987: 350).

Zech 6:11, since the text does not explicitly state that the crown is to be fabricated out of the two metals, but simply that a crown is to be made.

The description of the actual act is somewhat unusual, וְשַׂמְתָּ בְרֹאשׁ יְהוֹשֻׁעַ, 'and set it on the head of Joshua'. The phrase שִׂים ב ראש is mostly used with the preposition עַל (שִׂים עַל רֹאשׁ: Gen 48:18; Ex 29:6; 2 Sam 13:19 etc), and עַל is also used in a similar construction in Zech 3:5, יָשִׂימוּ צָנִיף טָהוֹר עַל־רֹאשׁוֹ, 'Let them put a clean turban on his head.' However, the prepositions עַל and ב are often interchangeable, and that is also the case in this expression. In Esther 2:17, Esther is crowned with a royal crown, and the expression used is שִׂים ב ראש, which shows that also in this particular phrase, there was no semantic difference between using עַל or ב. Nevertheless, van der Woude[1] has come up with a novel suggestion regarding this phrase, trying to understanding it in the light of the Akkadian phrase *ina rēši*,[2] and the Hebrew נתן לפני, meaning 'zur Verfügung stellen, anvertrauen'. This would mean that the high priest was never crowned, but only entrusted with the crown until a future time. However, his suggestion is not supported with any other example of that meaning for the phrase שִׂים ב ראש, and mere wishful thinking will not do, since there is a perfectly satisfying translation of the phrase already available.[3]

An act such as this is in fact described in 2 Sam 12:30 (=1 Chr 20:2). David symbolically takes the place of Milcom by having Milcom's golden crown transferred to David, וַיִּקַּח אֶת־עֲטֶרֶת־מַלְכָּם מֵעַל רֹאשׁוֹ ... וַתְּהִי עַל־רֹאשׁ דָּוִד, 'He took the crown of Milcom from his head ... and it was placed on David's head.' The emphasis here on the head is symptomatic of the description of the conventional act. The conventional act can only function as such if the proper, well-known procedure is followed, which is why the procedure of the transfer of the crown is made so explicit. Inherent in the description of the act of transferring the crown lies the meaning of transference of power, and through this particular act, royal power. It attempts to resemble a royal coronation, which it is not, but precisely for that reason it is even more important that the associative meaning of royal

---

[1] Woude (1988: 149-50).

[2] Soden (1972: 973-4).

[3] As a matter of fact, van der Woude seems to have overlooked Deut 1:13, which he could have made some use of in his argumentation. God says regarding the wise men, that וַאֲשִׂימֵם בְּרָאשֵׁיכֶם, 'I will set them over you', which could theoretically be made to mean 'I will put them at your disposal'. But that translation is as unlikely in Deut 1:13 as it is in Zech 6:11. A similar case can be made with 1 Kgs 21:9, 12, where the phrase יֹשֵׁב ב ראש is used. It is hard to see how Laato (1992: 246) can find this reference to be supportive of van der Woude's interpretation.

coronation is made even clearer.[1] In other words, it sounds as if it is a coronation, and if no questions are asked, David comes out of the event with an added
royal impetus. We have also mentioned Esther 2:17, where Esther is crowned by
having a royal crown placed on her head.[2] The procedure of the act in Zech 6:11
is therefore quite clear; a crown was put on the head of Joshua, as an imitation
of the conventional act of royal coronation.

The plural form of עֲטָרָה, 'crown' has been understood by some as a numerical plural, denoting two crowns that were meant for Joshua the high priest and
Zerubbabel the davidide.[3] The problem with this interpretation is that there is no
indication whatsoever in the text of a crowning or similar of the davidide Zerubbabel, in contrast to the described act of putting the crown on the head of Joshua
the high priest in v. 11. The most decisive argument against understanding the
term as a numerical plural, however, is the implicit reference to the one crown
commanded to be put on the head of Joshua, וְעָשִׂיתָ עֲטָרוֹת וְשַׂמְתָּ בְּרֹאשׁ יְהוֹשֻׁעַ,
'make a crown, and put (it) on the head of Joshua' (v. 11).[4] The pronominal object is commonly omitted in biblical Hebrew when it can easily be detected from
the context, and in particular when it relates to the verb שׂים, but only if the number of the object correlates to the number of the antecedent noun.[5] Since the object that is being implicitly referred to is decidedly singular, unless Joshua is
supposed to be crowned with more than one crown, the antecedent noun must
also be singular.[6]

---

[1] See Viberg (1992: 13-14). The act of royal coronation was not legal in the sense that it
achieved royal status for the one crowned; the decisive role in the legal sense was played by
the royal anointing, see Viberg (1992: 89-119). However, we find a similar case in 1 Kgs 2
concerning the royal anointing of Solomon. The author is at great pains to describe the anointing in detail in order to show that the proper procedure was followed. Nevertheless, the
anointing was not performed in the proper context with the representatives of the people present, which makes Solomon's entrance to the throne nothing but a coup d'état.

[2] The opposite of making someone king could be symbolized by having the crown removed,
see e.g. Jer 13:18, and Ez 21:21, where both the turban as well as the crown is part of the
royal ornaments, see Block (1997: 690, n 189).

[3] So e.g. Wallis (1972: 236), Petersen (1984: 275), Redditt (1992: 252), Cook (1995: 135).
Carroll (1979: 166-7, 238, n. 9) also seems to favour this view.

[4] It is very strange that this has gone unnoticed in earlier scholarship. A good example is
Cook (1995: 135), who makes a point of translating the passage, '... make crowns. Place [one]
on the head ...' with NPJS.

[5] Meyers (1987: 353) are mistaken in limiting this linguistic trait to only the singular.

[6] Meyers (1987: 353) acknowledges this as being 'not normal procedure'. But that is not good
enough. There is simply no example available that can show the number to be changing between the object and the antecedent noun. They apparently break the observable rules of

Not one instance can be found where שׂים refers implicitly to a preceding noun, where the reference and the noun do not agree numerically. The following are a few examples, according to the word-pattern found in Zech 6:11, noun + שׂים ו + prep + noun;[1]

Gen 9:23	‏וַיִּקַּח שֵׁם וָיֶפֶת אֶת־הַשִּׂמְלָה... ‏וַיָּשִׂימוּ עַל־שְׁכֶם שְׁנֵיהֶם.	Then Shem and Japheth took the garment, laid (it) on both their shoulders ...
Ex 3:22	‏כְּלֵי־כֶסֶף וּ...כְּלֵי זָהָב ‏וּ...שְׂמָלֹת וְשַׂמְתֶּם עַל־בְּנֵיכֶם ‏וְעַל־בְּנֹתֵיכֶם	... jewellery of silver and of gold, and clothing, and you shall put (them) on your sons and on your daughters ...[2]
Jer 13:2	‏וָאֶקְנֶה אֶת־הָאֵזוֹר כִּדְבַר ‏יְהוָה וָאָשִׂם עַל־מָתְנָי	I bought the loincloth according to the word of Yhwh, and put (it) on my loins.

When this common linguistic practise is allowed to shed some light on Zech 6:11, there can be no doubt that a singular sense must be involved:

Zech 6:11	‏וְלָקַחְתָּ כֶסֶף־וְזָהָב וְעָשִׂיתָ ‏עֲטָרוֹת וְשַׂמְתָּ בְּרֹאשׁ יְהוֹשֻׁעַ	Take the silver and gold and make a crown, and set (it) on the head of Joshua ...

It would be quite absurd to hold that two or more crowns were put on the head of Joshua, and therefore the only possible solution is that only one crown can be involved in the description of the act. The only, and very desperate, alternative would be to postulate that originally both Joshua and Zerubbabel were meant to be crowned, but that Zerubbabel was later removed. Needless to say, there is no textual indication in that direction. The quite common solution, that two crowns are involved and one is set on the head of Joshua, and the other one is intended for Zerubbabel, is therefore linguistically impossible, and should never have been seriously considered as a viable solution to the problem.

---

grammar deliberately in order to suit their preconceived ideas as to how the text is to be understood.

[1] Some further examples according to this strict pattern are Gen 22:6; Ex 17:14; Jud 16:3; Jer 40:10. If we broaden the search to include other verbs, preferably בוא and נתן, the examples are numerous. In Is 40:19 there is even a double case of implicit reference.

[2] Gesenius (1910, §117.f) considers the omission of the plural pronominal object as in this case to be remarkable, since it would open up to misunderstanding. However, the context can easily provide the necessary clues to a proper understanding.

The reason for the plural form must then be other than numerical, and the most probable function would be to create emphasis, which is understood by Tg., כליל רב, 'large crown'.[1] The defectively spelled plural in v. 14 is best understood as an originally singular form that was much later adapted to the plural form in v. 11 in the history of textual transmission. The originally singular form was used in v. 14 since there was apparently no need for the emphasis brought about earlier by the emphatic construction in v. 11.[2]

Why was a high-priest crowned?

The question why a high priest is said to be crowned instead of the davidide Zerubbabel has spurred the most diverse solutions, mostly redaction critical ones. The most popular solution has been that an original reference to a crowning of Zerubbabel was changed into the crowning of the high-priest Joshua.[3] This would have been due to the disappearance of Zerubbabel, or at least the disillusionment regarding the messianic visions centred on him as a davidide (Hag 2:24; Zech 4:7, 9). An originally singular form of 'crown' in v. 11 is then supposed to have been altered into a plural, in order to include the crowning of both Joshua as well as Zerubbabel, but, as has been shown above, a numerical plural form is impossible.[4] We must admit, however, that we know nothing of a 'disappearance' of Zerubbabel,[5] in fact the only disappearance we can speak of is the disappearance of references to Zerubbabel in the available sources, which is something quite different. The arguments behind this radical interpretation are basically two. 1. The crowning is followed by an accompanied oracle that does not concern Joshua, but the 'Branch', by most scholars identified as Zerubbabel. This is seen as a change of subject that is too illogical to be original, and so some scholars divide the text into various layers or separate oracles that have

---

[1] See *Textual Note* d.

[2] Se also the technical discussion in *Textual notes* a and b.

[3] So Mitchell, et al. (1951: 185-6), Elliger (1967: 128-9), Amsler, et al. (1988: 108-9), Redditt (1992: 256). The emendation is also done is NAB, see also BJ, n. *i* and NEB n. *g*. It is a common misconception that this view was held by Wellhausen (1898: 185), but his suggestion regarding v. 11 was more radical, 'Der Satz nach dem Atnach ist zu streichen; das Diadem ist von Sacharja für Serubbabel als künftigen König bestimmt, erst von einem späteren Diaskeuasten für den Hohenpriester Josua. ... Der Diaskeuast trug den Verhältnissen Rechnung, wie sie sich tatsächlich gestalteten; der Priester wurde das Haupt der Theokratie, nicht der Davidide.'.

[4] For a valuable critique of this alteration, see Woude (1988: 147-9).

[5] See Woude (1988: 139-40), ABD 6.1084-6, Carroll (1979: 162-8), Rose (1997: 11-3). Still, scholars keep imagining that he was e.g. accused of treason, so Luria (1990/1), or even assassinated, so Schneir (1996).

been brought together secondarily.[1] 2. A crowning is only supposed to be suitable in relation to a monarchic figure, which as far as conventional behaviour in the area of legal symbolic acts is concerned, is correct.[2] Should the required circumstances for the proper legal function not be in place, then the act would not have been able to achieve its intended purpose as a legal, conventional act.

However, two things need to be said in regard to this. First, no one can seriously suggest that a crowning by a prophet such as Zechariah would have been legally correct, according to customary practises and laws, so the purpose of the act must have been other than the proper, legal act of crowning the throne pretendent. Second, an all too rigid reading of the text denies the prophet any use of creative and unusual figurative language, in his nonverbal as well as in his verbal communication.

A striking comparison can be made with what I have elsewhere termed 'divine anointing'. A prophet is sometimes described as anointing a person with all the proper language, both verbal as well as nonverbal, pointing to a royal anointing. [3] However, the prophetic act of anointing never had the intention of making someone king in the legal sense, but only to make use of the emotive strength inherent in the connotative language and imagery related to the performance of the act. All is done in order to associate the act with the notion of divine election; as men select their leaders, so does God. And in Zech 6:9-15 it is precisely the same principle that is set in motion; the prophetic symbolic act makes use of the powerful associations connected with royal crowning, and they are innovatively set in relation to the high priest. By this act the prophet on the one hand made use of a strikingly new image, since although the priest were also anointed,[4] they were never crowned to be the leaders of the people as the kings were. On the other hand, the text does make use of conventional practise when the prophet is told to put something on the head of the high-priest, since some form of headdress was part of the institutionalised priestly dress (Ex 28:4, 40; 29:6; Zech 3:5, יָשִׂימוּ צָנִיף טָהוֹר עַל־רֹאשׁוֹ, 'Let them put a clean turban on his head'.) The priestly installation as it is described in Ex 29:6 makes the act of putting a headdress on the priest closely connected to the more formal acts of anointing and hand filling. It is therefore precisely here, in the association be-

---

[1] So e.g. Wallis (1972: 234-6), Petersen (1984: 273), Redditt (1992: 253).

[2] So e.g. Amsler, et al. (1988: 107-8).

[3] Viberg (1992)

[4] See Viberg (1992: 116-7). Fleming (1998) has finally shown that there is no need to view the priestly anointing as a late imaginative construction inspired by royal anointing, as e.g. Blenkinsopp (1996: 92).

tween the priest and the royal status, that the prophet accomplishes his provocative message, through his symbolic act; 'Can a priest really be a leader, like a king?' That is the rhetorical question that the prophet is seeking to put on the lips of his viewers, if indeed the act was ever performed. The rhetorical force of the intended act is accomplished through a combination of using traditional material and transforming it into a highly controversial message.

How many temples are involved?

A more difficult problem is that the 'branch', usually identified as Zerubbabel, is the one who is to build (יִבְנֶה) the temple (v. 13), while the crown is put away as a remembrance in the temple (v. 14). Since this relates to the handling of the item used in the prophetic symbolic act, it is a question that has to be dealt with at some length. The temple is yet to be built in v. 12-13, but has already been built in v. 14, and the apparent contradiction between the two verses seems hard to resolve. How can the temple be referred to as not yet built, but still be referred to as the place for keeping the crown? Does this not prove that certain verses presuppose the existence of the temple (v. 14) and some do not (v. 12-13)?[1] The common, redaction critical solution is to see an oracle concerning Zerubbabel as the builder of the temple yet to be. After some form of debacle on the part of Zerubbabel, Zechariah lost his faith in him, and so the oracle was integrated in the present form of the text. However, by then the temple was already built, and so v. 14 had to be added.[2] This solution is usually connected with the common redaction critical solution to the problem of the plural form of 'crown'. When the temple was built Zerubbabel was no longer on the political scene, and the crown was deposited as an item of sacral memorabilia, perhaps to be put on the head of a true messianic davidide to come.

However, the contradiction is more likely to be apparent and not real. Even though the temple is not yet built, it is being referred to as a future building project, and so it is natural to refer to this temple yet to be built as a place for the crown in a proleptic sense. We will show two examples where this is similarly done, and where scholars have had no difficulties in accepting this proleptic use.

> In Zech 5:11 the temple building is in the future, yet it is described how the interior of it is to be configured, לִבְנוֹת־לָהּ בַיִת בְּאֶרֶץ שִׁנְעָר וְהוּכַן וְהֻנִּיחָה שָׁם עַל־מְכֻנָתָהּ,

---

[1] So e.g. Laato (1992: 248-9).

[2] Variants of this view can be found in e.g. Ackroyd (1968: 174, 194-200), Laato (1992: 248-9). Those who see different oracles only later brought together all make this common distinction.

'To the land of Shinar, to build a house for it; and when it is prepared, they will set the basket down there on its base.' The temple is referred to as the place for the basket, yet it has not yet been built, but exists only in the mind of the characters, as well as the reader. That is all it takes for it to be referred to as a future location.

In Ezr 5:15, the Jehudites are in the middle of reciting the Persian decree permitting them to rebuild the temple. The Persian king decrees, וּבֵית אֱלָהָא יִתְבְּנֵא אֵלֶּה מָאנַיָּא שֵׂא אֵזֶל־אֲחֵת הִמּוֹ בְּהֵיכְלָא דִּי בִירוּשְׁלֶם, 'Take these vessels; go and put them in the temple in Jerusalem, and let the house of God be rebuilt'. The temple is not yet built, but that evidently does not stop him from referring to it, and order the temple vessels to be stored in it, *when it is built.*

There is therefore no need to see a contradiction between the putting of the crown in the temple and the building of the temple itself. This apparent contradiction has been caused by scholars all to eager to find a textual evolution that will provide us with further clues as to both the historical as well as ideological development in Jehud.[1]

There is also the matter of whether or not the temple in vv. 12-13 is the same temple being rebuilt when the night visions are dated, ca 520 BCE.[2] It is possible that what is referred to in the oracle is Zechariah's long-term strategy for the coming of the messianic era. What is referred to in v. 14 would then be the temple that was being built in his present time, and which formed part of his short-term plan.[3] Regardless of which alternative we choose, the temple is still in the future and the argument above still stands. However, if we opt for a more distant temple-building in vv. 12-13, v. 14 must refer to the temple being built in Zechariah's own time, since otherwise it would have been difficult to understand the very practical and concrete command to put the crown in the temple as a remembrance.

---

[1] From the way e.g. Hanson (1979: 256-8) and Carroll (1979) treats Zech 6 it is obvious that the multilayered text serves their purpose, in Hanson's case to exemplify how the messianic movement in the hierocratic tradition came to an end, and to Carroll the removal of Zerubbabel from the crowning is a good example of cognitive dissonance. According to Blenkinsopp (1996: 207), the history can even be 'read between the lines' of Zech 6:9-15!

[2] See Miller, and Hayes (1986: 456-60).

[3] The useful terminology of long-term and short-term strategy is from Tollington (1993: 179), 'Since the advent of the Branch was projected into the future, Zechariah also considered the matter of an interim rule to take effect as soon as the temple was finished'.

The symbolism of the prophetic act

The lack of an interpretation of the act in the form that we are accustomed to is problematic, since it means that the act was so self-evident to the original viewers/hearers, that there was apparently no need to provide one. Instead, the accompanying oracle concerns the figure 'Branch', and it is to this we must turn to understand the symbolism involved in the act. In the comparison between the symbolic act in Zech 6:11 and the so-called divine anointing made earlier, there is one important difference to be noted. In a divine anointing the symbolism works analogically, in the sense that although the person who is anointed by a prophet is not legally made king at that time, he is still a possible candidate to be made king, through the conventional practice of royal anointing. The reason why a divine anointing differs from a royal anointing is not that the one being anointed could not be imagined as being anointed in a legal sense, but because it is not performed in the proper context, e.g. the representatives of the people being present, the priest performing the act, etc. The analogical relationship between the divine anointing (the signifier) and the imagined royal anointing (the signified), however, was believable all the same. When e.g. David is anointed it must have appeared similar to a royal anointing (1 Sam 16:1), and there would have been nothing in principle that would have stood in the way of imagining David being anointed in a legal sense. It was not enough for the two acts to look the same, however, since it would have been necessary for the imagined reality, in this case a royal anointing, to have been a conceivable reality. In addition, it is precisely because it was conceivable that it formed the nucleus of the message of the symbolic act, 'as men make kings, so does God'.

However, a symbolism based on a similar form of analogy is not a viable alternative for the interpretation of the act in Zech 6:11, since no one could have imagined a priest being crowned in the proper, customary act of royal crowning.[1] The symbolism involved in this act must therefore have worked not through analogy, i.e. not through an iconic relationship between what is symbolized and that which symbolizes, but through association, i.e. through an indexical relationship between the two. Needless to say, we do find symbolism by means of analogy in the performance, since it looks like a royal crowning, and the crown might very well have looked like a crown used for such an occasion. Nevertheless, these items of symbolism are merely parts of the common, social construction of reality, materialised through conventions such as royal crown-

---

[1] Some scholars are close to this view, e.g. Schöttler (1987: 395-6). Of course, there are those who argue that the passage originally described the crowning of Zerubbabel to be king and when the name was replaced with Joshua, the problem occurred.

ing. They are taken for granted and used in the construction of the symbolism of the act. Instead, the focus of the prophetic message of the act lies not on the crowning as such, but on who is being crowned. Through the use of a priest involved in a crowning, the prophet challenges his viewers/listeners through the construction of a new and alternative reality.

Any attempt to understand the symbolism involved in this act must then begin by examining any possible indexical symbolism in the relationship between the act (signifier) and what it is meant to convey (signified). The clues can not only be found in the performance of the act itself, but in the subsequent oracle. It is perhaps because of this rather odd and demanding symbolism that modern scholars have felt themselves forced to recreate a simpler and more acceptable text. In this lack of analogies for the coming 'Branch' might very well lie an indication that Zechariah was more of an apocalyptic than is normally held.[1] There was nothing in his circumstances that could be used to signify that which was his ideal, and in his description he could paint no details but only a very rough picture of a throne with a priest nearby.

The crowning is meant to appear similar to a proper, royal crowning. Through this resemblance, one is meant to associate to what is achieved by royal crowning, namely such qualities as power, authority, divine election and leadership. Although no one would hold that this prophetic act could have been capable of achieving the same goals, still the mere performance forces one to associate in that direction. The high priest Joshua is therefore by means of this indexical symbolism attributed with these extraordinary qualities. Not in the sense that he might be king at a later stage, since that would have been inconceivable, but as the recipient of similar qualities. Zechariah could of course have tried to argue for Joshua as the new king, but it would have contradicted so much of the common, social reality and its conventions that it would simply have made him loose all credibility. The best evidence for this is that in the following oracle, Zechariah presents a future throne pretender. What we have gathered so far regarding the symbolic meaning of the act fits in well with how the future 'Branch' and the future priest will work together, וַעֲצַת שָׁלוֹם תִּהְיֶה בֵּין שְׁנֵיהֶם. 'with peaceful understanding between the two of them.' This implies that the priest in Zechariah's future does play a significant role in leading the people, which implies those characteristics which we saw is associated to by means of the symbolic act.

---

[1] See Cook (1995: 133).

In order to present his ideal picture of how the re-established society should be construed, [1] Zechariah starts with the elevation of priesthood and with the high priest as its representative, probably because he had no alternative since there was no king. Furthermore, Zechariah could see no acceptable candidate for the throne in his time. As Joshua was forgiven, symbolically by being provided with new clothes in ch. 3, and reinstalled in his office, so here in ch. 6 he is the first to be elevated to the heights of power and authority.[2] It is to this rekindled authority in Jehud, that God then speaks through the prophet concerning 'the Branch', who will personalize the resurrected monarchy, and who is to rebuild the temple (vv. 12-13). Zechariah seems to paint a picture of a society in which priest and king (and prophet?) are in harmony with each other, and dependent upon each other for the stability of the community, as has been described earlier in the book with the image of the two branches that both serve to provide the precious oil (4:3, 11-14).[3] His picture is one of compromise, the elevation of the high priest on the one hand and the monarch on the other, but none is elevated at the expense of the other. This is why he is so careful to describe how the priest is to be next to the royal throne (v. 13), ready with his council and oracular function. This does not mean that Zechariah imagines the priest being on the same level as the king, but still his picture has much of diarchy in itself. The oracle in 6:12-15 therefore presupposes and is balanced with a high priest being elevated to a position of power and authority. That is precisely what is accomplished in and through the symbolic act.[4]

---

[1] Eichrodt (1957) argues along similar lines, that the crowning of the priest foreshadowed the coming crowning of the 'Branch', the true davidide on the throne. The restitution of the cult would be a sign for the total restitution that was to come. Seybold (1972) argues in a similar way that the priest was to hold the crown as a substitute for the coming davidide, until the final diarchy had been established. See also Ackroyd (1968: 199), 'The high priest Joshua is here symbolically crowned in token of the coming of the Branch ...'. However, Ackroyd's suggestion that the symbolic act was performed in the Babylonian exile, and that Zechariah returned with Zerubbabel, lacks any credibility, as does his suggestion that originally both Joshua and Zerubbabel were mentioned as the objects of the coronation. According to Rose (1997: 69), the high priest Joshua is given the crown as 'a sign guaranteeing that YHWH will certainly fulfil his promise concerning the coming of Zemah.'

[2] There are several similarities between the chs 3 and 6: Joshua is restored, he is given promise and conditions (3:7, 6:15) and in both texts Joshua serves to point to 'the Branch' (3:8, 6:12-13).

[3] See Petersen (1984: 278), who tends to see the davidide as more elevated in the passage than is necessary. He is more to the point when he states, that 'The mention of a crown for Joshua in 6:11 represents a tilt in another direction, toward the high priest' (275).

[4] So Petersen (1984: 275).

We might find yet another indication that the priest is imbued with characteristics similar to that of a king. The normal recipient of a prophetic oracle is a king, and especially so when it concerns the building of a temple (cf. 2 Sam 7). It is remarkable in Zech 6:9-15 that the prophet directs his oracle to the high priest. It is through associating the high priest with the normal function of the king, i.e. being the recipient of a divine oracle concerning the building of a temple, that the priest is even more given an aura of authority, leadership and divine election. Although this is rather speculative, it would explain the odd choice of the symbolic act, as well as why the oracle is directed to the high priest even when it does not appear to concern him personally, but a future king. It is as if the prophet was challenged with the question, 'Why should we listen to a priest, when we can have a king?' The answer Zechariah gives is that the high priest can be a leader as well, not instead of the king, but the two together. In the choice of leadership in the bewildering times in Jehud when the people had begun to look for leadership on other grounds than that it was appointed by the Persian rulers, Zechariah comes with an alternative reality that refuses to take sides in the debate regarding the choice of king or priest.

The oracle shows that Joshua as a person is merely used as a representative for priesthood, since Zechariah is looking for a future where priesthood and monarchy will work together in harmony. However, since Joshua undeniably is available, he is the one who Zechariah elevates to a level of authority and leadership in his time.

Depositing the crown in the temple

To deposit the crown in the temple was not meant to be a symbolic act, but it does function symbolically. The phrase ל זכרון [ind obj] ב occurs only here, but if we widen it to [prep] + [ind obj] + ל זכרון ל we find certain priestly texts to be illuminating. In Ex 30:16 the atonement money is to be a reminder יִשְׂרָאֵל לִבְנֵי, 'to the Israelites', and לִפְנֵי־יְהוָה, 'before Yhwh'. In Num 10:10 the blowing of the trumpets will serve as a reminder לָכֶם, 'for you' לִפְנֵי אֱלֹהֵיכֶם, 'before your God'.[1] The similarities are so close that we must view this phrase as a typical priestly formulation for an item in the temple that is meant to be remembered. The phrase לִפְנֵי אֱלֹהִים/יְהוָה is the equivalent of בְּהֵיכַל יְהוָה in Zech 6:14, and Heldai, Tobijah, Jedaiah and Josiah are the indirect objects, preceded with the preposition ל. Nothing is said as to what the crown is to remind of, but we can not be far off if we see a symbolic reference to the coronation of the coming

---

[1] Cf. Ex 13:9; 28:29; 39:7; Num 17:5; 31:54; Josh 4:7; Mal 3:16. See also TDOT 4, 77-9, Meyers, and Meyers (1987: 363).

'Branch'. But who is to be reminded? It would seem natural to view the men referred to as those who will remember,[1] but the priestly texts show that it might just as well indicate that God would be remembered of his promise in the previous oracle.[2] However, it would seem impossible, and unnecessary, to choose between the two alternatives. The conclusion must be that the symbolism inherent in the symbolic act works hand in hand with the symbolic value of the crown as a deposited item of remembrance in the temple.

Indeed, van der Woude has gone so far as to identify the crown in the temple with the מוֹפֵת, 'sign', in Zech 3:8.[3] He understands אַנְשֵׁי מוֹפֵת as 'men assigned an omen', i.e., those priests that have been entrusted with the task of caring for the crown (cf. Gen 46:32, 34). He relies on his interpretation of שִׂים עַל רֹאשׁ as 'be entrusted with', which we have found to be unconvincing. However, there is nothing in the text that would indicate a connection between the crown and the מוֹפֵת. It is more likely that we should understand אַנְשֵׁי מוֹפֵת as a genitive of character (e.g. Gen 47:6; Ex 22:30; Jud 20:44; 2 Sam 19:29). This, in combination with the fact that prophets sometimes describe themselves as being a מוֹפֵת to the people (Is 8:18; 20:3; Ez 12:6; 11; 24:24, 27), makes it most likely that Joshua's friends are referred to as men who in some way point beyond themselves. Anything beyond that is mere speculation.

The symbolism inherent in this passage appears to run in two directions. The symbolic act elevates the priest by providing him with authority and leadership by associating him with royal authority and leadership, and the crown as a item of remembrance in the temple emphasizes the need for a king on the throne.

---

[1] So e.g. Petersen (1984: 279), Meyers, and Meyers (1987: 363).

[2] So e.g. Ackroyd (1968: 200).

[3] Woude (1988: 150-3), Woude (1988a: 244), followed by Cook (1995: 136).

Summary and Conclusions

1. There is no need to resort to source or redaction criticism in order to solve the riddles presented to us by Zech 6:9-15. A sensitive reading provides what is needed to not only understand the text as it stands, but also to reach a reasonable understanding of the prophetic symbolic act, together with the following oracle.

2. There is only one crown involved in the symbolic act.

3. The temple that is to be built according to the oracle (vv. 12-13) is the same temple where the crown is to be deposited as an item of memorabilia (vv. 14-15).

4. The performance of the symbolic act consists of putting a crown on the head of the high priest Joshua. There is no reason to postulate an earlier stage in the history of the text to explain how this description came about. It is instead in the nature of the prophetic symbolic act to be controversial.

5. The symbolic meaning of the act is primarily indexical, as it is based primarily on association and not analogy. The conventional act of crowning was used because of its capacity to evoke associations connected with royal authority and leadership. When the high-priest is crowned, he is thereby associated with these royal qualities, not in order to make him king, but to make him a credible leader.

7. The symbolic act is supplemented with the symbol of the crown being deposited in the temple, where it symbolizes the hope for a coming ruler. This indexical symbolism is also worked out by association, where the crown associates to a king.

8. There will be a priest *and* a king in Zechariah's ideal future. Through the symbolic act and the subsequent oracle, Zechariah envisages a future when priest and king work together harmoniously, which is symbolized through the very odd combination of royal crown and high priest.

H. General Conclusions

This study has displayed the construction, performance and symbolic meaning of each of the prophetic symbolic acts in the Old Testament, as was its purpose. This has been done through a detailed analysis of the texts in which the acts are described. However, some general conclusions still remain to be drawn.

1. No trace of a magical function has been found in any of the texts describing a prophetic symbolic act. The acts are created to communicate and persuade, along with the verbal communication by the prophets. That is not to say that there are no magical acts in the Old Testament, but only that the two forms of acts are separate categories, not to be confused with each other.

2. The analysis has shown it to be necessary to make a thorough and technical study of the texts in order to catch all forms of symbolism that are made use of in the construction of the symbolic acts. The symbolism is not found in some form of historical analysis, but through a serious attempt to find in the texts the clues to the meaning of the acts.

3. In the construction of the prophetic symbolic acts, various forms of symbolism have been used. It is clear that in this endeavour we see one of the most creative facets of the activity of the prophets. Various forms of symbolism from all forms of life were used in order to construe these very particular and highly nonconventional acts. All was done in order to convey an urgent message as persuasively as possible.

4. It is true that the historical veracity of these texts will always allude us in the end. However, it is very likely that it is precisely in this highly creative and nonconventional use of symbolism that we actually see the prophets in action.

I. Bibliography

Abrams, M. H., *A Glossary of Literary Terms* (Forth Worth, 1993).

Ackroyd, P. R., *Exile and Restoration: A Study of Hebrew Thought of the Sixth Century B. C.* (London, 1968).

Ahlström, G. W., *The History of Ancient Palestine from the Palaeolithic Period to Alexander's Conquest* (Sheffield, 1993).

Aichele, G., *Sign, Text, Scripture: Semiotics and the Bible* (Sheffield, 1997).

Aijmer, G., (ed.) *Symbolic Textures: Studies in Cultural Meaning* (Gothenburg, 1987).

Albrektson, B., "Translation and Emendation," *Language, Theology, and the Bible (FS J. Barr)* (Oxford, 1994) 27-39.

Albright, W. F., "Some Canaanite-Phoenician Sources of Hebrew Wisdom," *VTSup* 3 (1955) 1-15.

Allen, L. C., "The Rejected Sceptre in Ezekiel 21:15b, 18a," *VT* 39 (1989) 67-70.

Allen, L. C., *Ezekiel 20-48* (Waco, 1990).

Allen, L. C., *Ezekiel 1-19* (Waco, 1994).

Allwood, J., *Linguistic Communication as Action and Cooperation. A Study in Pragmatics* (Göteborg, 1987).

Alt, A., *Kleine Schriften zur Geschichte des Volkes Israel* (München, 1953).

Amiran, R., *Ancient Pottery of the Holy Land: From Its Beginnings in the Neolithic Period to the End of the Iron Age* (New Brunswick, 1970).

Amsler, S., "Les prophètes et la communication par les actes," *Werden und Wirken des Alten Testament (FS Westermann)* (Neukirchen-Vlyun, 1980) 194-201.

Amsler, S., *Les Actes des Prophètes* (Genève, 1985).

Amsler, S., et al., *Aggée, Zacharie, Malachie* (Geneve, 1988).

Andersen, F. I., and A. D. Forbes, *Spelling in the Hebrew Bible* (Rome, 1986).

Andersen, F. I., and D. N. Freedman, *Hosea* (New York, 1980).

Anderson, J. S., "The Metonymical Curse of Propaganda in the Book of Jeremiah," *BBR* 8 (1998a) 1-13.

Anderson, J. S., "The Social Function of Curses in the Hebrew Bible," *ZAW* 110 (1998b) 223-37.

Astour, M. C., "Sparagmos, Omophagia, and Ecstatic Prophecy at Mari," *UF* 24 (1992) 1-2.

Auld, A. G., "Prophets Through the Looking Glass: A Response to Robert Carroll and Hugh Williamson," *JSOT* 27 (1983) 41-4.

Auld, A. G., (ed.) *Understanding Poets and Prophets (FS G. W. Anderson)* (Sheffield, 1993).

Auld, A. G., *Kings Without Privilege: David and Moses in the Story of the Bible's Kings* (Edinburgh, 1994).

Austin, J. L., *How to Do Things with Words* (Oxford, 1975).

Avigad, N., "The Seal of Seraiah (Son of) Neriah (hebr)," *EI* 14 (1978) 86-7.

Bal, M., *Death and Dissymmetry: The Politcs of Coherence in the Book of Judges* (1988).

Baltzer, D., "Literarkritische und literarhistorische Anmerkungen zur Heilsprophetie im Ezekiel-Buch," *Ezekiel and His Book: Textual and Literary Criticism and their Interrelationship* (Leuven, 1986) 166-81.

Barakat, R. A., "Gesture Systems," *Keystone Folklore Quarterly* 14 (1969) 105-21.

Barasch, M., *Giotto and the Language of Gesture* (Cambridge, 1987).

Barcelona, A., *Metaphor and Metonymy at the Crossroads: A Cognitive Perspective* (Berlin; New York, 2000).

Barnes, W. E., "Two Trees Becomes One: Ezek. 37:16-17," *JTS* 39 (1938) 391-3.

Barr, J., *The Semantics of Biblical Language* (Oxford, 1961).

Barré, M. L., "Mesopotamian Light on the Idiom nasa' nepes," *CBQM Series* 52 (1990) 46-54.

Barstad, H. M., "No Prophets? Recent Developments in Biblical Prophetic Research and Ancient Near Eastern Prophecy," *JSOT* 57 (1993) 39-60.

Barth, C., "Ezechiel 37 als Einheit," *Beiträge zur alttestamentlichen Theologie (FS W. Zimmerli)* (Göttingen, 1977a) 39-52.

Barth, H., *Die Jesaja-Worte in der Josiazeit. Israel und Assur als Thema einer produktiven Neuinterpretation der Jesajaüberlieferung* (Neukirchen-Vlyun, 1977b).

Barthélemy, D., *Critique textuelle de l'Ancien Testament. Vol. 2. Isaïe, Jérémie, Lamentations* (Freiburg, 1986).

Bauer, H., *ZA* 40 (1928-9) 244-52.

Bauer, H., and P. Leander, *Grammatik des Biblisch-Aramäischen* (Halle, 1927).

Bauer, J. B., "Hes. 24:17," *VT* 7 (1957) 91-2.

Ben Zvi, E., "Prophets and Prophecy in the Compositional and Redactional Notes in I-II Kings," *ZAW* 105 (1993) 331-51.

Benson, R. G., *Medieval Body Language: A Study of the Use of Gesture in Chaucer's Poetry* (Copenhagen, 1980).

Bentzen, A., *Jesaja. Bind I: Jes. 1-39* (København, 1944).

Bentzen, A., "The Ritual Background of Amos 1:2-2:16," *OTSt* 8 (1950) 85-99.

Berger, P. L., and T. Luckmann, *The Social Construction of Reality: A Treatise in the Sociology of Knowledge* (New York, 1966).

Berlin, A., *Poetics and Interpretation of Biblical Narrative* (Sheffield, 1983).

Berridge, J. M., *Prophet, People, and the Word of Yahweh: An Examination of Form and Content in the Proclamation of the Prophet Jeremiah* (Zürich, 1970).

Birch, B. C., *The Rise of the Israelite Monarchy: The Growth and Development of 1 Sam. 7-15* (Missoula, 1976).

Birdwhistell, R. L., *Kinesics and Context: Essays on Body Motion Communication* (Philadelphia, 1970).

Bitter, S., *Die Ehe des Propheten Hosea: Eine auslegungsgeschichtliche Untersuchung* (Göttingen, 1975).

Blau, J., "Etymologische Untersuchungen auf Grund des Palaestinischen Arabisch," *VT* 5 (1955) 337-44.

Blenkinsopp, J., *Ezekiel* (Louisville, 1990).

Blenkinsopp, J., *Sage, Priest, Prophet: Religious and Intellectual Leadership in Ancient Israel* (Louisville, 1995).

Blenkinsopp, J., *A History of Prophecy in Israel* (Louisville, Ky., 1996).

Blenkinsopp, J., *Isaiah 1-39: a new translation with introduction and commentary* (New York, 2000).

Block, D. I., "Ezekiel's Boiling Cauldron: A Form-Critical Solution to Ezekiel 24," *VT* 41 (1991) 12-37.

Block, D. I., "Bringing Back David: Ezekiel's Messianic Hope," *The Lord's Anointed: Interpretation of Old Testament Messianic Texts* (Carlisle, 1995) 167-88.

Block, D. I., *The Book of Ezekiel Chapters 1-24* (Grand Rapids, 1997).

Boadt, L., "The Poetry of Prophetic Persuasion: Preserving the Prophet's Persona," *CBQ* 59 (1997) 1-21.

Bogaert, P.-M., "De Baruch à Jérémie: les deux rédactions conservées du livre de Jérémie," *Le Livre de Jérémie: Le Prophète et son Milieu, les Oracles et leur Transmission* (Leuven, 1981) 168-73.

Bokser, B. M., "The Wall Separating God and Israel (B Ber 32b)," *JQR* 73 (1983) 349-74.

Bolinger, D. L., *Aspects of Language* (New York, 1975).

Borger, R., *Die Inschriften Asarhaddons Königs von Assyrien* (Graz, 1956).

Borger, R., *Babylonisch-Assyrische Lesestücke: Heft 1: Die Texte in Umschrift, Heft 2: Elemente der Grammatik und der Schrift, Glossar, Die Texte in Keilschrift* (Rome, 1979).

Born, A. v. d., *De symbolische handelingen der oud-testamentische profeten* (Utrecht/Nijmegen, 1935).

Born, A. v. d., "Zu den symbolischen handlungen der Propheten," *SchwKiZ* (1946) 339-41.

Born, A. v. d., *Profetie metterdaad. Een studie over de symbolische handelingen der profeten* (Roermond/Maaseik, 1947).

Bourguet, D., *Des métaphores de Jérémie* (Paris, 1987).

Bowker, G. W., "Prophetic Action and Sacramental Form," *SE* 3 (1964) 129-37.

Brauner, R. A., "'To Grasp the hem' and 1 Samuel 15:27," *JANES* 6 (1974) 35-38.

Bright, J., *Jeremiah* (New York, 1965).

Briquel-Chatonnet, F., *Les relations entre les cités de la côte Phénicienne et les royaumes d'Israël et de Juda (Studia Phoenicia XII)* (Leuven, 1992).

Brownlee, W. H., "'Son of Man Set Your Face': Ezekiel the Refuge Prophet," *HUCA* 53 (1983) 83-110.

Brueggemann, W., *To Build, To Plant: A Commentary on Jeremiah 26-52* (Grand Rapids, 1991).

Buzy, D., *Les symboles de l'Ancien Testament* (Paris, 1923).

Caird, G. B., *The Language and Imagery of the Bible* (Philadelphia, 1980).

Campbell, A. F., *Of Prophets and Kings: A Late Ninth-Century Document (1 Samuel 1-2 Kings 10)* (Washington, 1986).

Campbell, E. F., *Ruth: A New Translation with Introduction, Notes and Commentary* (New York, 1975).

Carena, O., *La communicazione non-verbale nella Bibbia. Un approccio semiotico al ciclo di Elia ed Eliseo:1 Re 16,29-2 Re 13,25* (Turin, 1981).

Carroll, R., "Poets not Prophets," *JSOT* 27 (1983) 25-31.

Carroll, R. P., *When Prophecy Failed. Reactions and Responses to Failure in the Old Testament Prophetic Traditions* (London, 1979).

Carroll, R. P., *Jeremiah: A Commentary* (London, 1986).

Ceresko, A. R., *Job 29-31 in the Light of Northwest Semitic* (Rome, 1980).

Charlesworth, J. H., (ed.) *The Dead Sea Scrolls: Hebrew, Aramaic, and Greek Texts with English Translations. Volume 2: Damascus Document, War Scroll, and Related Documents* (Tübingen, 1995).

Chary, T., *Aggée, Zacharie, Malachie* (Paris, 1969).

Chatman, S. B., *Story and Discourse: Narrative Structure in Fiction and Film* (Ithaca, N.Y., 1978).

Childs, B. S., *Old Testament Theology in a Canonical Context* (London, 1985).

Clements, R. E., *Isaiah and the Deliverance of Jerusalem* (Sheffield, 1980).

Clements, R. E., *Isaiah 1-39* (Grand Rapids, 1980a).

Clements, R. E., *Jeremiah* (Atlanta, 1988).

Coggins, R. J., *Haggai, Zechariah, Malachi* (Sheffield, 1987).

Coggins, R. J., "Prophecy — True and False," *Of Prophets' Visions and the Wisdom of Sages (FS R. N. Whybray)* (Sheffield, 1993) 80-94.

Cohen, D., *La phrase nominale et l'évolution du système verbal en sémitique* (Leuven/Paris, 1984).

Cohn, R. L., "Literary Technique in the Jeroboam Narrative," *ZAW* 97 (1985) 23-35.

Conrad, D., "Samuel und die Mari Propheten. Bemerkungen zu 1 Sam 15:27," *ZDMG* suppl. 1 (1969) 273-80.

Contini, R., *Tipologie della frase nominale nel semitico nordoccidentale del I millenio A.C.* (Pisa, 1982).

Cook, S. L., *Prophecy and Apocalypticism: The Postexilic Social Setting* (Minneapolis, 1995).

Cooke, G. A., *The Book of Ezekiel* (Edinburgh, 1936).

Cooper, D. E., *Metaphor* (Oxford, 1986).

Cornill, C. H., *Das Buch des Propheten Ezechiel* (Leipzig, 1886).

Craghan, J. F., "Mari and its Prophets: The Contribution of Mari to the Understanding of Biblical Prophecy," *BTB* 5 (1975) 32-55.

Craigie, P. C., et al., *Jeremiah 1-25* (Dallas, 1991).

Crenshaw, J., *Prophetic Conflict: Its Effect Upon Israelite Religion* (Berlin, 1971).

Cross, F. M., *Canaanite Myth and Hebrew Epic: Essays in the History of the Religion of Israel* (1973).

Cruse, D. A., *Lexical Semantics* (Cambridge, 1986).

Dahood, M., "Textual Problems in Isaia," *CBQ* 22 (1960) 400-9.

Dalman, G., *Arbeit und Sitte in Palästina. Band II. Der Ackerbau* (Hildesheim, 1933 (Repr. 1964)).

Darr, K. F., "Write or True? A Response to Ellen Frances Davis," *Signs and Wonders* (New York, 1989) 239-47.

Darr, K. P., "Ezekiel Among the Prophets," *CR:BS* 2 (1994) 9-24.

Davies, G. I., *Hebrew Inscriptions. Corpus and Concordance* (Cambridge, 1991).

Davies, G. I., *Hosea* (London, 1992).

Davies, G. I., *Hosea* (Sheffield, 1993).

Davis, E. F., "Swallowing Hard: Reflections on Ezekiel's Dumbness," *Signs and Wonders* (New York, 1989a) 217-37.

Davis, E. F., *Swallowing the Scroll: Textuality and the Dynamics of Discourse in Ezekiel's Prophecy* (Sheffield, 1989b).

Dearman, J. A., "My Servants the Scribes: Composition and Context in Jeremiah 36," *JBL* 109 (1990) 403-421.

Debus, J., *Die Sünde Jerobeams. Studien zur Darstellung Jerobeams und der Geschichte des Nordeichs in der deuteronomistischen Geschichtsschreibung* (Göttingen, 1967).

Deissler, A., *Zwölf Propheten III: Zefanja, Haggai, Sacharja, Maleachi* (Stuttgart, 1988).

deJong Ellis, M., "Observations on Mesopotamian Oracles and Prophetic Texts: Literary and Historiographic Considerations," *JCS* 41 (1989) 127-86.

Delitzsch, F., *Jesaja* (Giessen, 1879).

Deutsch, C., *Hidden Wisdom and the Easy Yoke: Wisdom, Torah and Discipleship in Matthew 11:25-30* (Sheffield, 1987).

Dévényi, J., *Metonymy and Drama: Essays on Language and Dramatic Strategy* (Lewisburg, 1996).

DeVries, S. J., *Yesterday, Today and Tomorow* (London, 1975).

DeVries, S. J., *1 Kings* (Waco, Texas, 1985).

Dietrich, M., "Prophetie in den Keilschrifttexten," *Jahrbuch für Anthropologie und Religionsgeschichte* 1 (1973) 15-44.

Dietrich, W., *Prophetie und Geschichte: Eine redaktionsgeschichtliche Untersuchung zum deuteronomistischen Geschichtswerk* (Göttingen, 1972).

Dietrich, W., *Jesaja und die Politik* (Munich, 1976).

Dijk, J. v., "Zerbrechen der roten Töpfe," *LdE* 6 (1986) 1389-96.

Donner, H., *Israel under den Völkern. Die Stellung der klassischen Propheten des 8. Jahrhunderts v. Chr. zur Aussenpolitik der Könige von Israel und Juda* (Leiden, 1964).

Donner, H., *Die Verwerfung Des Königs Saul* (Wiesbaden, 1983).

Donner, H., *Geschichte des Volkes Israel und seiner Nachbarn in Grundzügen. Teil 2: Von der Königszeit bis zu Alexander dem Grossen. Mit einem Ausblick auf die Geschichte des Judentums bis Bar Kochba* (Göttingen, 1986).

Downing, F. G., "Words as Deeds and Deeds as Words," *BI* 3 (1995) 129-43.

Draffkorn Kilmer, A., "Symbolic Gestures in Akkadian Contracts from Alalakh and Ugarit," *JAOS* 94 (1974) 177-83.

Driver, G. R., "Some Hebrew Medical Expressions," *ZAW* 65 (1953) 259-60.

Driver, G. R., "Ezekiel: Linguistic and Textual Problems," *Bib* 35 (1954) 145-59.

Driver, G. R., "Rev. 'CAD 3'," *JSS* 5 (1960) 156-8.

Driver, G. R., "Review of ANET and ANEP," *JTS* 22 (1971) 548-52.

Duguid, I. M., *Ezekiel and the Leaders of Israel* (Leiden, 1994).

Duhm, B., *Das Buch Jesaia* (Göttingen, 1922).

Dupont-Sommer, A., "L'ostracon Araméen du Sabbat (Collection Clermont-Ganneau no 152)," *Sem* 2 (1949) 29-39.

Durand, J.-M., *Archives épistolaires de Mari I/1* (Paris, 1988).

Eco, U., *Semiotics and the Philosophy of Language* (Bloomington, 1984).

Eco, U., "Symbol and Semiotics," *Encyclopedic Dictionary of Semiotics* (Berlin/New York, 1986) 1029-30.

Eco, U., and T. A. Sebeok, *The Sign of Three: Dupin, Holmes, Peirce* (Bloomington, 1983).

Edwards, D. R., "Dress and Ornamentation," *ABD* 2 (1992) 232-38.

Efron, D., and S. v. Veen, *Gesture, Race and Culture* (The Hague, 1972).

Eichrodt, W., "Vom Symbol zum Typos: ein Beitrag zur Sacharja-Exegese," *TZ* 13 (1957) 509-22.

Eichrodt, W., *Ezekiel: A Commentary* (London, 1970).

Ekman, P., and W. V. Friesen, "The Reportoire of Nonverbal Behavior: Categories, Origins, Usage, and Coding," *Semiotica* 1 (1969) 49-98.

Elam, K., *The Semiotics of Theatre and Drama* (London/New York, 1980).

Ellermeier, F., *Prophetie in Mari und Israel* (Herzberg, 1968).

Elliger, K., *Das Buch der zwölf Kleinen Propheten: II: Nahum, Habakuk, Zephanja, Haggai, Sacharja, Maleachi* (Göttingen, 1967).

Eph'al, I., "The Assyrian Siege Ramp at Lachisch: Military and Lexical Aspects," *Tel Aviv* 11 (1984) 60-70.

Ewald, H., *The History of Israel. Vol. III: The Rise and Splendour of the Hebrew Monarchy (Germ. orig. 1853)* (London, 1878).

Finet, A., "Les symboles du cheveu, du bord du vêtement et de l'ongle en Mésopotamie," *Eschatologie et cosmologie* (Bruxelles, 1969) 101-30.

Finkelstein, J. J., "Cutting the sissiktu in Divorce Proceedings," *WO* 8 (1975) 236-40.

Firth, R., *Symbols. Public and Private* (London, 1973).

Fleming, D., "*Nābû* and *munabbiātu*: Two New Syrian Religious Personnel," *JAOS* 113 (1993a) 175-83.

Fleming, D. E., "The Etymological Origins of the Hebrew *nābî*: The One Who Invokes God," *CBQ* 55 (1993b) 217-24.

Fleming, D. E., "The Biblical Tradition of Anointing Priests," *JBL* 117 (1998) 401-14.

Fohrer, G., *Ezechiel* (Tübingen, 1955).

Fohrer, G., *Das Buch Jesaja. 1. Band Kapitel 1-23* (Zürich, 1966a).

Fohrer, G., "Prophetie und Magie," *ZAW* 78 (1966b) 25-47.

Fohrer, G., *Die symbolischen Handlungen der Propheten* (Zürich, 1968).

Fohrer, G., *Die Propheten des Alten Testaments. Band 7: Prophetenerzählungen* (Göttingen, 1977).

Freedy, K., "The Glosses in Ezekiel I-XXIV," *VT* 20 (1970) 129-52.

Friebel, K. G., *Jeremiah's and Ezekiel's Sign-Acts: Rhetorical Nonverbal Communication* (Sheffield, 1999).

Fuhs, H. F., "Ez 24 - Überlegungen zu Tradition und Redaktion des Ezechiel-buches," *Ezekiel and His Book: Textual and Literary Criticsm and their Interrrelation* (Leuven, 1986) 266-82.

Galling, K., and D. Irwin, "Pflug," *BRL* (1977) 255.

Garscha, J., *Studien zum Ezechielbuch* (Frankfurt, 1974).

Gaster, T. H., *Myth, Legend, and Custom in the Old Testament* (London, 1961).

Geertz, C., *The Interpretation of Culture* (New York, 1973).

Geller, S. A., "Were the Prophets Poets?," *Prooftexts* 3 (1983) 211-30.

Gesenius, W., *Gesenius' Hebrew Grammar as Edited and Enlarged by the Late E. Kautsch. Transl. A. E. Cowley* (Oxford, 1910).

Ginsberg, H. L., "Reflexes of Sargon in Isaiah after 715 B.C.E.," *JAOS* 88 (1968) 47-53.

Gitay, Y., (ed.) *Prophecy and Prophets: The Diversity of Contemporary Issues in Scholarship* (Atlanta, 1997).

Gooding, D. W., "The Septuagint's Rival Versions of Jeroboam's Rise to Power," *VT* 17 (1967) 173-89.

Gordis, R., *The Book of God and Man: A Study of Job* (Chicago, 1969).

Gordon, R. P., "The Second Septuagint Account of Jeroboam: History or Midrash?," *VT* 25 (1975) 368-93.

Gordon, R. P., "David's Rise and Saul's Demise: Narrative Analogy in 1 Samuel 24-26," *TynBul* 32 (1980) 37-64.

Gordon, R. P., "From Mari to Moses: Prophecy at Mari and in Ancient Israel," *Of Prophets' Visions and the Wisdom of Sages (FS R. N. Whybray)* (Sheffield, 1993) 63-79.

Gordon, R. P., (ed.) *'The Place is Too Small for Us': The Israelite Prophets in Recent Scholarship* (Winona Lake, 1995a).

Gordon, R. P., "Where Have All the Prophets Gone? The 'Disappearing' Israelite Prophet Against the Background of Ancient Near Eastern Prophecy," *BBR* 5 (1995b) 67-86.

Gorman, F. H. J., *The Ideology of Ritual: Space, Time and Status in the Priestly Theology* (Sheffield, 1990).

Gosse, B., "La malédiction contre Babylone de Jérémie 51:59-64 et les rédactions du livre de Jérémie," *ZAW* 98 (1986) 383-99.

Gosse, B., "La place primitive du recueil d'Oracles contre les Nations dans le livre de Jérémie," *BN* 74 (1994) 28-30.

Gosse, B., "La terminologie de Jér 25:15-18 et l'histoire de la rédaction du recueil d'Oracles contre les Nations du livre de Jérémie," *BN* 85 (1996) 11-13.

Grabbe, L. L., *Judaism from Cyrus to Hadrian* (London, 1992).

Grabbe, L. L., "Prophets, Priests, Diviners and Sages in Ancient Israel," *Of Prophets' Visions and the Wisdom of Sages (FS R. N. Whybray)* (Sheffield, 1993) 43-62.

Grabbe, L. L., *Priests, Prophets, Diviners, Sages: A Socio-Historical Study of Religious Specialists in Ancient Israel* (Valley Forge, 1995).

Graetz, N., "God is to Israel as Husband is to Wife: The Metaphoric Battering of Hosea's Wife," *A Feministic Companion to the Latter Prophets* (Sheffield, 1995) 126-145.

Graupner, A., *Auftrag und Geschick des Propheten Jeremia* (Neuckirchen-Vluyn, 1991).

Gray, G. B., *A Critical and Exegetical Commentary on the Book of Isaiah 1-39* (Edinburgh, 1928).

Gray, J., *I and II Kings: A Commentary* (London, 1970).

Grayson, A. K., *Assyrian and Babylonian Chronicles* (Locust Valley, 1975).

Greenberg, M., *Ezekiel 1-20* (New York, 1983).

Greenberg, M., *Ezekiel 21-37* (New York, 1997).

Greene, J. T., *The Role of the Messenger and Message in the Ancient Near East: Oral and Written Communication in the Ancient Near East and In the Hebrew Scriptures - Communicators and Communiques in Context* (Georgia, 1989).

Greengus, S., "The Old Babylonian Marriage Contract," *JAOS* 89 (1969) 505-32.

Greenstein, E. L., "'To Grasp the Hem' in Ugaritic Literature," *VT* 32 (1982) 217-8.

Grelot, P., *Documents araméens d'Egypte* (Paris, 1972).

Groenman, A. W., "De symbolische handelingen der Oudtestamentische profeten," *NedTTs* 31 (1942a) 101-14.

Groenman, A. W., *Hett Karakter van de Symbolische Handelingen der Oud-Testamentische Profeten* (Haarlem, 1942b).

Gross, W., *Die Pendenskonstruktion im Biblischen Hebräisch* (St. Ottilien, 1987).

Gruber, M. I., "The Tragedy of Cain and Abel: A Case of Depression," *JQR* 69 (1978) 89-97.

Gruber, M. I., *Aspects of Nonverbal Communication in the Ancient Near East* (Rome, 1980).

Gruber, M. I., "The Many Faces of Hebrew nasa' panim 'Lift up Face'," *ZAW* 95 (1983) 252-60.

Grønbaek, J. H., *Die Geschichte Vom Aufstieg Davids (1 Sam.15-2 Sam. 5): Tradition und Komposition* (Copenhagen, 1971).

Gunkel, H., *Die Propheten* (Göttingen, 1917).

Guthrie, H. H., "Ezekiel 21," *ZAW* 74 (1962) 268-81.

Görg, M., "Ezechiels unreine Speise," *BN* 19 (1982) 22-3.

Habel, N. C., *The Book of Job* (London, 1985).

Hals, R. M., *Ezekiel* (Grand Rapids, 1989).

Hanhart, R., *Sacharja* (Neukirchen-Vlyun, 1991).

Hanson, P. D., *The Dawn of Apocalyptic: The Historical and Sociological Roots of Jewish Apocalyptic Eschatology* (Philadelphia, 1979).

Hanson, P. D., *The People Called: The Growth of Community in the Bible* (San Francisco, 1986).

Hartley, J. E., *Leviticus* (Dallas, 1992).

Haulotte, E., *Symbolique du vêtement selon la Bible* (Paris, 1966).

Hausman, C. R., *Charles S. Peirce's Evolutionary Philosophy* (Cambridge, 1993).

Hayes, J. H., and S. A. Irvine, *Isaiah the Eighth Century Prophet: His Times and his Preaching* (Nashville, 1987).

Hedley, J., *Power in Verse: Metaphor and Metonymy in the Renaissance Lyric* (University Park, 1988).

Heintz, J.-G., "Oracles prophétiques et 'guerre sainte' selon les Archives Royales de Mari et l'Ancien Testament," *Congress Volume Rome 1968* (Leiden, 1968) 112-28.

Heisig, J. W., "Symbolism," *The Encyclopedia of Religion* (New York, 1987) 198-204.

Hempel, J., "Eine Vermutung zur Hes 24:15ff," *ZAW* 51 (1933) 312-3.

Herrmann, S., *Die prophetischen Heilserwartungen im Alten Testament* (Stuttgart, 1965).

Hillers, D. R., "A Convention in Hebrew Literature: The Reaction to Bad News," *ZAW* 77 (1965) 86-90.

Hillers, D. R., "Rite: Ceremonies of Law and Treaty in the Ancient Near East," *Religion and Law: Biblical-Judaic and Islamic Perspectives* (Winona Lake, 1990) 351-64.

Hitzig, F., *Der Prophet Ezechiel* (Leipzig, 1847).

Hoffmann, H.-D., *Reform und Reformen: Untersuchung zu einem Grundthema der deuteronomistischen Geschichtsschreibung* (Zürich, 1980).

Hoffmann, H. W., *Die Intention der Verkündigung Jesajas* (Berlin, 1974).

Holladay, W. L., *Jeremiah 1: A Commentary on the Book of the Prophet Jeremiah Chapters 1-25* (Philadelphia, 1986).

Holladay, W. L., *Jeremiah 2: A Commentary on the Book of the Prophet Jeremiah Chapters 26-52* (Philadelphia, 1989).

Holm-Nielsen, S., *Hodayot: Psalms from Qumran* (Aarhus, 1960).

Hooker, M. D., *The Signs of a Prophet: The Prophetic Actions of Jesus* (Harrisburg, 1997).

Horst, F., *Die zwölf kleinen Propheten: Nahum bis Maleachi* (Tübingen, 1964).

Hossfeld, F. L., and I. Meyer, *Prophet gegen Prophet: Eine Analyse der alttestamentlichen Texte zum Thema: Wahre und falsche Propheten* (Fribourg, 1973).

Houston, W., "What Did the Prophets Think They Were Doing? Speech Acts and Prophetic Discourse in the Old Testament," *BI* 1 (1993) 167-88.

Hubbard, R. L., "First and Second Kings," *Everyman's Bible Commentary* (Chicago, 1991)

Huber, F., *Jahwe, Juda und die anderen Völker beim Propheten Jesaja* (Berlin, 1976).

Hubmann, F. D., "Jeremia 13:1-11: Zweimal Euphrat retour, oder wie 'man' einen Propheten fertigmacht," *Ein Gott eine Offenbarung: Beiträge zur biblischen Exegese, Theologie und Spiritualität* (Würtzburg, 1991) 103-25.

Huffmon, H. B., "Prophecy in the Mari Letters," *BA* 31 (1968) 101-24.

Huffmon, H. B., "Prophecy (ANE)," *ABD*, 477-82.

Huffmon, H. B., "The Expansion of Prophecy in the Mari Archives: New Texts, New Readings, New Information," *Prophecy and Prophets: The Diversity of Contemporary Issues in Scholarship* (Atlanta, 1997) 7-22.

Hugenberger, G. P., *Marriage as a Covenant: A Study of Biblical Law and Ethics Governing Marriage Developed from the Perspective of Malachi* (Leiden, 1994).

Hutton, R. R., "Magic or Street-Theater? The Power of the Prophetic Word," *ZAW* 107 (1995) 247-60.

Huwyler, B., *Jeremia und die Völker: Untersuchungen zu den Völkersprüchen in Jeremia 46-49* (Tübingen, 1997).

Hylander, I., *Der literarische Samuel-Saul-Komplex (1 Sam. 1-15) traditionsgeschichtlich Untersucht* (diss, Uppsala, 1932).

Høgenhaven, J., *Gott und Volk Bei Jesaja. Eine Untersuchung zur biblischen Theologie* (Leiden, 1988).

Hönig, H. W., *Die Bekleidung des Hebräers. Eine biblisch-archäologische Untersuchung* (Zürich, 1957).

Irvine, S. A., "The Isaianic *Denkschrift*: Reconsidering an Old Hypothesis," *ZAW* 104 (1992) 216-31.

Iwry, S., "New Evidence for Belomancy in Ancient Palestine and Phoenicia," *JAOS* 81 (1961) 27-34.

Jacobsen, T., "Religious Drama in Ancient Mesopotamia," *Unity and Diversity: Essays in the History, Literature, and Religion of the Ancient Near East* (Baltimore, 1975) 65-97.

Jakobson, R., *Word and Language* (The Hague; Paris, 1971).

Janzen, J. G., *Studies in the Text of Jeremiah* (Cambridge, MA, 1973).

Janzen, J. G., "A Critique of Sven Soderlund's *The Greek Text of Jeremiah: A Revised Hypothesis*," *BIOSCS* 22 (1989) 16-47.

Jeffers, A., *Magic and Divination in Ancient Palestine and Syria* (Leiden, 1996).

Jeremias, J., *Der Prophet Hosea* (Göttingen, 1983).

Jirku, A., "Zur magischen Bedeutung der Kleidung in Israel," *ZAW* 37 (1917/18) 109-25.

Jones, D. R., *Jeremiah* (London, 1992).

Jones, G. H., *1 and 2 Kings* (Grand Rapids, 1984).

Joüon, P., and T. Muraoka, *A Grammar of Biblical Hebrew* (Rome, 1991).

Kaiser, O., *Isaiah 13-39* (London, 1974).

Kalluveettil, P., *Declaration and Covenant. A Comprehensive Review of Covenant Formulae from the OT and the ANE* (Rome, 1982).

Kaplan, J., "The Stronghold of Yamani at Ashdod-Yam," *IEJ* 19 (1969) 137-49.

Keefe, A. A., "The Female Body, the Body Politic and the Land: A Sociopolitical Reading of Hosea 1-2," *A Feministic Companion to the Latter Prophets* (Sheffield, 1995) 70-100.

Keil, C. F., *Biblical Commentary on the Prophecies of Ezekiel* (Edinburgh, 1876).

Kelso, J. L., *The Ceramic Vocabulary of the Old Testament* (New Haven, 1948).

Kendon, A., (ed.) *Nonverbal Communication, Interaction, and Gesture* (The Hague, 1981).

Kendon, A., "Gesture and Speech: How They Interact," *Nonverbal Interaction* (Beverly Hills, 1983) 13-43.

Keown, G. L., et al., *Jeremiah 26-52* (Dallas, 1995).

Key, M.-R., *The Relationship of Verbal and Nonverbal Communication* (The Hague, 1980).

Key, M. R., *Nonverbal Communication Today: Current Research* (Berlin, 1982).

Kilian, R., *Literarkritische und formgeschichtliche Untersuchung des Heiligkeitsgesetzes* (Bonn, 1963).

King, P. J., *Jeremiah: An Archeological Companion* (Louisville, 1993).

Kissane, E. J., *The Book of Isaiah. Vol. 1: 1-39* (Dublin, 1960).

Kitchen, K. A., *The Third Intermediate Period in Egypt (1100 650 B.C.)* (Warminster, 1986).

Kittay, E. F., *Metaphor: Its Cognitive Force and Linguistic Structure* (Oxford, 1987).

Kleber, A., "Ps. 2:9 in the Light of an Ancient Oriental Ceremony," *CBQ* 5 (1943) 63-7.

Klein, R. W., *1 Samuel* (Waco, 1983).

Knoppers, G. N., "Dynastic Oracle and Succession in 1 Kings 11," *Proceedings, Eastern Great Lakes and Midwest Biblical Societies* (1987) 159-172.

Knoppers, G. N., *Two Nations Under God: The Deuteronomistic History of Solomon and the Dual Monarchies. Volume 1: The Reign of Solomon and the Rise of Jeroboam* (Atlanta, 1993).

Koch, K., *The Growth of the Biblical Tradition: The Form-Critical Method* (London, 1969).

Koch, K., "Die Briefe 'prophetischen' Inhalts aus Mari. Bemerkungen zu Gattung und Sitz im Leben," *UF* 4 (1972) 53-77.

Korosec, V., "Les relations internationales d'apres les lettres de Mari," *XVe Rencontre Assyriologique Internationale* (Paris, 1967) 139-150.

Kruger, P. A., "On Non-Verbal Communication in the Baal Epic," *JSem* 1 (1989) 54-69.

Krüger, T., *Geschichtskonzepte im Ezechielbuch* (Berlin, 1989).

Laato, A., *Who is Immanuel? The Rise and the Foundering of Isaiah's Messianic Expectations* (1988).

Laato, A., *Josiah and David Redivivus: The Historical Josiah and the Messianic Expectations of Exilic and Postexilic Times* (Stockholm, 1992).

Lafont, B., "Le roi de Mari et les prophètes du dieu Adad," *RA* 78 (1984) 7-18.

Lambert, W. G., *Babylonian Wisdom Literature* (Oxford, 1960).

Lambert, W. G., and A. R. Millard, *Atra-Hasis: The Babylonian Story of the Flood* (Oxford, 1969).

Lang, B., *Kein Aufstand in Jerusalem: Die Politik des Propheten Ezechiel* (Stuttgart, 1978).

Lang, B., *Ezechiel: Der Prophet und das Buch* (Darmstadt, 1981a).

Lang, B., "Prophetie, prophetische Zeichenhandlung und Politik in Israel," *TQ* 161 (1981b)

Lang, B., "Ein babylonisches Motiv in Israels Schöpfungsmythologie (Jer 27:5-6)," *BZ* 27 (1983a) 236-7.

Lang, B., *Monotheism and the Prophetic Minority: An Essay in Biblical History and Sociology* (Sheffield, 1983b).

Lang, B., "Introduction: Anthropology as a New Model for Biblical Studies," *Anthropological Approaches to the Old Testament* (London, 1985) 1-20.

Lang, B., "Street Theater, Raising the Dead, and the Zoroastrian Connection in Ezekiel's Prophecy," *Ezekiel and His Book: Textual and Literary Criticism and their Interrelation* (Leuven, 1986) 297-316.

Lang, B., "Games Prophets Play: Street Theater and Symbolic Acts in Biblical Israel," *The Games of God and Man: Essays in Play and Performance* (Hamburg, 1997) 257-71.

Layton, S., "Biblical Hebrew 'To Set the Face' in Light of Akkadian and Ug-aritic," *UF* 17 (1986) 169-81.

Lemke, W. E., "'Nebuchadrezzar, My Servant'," *CBQ* 28 (1966) 45-50.

Levine, B. A., "The Epilogue to the Holiness Code: A Priestly Statement on the Destiny of Israel," *Judaic Perspectives on Ancient Israel* (Philadelphia, 1987) 9-34.

Levine, B. A., *Leviticus* (Philadelphia/NY, 1989).

Levine, B. A., *Numbers 1-20* (New York, 1993).

Lewis, D. K., *Convention: A Philosophical Study* (Cambridge, Ma., 1969).

Liddell, H. G., et al., *A Greek-English Lexicon* (Oxford, 1996).

Lie, A. G., *The Inscriptions of Sargon II King of Assyria. Part I: The Annals* (Paris, 1929).

Lindblom, J., *Profetismen i Israel* (Stockholm, 1934).

Lindblom, J., *Prophecy in Ancient Israel* (Oxford, 1962).

Lipinski, E., "'Se battre la cuisse'," *VT* 20 (1970) 495.

Lipínski, E., "Banquet en l'honneur de Baal: CTA 3 (V AB), A, 4-22," *UF* 2 (1970) 75-88.

Lods, A., "Le rôle des Idée magiques dans la mentalité Israélite," *Old Testament Essays: Collected Papers* (London, 1927) 55-76.

Lohfink, N., *Das Hauptgebot* (Rome, 1963).

Long, B. O., "Question and Answer Schemata in the Prophets," *JBL* 90 (1971) 129-39.

Lundbom, J. R., "Baruch, Seraiah, and Expanded Colophons in the Book of Jeremiah," *JSOT* 36 (1986) 89-114.

Lundbom, J. R., *Jeremiah 1-20* (New York, 1999).

Luria, B. Z., "What Happened to Zerubbabel? (hebr)," *BM* 36 (1990/1) 185-9.

Lyons, J., *Semantics* (Cambridge, 1977).

Macintosh, A. A., *A Critical and Exegetical Commentary on Hosea* (Edin-burgh, 1997).

Macky, P. W., *The Centrality of Metaphors to Biblical Thought: A Method for Interpreting the Bible* (Lewiston, NY, 1990).

Malamat, A., "The Twilight of Judah: In the Egyptian-Babylonian Mael-strom," *Congress Volume: Edinburgh 1974* (Leiden, 1975) 123-45.

Malamat, A., "A Mari Prophecy and Nathan's Dynastic Oracle," *Prophecy* (Berlin, 1980) 68-82.

Malamat, A., "A Forerunner of Biblical Prophecy: The Mari Documents," *Ancient Israelite Religion (FS F. M. Cross)* (Philadelphia, 1987) 33-52.

Malmberg, B., *Signes et symboles. Les bases du langage humain* (Paris, 1977).

Malul, M., "'Sissiktu' and 'sikku' - Their Meaning and Function," *BO* 43 (1986) 19-37.

Malul, M., *Studies in Mesopotamian Legal Symbolism* (Neukirchen-Vlyun, 1988).

Masson, E., *Recherches sur les plus anciens emprunts sémitiques en grec* (Paris, 1967).

Matthews, V. H., and D. C. Benjamin, *Social World of Ancient Israel 1250-587 BCE* (Peabody, 1993).

Mattingly, L., "An Archeological Analysis of Sargon's 712 Campaign Against Ashdod," *Near East Archeological Society Bulletin* 17 (1981) 47-64.

Mayer, W., "Sargons Feldzur gegen Urartu — 714 v. Chr. Text und Übersetzung," *MDOG* 115 (1983) 65-132.

Mayes, A. D. H., *The Story of Israel between Settlement and Exile: A Redactional Study of the Deuteronomistic History* (London, 1983).

McCarter, P. K., *1 Samuel* (NY, 1980).

McConville, J. G., *Grace in the End: A Study in Deuteronomic Theology* (Grand Rapids, 1993).

McKane, W., *Jeremiah: Volume One (1-25)* (Edinburgh, 1986).

McKane, W., "Jeremiah 27:5-8, Especially 'Nebuchadnezzar, My Servant'," *Prophet und Prophetenbuch (FS O. Kaiser)* (Berlin, 1989) 98-110.

McKane, W., *Jeremiah: Volume Two (26-52)* (Edinburgh, 1996).

McKenzie, S. L., *The Trouble with Kings: the Composition of the Book of Kings in the Deuteronomistic History* (Leiden, 1991).

Mettinger, T. N. D., "The Nomical Pattern qᵉtulla in Biblical Hebrew," *JSS* 16 (1971) 2-14.

Mettinger, T. N. D., *King and Messiah: The Civil and Sacral Legitimation of the Israelite Kings* (Lund, 1976).

Meyer, I., *Jeremia und die falschen Propheten* (Freiburg/Göttingen, 1977).

Meyer, R., *Hebräische Grammatik. III: Satzlehre* (Berlin, 1972).

Meyers, C. L., and E. M. Meyers, *Haggai, Zechariah 1-8* (New York, 1987).

Migsch, H., *Jeremias Ackerkauf: Eine Untersuchung von Jeremia 32* (Frankfurt am Main, 1996).

Milik, J. T., "Les papyrus araméens d'Hermoupolis et les cultes syro-phéniciens en Égypte perse," *Bib* 48 (1967) 546-622.

Miller, J. M., and J. H. Hayes, *A History of Ancient Israel and Judah* (London, 1986).

Mitchell, C. W., *The Meaning of BRK 'To Bless' in the Old Testament* (Atlanta, 1987).

Mitchell, H. G., et al., *Haggai, Zechariah, Malachi and Jonah* (Edinburgh, 1951).

Moor, J. C. d., *An Anthology of Religious Texts from Ugarit* (Leiden, 1987).

Moran, W. L., "New Evidence from Mari on the History of Prophecy," *Bib* 50 (1969) 15-56.

Morris, D., *Gestures: Their Origins and Distribution* (New York, 1979).

Mulder, M. J., "נפה," *TDOT* 15 (2006) 753-8.

Mullen, E. T. J., "Crime and Punishment: The Sins of the King and the Despoliation of the Treasuries," *CBQ* 54 (1992) 231-48.

Munn-Rankin, J. M., "Diplomacy in Western Asia in the Early Second Millenium B.C.," *Iraq* 18 (1956) 68-110.

Muraoka, T., *Emphatic Words and Structures in Biblical Hebrew* (Jerusalem, 1985).

Na'aman, N., "Sennacherib's 'Letter to God' on his Campaign to Judah," *BASOR* 214 (1974) 25-39.

Na'aman, N., "The Brook of Egypt and Assyrian Policy on the Border of Egypt," *Tel Aviv* 6 (1979) 68-90.

Nel, P. J., "Character in the Book of Judges," *OTE* 8 (1995) 191-204.

Nelson, R. D., *The Double Redaction of the Deuteronomistic History* (Sheffield, 1981).

Netzer, E., "Massive Structures: Processes in Construction and Deterioration," *The Architecture of Ancient Israel: From the Prehistoric to the Persian Period* (Jerusalem, 1992) 17-30.

Niccacci, A., *The Syntax of the Verb in Classical Hebrew Prose* (Sheffield, 1990).

Nicholson, E. W., *Preaching to the Exiles: A Study of the Prose Tradition in the Book of Jeremiah* (Oxford, 1970).

Nicholson, E. W., *The Book of the Prophet Jeremiah: Chapters 1-25* (Cambridge, 1973).

Nida, E. A., *Style and Discourse* (Cape Town, 1983).

Nielsen, K., *There is Hope for a Tree: The Tree as Metaphor in Isaiah* (Sheffield, 1989).

Nissinen, M., "Die Relevanz der neuassyrischen Prophetie für die alttestamentliche Forschung," *Mesopotamica - Ugaritica - Biblica* (Neukirchen-Vlyun, 1993) 217-58.

Nissinen, M., *References to Prophecy in Neo-Assyrian Sources* (Helsinki, 1998).

Noordtzij, A., *Ezechiël* (Kampen, 1932).

Noort, E., *Untersuchungen zum Gottesbescheid in Mari* (Neukirchen-Vlyun, 1977).

Noth, M., *Überlieferungsgeschichtliche Studien. I: Die Sammelten und Bearbeitenden Geschichtswerke im Alten Testament* (Halle, 1943).

Noth, M., *Könige. I. Teilband (1-16)* (Neukirchen-Vlyun, 1968).

Noth, M., *Aufsätze zur biblischen Landes- und Altertumskunde* (Neukirchen-Vlyun, 1971).

Nurmela, R., *Prophets in Dialogue: Inner-Biblical Allusions in Zechariah 1-8 and 9-14* (Åbo, 1996).

Nyberg, H. S., *Hoseaboken. Ny översättning med anmärkningar* (Uppsala, 1940).

Nyberg, H. S., *Hebreisk grammatik* (Stockholm, 1952).

Nötscher, F., "Prophetie im Umkreis des alten Israel," *BZ* 10 (1968) 161-97.

O'Brien, M., *The Deuteronomistic History Hypothesis: A Reassessment* (Freiburg/Göttingen, 1989).

Ochs, P., *Peirce, Pragmatism and the Logic of Scripture* (Cambridge, 1998).

Osswald, E., *Falsche Prophetie im Alten Testament* (Tübingen, 1962).

Oswalt, J. N., *The Book of Isaiah: Chapters 1-39* (Grand Rapids, 1986).

Otto, E., "Ächtungstexte," *LE* 1 (1975) 67-9.

Overholt, T. W., "King Nebuchadnezzar in the Jeremiah Tradition," *CBQ* 30 (1968) 39-48.

Overholt, T. W., *The Threat of Falsehood: A Study in the Theology of the Book of Jeremiah* (London, 1970).

Overholt, T. W., "Seeing is Believing: The Social Setting of Prophetic Acts of Power," *JSOT* 23 (1982) 3-31.

Overholt, T. W., *Channels of Prophecy: The Social Dynamics of Prophetic Activity* (1989).

Overholt, T. W., "Prophecy in History: The Social Reality of Intermediation," *JSOT* 48 (1990) 3-29.

Panther, K.-U., and G. Radden, *Metonymy in Language and Thought* (Amsterdam, 1999).

Parpola, S., *Assyrian Prophecies* (Helsinki, 1997).

Paterson, R. M., "Reinterpretation in the Book of Jeremiah," *JSOT* 28 (1984) 37-46.

Peirce, C. S. S., *Collected Papers* (Cambridge, 1931).

Perdue, L., *Wisdom in Revolt: Metaphorical Theology in the Book of Job* (Sheffield, 1991).

Petersen, D. L., *Haggai and Zechariah 1-8* (London, 1984).

Petersen, D. L., "Israelite Prophecy: Change versus Continuity," *Congress Volume: Leuven, 1989* (Leiden, 1991) 190-203.

Petersen, D. L., "Rethinking the Nature of Prophetic Literature," *Prophecy and Prophets: The Diversity of Contemporary Issues in Scholarship* (Atlanta, 1997) 23-40.

Petitjean, A., *Les Oracles du Proto-Zacharie: Un Programme de Restauration pour la Communauté Juive Après l'Exil* (Paris/Louvain, 1969).

Pham, X. H. T., *Mourning in the Ancient Near East and the Hebrew Bible* (Sheffield, England, 1999).

Plein, I., "Erwägungen zur Überlieferung von 1 Reg 11:26-14:20," *ZAW* 78 (1966) 8-24.

Pohlmann, K.-F., *Studien zum Jeremiabuch: Ein Beitrag zur Frage nach der Entstehung des Jeremiabuches* (Göttingen, 1978).

Pohlmann, K.-F., *Ezechielstudien: Zur Redaktionsgeschichte des Buches und zur Frage nach den ältesten Texten* (Berlin/New York, 1992).

Polk, T., "Paradigms, Parables and Mesalîm: On Reading the Masal in Scripture," *CBQ* 45 (1983) 564-83.

Pope, M. H., *Job* (New York, 1973).

Porten, B., *Archives from Elephantine: The Life of an Ancient Jewish Military Colony* (Berkeley/Los Angeles, 1968).

Poyatos, F., *New Perspectives in Nonverbal Communication: Studies in Cultural Anthropology, Social Psychology, Linguistics, Literature, and Semiotics* (Oxford, 1983).

Prince, G., *Narratology: The Form and Functioning of Narrative* (Berlin, 1982).

Provan, I., *Hezekiah and the Books of Kings* (Berlin, 1988).

Rabin, C., et al., *The book of Jeremiah* (Jerusalem, 1997).

Redditt, P. L., "Zerubbabel, Joshua, and the Night Visions of Zechariah," *CBQ* 54 (1992) 249-59.

Redford, D. B., "Sais and the Kushite Invasions of the Eighth Century B.C.," *Journal of the American Research Center in Egypt* 22 (1985) 5-15.

Redford, D. B., *Egypt, Canaan, and Israel in Ancient Times* (Princeton, 1992a).

Redford, D. B., "Execration and Execration Texts," *ABD* 2 (1992b) 681-2.

Reimer, D. J., *The Oracles against Babylon in Jeremiah 50-51: A Horror among the Nations* (San Francisco, 1993).

Ricoeur, P., *Interpretation Theory: Discourse and the Surplus of Meaning* (Fort Worth, 1976).

Ricoeur, P., *The Rule of Metaphor: Multi-Disciplinary Studies of the Creation of Meaning in Language* (London, 1978).

Ricoeur, P., and J. B. Thompson, *Hermeneutics and the Human Sciences: Essays on Language, Action and Interpretation* (Cambridge, 1981).

Rignell, L. G., *Die Nachtgesichte des Sacharja: Eine exegetische Studie* (Lund, 1950).

Ringgren, H., "The Place of Covenant in the Religion of Israel," *Ancient Israelite Religion (FS F. M. Cross)* (Philadelphia, 1987) 421-8.

Robinson, H. W., "Prophetic Symbolism," *Old Testament Essays: Collected Papers* (London, 1927) 1-17.

Rofé, A., *The Prophetical Stories: The Narratives about the Prophets in the Hebrew Bible - Their Literary Types and History* (Jerusalem, 1988).

Ronen, R., *Possible Worlds in Literary Theory* (Cambridge, 1994).

Rooke, D. W., *Zadok's Heirs: The Role and Development of the High Priesthood in Ancient Israel* (Oxford, 2000).

Rose, M., *Der Ausschliesslichkeitsanspruch Jahwehs* (Stuttgart, 1975).

Ross, J. F., "Prophecy in Hamath, Israel, and Mari," *HTR* 63 (1970) 1-28.

Rowley, H. H., "Ritual and the Hebrew Prophets," *JSS* 1 (1956) 338-60.

Rowley, H. H., *Men of God: Studies in Old Testament History and Prophecy* (London, 1963).

Rudolph, W., *Hosea* (Gütersloh, 1966).

Rudolph, W., *Jeremia* (Tübingen, 1968).

Rudolph, W., *Haggai, Sacharja, Maleachi* (Gütersloh, 1976).

Ruppert, L., "Beobachtungen zur Literar- und Kompositionskritik von Hos 1-3," *Künder des Wortes. Beiträge zur Theologie der Propheten (FS J. Schreiner)* (Würzburg, 1982a) 163-82.

Ruppert, L., "Erwägungen zur Kompositions- und Redaktionsgeschichte von Hosea 1-3," *BZ* 26 (1982b) 208-23.

Ryan, M.-L., *Possible Worlds, Artificial Intelligence, and Narrative Theory* (Bloomington, 1991).

Sanders, J. A., *From Sacred Story to Sacred Text* (Philadelphia, 1987).

Sasson, J. M., "The Posting of Letters with Divine Messages," *Florilegium marianum II (FS M. Birot)* (Paris, 1994) 299-316.

Saussure, F. d., et al., *Course in General Linguistics* (London, 1983).

Sawyer, J. F. A., "The Meaning of *barzel* in the Biblical Expressions 'Chariots of Iron', 'yoke of Iron', etc.," *Midian, Moab and Edom: The History and Archeology of Late Bronze and Iron Jordan and North-West Arabia* (Sheffield, 1983) 129-34.

Schaller, J. J., "Performative Language Theory: An Exercise in the Analysis of Ritual," *Worship* 62 (1988) 415-32.

Schmidt, K. W., "Prophetic Delegation: A Form-Critical Inquiry," *Bib* 63 (1982) 206-18.

Schmitt, A., *Prophetischer Gottesbescheid in Mari und Israel* (Stuttgart, 1982).

Schneider, W., *Grammatik des biblischen Hebräisch* (München, 1974).

Schneir, L., "Zerubbabel: A Riddle," *JBQ* 24 (1996) 14-7.

Schreiner, J., "Hoseas Ehe, ein Zeichen des Gerichts," *BZ* 21 (1977) 163-83.

Schreiner, J., *Jeremia 1-25* (Würzburg, 1981).

Schreiner, J., *Jeremia 26-52* (Würzburg, 1984).

Schreiner, J., "Tempeltheologie im Streit der Propheten: Zu Jer 27 und 28," *BZ* 31 (1987) 1-14.

Schumacher, G., "Der arabische Pflug," *ZDPV* 12 (1889) 157-66.

Schökel, L. A., *A Manual of Hebrew Poetics* (Rome, 1988).

Schöttler, H. G., *Gott inmitten seines Volkes: Die Neuordnung des Gottesvolkes nach Sacharja 1-6* (Trier, 1987).

Searle, J. A., *The Construction of Social Reality* (New York, 1995).

Searle, J. R., *Speech Acts: An Essay in the Philosophy of Language* (London,, 1969).

Searle, J. R., *Expression and Meaning: Studies in the Theory of Speech Acts* (Cambridge, Eng.; New York, 1979).

Searle, J. R., et al., *Speech act theory and pragmatics* (Boston, 1980).

Searle, J. R., and D. Vanderveken, *Foundations of Illocutionary Logic* (Cambridge, 1985).

Sebeok, T. A., *Nonverbal Communication, Interaction, and Gesture: Selections from Semiotica* (The Hague, 1981).

Seebass, H., "Die Verwerfung Jerobeams 1. und Salomos durch die Prophetie des Ahia von Silo," *WO* 4 (1963) 163-82.

Seebass, H., "Zur Teil und der Herrschaft Salomos nach 1 Reg 11:29-39," *ZAW* 88 (1976) 363-76.

Seidl, T., *Texte und Einheiten in Jeremia 27-29* (St. Ottilien, 1977).

Seifert, B., *Metaphorisches Reden von Gott im Hoseabuch* (Göttingen, 1996).

Seybold, K., "Die Königserwartung bei den Propheten Haggai und Sacharja," *Jud* 28 (1972) 69-78.

Sheppard, G. T., "True and False Prophecy within Scripture," *Canon, Theology, and Old Testament Interpretation (FS B. S. Childs)* (Philadelphia, 1988) 262-82.

Sheriff, J. K., *The Fate of Meaning: Charles Peirce, Structuralism, and Literature* (Princeton, 1989).

Sherwood, Y., "Boxing Gomer: Controlling the Deviant Woman in Hosea 1-3," *A Feministic Companion to the Latter Prophets* (Sheffield, 1995) 101-125.

Sherwood, Y., *The Prostitute and the Prophet: Hosea's Marriage in Literary-Theoretical Perspective* (Sheffield, 1996).

Sigrist, M., "Gestes symboliques et rituels à Emar," *Ritual and Sacrifice in the Ancient Near East* (Leuven, 1993) 381-40.

Sittl, K., *Die Gebärden der Griechen und Römer* (Leipzig, 1890).

Smith, D. E., *Gesture as a Stylistic Device in Kleist's "Michael Kohlhaas" and Kafka's "Der Prozess"* (Bern, 1976).

Smith, W. R., *The Old Testament in the Jewish Church* (London, 1908).

Soden, W. v., *Akkadisches Handwörterbuch II* (Wiesbaden, 1972).

Soderlund, S., *The Greek Text of Jeremiah: A Revised Hypothesis* (Sheffield, 1984).

Soggin, J. A., "Zum zweiten Psalm," *Wort - Gebot - Glaube: Beiträge zur Theologie des Alten Testaments* (Zürich, 1970) 191-207.

Soggin, J. A., *Introduction to the Old Testament* (London, 1989).

Soskice, J. M., *Metaphor and Religious Language* (Oxford, 1985).

Spalinger, A., "The Year 712 B.C. and its Implications for Egyptian History," *Journal of the American Research Center in Egypt* 10 (1973) 95-101.

Stacey, W. D., *Prophetic Drama in the Old Testament* (London, 1990).

Stephens, F. J., "The Ancient Significance of sisith," *JBL* 50 (1931) 59-70.

Stipp, H.-J., *Das masoretische und alexandrinische Sondergut des Jeremiabuches: Textgeschichtlicher Rang, Eigenarten, Triebkräfte* (Freiburg/Göttingen, 1994).

Stoebe, H. J., *Das erste Buch Samuelis* (Gütersloh, 1973).

Stroete, G. A., "Ezekiel 24:15-27: The Meaning of a Symbolic Act," *Bijdrag* 38 (1977) 163-75.

Stuart, D., *Hosea-Jonah* (Waco, 1987).

Stulman, L., *The Other Text of Jeremiah: A Reconstruction of the Hebrew Text Underlying the Greek Version of the Prose Sections of Jeremiah With English Translation* (New York, 1985).

Stulman, L., *The Prose Sermons of the Book of Jeremiah: A Redescription of the Correspondences with the Deuteronomistic Literature in the Light of Recent Text-critical Research* (Atlanta, 1986).

Stulman, L., "Insiders and Outsiders in the Book of Jeremiah: Shifts in Symbolic Arrangements," *JSOT* 66 (1995) 65-85.

Tadmor, H., "The Campaigns of Sargon II of Assur: A Chronological-Historical Study," *JCS* 12 (1958) 22-42, 77-100.

Tadmor, H., "Philistia Under Assyrian Rule," *BA* 29 (1966) 86-102.

Talshir, Z., "Is the Alternate Tradition of the Division of the Kindom (3 Kgds 12:24a-z) Non-deuteronomistic?," *Septuagint, Scrolls and Cognate Writings* (Atlanta, 1992) 599-621.

Talshir, Z., *The Alternative Story of the Division of the Kingdom (3 Kingdoms 12:24 a-z)* (Jerusalem, 1993).

Talstra, E., "Text Grammar and Hebrew Bible. I: Elements of a Theory," *BiOr* 35 (1978) 169-74.

Tambiah, S. J., *Culture, Thought, and Social Action: An Anthropological Perspective* (Cambridge, Mass., 1985).

Terrien, S., "Ezekiel's Dance of the Sword and Prophetic Theonomy (Ezek 21:14-22)," *A Gift of God in Due Season (FS J. A. Sanders)* (Sheffield, 1996) 119-132.

Thiel, W., *Die deuteronomistische Redaktion von Jeremia 1-25* (Neukirchen-Vlyun, 1973).

Thiel, W., *Die deuteronomistische Redaktion von Jeremia 26-46* (Neukirchen-Vlyun, 1981).

Thiselton, A. C., "The Supposed Power of Words in the Biblical Writings," *JTS* 25 (1974) 283-99.

Thompson, J. A., *The Book of Jeremiah* (Grand Rapids, 1980).

Thompson, R. C., *The Epic of Gilgamish: Text, Transliteration, and Notes* (Oxford, 1930).

Toews, W. I., *Monarchy and Religious Institution in Israel under Jeroboam I* (Atlanta, 1993).

Tollington, J. E., *Tradition and Innovation in Haggai and Zechariah 1-8* (Sheffield, 1993).

Tov, E., "Exegetical Notes on the Hebrew Vorlage of the LXX of Jeremiah 27 (34)," *ZAW* 91 (1979) 7393.

Tov, E., "Some Aspects of the Textual and Literary History of the Book of Jeremiah," *Le Livre de Jérémie: Le Prophète et son Milieu, les Oracles et leur Transmission* (Leuven, 1981a) 145-67.

Tov, E., *The Text-Critical Use of the Septuagint in Biblical Research* (Jerusalem, 1981b).

Tov, E., "4QJer^c (4Q72)," *Tradition of the Text (FS D. Barthélemy)* (Freiburg/Göttingen, 1991) 249-76.

Tov, E., *Textual Criticism of the Hebrew Bible* (Minneapolis, 1992a).

Tov, E., "Three Fragments of Jeremiah from Qumran Cave 4," *RevQ* 15(59) (1992b) 531-41.

Tov, E., (ed.) *The Dead Sea Scrolls on Microfiche: A Comprehensive Facsimile Edition of the Texts from the Judean Desert* (Leiden, 1993).

Tov, E., "4QJer^a — A Preliminary Edition," *Textus* 17 (1994) 1-41.

Trebolle Barrera, J., *Centena in libros Samuelis et Regum. Variantes textuales y composición literaria en los libros de Samuel y Reyes* (Madrid, 1989).

Trebolle Barrera, J. C., *Salomon y Jeroboan. Historia de la recensión y redacción de 1 Reyes, 2-12,14* (Salamanca, 1980).

Turkowski, L., "Peasant Agriculture in the Judean Hills," *PEQ* 101 (1969) 20-33, 101-12.

Törnkvist, R., *The Use and Abuse of Female Sexual Imagery in the Book of Hosea: A Feminist Critical Approach to Hos 1-3* (Uppsala, 1998).

Uehlinger, C., ""Zeichne eine Stadt ... und belagere sie!" Bild und Wort in einer Zeichenhandlung Ezechiels gegen Jerusalem (Ez 4f)," *Jerusalem: Texte - Bilder - Steine (FS H. and O. Keel)* (Freiburg/Göttingen, 1987) 111-200.

Ussishkin, D., "Excavations at Tel Lachisch 1978-1983," *Tel Aviv* 10 (1983) 137-46.

Waard, J. d., and E. A. Nida, *From One Language to Another: Functional Equivalence in Bible Translating* (Nashville, 1986).

Wacholder, B. Z., "The 'Sealed' Torah Versus the 'Revealed' Torah: An Exegesis of Damascus Covenant 5:1-6 and Jeremiah 32:10-14," *RevQ* 12 (1986) 351-68.

Wagner, M., *Die lexikalischen und grammatikalischen Aramaismen im alttestamentlichen Hebräisch* (Berlin, 1966).

Wallis, G., "Erwägungen zu Sacharja 6:9-15," *VTS* 22 (1972) 232-7.

Waltke, B. K., and M. O'Connor, *An Introduction to Biblical Hebrew Syntax* (Winona Lake, 1990).

Van Seters, J., *In Search of History: Historiography in the Ancient World and the Origins of Biblical History* (London/New Haven, 1983).

Wanke, G., *Untersuchungen zur sogenannten Baruchschrift* (Berlin, 1971).

Wanke, G., "Jeremias Ackerkauf: Heil im Gericht?," *Prophet und Prophetenbuch (FS O. Kaiser)* (Berlin, 1989) 265-76.

Vanoni, G., *Literarkritik und Grammatik: Untersuchung der Wiederholungen und Spannungen in 1 Kön 11-12* (St. Ottilien, 1984).

Watts, J. D. W., *Isaiah 1-33* (Waco, 1985).

Weems, R. J., "Gomer: Victim of Violence or Victim of Metaphor?," *Sem* 47 (1989) 87-104.

Veijola, T., *Die ewige Dynastie. David und die Entstehung seiner Dynastie nach der deuteronomistischen Darstellung* (Helsinki, 1975).

Weinfeld, M., *Deuteronomy and the Deuteronomic School* (Oxford, 1972).

Weippert, H., *Die Prosareden des Jeremiabuches* (Berlin, 1973).

Weippert, H., "Kleidung," *RLA* (1977) 185-88.

Weippert, H., "Die Ätiologie des Nordreiches und seines Königshauses (1 Reg 11:29-40)," *ZAW* 95 (1983) 344-75.

Weisbach, F. H., "Zu den Inschriften der Säle im Palaste Sargon's II. von Assyrien," *ZDMG* 72 (1918) 161-85.

Wellhausen, J., *Die kleinen Propheten* (Berlin, 1898).

Vermeylen, J., *Du Prophète Isaïe à L'Apocalyptique. Tome I. Isaïe, I-XXXV, miroir d'un demi-millénaire d'expérience religieuse en Israël* (Paris, 1977).

Westhuizen, J. P., "A Proposed Possible Solution to KTU 1.14 II 7 Based on Babylonian and Biblical Evidence," *UF* 17 (1986) 357-70.

Wevers, J. W., "The Septuagint Text of 1 Kings ii 12-xxi 43," *OTS* 8 (1950) 300-22.

Wevers, J. W., *Ezekiel* (London, 1969).

Viberg, Å., *Symbols of Law: A Contextual Analysis of Legal Symbolic Acts in the Old Testament* (Stockholm, 1992).

Viberg, Å., "Wakening the Sleeping Metaphor: A New Interpretation of Malachi 1:11," *TynBul* 45 (1994) 297-319.

Viberg, Å., "'A Mantle Torn is A Kingdom Lost': The Tradition History of a Deuteronomistic Theme (1 Kings xi 29-31)," *'Lasset uns Brücken bauen*

... '. *Collected Communications to the XVth Congress of the International Organization for the Study of the Old Testament, Cambridge 1995* (Frankfurt AM, 1998) 135-40.

Viberg, Å., "An Elusive Crown: An Analysis of the Performance of a Prophetic Symbolic Act (Zech 6:9-15)," *SEÅ* 65 (2000) 161-70.

Viberg, Å., "Saul Exposed by Irony: A New Understanding of 1 Samuel 15:27 Based on Two Symbolic Acts," *SEÅ* 65 (2005) 301-8.

Wildberger, H., *Jesaja: II Teilband: 13-27* (Neukirchen-Vlyun, 1974).

Williamson, H. G. M., "A Response to A.G. Auld," *JSOT* 27 (1983) 33-9.

Williamson, H. G. M., *Ezra, Nehemiah* (Waco, 1985).

Wilson, J. A., *The Burden of Egypt: An Interpretation of Ancient Egyptian Culture* (Chicago, 1951).

Wilson, R. R., "An Interpretation of Ezekiel's Dumbness," *VT* 22 (1972) 91-104.

Wilson, R. R., *Prophecy and Society in Ancient Israel* (Philadelphia, 1980).

Winckler, H., *Die Keilschrifttexte Sargons, I* (Leipzig, 1889).

Wiseman, D. J., *Chronicles of Chaldaean Kings (626-556 B.C.) in the British Museum* (London, 1956).

Wiseman, D. J., *Nebuchadrezzar and Babylon* (Oxford, 1985).

Witzenrath, H. H., *Das Buch Rut. Eine literaturwissenschaftliche Untersuchung* (München, 1975).

Vogels, W., "Hosea's Gift to Gomer (Hos 3:2)," *Bib* 69 (1988) 412-21.

Wolff, H. W., *Hosea* (Philadelphia, 1974).

Wood, J. R., "Prophecy and Poetic Dialogue," *SR* 24 (1995) 309-322.

Vorster, W. S., "Meaning and Reference: The Parables of Jesus in Mark 4," *Text and Reality. Aspects of Reference in Biblical Texts* (Atlanta, 1985) 27-65.

Vorwahl, H., *Die Gebärdensprache im Alten Testament* (Berlin, 1932).

Woude, A. S. v. d., "Serubbabel und die messianischen Erwartungen des Propheten Sacharja," ZAW (1988) 138-56.

Woude, A. S. v. d., "Zion as Primeval Stone in Zechariah 3 and 4," *Text and Context (FS F. C. Fensham)* (Sheffield, 1988a) 237-48.

Wright, D. P., *The Disposal of Impurity: Elimination Rites in the Bible and in Hittite and Mesopotamian Literature* (1987).

Wright, G. E., "Israelite Daily Life," *BA* 18 (1955) 50-79.

Würthwein, E., *Das erste Buch der Könige 1-16* (Göttingen, 1976).

Yadin, Y., *The Art of Warfare in Biblical Lands in the Light of Archeological Discovery* (London, 1963).

Ziegler, J., *Jeremias, Baruch, Threni, Epistula Ieremiae* (Göttingen, 1957).

Zimmerli, W., "Der Wahrheitserweis Jahwes nach der Botschaft der beiden Exilspropheten," *Tradition und Situation: Studien zur alttestamentlichen Prophetie (FS A. Weiser)* (Göttingen, 1963) 133-51.

Zimmerli, W., *Ezekiel: Volume I* (London, 1976).

Zimmerli, W., *Ezekiel: Volume II* (Philadelphia, 1983).

Itero

www.ehs.se/itero

1. Åke Viberg, *Symbols of Law: A Contextual Analysis of Legal Symbolic Acts in the Old Testament.* 2021. First published 1992 by Almqvist & Wiksell International.

2. Thomas Kazen, *Jesus and Purity* Halakhah*: Was Jesus Indifferent to Impurity?* 2021. First published 2002 by Almqvist & Wiksell International. Corrected reprint edition published 2010 by Eisenbrauns.

3. Åke Viberg, *Prophets in Action: An Analysis of Prophetic Symbolic Acts in the Old Testament.* 2021. First published 2007 by Almqvist & Wiksell International.

4. Thomas Kazen, *Issues of Impurity in Early Judaism.* 2021. First published 2010 by Eisenbrauns.

5. Rikard Roitto, *Behaving as a Christ-Believer: A Cognitive Perspective on Identity and Behavior Norms in Ephesians.* 2021. First published 2011 by Eisenbrauns.